MY NEW LIFE
in
VANCOUVER

我在温哥华的新生活

Written by
KARI KARLSBJERG
Translated by Yi Zheng

谨以此书献给我最亲爱的小侄子 —— 郑义最疼爱的孙子 —— 本杰明。他去年在温哥华降生，彼时，我正在筹备此书。令人欣慰的是，本杰明将在两种文化的熏陶下茁壮成长，他将天生的自然理解中英双语，也由此代表了下一代的无间融合和未来的无限希望。

Tellwell Talent
www.tellwell.ca

ISBN
978-1-77370-109-7 (Hardcover)
978-1-77370-108-0 (Paperback)
978-1-77370-110-3 (eBook)

Table of Contents
目录

How to Use This Book
如何使用这本书

There are Two Easy Ways to Use This Book:

使用这本书有两种简单的方法：

1. Find today's date and read the short text you find there – every day of the month is dedicated to a different category. Then tomorrow read the next section, and so on – one small daily reading will help you build your exciting new life in Vancouver one small step at a time.

1. 查找今天的日期，阅读找到的短文 - 每个月的同一天都是专门用于相同的类别。明天再看下一个类别，依此类推 - 每天读一小段，就会前跨出一小步，小小的阅读将会帮助您在温哥华建立起令人兴奋的新生活。

Or

或 者

2. Go directly to the index to find exactly the information you need in the different categories.

2. 直接翻到索引，按照不同类别找到您所需要的信息。

We invite you to join our "My New Life in Vancouver" Club and receive regular updates about Vancouver Life and invitations to classes and special events

www.mynewlifeinvancouver.com

我们诚挚地邀请您加入我们"温哥华新生活"俱乐部，定期收到有关温哥华生活的最新消息，并请您参加我们的研讨会和特别活动。

网址：www.mynewlifeinvancouver.com

Free Pronunciation Guides on Website

We have included basic **English For Everyday Life** lessons throughout the book that will help you in your daily life in Vancouver.

Please visit our website for free pronunciation guide videos for these lessons.

www.mynewlifeinvancouver.com

书里面包含了许多基本的日常生活英语课程，相信这些课程对你在温哥华的生活会有所帮助的。

请访问我们的网站去观看这些免费的发音视频指南课程。

www.mynewlifeinvancouver.com

January

Weather:	Average temperature: 1°C to 8°C
	Average rainfall days: 22, Average rainfall: 225 mm
Statutory holiday:	New Year's Day
Other special days:	Chinese New Year (Jan/Feb)
	Polar Bear Swim Jan 1

For some brave Vancouverites, the new year starts with a freezing cold Polar Bear Swim in English Bay. This annual event has happened since 1920. Around 3,000 brave Vancouverites join the quick swim in shallow water out to a marker and back, usually wearing crazy costumes, and many more warmly-dressed spectators watch from the beach and cheer them on. However, after the excitement and celebrations of Christmas and New Year's, January is usually a very quiet month in Vancouver. The weather is very cold and wet and the sun goes down in the late afternoon which makes Vancouverites feel like staying indoors at home. In addition, many people are recovering from spending so much money and eating so much food in December so they like to live very simply to give their bank accounts and stomach a rest.

New Year's Resolutions* is a popular topic of conversation as everyone compares the goals they have promised to work on for the New Year. The gyms are always temporarily very busy in January with people trying to keep their new fitness resolutions. School and work begin again in January and people settle back down into their regular daily life again after the excesses of the holidays.

When Chinese New Year falls in January, the celebrations and parade help brighten up the mood of the city. More than 50,000 people line Chinatown's streets to watch traditional lion dance teams as well as marching bands and dance troupes march in a big parade downtown.

Towards the end of the month (when people get sick of their diets) Dine Out Vancouver, Canada's largest food and drink festival, offers a very affordable 17-day calendar of food-related events and experiences at hundreds of restaurants and hotels throughout the city. Each restaurant offers three or more prix-fixe* meals at $20, $30 and $40 per person. This event gives people a chance to try new restaurants at an affordable price.

1月

气候： 平均温度：1°C 至 8°C
平均降雨天数：22， 平均降雨量： 225 毫米
公众节假日：元旦
其他特殊日：中国新的一年（1月/2月）
北极熊游泳1月1日

新的一年开始了，在这寒冷的季节里一些勇敢的温哥华人，将参加英吉利湾一个名为北极熊冬泳活动。这项年度盛会始于1920年，每年大约有3000名勇士游向浅水区的一个标记，然后快速地游回岸边，他们通常穿着怪异的泳装。海滩上有很多热情的观众在观看，并为他们加油。当人们兴奋的欢度了所有的庆祝活动如圣诞节和新年之后，一月的温哥华通常是很安静的。天气依然是非常的寒冷和潮湿，太阳早早地就下山了，这让当地的居民觉得还是待在家里更舒服些。人们又恢复了正常的生活，毕竟去年12月他们花掉了那么多钱，吃了那么多东西，所以他们只想过回简单的生活，让他们的银行账户有一些存款，同时也让他们的胃休息一下。

新年的决心是一个热门的话题，因为每个人都在比较他们曾许诺的在新的一年要达到的目标。一般来说，健身房一月份总是很忙的，因为人们试图实现他们新的健身计划。一月份学校开学了和工人们上班了，所有的假期结束之后，人们又重新回到他们的日常生活中去。

春节为农历新年，是中国与全世界各地华人的传统新年，又称新春，口头上亦称为过新年、过年、庆新春。春节也被视为一年的开始。届时将有5万多人在唐人街的街道两旁观看传统舞狮队，乐队和舞蹈团体举行的大游行。庆祝和游行给整个城市带来了喜庆的气氛。

每年1月底，温哥华旅游局组织全市范围内数百家餐馆和酒店，提供非常实惠的历时17天的餐饮节，这是加拿大最大的食品和饮料节。（当人们厌倦了他们日常的饮食） 此时正好可以外出就餐，体验一下，每个餐厅均提供三档或更多的套餐，定价为每人$20、 $30 和$40加元。这样就给了人们在合理的价格品尝试各大餐馆的机会，。

更多的信息：

（由温哥华市组织） 的北极熊游泳俱乐部： www.Vancouver.ca 中国慈善社网站提供有关在温哥华年度游行和中国新年庆祝活动的信息。http://www.cbavancouver.ca/

温哥华餐饮节：http://www.dineoutvancouver.com/

* New Year's Resolutions（新年的决心）： 您对自己新的一年的第一天所做出的承诺。做一些有益的事情，戒掉一些不好的毛病。比如：吃得更健康，多锻炼，戒烟，省钱等等。

* prix-fixe meals（固定价格套餐）：即全餐，它是一个完整的固定价格的套餐 （开胃菜，主菜，甜点）。它也被称为是定制的套餐

Birthday Celebrations

Canadians love to celebrate their birthday no matter how old they are. The only thing that changes is the kind of party that is given.

- For **young children up until pre-teens**: parties are held at the home or at a restaurant like McDonalds or special entertainment centre like Chuck E Cheese. Fun food is served like hot dogs or pizza and there is always a birthday cake with candles to blow out. The cake is usually decorated with the child's favourite cartoon character. All the guests bring the birthday child a present and the birthday child gives all the guests a little 'goodie' bag of candy and inexpensive small games or toys at the end of the party.

- **Teenagers** usually go out for dinner or a movie to celebrate their birthday. Sometimes they have a sleepover at the home of the birthday teen. All the teens sleep at the house – usually in sleeping bags on the floor of the living room –and watch a movie, eat junk food and candy and have birthday cake. The guests all bring a present for the birthday teen.

- **Adults** also celebrate their birthday by going out for a meal or having friends come to their home. There will always be a birthday cake but sometimes the birthday person does not want any presents.

- The **"big" birthdays** that are celebrated with special parties are 1, 13, 16 (sweet sixteen for girls), 19 and then 30, 40, 50, 60, 70, 80 and so on.

生日庆祝活动

加拿大人庆祝他们的生日，是不分年龄的，唯一的区别是派对的形式。

* **从婴幼儿到学前儿童**：派对在家里或在餐厅如麦当劳或特殊的娱乐中心像Chuck E Cheese举行。吃一些有趣的食物像热狗或比萨饼，吹灭插在蜡烛上的生日蛋糕之后与大家分享。蛋糕通常是用孩子最喜欢的卡通人物装饰。每一位客人都会带来一份生日礼物，在聚会结束的时候，过生日的孩子也会给所有的来宾发一个小的"goodie"袋装的糖果和便宜的小玩具。
* **青少年**：通常出去吃饭或看一部电影来庆祝他们的生日。有时候，他们会在过生日的青少年的家中过夜。大家都挤在同一间房子里 – 通常在客厅的地板上套上睡袋 – 一起看电视，吃垃圾食品，糖果和生日蛋糕然后睡在一起。 所有的来宾都会带来一份生日礼物。
* **成年人**：也是出去吃一顿饭或约朋友们到家里来庆祝他们的生日。生日蛋糕是少不了的，但也有过生日的人不想收任何礼物。
* 特别"重大"的生日庆祝派对是：1岁，13岁，16岁（特指女孩甜美的十六岁）19岁，然后是30岁，40岁，50岁，60岁，70岁，80岁等等。

English for Everyday Life
日常生活英语

在这里是大家最熟悉的生日快乐歌的歌词，唱给所有过生日的人，我们用蜡烛来装饰生日蛋糕：

Happy Birthday to you
Happy Birthday to you
Happy Birthday dear (name of person)
Happy Birthday to you.

祝你生日快乐
祝你生日快乐
亲爱的（人的名字）生日快乐
祝你生日快乐

在过生日的人吹灭蜡烛之前我们说：

"Make a wish and blow out the candles!"
"把蜡烛吹灭之前先许个愿吧 ！"

　　这样做的意思是，他们心里最想要的是什么，先许个愿，再吹灭蜡烛，然后蜡烛冒出的烟会带着他们的愿望去天堂，最终帮助他们实现愿望。

　　如果有几只蜡烛没有吹灭，我们数一下，然后和他开个玩笑，假如过生日的人是个男的，且有三根蜡烛尚在燃烧。 这时会戏弄他说，

```
"You have three girlfriends!"
```
"你有三个女朋友 ！"

　　当小伙子听到这句玩笑话的时候，通常是会脸红的。

January 2   # Parenting in Vancouver

1月2日   在温哥华养育子女

BC Parent Magazine and Website

BC Parent magazine has been providing up to date and trustworthy information for families for more than twenty five years. In addition to a magazine that is published six times per year full of helpful articles about parenting infant to teenage children in Vancouver, their website also has excellent information about family friendly events and children's activities and services in Vancouver.

BC省育儿杂志和网站   www.bcparent.ca

　　这家杂志社已经独立经营了超过二十五年，它一直为家庭提供最新和最值得信赖的信息。除了每年出版六期，从如何养育婴幼儿到十几岁大的儿童的文章之外，其网站也提供关于温哥华亲子活动，儿童活动和相关服务的信息。

Stories and Advice for Newcomers

新 移 民 的 故 事

Athina

使用语言远远比学习它重要的多

我是2015年6月来到温哥华的，我来温哥华的主要目的是陪读，因为女儿在U-HILL中学读书，当然我也很乐意在国外体验一种不同的生活。再加上温哥华是一个如此美丽的花园城市，空气清新，食品安全。在来温哥华之前，我就认为无论生活在哪里，我都能安排好自己的生活，一样生活得自在幸福。然而，事情并不是想象中的那么简单，这里的生活和中国有着很大的不同。首先最大的挑战就是语言，刚来的时候，我根本听不懂别人说什么，也无法表达我的意思尽管我在中国学了很多年的英文，我非常崩溃。这时候我意识到学英语是我目前最重要的事。于是我参加了各种英语班和英语讲座，现在我还在RICHMOND中侨上CCW（CLEAR COMMUNICATION IN WORKPLACE）的课程。另外我还做了各种义工：中侨、温哥华教育局、公共图书馆、UNA COOKING CLUB, WESBROOK 社区中心和2017年温哥华POINT GREY的省选。所有这些都是为了学习语言，了解当地文化，尽快融入和适应在温哥华的生活。我认为学习语言一定是和文化结合的，使用语言远远比学习重要的多，所以尽可能地主动去找说英语的场所和机会。（因为这里中国朋友太多了，没有太多机会说英语）。当我去上课和参加各种活动时，我认识了很多新朋友，所以我一点也不觉得孤单了。我从她们那里获取了很多信息。我参加了跳舞班，每周2次4小时的跳舞，这是我最喜欢的事情，在中国因为太忙根本没有时间去跳舞。另外我又开始学打高尔夫，我觉得生活越来越有意思，我很享受目前在温哥华的生活。

所以给像我一样的新移民以下几点建议：

1）学习英语并尽量多去使用。
2）做一个在温哥华1-3年的计划，选2、3件去做（可以是对你来说重要的事或是喜欢做的事）
3）走出家门参加各种适合你的活动，了解当地文化，尽早融入社会。
4）学会怎样和孩子处理好关系。
5）积极地面对和接受生活中的挑战及各种与你自己国家的不同。

Casinos, Gaming, and Horse Racing

There are five casinos in the greater Vancouver area. They are a popular place for entertainment as they have upscale restaurants, lounges, live concerts and shows in addition to the gaming.

1. ***Edgewater Casino (downtown Vancouver)***

   Downtown Vancouver's only casino, Edgewater Casino is located right on the waterfront and offers 600 exciting slots machines and 70 table games—including blackjack, roulette, baccarat, and poker. They also simulcast boxing matches from around the world. The casino has two restaurants and is an enjoyable place to have a meal or a relaxing drink while enjoying the wonderful views across False Creek. Edgewater is open 24 hours, 7 days a week.

2. ***River Rock Casino (Richmond)***

   Located in nearby Richmond, River Rock Casino is a four-star resort and casino. On the gaming floor, you'll find all your favourite table games, more than 1,100 slots, and a dedicated Poker room. Their two high-end restaurants Tramonto and Sea Harbour offer fine cuisine. There is also a fantastic buffet restaurant and a food court, so there is something for everyone. The River Rock also has a large Show Theatre that attracts high quality shows and celebrities. Finally, there is free live entertainment at Lulu's Lounge and Curve.

3. ***Hastings Racecourse (Burnaby)***

   Visit Hastings Racecourse for live thoroughbred horse racing in a great location with beautiful mountain and waterfront views. You can also watch simulcast racing from many of the world's most prestigious horseracing tracks. They offer casino slots and a variety of dining experiences. The live horse races run from May to October at the racecourse.

4. *Grand Villa Casino (Burnaby)*

   This Burnaby casino features two high-energy casino floors with the newest and most exciting slot machines and table games and a brand-new Poker room. There is also high stakes and private gaming salons in the luxurious Cypress Room. For drinking and dining, the Grand Villa Casino offers 7 dining and lounge choices where you can enjoy live entertainment.

5. *Hard Rock Casino Vancouver (Coquitlam)*

   Hard Rock Casino Vancouver's 80,000 square foot gaming floor is the largest of any Metro Vancouver casino. They have over 950 slot machines, and all the best table games like roulette, baccarat, poker, blackjack, craps, pai gow, and more.

赌场，赌博和赛马

在大温哥华地区有五个赌场。 他们是娱乐的热门场所，除了赌博之外，还设有高档餐厅、休息室、现场音乐会和各种表演。

1. **艾吉水滨赌场**（位于温哥华市中心）
    艾吉水滨赌场是温哥华市区唯一的赌场，位于海滨，有600台老虎机和70桌赌博游戏，包括21点、轮盘赌、百家乐和扑克牌。他们还同步直播来自世界各地的拳击比赛。赌场内有两间个厅，在享用美食和美酒的同时，看看窗外菲沙河那美妙的景色，能让人无比的愉快和放松。赌场全天24小时，每周7天对外开放。

2. **河石赌场**（里士满）
    河石赌场位于里士满附近，是一家四星级度假村和赌场。在赌博大厅，您会看到各种桌面游戏，1100多台老虎机，以及专用的扑克室。有两个高档餐厅拉蒙和海港为客人们提供精美的菜肴。另外还有一个美味的自助餐厅和一个美食广场，对于赌客来说是一应俱全。赌场内还有一个大型的剧场，经常上演高品味的节目，吸引许多达官贵人前来观看。在露露的休息室还有免费的现场娱乐表演。

3. **黑斯廷斯赛马场**（本拿比）
    黑斯廷斯赛马场近山靠海，地理位置优越，在这里还可以观看来自世界上最负盛名的赛马联播。他们也提供赌场用的老虎机，和各种美食。赛马场每年从五月至十月对外开放。

4. **大别墅赌场**（本拿比）
    本拿比大别墅赌场有两个楼层，配备了最新式和最令人兴奋的老虎机和桌面赌博游戏以及全新的扑克室。还有高额下注超豪华的赛普拉斯私人贵宾房。赌场为客人们提供饮料和饮食服务，共有7个餐厅和休息室，您可以在那里观看现场娱乐表演。

5. **硬石赌场**（高贵林）
    硬石赌场大楼占地8万平方英尺，是温哥华赌场中最大的一个。老虎机950多台，桌面游戏最全，如轮盘赌、百家乐、扑克、二十一点、骰子和牌九等等。

Best Elementary Schools

1月5日   温哥华著名的小学

Irwin Park Elementary School (public)

Here is the description of the school from their website: "Irwin Park is a K – 7 school situated in Dundarave, a part of West Vancouver, with a population of 396 students. Irwin Park is a welcoming school where all members of our school community value and promote respect, caring, acceptance and responsibility. It enjoys a diverse ethnic mix of students (with not one dominating) including many new immigrants to Canada. The school is located within three blocks of commercial business properties that support and service this small community. The school's parent group is very involved and actively supports school and classroom-based activities in numerous ways."

欧文公园小学（公立）

　　以下是其网站上的概述：

　　"欧文公园学校坐落在西温哥华邓达拉夫的一所K-7学校，有396名学生，包括许多新移民的孩子。它是一所颇受欢迎的学校，校内所有成员都受到重视、尊重、关怀、接纳和负有责任。我们提倡不同民族的融合（不存在谁是主宰）。我校位于商业区的三个街区内，欧文公园小学支持和服务这里的社区。学校的家长委员会非常投入，并以多种方式积极支持学校和课堂活动。"

January 6

A Different Way of Thinking

1月6日   不同的思维方式

Standing in Line

> *"The simple act of taking one's turn is one of the things that holds our country together."*
>
> **-U.K. immigration minister Phil Woolas**

A line (or a queue as the British call it) is an orderly line of people waiting their turn to do something such as get on a bus, go into a show, buy groceries, use the bank machine and so on. Canadians take these lines very seriously and will get quite upset and frustrated if people do not respect the line and try to jump ahead in line. Canadians are very good at forming and respecting lines as they believe it contributes to a calm, peaceful and civilized culture. At automatic banking machines in shopping centres or with street-access, for example, we form a single line that starts about two metres behind the people using the machines. We leave room for passersby and give the people at the machines privacy to conduct their business, and as each person finishes his/her banking, the next in line moves to that machine. The same procedure happens at bus stops, even for very popular bus routes during the busiest times. Trying to cut into the line and go ahead of the other people is considered one of the most rude and selfish behaviours that you can do. Just try to be patient in a line-up and use the time to take a little break and have a few free moments to relax. Standing in a line is also a really great time to practice a little small talk with the person beside you.

Canadian children learn about the importance of forming lines very early in elementary school. The classes are taught to line up in an orderly and polite way before leaving the class and during field trips and so on.

排队

> "把我们国民团结起来的方式就是简单的轮到自己去做的行为。"

> ——英国移民部长菲尔·沃拉斯

排队（英国人称为队列）是有秩序的人等着轮到他们去做一些事情。比如上公共汽车，去看表演，买杂货，使用银行取款机等等。加拿大人很严肃地对待排队一事，如果有人不遵守排队试图插队儿，那么可能会使到正在排队的人士感到非常失望和不满。加拿大人非常习惯和尊重排队，因为他们认为排队是平静、和平与文明的体现。例如，在购物中心的银行自助取款机通道处，我们一字排开。并且距离正在机器提款的人后面，我们为其他路人留下大约两米的空间，这样就保护了前者的隐私。等他/她办完了银行业务离开，下一位才会走过去。巴士站也是如此，即使在最繁忙的时段，人们也会耐心排队等候。凡试图加塞儿，抢在其他人面前，都被认为是最无礼和最自私的行为。排队的时候要保持耐心，利用这个时间休息一下，放松一下。顺便还可以和身边的人聊上几句，练练口语。

加拿大的孩子们在小学很早就学会了排队的重要性。上课前或者去校外参观学习，要有秩序、有礼貌地排好队。

English for Everyday Life
日常生活英语

这里是与排队有关的一些词语：

有时会看到有人在排队，不清楚大家为什么排队。 这时您可以这样问：

"Is this the line for _____?" Ex. "Is this the line for the 99B bus?"
"这是排队等_____吗？" 如 "这是排队等99B巴士的吗？"

在一个拥挤的地方，有时很难判断人们是站在您周围还是站成一列。要确认时，可以问：

"Are you in line?"
"您是在排队吗？"

如果有人想要在您前面插队，您可以简单地说：

"Don' t butt in line"
"不要插队"

January 7   Best High Schools

1月7日   温哥华著名的中学

University Hill High School (public)

Here is the description of the school from their website: "University Hill Secondary is an exceptional school in a number of respects. The first Vancouver Secondary School constructed in the 21st Century, with a capacity of 1000 students, it is one of the smallest schools in the VSB. We have a strong sense of community with parents, students, and staff working together to create and maintain high quality educational programs in a safe and supportive learning and social environment. University Hill takes pride in its traditions of excellence and service. Our school culture is characterized by a strong commitment to academics and a record of active participation in the fine and performing arts, and athletics. University Hill Secondary ranks among the top academic schools in the province and consistently performs extremely well in relation to other British Columbia schools."

大学山中学（公立）

以下是学校网站上的描述：

"大学山中学在许多方面都是独一无二的。它是二十一世纪建造的温哥华第一所中学，可容纳1000名学生，是VSB中最小的学校之一。我们有强烈的社会责任感，我们与家长，学生和教职员工一道，在一个安全的学习环境中共同创建和维护高质量的教育计划。大学山中学以其卓越的传统和服务而自豪。我校的文化特点是对学术界的坚定承诺，积极参与表演艺术，保持田径运动会的纪录。大学山中学与其他省校相比表现非常出色，已跻身我省顶尖的学术学校之列。"

January 8   The Homes of Vancouver

1月8日   温哥华住宅

A Grand Home
大宅子

Best Extracurricular Activities for Kids

最佳儿童课外活动

Goh Ballet Academy

"One of the most respected ballet schools in Canada... Ballet companies all over the world can boast Goh trained dancers in their number"

Luke Rittner – Former Chief Executive, Royal Academy of Dance

The Goh Ballet Academy was founded by Choo Chiat Goh and Lin Yee Goh and Chan Hon Goh is the Director. The Goh Ballet Academy provides the highest quality ballet education for all ages and levels – from beginner to advanced levels.

Goh芭蕾舞学院

"加国境内最具声誉的芭蕾舞学校之一…… 它在世界各地的芭蕾舞团体中拥有Goh式训练有素的"相当数量"舞蹈演员而自豪，

卢克·里特纳——皇家舞蹈学院前首席执行官

Goh芭蕾舞学院是由中国国家芭蕾舞团首席舞者Choo Chiat Goh和Lin Yee Goh携手创办。Goh芭蕾舞学院为所有年龄舞者提供从初级到高级最优质的芭蕾舞教育 。

January 10

January 10   Meeting Locals in Vancouver

1月10日   与当地人接触

One of the Main Goals of our Book

Yi and I decided to write this book because we wanted to remove any barriers to communication between newcomers and locals. All the information in the book about culture and language is to help you have a good understanding of the basics of everyday life in Vancouver so that you will feel more relaxed and comfortable living here. It is difficult to feel brave enough to take a chance talking to local people when you feel absolutely lost and confused by all the new things in your city. We really hope that this guide to your first year in Vancouver will reduce any anxiety you have and give you confidence to take a chance once in a while and reach out and meet new people in Vancouver – newcomers, oldtimers, local -everyone!

本书的主要目标之一

义和我决定写这本书是因为我们想消除新移民与当地人之间沟通的障碍。书中涉及到有关文化和语言等所有的信息都是为了帮助您更好地了解温哥华日常生活的基本常识，这样您在这里生活会感到更加轻松和舒适。当您在新的城市中遇到新事物感到困惑和迷茫的时候，很难会鼓足勇气去和当地人交谈。我们真诚的希望这本指南，您在温哥华新生活这本书会最大限度地减少您所担心的任何问题。让您有信心在短时间内有机会在温哥华接触到更多的新朋友——新移民、本地人以及其他所有居住在温哥华的人！

Restaurant Customs and Etiquette

1月11日   温哥华餐厅的习俗与礼仪

Finding the Best Restaurants in Vancouver

There are so many restaurants in Vancouver- how to choose a good one? Fortunately, there is an annual list published of the very best restaurants in Vancouver. This list is published by the Georgia Straight Newspaper who survey thousands of their readers to find out which restaurants deserve the prestigious Golden Plate Award. They have several categories of restaurants and they choose the top three winners in each category. Choosing a restaurant from this list will ensure that you have a very good dining experience in Vancouver no matter what type of restaurant you go to.

寻找温哥华最好的餐馆：佐治亚直报年度金盘子排行榜

温哥华的餐馆太多了，可究竟怎样才能选出一家好的餐厅呢？很幸运，我们这里有一份温哥华最好的餐馆年度排行榜。这份榜单是由佐治亚直报公布，他们每年都会对数以千计的读者进行问卷调查。 他们将餐馆分成几类进行统计，根据票数每个类别中再选出前三名优胜者。从这个榜单中您可以任选一家餐厅去用餐，无论您去哪一间或什么类型的餐厅，您都将会得到很好的用餐体验。

January 12   Top English Programs for Adults

1月12日   成人高级英语课程

Vancouver Community College (VCC)

Vancouver Community College provides adult learners with first-class English language instruction. They have been the number one provider of English language courses to adult newcomers for decades. Not only does VCC offer a variety of high quality, award-winning Pathways English language courses, but they also provide exceptional support to their students with free, daily one-on-one English tutoring in their Learning Centres with professional, fully certified English tutors. Also, there are two libraries, plenty of study spaces, sports and activities and cafeterias serving high quality, gourmet food prepared by the culinary students.

Language Instruction for Newcomers to Canada (LINC) courses are offered by VCC as well as the gold-medal award winning **Pathways English** courses. The Pathways courses help prepare students for employment or further academic and skill training. In addition, VCC has innovative career training programs that combine ESL classes with skills training such as hairstyling, cooking and health care aid programs. The English language courses take place at the Broadway campus which is easily accessible by bus and Skytrain. Also, fulltime students are eligible for a Transit UPASS which allows unlimited use of transit for a very low monthly fee of $30.

温哥华社区学院（VCC）LINC，途径与职业英语课程

　　温哥华社区学院（简称VCC）为成年人提供一流的英语教学。 几十年来，一直把成人移民的英语课程放在首位。提供多门高品质屡获殊荣的英语课程，有很多专业的和经过认证的英语导师，在学习中心免费提供日常一对一的英语辅导，为学生提供额外的支持。温哥华社区学院设有两座校园，分别位于百老汇街和温哥华市中心。有两个图书馆，超大的自习室和体育活动场所，餐厅提供高质量的由烹饪学生准备的美食。

　　VCC提供加拿大新移民语言教学（LINC）课程以及获得过金奖的途径英语课程。途径课程帮助学生准备就业，研究学术和提高技能。此外，VCC还创办了各种职业培训课程，将ESL课程、烹饪、发型设计、医疗援助计划与技能培训相结合。LINC课程安排在百老汇校园，交通很便利，可以乘坐公交车和轻轨。全日制学生有资格获得通票U-PASS，每月只需付30加元。可以无限制地使用。

January 13   # Vancouver Backyard Wildlife

1月13日   温哥华后院的小鸟和动物

Eastern Grey Squirrel

The Grey Squirrel is the most common squirrel in British Columbia's biggest cities. In 1909, the Mayor of New York city gave the city a gift of some Eastern Grey Squirrel breeding pairs and the population has grown since that time. The squirrels are very well suited to an urban environment. The Eastern Grey Squirrel varies widely in colour from black and brown to gray. Grey squirrels are mainly herbivorous, eating acorns and hazel nuts, berries, and berries.

东部地区的灰松鼠

灰松鼠在不列颠哥伦比亚省各大城市里是最常见的小动物。 1909年，纽约市市长将东部地区的灰松鼠作为礼物送给了温哥华市。这种松鼠非常适合城市环境，繁殖的很快。颜色有黑色、棕色和灰色，差别很大。灰松鼠主要是食草动物，吃橡子、坚果和浆果。

January 14   ## Support for Newcomers

1月14日   支持新移民

Welcome BC

The government of British Columbia runs this website. It has information to help newcomers get settled, find employment, join the community and be a part of the social and economic activities in BC. WelcomeBC has information, tools, resources, and links to resources. It also has a very useful "cost of living calculator" that will allow newcomers to estimate the cost of living in different parts of BC. They also provide a Newcomer's Guide in 14 different languages.

BC省欢迎您 https://www.welcomebc.ca/

这是不列颠哥伦比亚省政府官网。有许多实用的信息，它帮助新移民解决定居、找工作、加入社区、并成为卑诗省社会经济活动的一部分。WelcomeBC上面有信息、工具、资源和资源链接。它还有一个非常有用的"生活成本计算器"，它可以帮您估算居住在BC省不同地区的生活费用。网站提供用14种不同语言编写的"新移民指南"。

Vancouver Neighbourhoods

温哥华社区

Kerrisdale Village

Kerrisdale is a beautiful and elegant neighbourhood on the west side of Vancouver with grand houses and tree-lined streets that is popular with families and seniors. Kerrisdale Village is the main shopping area on West 41st Avenue. There are many charming boutiques that sell a wide variety of products; many of them family owned businesses that have been in business for many years such as the clothing store Hills, the bookstore Hager Books and the stationary store, Buchan's. There are also speciality food stores including a cheese market, Asian bakery, fine chocolates store and liquor store. The restaurants reflect the diversity of the neighbourhood with busy dim sum restaurants like the popular Golden Ocean Seafood Restaurant to family dining at Minerva's Pizza and Steakhouse Restaurant and everything in between. Kerrisdale Village has many different coffee shops to relax in from the Parisian style Faubourg Café to the Italian style Artigiano Café. There are also two famous teahouses in Kerrisdale where you can enjoy high tea at the Secret Garden and at Adonia Café.

克里斯戴尔http://www.kerrisdalevillage.com/

　　温哥华西侧有一个美丽而优雅的社区叫做克里斯戴尔社区，它拥有高大的建筑和绿树成荫的街道，深受当地居民特别是老年人的喜爱。主要购物区位于西41大道。那里有许多可爱的小店铺出售各种各样的产品；其中许多家族企业在那里经营了多年，如希尔斯服装店，海格书店和巴肯文具商店。此外还有特色食品商店，像奶酪市场、亚洲面包店、精美巧克力店和酒品店。餐厅同样反映了该社区的多样性，如广受欢迎的金海阁海鲜餐厅，还有一个像在家里用餐的密涅瓦式披萨和牛排餐厅，等等。克里斯戴尔社区还有许多不同类型的咖啡厅，从巴黎风格的Faubourg咖啡厅到意大利风格的ArtegianoCafé咖啡厅，在那里你可以充分放松自己。另有两个著名的喝下午茶的茶馆，也在克里斯戴尔社区，一个是秘密花园，另一个是阿多尼亚咖啡馆。

Basic Everyday English

基本日常生活用语

Greetings, Introductions, and Goodbyes

It is very common to say hello and give a little smile to people you pass on the street, even if you don't know them. Remember that a smile is always welcome and can be a great way to send a friendly message even if you can't speak English yet! Please visit our website to hear audio clips of the English phrases below that you can use to practice pronunciation.

"A smile is the shortest distance between two people".

-anonymous

问候、介绍和道别

在街上向对面走过来的人问好和微笑是很常见的，即使您不认识他们。记住，微笑总是受欢迎的，即使您不会讲英语，也同样可以传递友好的信息！

"两个人之间最短的距离是微笑"。

——无名氏

English for Everyday Life
日常生活英语

下面是一些基本英语短语，您也许听到过，您可以用来问候、介绍和告别。请访问我们的网站——，听一听这些短语的发音并练习会话。

Hi, I'm Yi.
Hello, my name is Yi.
Hello, I'm Yi and this is my wife, Qi and my son, Jason
What's your name?
It was nice talking to you
See you later
I have to get going now
Goodbye

您好，我是义。
您好，我叫义。
您好，我是义，这是我的妻子琪和我的儿子杰森。
您叫什么名字？
和您谈话很愉快。
稍后见
我现在得走了。
再见

Education

1月17日   教育

Vancouver School Board Parent Information Brochures

The Vancouver School Board has prepared many brochures for parents to help answer their general questions about BC schools. It is very important to them that all parents are informed about the education system and so they have ensured that the brochures are also available in many languages. To see the brochures in Chinese, visit their website.

温哥华学校董事会家长信息手册
https://www.vsb.bc.ca/multilanguage-brochures

　　温哥华学校董事会为家长准备了许多手册，帮助解答他们关心的卑诗省学校的一般问题。 对董事会而言，所有家长都能够了解教育制度非常重要，因此他们确保手册有多种语言版本。 要查看中文手册，请点击上面的多语言手册的网页。

Scenes from Daily Life

1月18日   温哥华日常生活中的一些镜头

Busy Downtown Sidewalk
繁忙的市区人行道

Outdoor Life in Vancouver

1月19日 温哥华户外生活

A Walker's Paradise — Walk BC

Vancouver is a city that is perfect for walking. The air is fresh, the scenery is beautiful and the many different walking choices are endless. In fact, there are several books and websites dedicated to documenting all the different walking paths and routes in Vancouver. The best website for finding all the information you need about walking routes and paths throughout Vancouver and BC is the WalkBC website. It is maintained by the BC Parks and Recreation Association and the information and maps are always reliable and kept up to date.

健走者的天堂 – BC省徒步网站 http://www.walkbc.ca/

温哥华是一座非常适合健走的城市。空气清新，风景秀丽，有数不清的步行路线。事实上，有几本书籍和网站专门记载温哥华所有不同的行走路径和线路。浏览上面的网站，可以找到您需要的温哥华和BC省行走的所有路径和线路的详细信息。该网站是由卑诗省公园和娱乐协会维护，所提供的信息和地图都是可靠的，而且内容随时更新。

Tips to Learning English

1月20日 资深英语老师提供学习英语的小贴士

Start Where You Are

Sometimes newcomers are worried about their English abilities when they first arrive. If they get an English Assessment test, they also worry about the level they have been assigned and how it isn't as high as they want or think it should be. As an English Instructor, I wish that these English level labels could be eliminated as they simply don't matter for the real world and they give newcomers such stress. What really matters is that a newcomer just 'Start where you are". Whatever English level you are, that is your starting point and you can build your skills every single day from there. Wherever you start, no matter how low, this is just a temporary starting place from which you will build and improve – a little at a time, day by day, and step-by-step. Before you know it, time will pass by so quickly and your English will be dramatically improved.

从哪里开始

当新移民初到温哥华的时候，他们往往会担心自己的英语能力。为了参加成人英语培训，他们先要进行英语评估测试，这时，他们又担心测试的结果，会不会被评估的太高，超出他们的实际水平。以至于听不懂或者跟不上学习的进度。作为一名英语教师，我希望可以取消这些英语级别的测试，因为他们根本不关心现实世界，他们只会给新移民带来心理压力。其实最重要的是，无论你的英语水平如何，此刻就是你的起点，你可以从这里起步，每天坚持。无论你的英语水平多么低，它只是一个临时的起点，此后，一点一点，一天一天，一步一步，你将逐步提高。随着时间的推移，你会发现，你的英语已经有了长足的进步。

January 21   A Little Canadian Inspiration

1月21日   一点点启示

"Canada is not a melting-pot. Canada is an association of peoples who have, and cherish, great differences but who work together because they can respect themselves and each other."

-Vincent Massey*"

The concept of "**not** being a melting pot" is a very popular ideal in Canada. Canadians take pride in being a country that is a 'mosaic' (from the term used to describe a picture made from thousands of different coloured tiles). The idea of a cultural mosaic describes a form of multiculturalism, different from other systems such as the melting pot, which is often used to describe the United States' ideal of assimilation. In Canada, immigrants are encouraged to retain their culture, language and heritage while at the same time learning the language and customs of Canada.

"加拿大不是一个大熔炉。加拿大是一个拥有和珍视巨大差异的民族，因为他们能够尊重彼此，共同合作。"

——文森特·梅西

"不是熔炉"这一概念在加拿大是家喻户晓深入民心的。让加拿大人感到自豪的是，这个国家的特点就是"马赛克"（马赛克一词是用于描述由数千种不同颜色瓷砖制成的图片）。马赛克体现了一种多元文化。它不同于其他的体系，如熔炉，它常常被用来描述美国的同化理想。在加拿大，鼓励移民保留他们的文化、语言和遗产，同时学习加拿大的语言和习俗。

Volunteer in Vancouver

1月22日　在温哥华做义工

Being a Volunteer in Vancouver

Over 50% of Canadians do volunteer work and contribute their time, energy and skills to groups and organizations such as charities and non-profit organizations. This volunteer work is not only very important to the individual organizations, but it is also very important to Canadian society as a whole and is part of our national identity as a compassionate nation. There are many types of volunteer positions including visiting seniors, coaching sports teams, preparing and delivering food to homeless people, helping to preserve the environment, working in thrift stores and helping with arts and culture festivals. Local schools and community centres also rely on many volunteers for their daily operations. Volunteers help shape their communities by showing kindness and service to their fellow Canadians. The Employment Standards Act of Canada ensures that volunteers are not used in positions that should be paid, so volunteer jobs usually have a maximum weekly hour limit of approximately 10 to 15 hours. On the other hand, volunteer positions are taken seriously and the organizations will expect you to be punctual and reliable.

在温哥华做义工

在温哥华有超过50% 的加拿大人从事各种志愿服务工作，为慈善和非营利机构等团体和组织贡献他们的时间、精力和技能。义工的工作不仅对各个组织非常重要，而且对整个加拿大社会也是不可或缺的，它是我们作为一个富有同情心的国家和整个民族认同的一部分。义工的岗位有很多种，包括看望老年人、指导运动队、为无家可归的人准备和提供食物、帮助保护环境、在旧货商店工作、帮助组织艺术和文化节。当地学校和社区中心的许多日常工作也依靠义工们的参与。他们通过友善的服务来塑造自己的社区。加拿大《就业标准法》规定，义工不得按照付酬的岗位使用。因此义工每周工作时间的上限大约为10至15小时。另一方面，义工要认真负责，相关的组织期望您守时可靠。

Healthcare in Vancouver

温哥华的医疗保健

BC Medical Services (MSP) and Private Plans

All BC residents must register with the BC Medical Services Plan and will receive a BC Services Card. The BC MSP card will pay for many health costs, including doctors, most medical tests and treatments. It may take up to three months before you receive your card, so you must purchase private medical coverage for this time. If you do not have medical insurance, you must pay the doctor or hospital yourself, which can be expensive.

Always take your card with you when you go to a doctor, clinic or hospital. You will also need a valid BC Services Card for prescriptions.

Unfortunately, not all healthcare services are covered by MSP. All of the following are not covered by the Medical Services Plan and the patient must pay the total cost: Dentists, eye exams, hearing aids, private hospital rooms, psychologists, counsellors, physiotherapists, cosmetic surgery and tests required for immigration papers, driver's licences and insurance.

Therefore, many people also purchase private extended health care plans for their families which have a monthly fee that ensures you only pay a percentage of the cost of these services instead of the whole amount. The amount of total bill that you have to pay depends on how much of a monthly premium you have agreed to. It is possible to buy extended health care plans from most insurance offices. Also, many of the colleges, professional associations and auto associations (such as BC Automobile Association) offer discounted extended health plans to their students and members. Finally, Pacific Blue Cross is the largest non-profit provider of extended health plans in the province and offers a wide selection of plans to fit every budget.

卑诗省医疗服务计划（MSP）和私人扩展保健计划

> BC省医疗服务计划 www.hibc.gov.bc.ca/
> BCAA保险计划 https://www.bcaa.com/insurance/
> 太平洋蓝十字保险 http://www.pac.bluecross.ca/

所有BC居民都必须向BC省医疗服务计划（简称MSP）登记注册，并将收到BC服务卡。 此卡将支付许多医疗费用，包括看病、大多数医疗检查和治疗费用。申请之后可能需要等上三个月才能收到您的医疗卡。因此您必须先购买私人医疗保险。 如果您没有医疗保险，您必须自己支付医生或医院的费用，这将是非常昂贵的。

当您去诊所或医院看医生时，一定要带上医疗卡。去药房取处方药的时候也同样需要它。

不幸的是，并非所有的医疗保健服务都包括在医疗服务计划MSP中。患者必须全额支付以下未涵盖的费用：牙医、眼睛检查、助听器、私人病房、心理医生、辅导员、物理治疗师和整容手术，还有移民文件、驾驶执照和保险所需要的各项体检。

因此，许多人也会为他们的家庭购买私人扩展保健计划，这些计划每月收费一次，您只需要按百分比支付部分服务费用，而不是全部的。您要付的金额取决于您同意每月的保费额是多少。您可以从大多数保险机构购买扩展医疗保健计划。此外，许多学院、专业协会和汽车协会（如卑诗省汽车协会）也向学生和会员提供优惠的扩展健康计划。最后，太平洋蓝十字是全省最大的非营利性健康计划提供商，它提供多种计划可供选择，以适应各种预算方案。

January 24   Interesting Facts About Vancouver

1月24日   温哥华趣闻

A Winning City

According to Tourism Vancouver, here is just a small selection of the many awards that the city of Vancouver has been given:

- *Most Livable City in North America* – Mercer Quality of Living Survey (March 2017). It is also ranked the fifth most livable city in the world. This annual survey looks at factors such as political and social environment; sociocultural factors; housing; and natural environment.

- *Top Destination in Canada* – TripAdvisor's 2017 Travelers' Choice Awards (March 2017). The visitors love the mountains, forests, city beaches, Olympic history and the suspension bridge.

- *Vancouver is a favourite destination for Chinese Millennial travellers - Ctrip* (February 2017). This award is voted by travellers born after the year 1980. Ctrip is China's leading online travel agency and its voters judge the city by factors including destinations, attractons, hotels, culinary, cruises, shopping, airlines and car rentals. The Ctrip voters voted Stanley Park, Capilano Suspension Bridge Park and Canada Place as the top three attractions in Vancouver.

- *'Greenest' City in the World* - World Economic Forum (January 2017). This group measures and compares the cities' green canopies and how dense they are. Vancouver had the largest tree canopy of all the major cities looked at.

- *Vancouver is a Top 2017 Travel Destination* – Forbes (January 2017). Forbes Magazine has placed Vancouver on its Top 10 List of Travel Destinations.

屡获殊荣的城市

　　据温哥华旅游局介绍，下面是颁发给温哥华市众多荣誉奖项的一小部分：

- **北美洲最宜居城市**——美世生活品质调查（2017年3月）温哥华被列为世界上第五个最宜居的城市。这项年度调查着眼于政治、住房、社会环境、社会文化和自然环境等因素。
- **加拿大荣获首选旅游目的地**——荣获国际旅游网站TripAdvisor的"2017年旅客选择奖"（2017年3月）。游客喜欢这里的山、森林、城市海滩、奥运历史和吊桥。
- **温哥华是中国千禧年游客最喜欢的目的地 - 携程网** ——（2017年2月）。该奖项是由1980年以后出生的旅客投票。携程网是中国大型的在线旅行社，其选民通过包括目的地、吸引力、酒店、美食、游轮、购物、航空公司和汽车租赁等因素来评判城市。携程选民投票选出了斯坦利公园、卡皮拉诺吊桥公园和加拿大广场，是温哥华的三大景点。
- 世界**"最绿色的城市"** —— 世界经济论坛（2017年1月）。通过测量和比较所有主要城市的绿色檐篷和它们的密度。结果温哥华拥有最大的树冠。
- **温哥华是2017热门的旅游目的地** —— 福布斯（2017年1月），"福布斯"杂志已将温哥华列为10大旅游目的地的名单。

Finding Work in Vancouver

1月25日　　在温哥华找份工作

International Credentials Evaluation Service (ICES at BCIT)

It can be very useful for planning your career in Canada to get your non-Canadian education assessed by ICES in a report that can be given to future employers and educational institutions. These documents make it easier to compare your education to the Canadian equivalent. There are three kinds of reports that you can get: Basic Report, Comprehensive Report and an ECA Report.

1. The **Basic Report** is most useful to those seeking general employment. It identifies each fully or partially completed educational credential and indicates the comparable credential in Canada.

2. The **Comprehensive Report** is most useful to those seeking employment in a professional occupation or admission to a post-secondary institution. Some organizations require a Supplemental Report that has additional research completed by ICES to meet the needs of the organization.

3. **Educational Credential Assessment (ECA) Reports** are prepared by ICES for Citizenship and Immigration Canada (CIC) for Canadian immigration purposes (Express Entry and Permanent Residency). Under the guidelines provided by the Citizenship and Immigration Canada (CIC) ICES will only provide ECA reports for completed academic credentials.

成绩单和国际证书评估服务（BCIT的ICIT）

国际认证评估服务（ICES）http://www.bcit.ca/ices/

　　获得一份对于那些没有加拿大教育机构学历的人来说，ICES的评估报告在加拿大规划你的职业生涯是非常有用的，可以把它出示给未来的雇主和教育机构。 这些文件可以证明你曾受到教育的程度与加拿大是相等的。 您可以获得一下三种报告：

　　1. **基本报告**：对寻求一般就业的人来讲最为有用。 它用来甄别某人是否曾经受过全面或者部分的教育凭证，并等同于在加拿大受教育的程度。

　　2. **综合报告**：对那些寻求特殊职业或者注册某些专业课程的人士最有用。一些机构需要一份补充报告，该报告由ICES完成，以满足该机构的额外需求。

　　3. **教育证书评估（ECA）报告**：由加拿大移民局（CIC）为那些加拿大移民（快速入境和永久居留）准备。根据加拿大移民局（CIC）提供的指导方针，ICES只提供已完成学历证书的ECA报告。

January 26 Vancouver Sightseeing

1月26日   观光

Grouse Mountain

Grouse Mountain is one of the beautiful mountains towering over the city of Vancouver. It is a wonderful place to visit all year round. The foot of the mountain is just 15 minutes from downtown Vancouver and the Grouse Mountain Gondola takes you to the top of the mountain. In the spring and summer, you can enjoy the city view while eating a meal at the restaurant, or you can be more active and walk the forest trails, visit the grizzly bear enclosure, try the Zipline and enjoy the Birds of Prey and Lumberjack shows. For a fitness challenge in the summer months, you can skip the Gondola and walk up the famously difficult hiking trail called the Grouse Grind. It is popular with locals looking for a workout. In the winter months, the mountaintop becomes a winter wonderland with an outdoor skating rink, skiing, snowshoeing and sliding.

松鸡山https://www.grousemountain.com/

　　松鸡山是温哥华市最美丽的山峰之一，一年四季都可以游览。从温哥华市中心开车到松鸡山脚下只需 15分钟的车程，然后乘坐松鸡山的缆车直达山顶的滑雪场。春季和夏季，您在餐厅用餐时可以鸟瞰城市的美景，或者漫步在森林的小径中，中途还可以参观一下灰熊围场，尝试一下高空滑索，观赏猎鸟表演和伐木秀 。 夏季你可以挑战自我，不坐缆车，沿着著名陡峭的松鸡山径一路往上爬，这是很受当地人欢迎的健身方式。冬天，整个山顶仿佛仙境一般，那里有一个室外溜冰场，和不同级别的滑雪道。

January 27   # Vancouver Transportation

1月27日   温哥华交通运输

Translink

Translink is the name of the organization that takes care of Vancouver's transportation network including buses, trains, major roads and bridges. Their website has many helpful features that can help you figure out how to get to your destination in the fastest and most efficient way. The Trip Planning feature allows you to enter the address of where you are and the address of your destination and the time you want to arrive and then it figures out your route and timing.

运输联线 http://www.translink.ca/

　　运输联线(TransLink)，简称运联，是负责加拿大卑诗省大温哥华地区运输网络组织的名称，包括公共汽车，火车，主要道路和桥梁。 他们的网站有许多有用的功能，可以帮助您以最快和最有效的方式到达您的目的地。 旅行规划功能允许输入您所在的位置，目的地和您想要到达的时间，然后计算您的路线和时间。

English for Everyday Life
日常生活英语

这里是如何向公共汽车司机询问信息：

　"Can you please tell me which bus goes to Metrotown Mall?"
　"Does this bus go to Metrotown mall?"

　"您能告诉我吗，哪辆巴士去铁道镇购物中心？"
　"这辆车到不到铁道镇购物中心？"

Sports Teams and Special Events

1月28日   专业体育赛事和活动

Vancouver Canucks Team

Canadians are well-known for their love of ice hockey. They closely follow the Hockey World Championships and the hockey matches in the Winter Olympics. But the most popular hockey teams play in the National Hockey League which has 30 teams based in different provinces and states in Canada and the USA. The NHL team based in British Columbia is called the Vancouver Canucks. The NHL hockey season runs from October to April each year. At the end of the season there is the big **Stanley Cup** playoffs and final championship. NHL hockey games are a popular sport to watch. People go to the actual games, or they gather to watch the games on television in bars or at home. It is possible to buy tickets to single games or buy "season tickets" to go see all the local Vancouver Canucks games all year. On game day in Vancouver, it is common to see many people wearing a Vancouver Canucks shirt to show their support for the team. The Vancouver Canucks play their home games at Rogers Arena.

温哥华加人队https://www.nhl.com/canucks

　　加拿大人因喜爱冰球而闻名。他们总是密切关注冰球的世界锦标赛和冬季奥运会的冰球比赛。 但最受欢迎的则是观看全国冰球联盟赛，总共有30支冰球队，分别来自加拿大不同的省份和美国各个州。不列颠哥伦比亚省的NHL冰球队被称为温哥华加人队。NHL冰球赛季从每年的十月至来年的四月。在赛季结束时举行大的斯坦利杯季后赛和最后的冠军决赛。每逢NHL冰球比赛总会吸引大批的观众。人们聚集在酒吧里观看或者在家里看电视，超级球迷们则直接去现场观看。门票分为单次的和赛季的。在比赛当天，很多球迷都穿着温哥华加人队的球衣来表达他们对该球队的支持。温哥华加人队的主场设在罗杰斯体育馆。

January 29   Vancouver Parks

1月29日   温哥华公园

Queen Elizabeth Park

Queen Elizabeth Park, at 152 metres above sea level, is the highest point in Vancouver and has spectacular views of the park, city, and mountains on the North Shore. The Park is located at the corner of Cambie Street and West 33rd Avenue. There are entrances on several sides of the park, including Ontario Street and West 33rd Avenue, or along West 37th Avenue between Columbia and Mackie streets. Some highlights of the park are:

- The Bloedel Conservatory: An indoor tropical garden underneath a large glass dome
- A beautiful garden built in a former rock quarry
- An arboretum with a collection of exotic and native trees and sculptures
- Recreational activities such as tennis, lawn bowling and pitch & putt golf
- Fine dining at Seasons in the Park Restaurant
- Many places for picnics

伊丽莎白女王公园

伊丽莎白女王公园位于海拔152米处，是温哥华市的最高点，可以俯瞰城市和山脉的壮丽景色。 公园位于甘比街夹33街一带。 公园有几处入口，包括安大略街和西33街，以及在哥伦比亚和麦基街之间的西37街。 公园的一些亮点是：

- 布洛德尔温室：在一个大玻璃圆顶下面的室内热带花园
- 一个建在前荒废的采石场上面的美丽花园
- 有一个植物园，它收集了异国情调的树木和雕塑
- 有各种娱乐设施，如网球，草地保龄球和推杆高尔夫球
- 在公园的四季餐厅享用美食
- 有许多可以野餐的地方

January 30 ## Stories and Advice for Newcomers

1月30日　　移民的故事和建议

Yi

当代的白求恩

移民后，我发现，自己原来学的英语在这里不太灵光，自己说的话，西人听不懂。生病了，说不清楚自己的症状；去西餐厅，看不懂菜单；电话铃响了，拿起话筒不知道对方在讲些什么。为此，我报读了温哥华社区学院(VCC)的成人英语课程LINC 。我在这里遇到了一位备受移民们尊敬的导师Kari。在她耐心的日复一日的帮助下，我进步得很快。日常交流、看病甚至接听电话都没有问题。Kari和我在一起经常讨论加拿大和中国的文化，探讨各种问题。也交流个人的经历。听到我讲自己小时候的艰苦生活，Kari流下了热泪。

除了学习英语之外，我爱好摄影。 经常作为自媒体人参加各种活动。2015年6月，温哥华举办国际龙舟赛期间、Kari推荐我参加龙舟赛的媒体采访组，亲历了大赛。媒体采访组一共8人，除我之外，都是报社、电视台的摄影记者。我所拍的40多幅作品均被龙舟赛组委会选用。其中的两幅还被选登在龙舟赛的官方网站上。

Kari把移民的事情当作自己的事情，她经常利用自己周末休息时间，为广大的移民朋友排忧解难。2015年，在Kari的倡导下我们组建了一个英语学习团队，定期组织活动。凡是接触过Kari的移民朋友，都有这样的一种感觉，那就是，她处处为他人服务，毫不利己，专门利人，对移民极端的热忱。借此机会我想说出大家的心声 —— Kari是当代的白求恩。

Diverse Vancouver

1月31日　　**多元文化的温哥华**

Friday Night Ukrainian Perogy Suppers

Get to know your Ukrainian neighbours at their delicious monthly **Friday Night Perogy** dinners served once per month on the first Friday of each month from 5:00 pm to 8:00 pm. These dinners have been happening in Vancouver since 1995 and are very popular with the locals so it is a good idea to come early. All of the food is prepared by volunteer church members and is very affordably priced. Perogies, cabbage rolls, koubassa sausage and borsch soup are some of the favourite items on the menu.

周五晚上乌克兰Perogy晚餐

先来介绍一下乌克兰社区，每月的第一个星期五晚上从下午5:00开始到晚上8:00提供美味的每月一次周五Perogy晚餐。此晚餐在温哥华始于1995年，非常受当地人的欢迎，所以最好早点去。所有的食物均是由教会的志愿者准备的，价格不贵。晚餐备有番石榴、卷心菜等等，其中乌克兰Koubassa香肠和罗宋汤是菜单上最受欢迎的。

February

Weather:	Average temperature: 1°C to 9°C
	Average rainfall days: 18, Average rainfall: 70 mm
Statutory holiday:	Family Day
Other special days:	Valentine's Day
	Vancouver International Wine Festival (Feb/March)

In February, the mood improves a little bit as the weather starts to get a little drier and the Family Day long weekend gives everyone a nice three-day weekend. Family Day always occurs on the second Monday of February. The purpose of Family Day is to enable workers to take a break from their busy working lives to spend some quality time with their family and friends. There are no traditional ways to celebrate the day and every family uses the time in their own way. However, many of the sightseeing attractions and community centres and parks arrange family-themed activities during that long weekend.

Valentine's Day is always on the 14th of February and it is the day when everyone celebrates love – especially romantic love – but also the love between friends and family, too. In elementary schools, the children have a class party and celebrate with cookies and cakes that are shaped like hearts and have pink and red icing. Also, the children will give each other little Valentine's Day cards that have their favourite cartoon characters on them. Finally, adult couples go out to dinner in restaurants and give each other romantic presents such as roses, a box of chocolates or jewelry. Many restaurants offer special Valentine's Day dinner special set menus for couples.

In late February until early March there is also the Annual Vancouver International Wine Festival where wineries from around the world showcase their wine at North America's number one wine festival. You can go to seminars and learn more about wine and food pairings and taste some gourmet lunches and dinners.

2月

气候：　平均温度：1°C 至 9°C
　　　　平均降雨天数：18，平均降雨量：70毫米
公众节假日：家庭日
其他特殊日：情人节
　　　　　温哥华国际葡萄酒节（2月/3月）

到了二月份，大家的心情好转了一点，因为天气开始变得有点不那么潮湿，家庭日为大家提供了一个为期三天的长周末。家庭日是在二月的第二个星期一。家庭日的目的是使员工从他们忙碌的工作中解脱出来，安排好生活和休息，多花一些时间与他们的家人和朋友一起共度美好的时光。家庭日没有传统的庆祝方式，每个家庭都是按照自己的方式来庆祝。许多的观光景点、社区中心和公园都会利用这个漫长的周末安排以家庭为主题的活动。

情人节（Valentine's Day），在每年的2月14日。这是人人都会庆祝爱情的日子，特别是指浪漫的爱情，当然还有朋友和家人之间的爱。在小学，孩子们举行一个班级聚会，用饼干和心形蛋糕，粉色和红色的冰糖来庆祝。孩子们会互赠小小的情人节卡片，上面有他们最喜欢的卡通人物。成年情侣去餐馆吃饭，赠送浪漫的礼物给对方，例如玫瑰花，巧克力或珠宝等，表达爱慕之心。许多餐馆还特意推出情侣套餐，专门为情侣们提供特别的情人节晚餐。

在2月下旬至3月初还有一年一度的温哥华国际葡萄酒节，来自世界各地的葡萄酒厂商将在北美地区排名第一的葡萄酒节上展示他们的葡萄酒。您可以去研讨会学习更多关于酒和食物的搭配并品尝美味的午餐和晚餐。

Local Customs

Pre-wedding Parties and Celebrations

Over the last twenty years, weddings have become "big business" and there are increasing expectations of how an engagement and wedding should proceed. Couples always have a choice to have a modest engagement and wedding, or to elope (secretly leave town and get married on their own in another city without telling anyone). However, for the couples who want to fully celebrate, here is a list of pre-wedding parties, traditions and celebrations:

- **Engagement announcements, photos, parties and "save the date":** Couples can formally announce their engagement by placing a special announcement in the personal section of the newspaper or by sending out engagement announcement cards or emails. These are often accompanied by an official engagement photograph of the couple. The parents of the couple can also host an engagement party to celebrate the engagement of their child. Some couples also let everyone know of their wedding date at this time by telling them to "Save the Date" and mark their calendars with the wedding day before the official wedding invitations are sent out.

- **Bachelor/bachelorette/stag parties**: A Bachelor party, also known as a Stag Party is a male-only outing with the Groom and his friends going out and having "one last big celebration as a single man". Usually the outings include playing sports, going drinking and possibly going to a strip bar. The bride and her friends also go out for an evening of women-only fun called a Bachelorette party.

- **Bridal Showers** A bridal shower is a gift-giving party held for a bride-to-be in anticipation of her wedding. It is only attended by the Bride's closest female friends and family members. Also, every shower guest must already be on the wedding guest invitation list. Guests bring presents that are only meant for the bride such as beautiful nightwear or beauty products.

- **Wedding Rehearsal Dinners** For big church weddings, there is often a wedding rehearsal the night before with all the members of the wedding party (bridesmaids, groomsmen, parents of the couple). The rehearsal dinner is usually held after the rehearsal as a way of thanking the wedding party for their participation.

婚礼前的聚会和庆祝活动

在过去二十年里，婚礼已经成为一桩"大生意"，对于订婚和结婚仪式的期望越来越高。夫妻总是要做出一个选择，要么举行一场温馨的婚礼，要么就采取elope私奔（偷偷离开城镇，在另一个城市结婚，而不告诉任何人）。然而，对于那些想要举行传统婚礼庆祝活动的夫妇，这里有一个婚礼前聚会庆祝活动的列表：

- 订婚公告、照片、聚会和"约定日子"：夫妇可以通过在报纸个人版面上正式刊登他们订婚的消息，通常要附上这对夫妇正式订婚的照片。有的夫妇寄送邀请函，或者通过电子邮件通知亲朋好友。这对新婚夫妇的父母还可以主办一个订婚晚会来庆祝孩子的订婚。有的夫妇也会在这个时候让每个人都知道他们的婚礼日期，即"约定日子"，并当他们收到婚礼邀请函的时候，将婚礼日期标记在他们的日历上。
- 单身男子、单身女郎和单身派对：单身派对，也被称为一个男人的聚会，是新郎和他的朋友们出去玩耍，"最后一次庆祝作为单身男子大的外出活动"。通常的活动包括体育运动，去喝酒，甚至去脱衣舞酒吧。女人也要有一个大的庆祝活动，新娘也会约上她的朋友们出去搞一个只有单身女人最后一晚上的剩女派对。包括最后去修个指甲，去沙龙喝酒和跳舞
- 新娘送礼会：是新娘最亲密的女性朋友和家人为准新娘举行的送礼聚会。每一位来宾必须是列在婚礼邀请的客人名单上。送礼会上会收到许多实用的礼品如漂亮的睡衣或美容产品作为一种嫁妆，为新娘即将承担妻子的角色做准备。
- 婚礼彩排晚宴：往往是婚礼前一天晚上在大教堂与所有参加婚礼的成员（伴娘、新郎、新婚和双方的父母）举行婚礼排练。预演后设晚宴招待大家，作为一种酬谢的方式。

Parenting in Vancouver

2月2日   在温哥华养育子女

Elementary and High School Rankings

Every year the Fraser Institute prepares a report card for all the elementary and high schools in British Columbia. These annual reports provide information about the performance and success of the schools to help parents make choices about the different schools in the city. However, most Vancouver parents also go and look at the schools in person as well so that they decide if the school atmosphere is a good fit for their child.

中小学排名http://compareschoolrankings.org/

　　每年菲沙研究所都会为所有的不列颠哥伦比亚省中小学准备一份年度报告卡，提供有关学校的绩效和成功的信息，以帮助家长对不同学校做出明智的选择。然而，多数家长也会亲自去这些学校看看，实地考察一下学校的氛围是否适合他们的孩子，然后再做出决定。

Stories and Advice for Newcomers

2月3日 新移民的故事

Joshua

我们尚未达到我们的理想目标，但我们正处在正确的轨道上。

1. 知道你的英语水平，找到一个方法来改善它。这是在加拿大生存和发展的首要任务。根据我们的经验，提高英语水平的最佳途径是参加当地公立中学或大学的热门课程。为下一个具体的人生计划铺设道路。我首先参加了道格拉斯学院的医疗保健工作者计划，它帮助我找到了我的第一份工作。后来，我又报名参加了VCC的医学英语课程，在那儿我遇到了许多著名的导师，如Kari。

2. 位置！位置！位置！找到一个合适的位置和工作安顿下来。这一部分，你必须做你自己的研究，找出合适的城市去追求你的梦想。同时，我们必须务实，选择一个你能负担得起的。例如，UBC地区可能是医学在温哥华的一个理想的位置。

3. 另一点是扩大与你的领域相关的人脉关系。这一点通过申请志愿者工作就可以实现。与我们的专业有关的义工工作也有利于我们的事业。作为国际医生，我已连续两年自愿参加VGH，BH，GPC的义工工作。就个人而言，除了人际交往，我还从这些经历中学到了医疗系统和它的工作原理。

4. 加拿大是一个多元文化的国家，她拥抱来自世界各地的人们。因此，我们需要对周围的人敞开心扉，尊重他们，感激他们为你所做的一切。

5. 理性地对待过去取得的成就对未来第二个家园有实际意义。实事求是，面对未来。一切从头开始，如何调整好我们的心态，是前进的关键。生活就是选择。它不只是黑或白，对或错。每当我们做出重大决定时，都会有灰色地带。永远要保持健康的心态。

6. 无论如何不要忘了你最初追求的梦想。为什么我们会在加拿大？

February 4 Vancouver Entertainment

2月4日 温哥华娱乐

Karaoke

There are two styles of karaoke bars in Vancouver. The more popular style with the locals is to go to a regular bar, restaurant, club, or lounge for Karaoke Night on a certain night of the week. The venue provides a karaoke machine, a microphone, and a small stage so that people can sing publicly. Usually there is no cost as they offer it as a type of entertainment to attract customers. They make their money from selling food and drinks to the singers and the audience. These nights can be very popular with a waiting list for singers who want to try it. It also means that whether you are a good or bad singer, everyone in the bar can hear you and cheer (or not!) depending on your skill. Many times, people will go up and sing even though they know they are not very talented singers. The whole point is to just have fun and have a good time.

Over the last few years, more and more private karaoke rooms, similar to Asia's karaoke boxes, have opened in Vancouver where guests can reserve private rooms and enjoy their singing, food and drinks with their friends in private. Many of these new venues offer large selections of music choices in Cantonese, Mandarin and Korean. The website called Vancity Karaoke has a complete and updated guide to all types of karaoke in the greater Vancouver area on every night of the week.

卡拉OK

　　大温哥华地区所有卡拉OK场馆的完整指南：https：//www.vancitykaraoke.com/

　　在温哥华有两种风格迥异的卡拉OK场所，一个是酒吧，另一个是私人歌厅。当地人通常每周的某个夜晚去一个普通的酒吧、餐厅、俱乐部或夜总会的休息室去放松一下。酒吧提供卡拉OK机，麦克风和小舞台，让客人们尽情地唱歌。设备通常是不计成本的，因为店家把它作为一种吸引顾客娱乐的手段。他们靠卖给歌手和听众食物和饮料赚钱。朋友们愿意在这里消磨时光，任何人都有机会进入等待的名单，一展歌喉。无论您唱的好或不好，酒吧里的每个人都可以听到您的歌声并给您送出掌声和喝彩声（也许不），当然这取决于您演唱的技巧。大多数人都不是很有天赋的专业歌手，但这并不妨碍上台演唱。总的来说，只要和朋友们一起度过一个愉快的时光玩得开心就足够了。

　　近几年，越来越多的私人卡拉OK歌厅出现在温哥华，类似于亚洲的歌厅，客人可以预约私人房间，与好友们聚在一起歌唱，享受美食和饮料。这种歌厅一般都提供粤语，国语和韩语等多语种曲目供客人们挑选。上面的网站对大温哥华地区每天晚上的各种类型的卡拉OK场所都有完整的指南，并定期更新。

Best Elementary Schools

2月5日 温哥华著名的小学

Crofton House Junior School
Elementary School (private)

Here is the description of the school from their website: "The Junior School is a dynamic, energetic centre of learning for girls from Junior Kindergarten to Grade 7. The program develops the whole child by offering an enriched and challenging curriculum with caring and enthusiastic teachers. Exciting lessons, field trips, in-depth projects, the integration of technology, and a positive partnership with parents all contribute to the environment of high expectations for each girl."

克罗夫顿之家小学（私立）http://www.croftonhouse.ca

以下是学校网站上的描述：

"从幼儿园女童到七年级的女孩是充满活力的。学习中心的教师们极富爱心，他们通过设置丰富且具有挑战性的课程计划，来培养孩子。那些令人兴奋的课程、实地考察、具体项目、技术整合以及与家长们的积极配合，都有助于为每个女孩营造一个高期望的环境。"

February 6   A Different Way of Thinking

2月6日   不同的思维方式

A Welcoming Homefront

Vancouverites don't usually drop in uninvited or casually to each others' homes. Instead, they will schedule a gettogether for a certain date and time. Even neighbours who have lived beside each other for many years might never see the inside of each other's houses. However, locals like to send a welcoming message out to the neighbourhood with their home. They like their home to look open and inviting. Therefore, they open all the drapes and blinds during the daytime and then only close them again at nighttime. When a home always has all its blinds and drapes completely closed all the time, it sends a message of "do not come near, stay away". Also, it is common to always turn on the front light above the front door at night. Again, this gives a feeling of safety and warmth. The open blinds in the daytime and the front door light at night time send a message that if you need something, we are here to help the community. It sends a message that the homeowners are looking out for each other in a community and ensuring all is safe and well.

打开门前的夜灯

温哥华人通常不会不请自来或随便去串门的。相反，他们会安排一个特定的会客时间。即便是隔壁住了多年的邻居也可能从未看到过彼此房屋的内部。可是当地人喜欢向邻居发出欢迎来家做客的邀请。他们喜欢让别人感觉自己很开放，很好客。因此，他们在白天打开所有的窗帘和百叶窗，然后到了晚上再关上。当某个家庭总是把所有的窗帘和百叶窗完全关闭的时候，它会传递一个信息："不要走近，请离开"。另外，夜里前门上方的灯总是亮着也很常见。这给人一种安全和温暖的感觉。白天打开百叶窗以及夜晚把前门的灯打开，是向路人发出一个信息：如果您有需要的话，房主乐于提供帮助，以确保社区所有的人平平安安。

Best High Schools

2月7日 温哥华著名的中学

York House Senior School (private)

Here is the description of the school from their website: "Finding her voice. Discovering her passions. A Yorkie can do anything! Whether it's completing a design challenge, testing predictions in a science lab, performing in the senior concert band, making the final shot in the game for the Tigers, working with children at Project Somos in Guatemala or the YWCA right here in Vancouver, the Senior School is a place where girls can further explore their talents and discover their passions. Our Senior School teachers are subject specialists who offer challenging and individualized instruction that caters to each girl's learning needs and interests. The Senior School offers a comprehensive and rigorous academic program that prepares young women for success in a university of their choice, and for a life-long career in learning. University offers are made to 100% of the graduating class."

约克屋中学（私立）https://www.yorkhouse.ca

以下是学校网站上的描述：

"找到她的声音，发现她的激情，无论是否完成一项挑战，约克屋可以做任何事情！例如在科学实验室里的预测、在高级音乐会上的表演、在老虎游戏中的最后一枪、在危地马拉或温哥华基督教女青年会从事儿童工作的项目等等。女孩们可以进一步发掘她们的才能，我们学校是一个发现自我激情的地方。 我们的教师是各学科的专家，提供具有挑战性和个性化的教学，以满足每一个女孩的学习需要和兴趣。学校提供全面而严谨的学术计划，为年轻女性在自己选择的大学里取得成功和终身学习的过程中奠定基础。大学预科课程提供100%的毕业生。

The Homes of Vancouver

2月8日 温哥华住宅

A Charming Home
迷人的住房

February 9   Best Extracurricular Activities for Kids

2月9日   最佳儿童课外活动

Public Speaking for Kids

Being able to express yourself clearly and confidently is a very important skill nowadays. For young newcomers who must do presentations and public speaking in a second language, this can feel intimidating and cause anxiety. Fortunately, there are organizations with training programs designed to develop public speaking skills and confidence. Pear Tree Education helps young children build their speaking confidence. The Bolton Academy of Spoken Arts (BASA) helps prepare students for "all types of performances, from interviews and school projects to speeches, debates, networking, and life." Finally, Debate Camp Canada provides "one-week summer camp programs in Public Speaking, Debating and Model United Nations for students eager for new ideas and a boost in their skills, confidence and ability with the spoken word!". BASA and Debate Camp can help teenage newcomers express themselves persuasively and confidently for school and for their future professional careers.

儿童在公众场合演讲

梨树教育（儿童） http://www.pear-tree.ca/public-speaking-for-kids-vancouver/
博尔顿说唱艺术学院（为儿童和青少年开办）
http://www.theboltonacademy.com/
加拿大辩论营（青少年） http://www.debatecamp.org/

　　能够清楚地、 自信地表达自己是当今一项非常重要的技能。对于必须用第二种语言做报告和在公开场合演讲的年轻人来说，这可能会让他们感到恐惧和焦虑。幸运的是，有些组织设有培训计划，旨在发展公众演讲技巧和自信。梨树教育帮助培养孩子说话的信心。博尔顿的说唱艺术学院（BASA）帮助学生准备"所有类型的表现，从采访、演讲、 辩论、 联网、生活和学校项目取得成功"。最后，加拿大辩论营提供为期一周暑期夏令营计划"在公众演讲、 辩论和模拟联合国发言，学生们渴望新思想，提升他们的技能、 信心和能力与口头交流！"BASA和辩论营可以帮助新来的少年能够自信地表达自己对学校和未来职业生涯的信心。

Meeting Locals in Vancouver

2月10日   与当地人接触

Join our My New Life in Vancouver Club

We know exactly what it is like to be a newcomer in this city and not know many people. My adult newcomer students often ask me how they can meet local people. Therefore, Yi and I have started a social club for our readers. We organize regular get-togethers for newcomers to meet locals, and we have guest speakers who come and give presentations about the topics that we cover in this book. We can also help answer any of your questions about your new life in Vancouver. Come join us and meet new people, learn new things and make your first year in Vancouver a little more fun!

请加入我们"温哥华新生活"俱乐部

我们诚挚地邀请您加入我们"温哥华新生活"俱乐部，请在我们的网站上注册，以定期收到有关温哥华生活的最新消息，同时可参加我们定期组织的研讨会和特别活动。

我们的网址是：www.mynewlifeinvancouver.com

我们很清楚新移民刚刚来到这个城市人地生疏，举目无亲。新来的学生经常问我这样的问题，他们如何才能与当地人结识。为此，义和我为我们的读者成立了一个社交俱乐部。我们将定期组织新移民与当地人聚会，邀请我们的嘉宾就本书中涵盖的主题给大家做专题演讲。我们也可以回答您关于在温哥华开始新生活的任何问题。来加入我们吧，认识新的朋友，学习新的事物，让您在温哥华的第一年更有乐趣！

February 11   Restaurant Customs and Etiquette

2月11日   餐厅的习俗与礼仪

Making Restaurant Reservations

Restaurant reservations are not necessary for casual restaurants, but it is a good idea to make a reservation at all the other types of restaurants. The most popular timeframe to eat dinner in a restaurant are between 6 and 8:30 pm, so if you arrive during this time without a reservation, you might be waiting a long time for your table. It is especially important to make a reservation if you are part of a large group, or if you want to make a special request such as reserving a table with a good view. Fortunately, it is possible to make reservations online.

Open Table is a free website that makes it very easy and efficient to make dinner reservations at most restaurants in Vancouver. It also removes any worries about having to speak English on the phone to call and make a reservation at a restaurant. Also, it is very easy to cancel or change your reservation online.

预定座位

免费在线预订餐厅座位<u>https://www.opentable.com/vancouver-restaurants</u>

预订餐厅对普通小众餐厅来说是没有必要的，但对于那些知名的或有特色的餐厅则需要提前预订座位。在餐厅吃饭最理想的时间段是晚上的6点到8点半，如果您在这段时间没有预订上座位，可能会等很长时间才会有空位。如果您要包间，或者您有特殊的要求，比如订一张视野好的桌子，那么预订尤为重要。

Open Table是一个免费的订位网站，有了它人们在网上预订温哥华大多数餐馆的晚餐变得非常简单和高效。 它也消除了给餐厅打电话预约座位时不得不讲英语的顾虑。还有，当您想取消或更改您的预订时间也非常方便。

English for Everyday Life
日常生活英语

当您到达餐厅时，请务必告知迎宾员您有预订：

"Hello, my name is Judy Chen and I have a reservation for six people at 8 pm"
"您好，我的名字是朱迪陈，今晚8点我预订了六个人的座位。"

February 12   Top English Programs for Adults

2月12日   成人高级英语课程

Immigrant Services Society of British Columbia (ISSBC)

In addition to providing many settlement services for newcomers, ISSBC runs English programs as well. They have Language Instruction for Newcomers to Canada (LINC) classes and LINC for Employment classes. They also operate a **Language and Career College (LCC)** where they teach many different English classes including Business English.

卑诗省移民服务协会（ISSBC）https://issbc.org/

卑诗省移民服务协会除了为新移民提供许多安置服务外，他们也开设英语课程。有加拿大新移民语言教学（LINC）课程和就业培训课程。 他们还有一个附属的语言和职业学院（LCC），在那里他们教授许多不同的专业英语课程，包括商务英语。

Vancouver Backyard Wildlife

温哥华后院的小鸟和动物

Raccoons

With their distinctive black eye masks and habit of washing their food with their front paws, raccoons are loved and considered very cute. They thrive in the urban environment and only need a variety of food, a source of water and a protected area for their den, or living space, to survive. Raccoons are not normally aggressive and rarely injure people; however, they can be dangerous when threatened or cornered. It is important not to put out food for raccoons as the raccoons will then attract the larger predators which will cause problems. Dogs are not an effective method of keeping raccoons away so keep your pets indoors at night to keep them safe.

浣熊

　　浣熊眼睛周围呈黑色，因其食前要将食物在水中洗濯，故名浣熊。浣熊非常可爱。虽然是野生动物，但其非常适应人类城市的生活，它们以都市为栖地，杂食性，常会潜入民宅偷窃食物。通常浣熊不会主动攻击人，很少伤害到人。然而，一旦受到威胁或走投无路的时候，它将是非常危险的。千万不要投放食物给它，这会招来更大的捕食动物，引来安全问题。也不要放狗驱赶它们，狗被浣熊袭击受伤甚至致死的事件时有发生。所以晚间要格外小心，要把宠物关在室内，以确保它们的安全。

Support for Newcomers

2月14日   支持新移民

Immigrant Services Society of BC (ISSBC)

Since 1972, this organization (the largest of its kind in Western Canada) has been assisting immigrants and refugees in setting up their new life in Vancouver. Their large team include staff, volunteers and community partners who provide settlement, education, language and employment services to newcomers.

卑诗省移民服务协会(ISSBC) https://issbc.org/

自1972年以来，这个组织（加拿大西部最大的组织）一直在帮助移民和难民在温哥华建立新的生活。他们有一个庞大的团队，有工作人员、志愿者和社区合作伙伴。他们为新移民提供定居、教育、语言和就业服务。

Vancouver Neighbourhoods

2月15日 温哥华社区

Kitsilano

Kitsilano is the fashionable neighbourhood for young, trendy, health conscious professionals who want to live a healthy active life close to the famous Kits Beach—named one of the "top 10 best city beaches in the world" by international travel magazines, and perfect for outdoor fitness. Exploring Kitsilano will give you a true taste of "West Coast living" with its focus on living a more relaxed life with a focus on wellbeing and fitness. Condominiums are the main style of housing for the busy residents who spend more time outdoors than inside. Kits is one of the city's most desirable neighbourhoods with its famous beach and outdoor pool, parks and excellent selection of trendy shops and restaurants in the shopping district on West Fourth Avenue. In addition to the usual selection of coffee shops, Kitsilano Village also a has a number of bars where you can grab a snack, dine and enjoy a cocktail while you watch the "beautiful people" of Kitsilano and the beautiful views of the beach and the mountains in the distance.

基茨兰诺 http://www.kitsilano.ca/

　　基茨兰诺(简称"Kits")是温哥华市的一个小区,位于市区的南部。它年轻,时尚,是完美的户外健身运动的场所,对于那些有健康意识的喜欢靠近海边生活的年轻一族来说它是一个非常理想的居所。基茨兰诺海滩被国际旅游杂志评为"世界10大最佳城市海滩之一"。来这里游泳者,年轻漂亮,而且富有,在这里可以体会到什么才是真正的'西海岸生活',居住在这里的人们更加休闲,他们似乎更加专注于健康和健身,除了游泳,晒太阳,放风筝,还可以打沙滩排球。对于那些比较忙碌且宁愿花更多的时间在户外活动的人们来说公寓是不错的选择。基茨兰诺是温哥华最理想的社区之一,它不仅拥有著名的海滩和室外游泳池,还有公园,街道绿化的也很漂亮。西第四大道是整个社区的购物和活动中心,大街两旁都是咖啡店、酒吧和餐馆,你可以在这里品尝小吃、用餐和享用鸡尾酒,同时还可以欣赏基茨兰诺的俊男靓女,以及隔海相望的北温群山美景。

February 16   # Basic Everyday English

2月16日   基本日常生活用语

What to Say When You Don't Understand

When you are a newcomer, there are going to be many times when you are going to have trouble understanding what people are saying. When this happens, there are two important things to remember: 1) don't panic! This is a completely normal situation; and 2) remember that body language can be a great help in these situations. It is quite surprising how much of a message you can send with simple hand movements and facial expressions – don't be afraid to try. After all, communication is the goal, whether it is from words or from body language. The basic phrases in the English for Everyday Life section will be helpful for you to learn.

"Body language is a very important tool. We had body language before we had speech....80% of what you understand is read through the body, not the words."

- Deborah Bull

当您不明白对方说的是什么的时候

初到温哥华，您经常不明白别人在讲些什么。下一次再遇到这种情况时，请记住两件重要的事情：1）不要慌！ 这很正常；2）记住肢体语言在这种情况下会有很大的帮助。您会惊奇地发现，您完全可以用简单的手势和面部表情来传递很多信息——不要害怕去尝试。 毕竟，沟通才是目的，无论是来自语言的还是肢体的。下面的几个基本短语会帮助您走出困境。

"肢体语言是一个非常重要的工具。 在讲话之前，我们可以运用肢体语言...其实，80%的理解是通过身体而不是文字来解读的。

——德博拉·布尔

English for Everyday Life
日常生活英语

下面是一些基本英语短语，您也许听到过，您可以在听不明白的时候使用。请访问我们的网站www.mynewlifeinvancouver.com，听一听这些短语的发音并练习会话。

Can you please say that again?
Please speak slower thank you
I'm sorry, I don't understand.
Can you write it down?
Can you say that another way?

请再说一遍好吗？
请说慢一点谢谢。
很抱歉，我不明白。
您能把它写下来吗？
您能换一种方式说吗？

February 17   Education

2月17日   教育

School Forms in Elementary and Secondary School

During the school year, the school administration and the teachers maintain communication with parents through many different documents. These will be mailed to your home or given to your child to take home and give to their parents. Sometimes the forms are just information: A list of important school calendar dates or newsletters about school activities. However, sometimes the forms are important consent forms where you need to complete and the sign the form to give your consent for an activity for your child. It is very important that these forms are signed and returned as soon as possible so as not to create problems for the teacher. An example of an important consent form is a Field Trip Permission Form. Your signature on the form means that your child can take part in a trip to another location away from school which is an important part of student learning. Sometimes you will be asked to send some money for the field trip as well. Many teachers also ask for parent volunteers to come along the field trip to assist with controlling the group. A detailed description in Chinese of "Forms You May See in September" for both elementary and secondary schools is found on the website.

开学初小学和初中的 家长收到的 通告及表格

https://www.vsb.bc.ca

在学年期间，学校行政管理部门和教师通过许多不同的文件与父母保持沟通。这些将邮寄到你的家或给你的孩子带回家并交给他们的父母。有的时候只是发个通知单：学校重要的事件的安排和相关活动的列表。然而，有些表格是需要你签署同意的重要的文件，它表示你同意让你的孩子参加学校安排的活动。这些表格通常需要尽快签署并交还给学校，这非常重要，否则会对教师造成问题。校外考察同意书就是一个例子。家长签署同意，你的孩子便可参加校外考察，它是学习的重要一环；有些考察活动需要收费。许多教师还鼓励家长担当志愿者来参与实地考察，同时协助组织小组活动。在多语种的家长信息小册子页面上可以找到有关中小学的"开学初家长收到的通告及表格"的中文页面。

February 18   ## Scenes from Daily Life

2月18日   日常生活中的一些镜头

A Peaceful Walk in the Snow
在雪地里散步

February 19   Outdoor Life in Vancouver

2月19日   *温哥华户外生活*

Best Public Golf Course in Vancouver: The University Golf Club

The very scenic University Golf Club has been voted the number one public golf course for ten years in a row by the readers of the Vancouver Courier newspaper. Located close to UBC, this golf course has long narrow fairways that are surrounded by beautiful trees and nature. The golf course is accessible to all levels of players and can be walked or driven in a golf cart at a relaxed pace. In addition to the golf course, there is a large clubhouse with a restaurant, bar and event space that can be reserved for weddings and large social events. The UBC Golf Club also has a large driving range for practicing shots and offers private and group golf instruction for beginners to advanced players.

温哥华最佳公共高尔夫球场：UBC高尔夫俱乐部

大学高尔夫俱乐部 http://universitygolf.com/

这座风景秀丽的大学高尔夫俱乐部已连续十年被温哥华快递报评为"最佳公共高尔夫球场"。这个高尔夫球场位于不列颠哥伦比亚大学，有狭长的球道，四周都是美丽的树木和自然景观。高尔夫球场可供所有级别的玩家使用，可以悠闲的步行或驾驶高尔夫球车代步。除了高尔夫球场，还有一个大型的会所，设有餐厅，酒吧和活动空间，可供预订婚礼和大型社交活动使用。 UBC高尔夫俱乐部还有一个很大的练习击球的训练场，并为初学者提供私人和团体高尔夫教练。

English for Everyday Life
日常生活英语

新词汇:

Round of golf（一场高尔夫）：打18洞一轮的高尔夫球活动。打一场高尔夫大约4小时。

Green fees（果岭费）： 在高尔夫球场打一轮或是打球的费用。

Tee time（开球时间）：预订高尔夫球场时，需要跟球场预约开球时间。

Par（标准杆）： 一个好的高尔夫球手完成一个高尔夫球洞的击球次数或摆动次数。"这是一个标准杆6洞"

Driving range（高尔夫练球场）：高尔夫球手练习击球挥杆的特殊练习区。

Public Golf Course（公共高尔夫球场）：高尔夫球场和俱乐部向所有市民开放。

Fairway（球道）： 高尔夫球场的一部分，球座与果岭之间球洞所在的区域。

Sand trap（沙坑）：高尔夫球场上的一种人为设置的障碍，由沙丘的凹陷或浅洞所组成。

Water hazard（水上障碍）：是指在高尔夫球场旁边的池塘、湖泊、河流、小溪、海洋、海湾，这对运动员击球来说更为困难。

February 20   Tips to Learning English

2月20日   资深英语老师提供学习英语的小贴士

You Are NOT too Old to Learn English

It used to be that we all thought our brain became less capable of learning new things as we get older. However, recent research done in 2000 (Macguire et al) on older London Taxi drivers proved that their brains were still constantly developing and changing as they learned new driving routes in the large city. This ability of the brain to change is called neuroplasticity and it refers to the brain's ability to change and form new neural connections which is exactly what happens when we learn new things. New neuroplasticity research has proven that training can change your brain even after only a few training sessions, and the longer the period of time of regular training sessions, the stronger the effect. In 2010, a group of Swedish scientists tested a group of younger (21-30) and older (65-80) adults for six months, and "did not detect any significant age-related differences in plasticity". Translation: Older brains can change too, which means you are never too old to learn. It might take longer than for your children, but that is simply related to time spent practicing. Younger children are in school all day long and practicing English for 50 or more hours each week. Most newcomer adults don't have that amount of time to study and practice English, so their progress is slower.

什么岁数学英语都不晚

　　过去我们都认为随着年龄的增长，我们的大脑学习新事物的能力会变差了。然而，在2000年（麦圭尔等人）通过对伦敦老出租车司机的最新研究证明他们的大脑仍在不断发展和变化，因为他们在大城市中学习新的驾驶路线。这种大脑改变的能力被称为神经可塑性，它指的是大脑改变和形成新的神经连接的能力 – 正是当我们学习新事物时到底会发生什么。新的神经可塑性研究已经证明，训练可以改变你的大脑，即使只有几次训练课程，而定期训练课程的时间越长，效果就越明显。 2010年，瑞典科学家对一组年轻（21-30岁）和年长（65-80岁）的老年人进行了6个月的测试，"没有发现任何明显与年龄相关的可塑性差异"。年长的大脑也可以改变，这意味着在学习上你永远都不会太老，与你的孩子比起来可能需要更长的时间，只是与练习的时间有关。孩子们整天都泡在学校里学习，每周练习50小时以上的英语。而大多数新来的成年人根本没有那么多时间来学习和练习英语，所以他们的进步显得比较慢。

February 21   A Little Canadian Inspiration

2月21日   一点点启示

"When I'm in Canada, I feel like this is what the world should be like."

——Jane Fonda, actress

"当我在加拿大的时候，我觉得这个世界就应该是这个样子。"

——女演员简·达方，

Volunteer in Vancouver

2月22日　　在温哥华做义工

Green Volunteer Opportunities

There are many different volunteer positions that help keep Vancouver green and pleasant. Here are three park and garden organizations that rely on many volunteers to help run all aspects of their organizations.

- **Stanley Park Ecology Society (SPES)**

  Volunteer in Stanley Park, one of the greatest parks in the world. SPES volunteers help with everything from education, conservation, wildlife monitoring, and office tasks.

- **UBC Botanical Garden**

  When you volunteer with the UBC Botanical Garden, you will get to learn a lot about plants and gardening, meet new people and share your love of gardening with others.

- **VanDusen Garden**

  VanDusen Garden has many volunteer opportunities in the garden and in their daily operations.

绿色志愿者的机会

有许多不同的志愿者岗位可以帮助温哥华保持绿色和令人愉快的环境。这里有三个公园和花园需要依靠许多志愿者来帮助他们组织和完成各方面的工作。

斯坦利公园生态学会（SPES）
斯坦利公园是世界上最伟大的公园之一。 志愿者在园内帮助从教育，保护，野生动物监测和办公室的一切工作。

不列颠哥伦比亚大学UBC植物园
当您志愿在UBC植物园工作时，您会学到很多关于植物和园艺方面的知识，认识新的朋友，分享您与他人的园艺爱好。

范渡森花园
范渡森花园园内给志愿者提供了很多日常工作的机会。

Healthcare in Vancouver

2月23日   温哥华的医疗保健

Fair PharmaCare Prescription Drug Program

The Medical Services Plan (MSP) does not cover the cost of prescription medicine. This can be challenging for BC residents with a low income. So, to help pay some of the cost of prescription drugs, there is a program called Fair PharmaCare. It is for all BC families, and the coverage is based on your income. The lower your income, the more help you will get to pay for prescription drugs. As soon as you get your BC Services Card, register with PharmaCare. To qualify, you must be a permanent resident of BC and already have Medical Services Plan coverage.

公平医药保健处方药计划

医疗服务计划（MSP）不包括处方药的费用。对于低收入的卑诗省居民而言，这可能是一个挑战。所以，为了帮助支付一些处方药费，有一个为所有卑诗家庭推出的名为"公平医药保健处方药"的计划。是根据您的收入，减免处方药的支付。收入越低，得到的帮助就越多，一旦您获得BC医疗卡，请向PharmaCare注册。条件是您必须是BC省的永久居民。并且已经有资格获得医疗服务计划。

February 24   Interesting Facts About Vancouver

2月24日   温哥华趣闻

Vancouver is Known as Hollywood North

Vancouver is the third largest movie production center in North America after Los Angeles and New York City. According to the Vancouver Economic Commission, the film and tv production industry in Vancouver totalled more than $2 billion. There are three world-class film and tv studios in the city that make an average of thirty movies and TV series annually. In addition, they also make commercials and other small films for private companies.

温哥华被誉为北好莱坞

温哥华在北美是继洛杉矶和纽约的最大电影制作中心。 据温哥华经济委员会统计，温哥华电影和电视制作产业总额超过20亿美元。 这个城市有三个世界级的电影厂和电视台，每年平均播放三十部电影和电视剧。 此外，他们还为私营公司制作广告和其他小电影。

Finding Work in Vancouver

2月25日 在温哥华找份工作

Important Career Documents

When looking for work in Canada, Job-hunters need to prepare three documents.

1. **A resume** is a one to two-page formal document that lists a job applicant's work experience, education and skills.

2. **A cover letter** is a written document submitted with a job application explaining the applicant's credentials and interest in the open position. Since a cover letter is often one of only two documents sent to a potential employer, it is often extremely important in determining whether the applicant will obtain an interview for the position.

3. A **Reference sheet** is a single sheet of paper that lists your references – usually three names is sufficient. The people listed should be able to speak directly about your qualifications and experience. If possible, include at least one Canadian reference. Doing volunteer work in Vancouver is an excellent way of obtaining a Canadian reference that can be used for job-hunting.

重要的职业文件：简历，求职信，推荐信

在加拿大寻找工作时，求职者需要准备三份文件：

1.**简历**：是一份一页到两页的正式文件，列出求职者的工作经历、教育和技能。

2.**求职信**：是一份随工作申请一起提交的书面文件，说明申请人的资历和对所求职位的兴趣。 由于求职信通常是发送给潜在雇主的两份文件之一，因此确定应聘者是否能获得该职位的面试通常是极其重要的。

3. **推荐信**：是一张单页，上面列出了您的推荐人 – 通常有三位就够了。 列出的人员应该能够直接说明您的资历和经验。 如果可能，至少包括一个加拿大推荐人。 通过在温哥华做义工可以结交加拿大人并请其做您的推荐人，这是求职的一种极好方法。

Vancouver Sightseeing

2月26日　　观光

Hop on/Hop Off Buses

The Hop-On/Hop-off buses are a great way to get to know your new city. These buses follow a set circuit of stops within the city. They stop at all the major attractions in Vancouver. You can buy a one to three-day pass and get on and off the bus at any stop that you wish. You can even just stay on the bus for the whole circuit so that you get an overview of the city and enjoy listening to the commentary that describes the major cultural and historical background of the attractions. The buses all provide commentary in many different languages.

随上随落观光旅游巴士：
    温哥华电车公司
    海岸旅游

    随上随落观光旅游巴士是了解一个城市的好方法。 这种观光车在市内有一个循环路线，在温哥华市里所有主要的景点停靠。 你可以购买一到三天的通票，你可以在任何你想要去的景点上下车。 你甚至可以呆在在车上，随着汽车通览整个城市，静静地享受温哥华主要文化和历史背景以及各个景点的讲解。 车上提供多语种的讲解。

February 27   Vancouver Transportation

2月27日   温哥华交通运输

Parking in Vancouver

Information about parking in Vancouver can be found on the City of Vancouver's website. The information is in English, however if you call the main city number 311, you can have someone explain the details to you in Mandarin.

In downtown Vancouver, parking spots are paid at a street meter (most spots you can pay up to 2 hours at a time) or at a paid parking lot. There are very few free parking spaces in the downtown area. You can add an app to your phone called PayByPhone that you can use to pay your parking fees. Most big shopping malls have free parking for their shoppers only. If you park in a shopping mall parking lot and don't shop in their stores, you can get a ticket or get towed.

For residential street parking on streets where there are no parking information signs, it is important to park as close to the front of your own home as possible. The city has a 3-hour bylaw that restricts all-day commuter (people coming from other areas) parking to allow daytime access for residents to their homes. Between 8:00am and 6:00pm every day, do not park your vehicle for more than 3 hours in front of residential or commercial properties that you do not own or work at.

在温哥华停车http://vancouver.ca/streets-transportation/parking.aspx

上面的链接包含关于在温哥华停车的所有信息。信息是英文的，但是如果您拨打电话号码311给城市信息台，会有人用普通话向您介绍停车的详细信息。

在温哥华市中心，马路边上划有停车位，旁边竖着收费表（可一次付费2小时）或在付费停车场付费。在市中心很少有免费停车位。您可以在手机中添加一个称为"电话支付"的应用程序，这样您就可以使用该应用程序支付停车费了。

大多数大型购物中心只为本店购物者提供免费停车位。如果您在某个商场的停车场里面停车，而不在他们的商店购物，您可能吃一张罚单或车被拖走。

对于没有停车标志的住宅街道上停车，尽可能靠近自家门前停车是很重要的。该市有一个3小时章程，限制全天通勤（从其他地区过来的人）停车，每天上午8:00至下午6:00之间，允许居民的朋友白天到家里访问。但不要将车辆停放在不属于您朋友的住宅或商业物业前面超过3小时。

Sports Teams and Special Events

专业体育赛事和活动

BC LIONS Team

The BC Lions is a local Canadian Football League (CFL) team. It is a very special and beloved organization because this football league is completely Canadian and all 9 teams are based in Canada and follow uniquely Canadian rules. It is quite an accomplishment as the much more powerful American National Football League (NFL) has wanted to come into Canada for a long time. The CFL football season runs from June to November each year. At the end of the season there is the big **Grey Cup** playoffs and final championship. CFL football games are a popular sport to watch. People go to the actual games, or they gather to watch the games on television in bars or at home. It is possible to buy tickets to single games or buy "season tickets" to go see all the local BC Lions games all year. On game day in Vancouver, it is common to see many people wearing their BC Lions shirts to show their support for the team. The BC Lions play their home matches at BC Place Stadium.

卑诗雄狮队http://www.bclions.com/

卑诗雄狮队(BC Lions)是当地加拿大加式足球联盟(Canadian Football League简称CFL)的一支职业球队。它是一个非常特殊的和有爱心的组织。因为这个足球联赛是在加拿大国内进行的，所有9支球队都来自加拿大，并遵循加拿大独特的规则。而且取得了相当大的成就，因为长期以来，更强大的美国国家足球联赛（NFL）一直想进入加拿大参加比赛。 CFL足球赛季每年从6月至11月展开。 在赛季结束时有大灰杯季后赛和最后的总决赛。加拿大人喜欢观看 CFL足球比赛。人们或去现场观看，或聚集在酒吧里观看，或者在自己家里看电视直播。 门票分为一次性的或者赛季的。在温哥华观看比赛的当天，可以看到很多球迷都穿着卑诗雄狮队的球衣来表达他们对该球队的支持。卑诗雄狮队的主场设在BC广场的体育馆。

Vancouver Parks

2月29日   温哥华公园

Stanley Park

Stanley Park is the much beloved and treasured park of all Vancouverites and tourists. It is a wonderful large area of green and nature right in the middle of the city. The 400-hectare park features natural West Coast rainforest, scenic views of water, mountains, sky, and majestic trees along Stanley Park's famous Seawall. Here are just a few of the many amazing sights to visit in the park:

- Kilometres of walking trails winding through the forest, as well as the 8 km seawall path that surrounds the park, perfect for walking and cycling
- Beautiful beaches, a waterpark for children and a heated outdoor pool open in the summer
- Casual to elegant dining opportunities
- A pitch & putt course, tennis courts and lawn bowling
- Canada's largest Aquarium
- A charming train ride to delight the children
- Horse and carriage rides
- Formal rose garden
- First Nations Totem poles

史丹利公园

欢迎来到史丹利公园，它是温哥华最大的市区公园。

史丹利公园深受所有温哥华人和游客们喜爱的公园。 公园里长满了绿色的植物。 占地面积有400公顷(1000英亩)，拥有天然的西海岸热带雨林，沿着史丹利公园著名的海堤散步，仿佛来到一个世外桃源，这里有山，有水，有蓝天，还有原始森林。这里只是简要地介绍一下公园里的的几个主要的景点：

- 数公里的步行小径蜿蜒穿过森林，和一条8公里(5.5英里)长的路径环绕整个公园,以供游人步行和骑自行车
- 美丽的海滩，儿童水上乐园和一个在夏季开放的室外温水游泳池
- 休闲优雅的餐厅
- 推杆球场、网球场、草地保龄球场
- 加拿大最大的水族馆
- 让孩子们着迷的火车
- 骑马和马车游乐设施
- 玫瑰花园
- 第一民族图腾柱

March

Weather:	Average temperature: 3°C to 11°C
	Average rainfall days: 21, Average rainfall: 110 mm
Statutory holiday:	None
Other special days:	Spring Break in elementary and high schools
	St. Patrick's Day
	Pacific Daylight Time (PDT)

There is a common expression to describe the month of March: *"In like a lion and out like a lamb"*. This expression refers to the weather which starts the month like an angry lion with very cold, dark, wet and windy conditions, but then changes at the end of the month to be gentler, lighter and brighter like a lamb. By the end of March, the air is fresher, the grass and trees greener and the spring flowers start to bloom.

The Spring Equinox* or first day of spring happens on March 21 and the official time also changes forward one hour for Pacific Daylight Savings Time (PDT)*. March is also the month that Vancouverites begin seriously working in the garden and clear out the dead branches and leaves, do some weeding and begin planting vegetable seeds and plants.

The children enjoy a two-week spring break from elementary and high school. Many of them will register for spring break day camps over the period. Some of the camps focus on a variety of play and activities, and others focus on sports such as soccer or tennis or academic activities like computer and science camps. The local sightseeing and community organizations also offer Spring Break activities for the whole family.

St. Patrick's Day is not a statutory holiday, but it is widely celebrated in Canada as many of the early settlers to Canada came from Ireland. Saint Patrick's Day is a cultural and religious celebration held on 17 March, the traditional death date of Saint Patrick (c. AD 385−461) - the most famous saint of Ireland. On this day, many people dress up in green clothes and even drink green food and drink green beer! Many people go to Irish pubs in the city to drink and have fun with their friends on this day. There is also a big St. Patrick's Day parade that winds its way through downtown Vancouver with marching bands and a fun and happy mood.

March also marks the beginning of the Spring Skiing* season which lasts until the end of April. Grouse, Seymour and Cyprus Mountains often offer discounted ski lift passes for the spring skiing season.

3月

气候： 平均温度：3 ° C ~ 11° C
平均降雨天：21， 平均降雨量： 110 毫米
公众节假日： 无
其他特殊日：中小学的春假
圣帕特里克日
太平洋夏令时 （PDT）

有这样一句话来形容3月的天气："月初像雄狮，月末像羔羊"。指的是月初天气很恶劣就像一头愤怒的狮子，非常的寒冷、阴暗、潮湿、多风，但随着气温的回暖，到了月底天气就变得温和明亮，空气清新，如羔羊。草地和树木开始变绿，春天的花朵开始绽放。

春分，春季的第一天，每年的3月21日，官方时间也依照太平洋照时间（PDT）*相应地向前调整一个小时。春天是草木生长的萌芽期，温哥华人开始着手在花园里工作，清除枯枝落叶，除草并开始种植蔬菜和植物。

　　小学和高中的孩子们非常享受为期两周的春假。他们中的许多人将在这段时间内注册春令营。春令营的内容很丰富，有的安排各种游戏和活动，有的重点是体育，如足球或者网球，其他的则专注于学术活动，比如计算机和科学营的学术活动。当地的观光和社区组织也为整个家庭提供了春假期间的活动

　　圣帕特里克节（Saint Patrick's Day），不是一个法定的节假日，但它在加拿大被广为庆祝，因为有许多早期的移民是来自爱尔兰的。圣帕特里克节是纪念爱尔兰的主保圣人，圣博德主教，爱尔兰最著名的圣人（约385 - 461年）的文化和宗教庆祝活动的节日，在每年3月17日举行。在这一天，许多人都穿着绿色的衣服，甚至吃绿色的食品，喝绿色的啤酒！有人甚至在当天把头发染成绿色。许多人会去城里的爱尔兰酒吧喝酒，在这一天和他们的朋友玩得很开心。另外还要举办一个大的联欢和游行，依据传统，游行队伍要蜿蜒穿过温哥华市中心，所有的人全都沉浸在欢乐的节日气氛中。

　　3月也是春季滑雪季节的开始，一直持续到四月底。松鸡山、 西摩山和塞浦路斯山三大滑雪场地经常提供打折的滑雪缆车票。

更多的信息：

圣帕特里克节游行：

http://www.celticfestvancouver.com/parade/

* **Spring Equinox春分**：通常指阳光直射赤道的那一天，通常发生在3月21日。整个地球的昼夜几乎等长。

* **Spring Skiing春天滑雪**：当地的滑雪山上的天气温暖，阳光充足，但雪仍然很厚。有的人只是穿一件T恤在雪山上享受日光浴。

* **Pacific Daylight time(PDT)太平洋夏令时**：时间往前拨一小时，这样晚上将会有更多光亮的时间。

Local Customs

Weddings and Wedding Anniversaries

There is no such thing as a standard wedding any more. Nowadays, weddings can be large, formal and traditional to very casual and unique. Here is a brief description of both types of weddings:

- *Formal traditional weddings* begin with a church wedding ceremony. The bride wears a long white dress and the groom wears a tuxedo suit. The bride has a maid-of-honour and three or more bridesmaids who all wear matching dresses. The groom has a best man and three or more groomsmen who all wear matching tuxedos or suits. The ceremony is followed by the formal photography session with the bride, groom and wedding party. Then some time after that there is the wedding reception with food, drinks, speeches, toasts and dancing – especially the traditional first dance with the bride and groom. The wedding presents are displayed on a table but are not opened in front of the guests. Families usually hire professional **Wedding Planners** to help plan and organize every detail of these big weddings.

- **Non-traditional weddings** are more and more popular in recent years as people are less religious and want a more unique and personalized wedding. The wedding ceremony can take place anywhere that the couple wants – from the beach to the mountains to their home or a restaurant. The ceremony is performed by a **Wedding Officiant** who is legally approved to perform wedding ceremonies in BC. After the ceremony and photos, there is some sort of meal to celebrate the event.

Canadian celebrate the anniversary of their wedding date. Usually a couple will celebrate their anniversary privately with a nice dinner in a restaurant and exchange gifts with each other. However, there are a few special wedding anniversaries that many couples celebrate with a special party. The big anniversaries are:

- The 25th wedding anniversary, also called the "silver anniversary"

- The 50th wedding anniversary, also called the "gold anniversary"

- Many also celebrate the 60th, 65th, 70th and any wedding anniversary after that with a celebration.

Couples can receive a message from the Governor General of Canada for their 50th anniversary and every fifth anniversary after that. Canadians can also receive a written message from the Queen for their 60th, 65th and 70th wedding anniversary if they apply to Buckingham Palace or to the Governor-General's office in Canada.

婚礼和结婚纪念日

婚礼没有固定的形式。 如今，婚礼的规模可大、可正式和传统的，也可以是非常休闲和独特的。 下面对两种不同类型的婚礼做一个简要的说明：

婚礼类型
- **正式的传统婚礼**：从教堂婚礼仪式开始。新娘穿着长长的白色连衣裙，新郎穿着燕尾服。新娘有一个首席伴娘和三个或更多的伴娘穿着伴服。而新郎也跟着一个最要好的朋友和三个或更多的伴郎，一律身着晚礼服或西装。仪式之后由摄影师给新娘、新郎和婚礼现场拍合影留念。然后，大家进入接待室里，那里有食物，饮料，婚宴演讲，烤面包和婚礼舞蹈 – 由新娘和新郎单独跳第一个传统的舞。婚礼上的所有礼物均摆放在桌子上，但不要在客人面前打开。一般家庭通常会聘请专业的**婚礼策划师**，帮助他们规划和组织这些大型婚礼的每一个细节。
- **非传统婚礼**：在最近几年越来越受人们的欢迎，因为人们的宗教信仰越来越淡薄，他们想要搞一个别开生面的婚礼。婚礼可以在任何地方举办，从海滩到山上，在自己的家中或餐馆。婚礼仪式由BC省在法律上认可的**婚礼官**主持，婚礼仪式和拍照后，举办一个庆祝宴会。

婚礼周年纪念活动

加拿大人庆祝他们的周年婚礼纪念日。通常夫妇会选一家饭店享用一顿丰盛而美好的晚餐私下庆祝他们的周年纪念日，席间相互交换礼物。当然，还有一些特别重大的婚礼纪念日，这些大的周年纪念日是：

- 25周年结婚纪念日，被称为"银婚纪念日"
- 50周年结婚纪念日，被称为"金婚纪念日"
- 许多人还庆祝60周年、65周年、70周年以及从那以后年年举办庆祝他们的结婚纪念日活动。

凡是加拿大夫妇，当他们庆祝50周年纪念日的时候会收到来自加拿大总督发来的贺信，并在那之后每五周年收到一封贺信。如果他们向白金汉宫或加拿大总督办公室递交申请的话，还可以收到女王发来的60周年，65周年和70周年结婚纪念日的书面贺信。

Parenting in Vancouver

在温哥华养育子女

Parent Support Services of BC

This charity organization is dedicated to helping parents have the information and support they need to be the best parents they can be and create healthy, successful families. They offer courses in parenting and they offer "parenting circles", which is a group of parents that meet once per week (childcare is provided) and talk about their children, parenting challenges, successes and failures, the stress or worries in their lives, receive support and learn more about parenting skills. Support Circles are free, confidential, and anonymous. Meetings are held in English and in many other languages, including Mandarin.

卑诗省家长支持服务协会 http://parentsupportbc.ca/home

　　这个慈善组织致力于帮助父母获得信息和支持，他们需要成为最好的父母，他们可以创建健康，成功的家庭。 他们提供育儿课程，他们提供"育儿圈"，家长们每周见面一次（提供看护），谈论他们的孩子，面临的育儿挑战，成功和失败，他们生活中的各种压力或忧虑，接受支持和养育技能。支持圈子是免费、保密和匿名的。 会议使用英语和许多其他语言，包括普通话。

March 3   Stories and Advice for Newcomers

3月3日   新移民的故事

Shirley

保持乐观积极的心态，很重要

时间都去哪儿了，转眼来温哥华四年了，已经不算新移民了。我很愿意和大家分享在这四年中的感受和体验。首先我有一颗好奇和乐观的心，来迎接新生活。既然我们选择了移民，那么我们就要敞开心扉去接受和学习新的文化和生活方式。

我喜欢尝试新鲜事物，比如去做义工，就是一个很好的认识新朋友的机会，了解这边工作的方式方法。而且没有压力，大多数人都很友善乐于帮助新人。其次去参加喜欢的社会活动，或者参加专为新移民安排的一些活动。当然我知道去参加这些活动需要勇气，需要勇敢，因为总是担心语言的问题。但当我做了以后，我会为自己感到骄傲而且更加的自信。比如有一次我想参加温哥华市代表组织的一个早餐会，同时请的嘉宾现场讲座。但是我不敢去，我就和我的一个老师说了这件事， 最后老师决定陪我一起去参加。只要保持积极心态，好事总会主动找上门来。当然我更感谢这位老师对我的帮助和支持。

然后是坚持学习英语，我是从LINC 二级开始学起的，现在是七级，我是从内心喜欢英语并有很强的愿望想说的流利。虽然我不是特别用功的一个，但我坚持不懈。今年年底我就可以申请入籍了。同时我在考虑开一个自己小店，相信那个时候我会觉得自己是真正的加拿大人了。记得保持乐观积极的心态，很重要。

Vancouver Entertainment

温哥华娱乐

Vancouver Nightlife

Vancouver's nightlife is divided into various districts around the city. The nightlife has a different style and feeling in the different areas. Various age groups prefer the type of nightlife in some neighbourhoods over others. Nightlife venues are divided into clubs, bars and pubs.

Club Hopping in the Granville Entertainment District

Downtown Vancouver's Granville Street is the place to go for loud clubs and dancing. The area of Granville Street from Nelson Street to Robson Street is full of bars and clubs which makes it easy to club hop from one club to another. These clubs are most popular with people in their twenties and early thirties. Be prepared for line-ups to get into the clubs on the weekend.

Trendy Bars in Yaletown

The business professionals like to hang out in the stylish Vancouver district of Yaletown. Most of the trendy and fashionable bars are located on Hamilton and Mainland streets located in that neighbourhood.

Pubs and Cocktails in Historic Gastown

Vancouver's historic centre, Gastown, is a popular place to sightsee and shop for souvenirs in the daytime, but at night, it is a popular district with comfortable pubs to meet for a beer or visit one of the sophisticated bars where you can enjoy very chic cocktails. These Gastown venues attract customers of all ages.

Live Music on Main Street

Vancouver's Main Street has a more casual and relaxed feeling, with a few clubs that focus more on creating a unique and hip atmosphere than on creating an exciting mood like the downtown clubs.

温哥华夜生活

温哥华的夜生活分布在城市的各个角落。不同地区的夜生活方式和感受都不尽相同。不同年龄段的人喜欢在某个地区的过夜生活超过其他年龄段。夜生活场所分为俱乐部，会所和酒吧。

English for Everyday Life
日常生活英语

小酒馆，酒吧和俱乐部之间的区别：

Pubs小酒馆：比较传统，朋友们喝着啤酒，聊聊天，是一个很放松的地方。一些小酒馆可以自己酿造啤酒。被人们称为酿酒吧或小棚屋，柜台上摆放着带有水龙头的大啤酒桶。 这类酿酒吧在温哥华很受欢迎。

Bars酒吧：这些地方到了晚上，会播放震耳欲聋的音乐，提供特色饮料，各种鸡尾酒和混合饮料，如马提尼酒和伏特加苏打水。

Clubs or Nightclubs俱乐部或夜总会：这些是与朋友相约（通常是年轻人）夜晚跳舞的场所，俱乐部或夜总会一般都配有非常专业的音响设备和很大的舞池，没有太多的空间提供座位。 大多数俱乐部一般在晚上10点之后开始忙碌起来，直至次日凌晨3点结束。

格兰维尔娱乐区的狂欢俱乐部

温哥华市中心的格兰维尔街是夜生活跳舞的地方。 沿着格兰维尔街从尼尔森街一直到罗布森街到处都是酒吧和俱乐部，每当夜幕降临，整个格兰维尔街变得动感起来，这些俱乐部最受二三十岁的年轻人的热捧。周末人最多，往往需要排队等候进场。

耶鲁镇时尚酒吧

商业人士往往喜欢在温哥华时尚的耶鲁镇地区消磨时光。大部分新潮时尚的酒吧都位于汉密尔顿和附近的街道上。

历史悠久的盖斯镇酒吧和鸡尾酒

温哥华的历史中心，盖斯镇，白天是观光和购买纪念品的热点地区，夜晚形形色色的"吧"开始引领热闹的夜生活舞台。来这里喝上一杯啤酒或造访一间别致酒吧，品尝一下口味非常独特的鸡尾酒。这里吸引着不同年龄段的人。

主街现场音乐

温哥华主街上的俱乐部则显得更加休闲和放松，这里不同于市中心俱乐部营造出令人激动人心的场面，它似乎更注重通过装饰来营造气氛。

Best Elementary Schools

3月5日　　　温哥华著名的小学

Dr. R.E. McKechnie Elementary School (public)

Here is the description of the school from their website: "We want to welcome all students, staff and parents to Dr. R. E. Mckechnie Elementary School. Our school is committed to supporting engaged learners and fostering a caring and inclusive school community. We welcome learners of all types and invite you to contact our staff to learn more about the wide-range of excellent educational programs and services we offer at our school."

R.E. 麦肯尼博士小学（公立）
http://go.vsb.bc.ca/schools/mckechnie

　　下面是学校网站的描述：

　　"我们欢迎所有的学生、员工和家长来R. E. 麦肯尼博士小学。我们承诺支持参与学习和培养一个有爱心和有包容心的学校社区。我们欢迎所有类型的学习者，并邀请您与我们的员工联系，了解我们学校提供的各种优质的教育计划和服务。

March 6	A Different Way of Thinking
3月6日	不同的思维方式

Driving manners and etiquette – the friendly wave

When driving in Vancouver, people try to be helpful to others and do things such as letting someone merge in front of your car. When you do this, you will sometimes see the driver give a friendly little wave. This wave is a way to show your appreciation to the other driver for letting you move in front of him, or for pulling over to let you pass – basically you give the little wave any time that another driver does something that makes it easier for you on the road. Drivers will give this wave even when the other driver is just obeying the law and doing the right thing. It is just a little action, but locals think it is a nice way to be polite to each other.

驾驶的礼仪和礼节——挥手致意

在温哥华开车的时候，人们会礼让，尽力帮助别人，而不会超车抢行，比如让别人在您的车前面并线先行。当您这样做时，有时会看到对方司机友好的向您挥挥手。这种挥手是对您的一种答谢。挥手是一种表达您欣赏其他司机的做法。别的司机为了让您在他前面先行通过，会把车开到慢行车道，甚至有时会靠边停车让行。总的说来，只要是遇到他人礼让，都要挥手致意。即使其他司机只是遵守交通法规，处理得当。彼此也会发出这个友好的信号。虽然这只是一个小小的动作，但当地人认为这是一个很好的礼貌待人的好习惯。

March 7   Best High Schools

3月7日   温哥华著名的中学

Lord Byng High School (public)

Here is the description of the school from their website: "Lord Byng Secondary School is a public secondary school located in the West Point Grey neighbourhood on the west side of Vancouver, British Columbia, Canada. The school officially opened in 1925 and was named in honor of Julian Hedworth George Byng, the Lord Byng of Vimy, a hero of Vimy Ridge and the Governor General of Canada at the time. Lord Byng underwent a seismic upgrade, completed in 2005 and with a new library and gymnasium, as well as a gallery, studios and classrooms added. The school is well-known for its Byng Arts Mini School program and their wide range of sports and music programs."

劳宾中学（公立）http://go.vsb.bc.ca/schools/byng

宾艺术： http://byng2.vsb.bc.ca/byngarts/

以下是学校网站上的描述：

"劳宾中学位于加拿大不列颠哥伦比亚省温哥华西侧西点灰附近的一所公立中学。学校正式创办于 1925 年，并以当时维米岭战役的英雄劳宾，加拿大总督拜恩勋爵的名字命名。劳宾中学经历了一次扩建，于2005年完成，增设了一个新的图书馆，一个体育馆和一个画廊，还添加了许多工作室和教室。我校以迷你宾艺术计划和各种体育和音乐课程而闻名。

March 8   The Homes of Vancouver

3月8日   温哥华住宅

High-rise Condominiums

高层公寓

　　在温哥华市中心建造的许多现代公寓楼都是高层建筑。　温哥华最高的高层公寓大楼是香格里拉大酒店，共62层。

Best Extracurricular Activities for Kids

3月9日   **最佳儿童课外活动**

Arts Umbrella

Vancouverites have been trusting the Arts Umbrella for their children's visual arts, music, theatre, dance and media arts education since 1979. They offer over 785 classes per year in four different locations around the city for students from 2 to 19 years of age. Highly experienced practicing artists lead the classes and only top-quality supplies are used. The Arts Umbrella's reputation for teaching excellence and satisfied parents has ensured their continued success in the future.

艺术伞http://www.artsumbrella.com/

自1979年以来，温哥华人绝对信任艺术伞为儿童提供的视觉艺术、音乐、戏剧、舞蹈和媒体艺术教育。他们每年在温哥华四个不同地点为2至19岁的学生提供超过785门课程。 由经验丰富的艺术家执教，老师使用高品质的教具。 艺术伞在卓越教学和满足父母需求的声誉确保了他们未来的持续的成功。

Meeting Locals in Vancouver

与当地人接触

Don't Wait Until Your English is Perfect

Adult newcomers often feel worried that their language skills are not good enough to speak with locals. They think it will be better to just wait until they take more classes or improve their English skills. They worry that they have an accent or they don't know enough vocabulary. However, it is important to remember that Canada is a country of immigrants, especially Vancouver. Residents here are very used to hearing English spoken in many ways and levels and accents – and it doesn't matter!

The reason we communicate with each other is to share feelings and opinions and to feel closer to each other. The purpose of the communication is the most important thing. A little communication with your smaller vocabulary is still much better than zero communication. Also, the more you try, the easier it will become.

不要等到您的英文完美了再开口

新移民常常担心自己的语言能力不够好，不能和当地人交谈。他们认为只有参加更多的英语课程或等到他们的英语水平提高之后再与当地人交谈。他们担心自己的发音不准或者词汇量太少。然而，请记住，加拿大是一个移民国家，尤其是温哥华。这里的居民都非常习惯于听到用不同方式和不同水平讲的英语。 因此，语言能力并不重要！

我们交流的原因是为了分享彼此的感受和看法，使得彼此更加亲近。沟通才是最重要的。用有限的词汇量去交流总比零沟通要好得多。而且，您越尝试，沟通就会变得越容易。

March 11   Restaurant Customs and Etiquette

3月11日   餐厅的习俗与礼仪

Restaurant Staff

Vancouver restaurant owners work hard to keep their costs down as it is very expensive to run a restaurant in Vancouver. One way they do this is by limiting how many restaurant staff work at one time. This means that you will see far fewer staff members working in restaurants here compared to Asian countries. Therefore, fewer staff are responsible for more tables and can't always be there right away. Locals are used to this and just wait patiently until the server comes to their table. When possible, they try to avoid calling over the server unnecessarily, as it is considered very rude to whistle or call for a server. If you need to get the staff's attention, just "catch their eye" or slightly lift a hand in the air. These are the typical restaurant staff workers that you will see:

- *Hostess:* When you first arrive at the restaurant, the hostess will welcome you and take you to your table. If it is a formal restaurant, then this will be a different person than your server.

- *Server:* Each section has one server who takes care of the tables in their section. If you have a question about the food, or need something, you usually need to wait until your own server comes to your table and not ask the other servers.

- *Busperson:* The busperson clears the dirty dishes off the table, refills water and sets the table for new guests. They usually do not interact with the guests.

- *Coat Check (upscale restaurants only)* In high-end restaurants, there will be a coat check staff member who will take your coat and give you a ticket that you use to pick it up again at the end of the night.

- ***Valet Parking Attendant (upscale restaurants only):*** If the restaurant has valet parking, then the Car Attendant will park your car and hold your car keys until the end of the evening when they will retrieve your car for you again.

餐厅员工岗位职责

温哥华餐馆的老板都会努力地工作，以降低成本，因为在温哥华经营一家餐厅的费用相当高。他们采取的方法是尽量限制餐馆员工的人数和工作时间。您会看到，与亚洲国家相比，这里餐厅工作的服务员要少得多。因此，每位服务员要负责更多的桌子，不能总是一直呆在一个地方让客人们随叫随到。当地人早已对此习以为常，他们会耐心等待，直到服务员巡台来到他们的桌子跟前招呼他们。如果可能的话，他们尽量避免不是必须的服务，吹口哨，或召唤服务员都被认为是非常粗鲁的行为。如果您需要引起餐厅服务员的注意，只需等到她看到您，再向她招招手。下面是餐厅职工的岗位：

- **女迎宾员**：当您到达餐厅的时候，迎宾员将打招呼欢迎，然后领您到预订的座位上。如果是正式的餐厅，那么迎宾员是专职的。有别于服务员。

- **服务员**：每个区域都有一个服务员，负责照顾餐厅的几张桌子。如果您对菜单上的菜品有不明白的地方或需要点菜的时候，通常需要耐心等待您自己的服务员来到您的餐桌前为您服务，而不要召唤其他区域的服务员。

- **清洁员**：清洁员负责将台面清理干净，拿走桌子上的剩菜盘子，为客人加水，以及为下一桌客人布置台面。他们通常不与客人互动。

- **衣帽员**（仅适用于高档餐厅）：客人到了餐厅，将外套脱下来交给衣帽员，他/她会帮您收好外套和帽子，给您开一张收条，等您用餐结束时再将衣帽交换给您。

- **代客泊车服务员**（仅限于高档餐厅）：如果餐厅有代客泊车服务，那么泊车员将会把您的汽车停放好，并负责保管车钥匙，直到晚餐结束，再次为您取回车辆。

Top English Programs for Adults

3月12日　　成人高级英语课程

SUCCESS BC

SUCCESS BC offers Language Instruction for Newcomers to Canada (LINC) classes and an English program called **"Project Based Languages Services (PBLT)** which helps students learn and practice English terminology for the employment field. The website explains that students will "learn job-specific English language skills needed to succeed in high-demand, growing B.C. industries." During the PBLT courses, students will meet employers, career advisors and go on field trips to local employers. SUCCESS BC currently runs PBLT courses for the retail industry and the construction industry.

中侨互助会 http://www.successbc.ca/

　　中侨互助会（简称中侨）是加拿大卑诗省最大的社会服务团体之一，提供加拿大新移民语言教学（LINC）课程和帮助学生学习和实践就业领域的（PBLT）英语课程。该网页介绍，学生将定向学习卑诗省高增长产业所需要的特定工作的英语语言技能。在PBLT课程学习期间，学生将会与雇主，职业顾问见面，并对当地的企业进行实地考察。目前开设的PBLT课程有零售业和建筑业。

March 13 # Vancouver Backyard Wildlife

3月13日 温哥华后院的小鸟和动物

Skunks

Vancouverites know that if they see a skunk, they need to stay far away! Although they are very adorable with their black and white fur, they have very strong scent glands that will spray a very bad smelling musk. The spray of a skunk can go as far as six meters and the terrible odour can be carried up to one kilometer by the wind. The spray can be dangerous for dogs if it gets into their eyes. It is almost impossible to remove the smell from clothes and they must be thrown away. The good news is that the skunks only come out at nighttime when they leave their small dens and go hunting for fruit, plants, insects, bird eggs and small rodents. Skunks eat a lot of food over the summer so that they are covered with a very warm layer of fat by the winter time when they hibernate until February when they wake up again for breeding season.

臭鼬

臭鼬的体毛为黑色，身体两边为白色条纹。温哥华人都知道，如果遇见它，一定要保持相当的距离！尽管它们看上去非常可爱，但它们有很强的气味腺，可以放出奇臭无比的气味，这种气味常在遇到威胁时释放出来。臭鼬喷出恶臭的液体可达六米远，其强烈的臭味在约一公里的范围内都可以闻到。如果这种液体进入狗的眼睛会导致其短时间失明。如果喷到衣服上，几乎不可能把它去除，必须扔掉。好在臭鼬只会在夜晚出来活动。去寻找水果，植物，昆虫，鸟蛋和小型啮齿动物。臭鼬在夏季要吃大量的食物，在秋末，它们会变得非常胖，有一层很温暖厚厚的脂肪进入冬眠，交配期通常为每年的二月。

MOSAIC

MOSAIC is a registered charity serving immigrant, newcomer, and refugee communities in Greater Vancouver. While they do offer settlement assistance and language training, their focus and success has been with providing employment support and programs to newcomers. In fact, they are the only immigrant serving organization that offers programs for the B.C. Government's Employment Program.

马赛克MOSAIC是在大温哥华地区注册的慈善机构。他们为新移民和难民提供定居援助和语言培训，并把重点放在为新移民提供就业支持和相关的课程。事实上，他们是唯一一家为卑诗省政府就业计划提供服务的移民组织。

March 15   Vancouver Neighbourhoods

3月15日   温哥华社区

Gastown

To get a sense of Vancouver's history, explore its oldest neighbourhood, Gastown. It was started in 1867 by a famous Vancouverite, John "Gassy Jack" Deighton. The area is an interesting mix of old and new. There are many old buildings and warehouses that have been renovated into trendy new restaurants and stores, there are cobblestone streets, vintage lampposts and the famous Gastown Steam Clock. There is also a statue of old Gassy Jack too. Gastown reflects Vancouver's old history as a dynamic harbour town with a diverse population. Gastown is home to many of the city's hottest restaurants serving a diversity of cuisine. This neighbourhood is also the centre of the city's cocktail scene with many bars serving classic drinks with artistic flair. Finally, you can get a bird's eye view of the area from the Vancouver Lookout, which rises 167-metres to give visitors a 360° panorama of the city. Gastown is also home to many traditional souvenir stores and art galleries as well as lot of independent fashion boutiques and modern gift stores. The area has some excellent First Nations art galleries which are worth checking out for unique keepsakes such as silver jewellery, art pieces and carvings.

煤气镇

　　煤气镇又名盖斯镇是温哥华历史文化的发源地。其古老的街道至今还完好地保留着。煤气镇是由著名的温哥华人约翰·盖斯·杰克·德顿于1867 年创办的。这个是一个有趣的新旧组合的地区。许多古老的建筑和仓库已经被改建成时髦的现代餐馆和商店，有鹅卵石街道，老式复古的路灯柱，著名的盖斯镇蒸汽钟和老盖斯杰克的铜像。煤气镇不仅反映了温哥华悠久的历史，同时也是一个人口众多充满活力多元化的港口。这里有最热门的餐厅提供多样的美食。这一带也是这个城市鸡尾酒会的中心，人们常来这里消闲，喝咖啡。最后，你可以从温哥华观景塔上欣赏到该地区的全貌，塔高167米，为游客提供了360度的鸟瞰整个城市的全景。煤气镇还有许多传统的纪念品商店、艺术画廊以及许多独特的时尚精品店和现代礼品店。最值得一提的是具有美洲艺术风格的第一民族艺术画廊和纪念品，如银首饰，手工艺术品和雕刻品等等，很有收藏价值。

March 16 Basic Everyday English

3月16日 基本日常生活用语

Talking to Neighbours

Many newcomers think that they need to wait until they can speak English perfectly before they speak to their neighbours. In Vancouver, it is common to give neighbours a little smile and say hello whenever you see them; however, it doesn't mean that you must become good friends. For the safety of your home and neighbourhood, it is good to have a polite relationship with them. When you first move into the neighbourhood, it can be a nice gesture to give your new neighbours a small card to introduce yourself.

"A good neighbour is a priceless treasure."

-Chinese proverb

跟邻居聊天

许多新移民认为需要等到他们的英语说得非常流利时再和邻居们聊天。在温哥华，当您遇见邻居时，给他们一个微笑并打声招呼很平常，这并不意味着你们必须成为好朋友。为了您家和邻里的安全，有礼貌地与他们友好相处是必要的。当您刚搬进来时，送给邻居一张自我介绍的小卡片是一个不错的友好举动。

"邻居好, 胜金宝" —— 中国谚语

English for Everyday Life
日常生活英语

下面是一些基本英语短语，您也许听到过，您可以直接用它们和您的邻居交谈。

Hello, how are you today?
I'm fine thank you
It is a beautiful day
It is so rainy today.
Your garden looks pretty.
I have to go now, have a great day.
It was nice talking to you.
Would you like to come in for some tea and cookies?

您好，今天感觉如何？
我很好，谢谢您。
真是美好的一天
今天雨这么大。
您的花园看起来很漂亮。
我现在得走了，祝您愉快。
和您谈话很开心。
您想进来喝点茶吃块饼干吗？

March 17   Education

3月17日   教育

Amount of Homework in Elementary and Secondary School

Many newcomers are often surprised at how little homework students are assigned on a daily basis. This is because in BC, the teachers see more value in the *quality* of the work, rather than the *quantity*. In addition, the teachers must follow the guidelines set by the BC Ministry of Education about the amount of homework to be given to elementary and secondary students. The guidelines are as follows:

Elementary School

- From Kindergarten to Grade 3: no homework is given
- From Grade 4 to Grade 7: ½ hour per night of homework is given
- Some examples of homework given are: Complete work given in class, read a book for a specified time, write a journal entry and work with classmates on a class project.

Secondary School

- Grades 8 to 12: 1 to 2 hours per night, however students learning English will take longer.
- Some examples of homework given are: Gather information from various sources, think or reflect on a given topic and write about it, read chapters of a book or work with classmates on a group or class project.

For more detailed descriptions of the homework assigned to students, please see the homework brochures on the Multilanguage parent information brochures page on the VSB website.

关于中小学家庭作业数量的规定

　　许多新移民对于学校每天给学生布置的家庭作业少而感到惊讶。这是因为在卑诗省，老师更注重作业质量而非数量。

　　教师必须遵循卑诗省教育局制定的关于中小学生家庭作业数量的指导原则。这些指导原则是：

小学

- 幼儿园到三年级：无家庭作业
- 四年级至七年级：每晚半小时的家庭作业
- 举例来说，家庭作业有：完成课堂上未完成的功课、安排一个特定时间读书、写日记、重复观看某一个英语电视节目以及与同学合作完成小组项目。

中学

- 八年级至十二年级：每晚一至两个小时，正在学习英语的学生用的时间会长一些。
- 举例来说，家庭作业有：收集不同来源的信息、对一个指定题目进行思考或预习笔记并将想法写下来、阅读或重复阅读课文或小说中的某一章节、与同学合作完成一个课堂或小组项目。

　　有关分配给学生的家庭作业的更多更详细的说明，请参阅上面的多语言父母信息手册页面上的家庭作业手册。

March 18   # Scenes from Daily Life

3月18日   日常生活中的一些镜头

Shopping for Fresh Fruit and Vegetables at the Market
在市场上购买新鲜水果和蔬菜

Outdoor Life in Vancouver

3月19日　　温哥华户外生活

Getting Naked at Wreck Beach

The internationally famous Wreck Beach, North America's largest nude beach, is only 15 minutes away from downtown Vancouver located at the bottom of a very steep cliff near UBC. The Wreck Beach Preservation Society (WBPS) works very hard all year to maintain the beautiful nature reserve that surrounds the beach. Also, the WBPS ensures that there is a warm, welcoming environment at the beach and especially encourage an attitude of body acceptance. Wreck Beach is popular with people of all ages, shapes, and sizes. An average of 12 to 14,000 visitors from all over the world visit the beach every day during the summer season.

沉船裸体海滩

国际著名的沉船海滩，是北美洲最大的裸体海滩，距温哥华市中心只有15分钟的车程，位于UBC非常陡峭的悬崖底部。沉船海滩保护协会（WBPS）的工作尽职尽责，常年对海滩周围的自然保护区进行维护。以确保给游客们提供一个温暖和舒适的环境。在沙滩上，特别提倡人们对身体接纳的态度。沉船海滩受到所有年龄、体形和体质的欢迎。到了夏季，每天平均有近14,000名来自世界各地的游客访问此海滩。

English for Everyday Life
日常生活英语

新词汇：

Clothing optional beach（可穿可不穿沙滩）：这意味着人们可以自由选择是否要在海滩上穿泳衣。完全或部分的裸露是完全可以接受的。

Skinny dipping（裸泳）：这是裸露的俚语表达方式。"we went skinny-dipping in the pool last night" "我们昨晚去泳池裸泳了"

Birthday suit（生日礼服）：是裸体的另一种俚语表达。"I was only wearing my birthday suit" "我只穿着我的生日礼服"

Nudist or naturist（裸体主义者或天然主义者）：这些人认为裸体有益于健康。

March 20 Tips to Learning English

3月20日 资深英语老师提供学习英语的小贴士

Know and Believe it is Possible

I have been an English teacher for more than sixteen years. In that time, I have seen numerous adults become comfortably fluent in English for everyday life. Most of them began with very limited skills. All of them improved a little bit every day, step-by-step, day by day until they were comfortable to speak English with anyone about almost any topic. I wish I could say that it was due to magic, or an excellent website or due to my teaching skills, but the truth is, it was entirely due to the most important characteristic they all had: PERSISTENCE. They never gave up and they never stopped. They started where they were, no matter how low, and they began to learn English a tiny bit every day. They all had setbacks, certainly, and times when it felt impossible and they wanted to give up. However, they didn't give up, they just kept going and kept persisting. They realized that even learning a single new word in a day is step forward. If you don't believe that it is possible to learn, maybe it would help you to know that I believe and know 100% that you can be fluent in English. So, feel free to "borrow" my unshakeable belief in your ability to learn English until you can believe it yourself!

知道并相信这是可能的

我一直在教英语，有十六年多的教学经验。在此期间，我看到许多成年人完全可以轻松的讲一口流利的日常生活英语。他们当中绝大多数人的英语基础开始的时候都非常有限。但我每天都能感觉到他们会有一点点进步，就这样一步一步地，一天一天地，直到他们能轻松地和任何人讲英语，而且无论是什么话题。我想说的是，这简直就是魔法，或许是由于我的教学技巧。但事实是，这完全归功于他们身上所具有最重要的特征：坚持不懈。他们从不放弃，他们从来没有停止过。不管最初英语水平有多低，他们就从这里起步。他们每天都坚持学一点点。当然，他们都遇到过挫折，有时感到不大可能，他们也曾产生过想放弃的念头。然而，最终他们没有放弃，他们继续前进，一直坚持学下去。他们意识到，即使在一天中学习一个新词，也是向前又迈进了一步。我百分之百地相信您可以流利的讲英语，您有这个能力。对此我深信不疑。

March 21   A Little Canadian Inspiration
3月21日   一点点启示

"For over a century, hard-working and independently minded people have been coming here [to Canada] from all over the world to make a better life for themselves and their families. As they have pursued their dreams, they have enriched this province, and our country. Now all these diverse peoples live together in harmony."

-*Former Governor General of Canada, Michaëlle Jean*
(the Queen's representative in Canada)

The only true "locals" are the First Nations peoples of Canada. All the other residents are either first generation immigrants or they are second, third or fourth generation immigrants from all over the world. This unique mixture of people and cultures makes Canada a special and welcoming place to live.

"一个多世纪以来，勤劳和独立的人们从世界各地来到加拿大，为自己和家人创造更加美好的生活。他们追求自己的梦的同时丰富了我们省和国家。现在所有不同文化的民族都和谐地生活在一起。"

——加拿大总督米歇尔·让（加拿大女王的代表）

唯一真正的"当地人"是指加拿大的第一民族。所有其他居民都是来自世界各地的第一代移民，第二代移民或者是第三代移民。这种独特的人文混合使得加拿大成为一个特别温馨的居住场所。

Volunteer in Vancouver

在温哥华做义工

Go Volunteer Website for Volunteer Job Listings

The Go Volunteer website lists all the volunteer jobs available in the city. Just by browsing through the listings you can get an idea of all the interesting volunteer work that is available in the city. The website allows you to search through the listings depending on your area of interest and location.

Please note that in the "advanced options" search form, you can search for jobs that are "suitable for English as Second Language (ESL)". This will help you feel confident that the volunteer organizations will be very welcoming to you, even if your English skills are not advanced.

上网站查看志愿者工作清单

http://www.govolunteer.ca/volunteer-opportunities

　　志愿者网站列出了温哥华市所有最新的志愿者工作。 浏览一下，您就可以了解到城市中所有有趣的志愿者工作。 该网站允许您根据兴趣、技能和地理位置进行搜索。

　　请注意，在"高级选项"搜索栏中，您可以搜索"适合英语作为第二语言（ESL）"的工作。即使您的英语水平不高，也能让您感觉到志愿者的组织会非常的欢迎您。

March 23	Healthcare in Vancouver
3月23日	温哥华的医疗保健

How to Find a Family Doctor and Medical Specialists

Family Physicians (also called General Practitioners or GPs) are trained to treat the whole person in an integrated care model. They treat patients of all ages, and they treat each organ and disease. Typically, every member of the family will have the same Family Physician. Family Physician offices can be contacted directly by patients; however, any contact with Medical Specialists can only be made by referral from a Family Physician. If your Family Physician feels that you will need to be seen by a specialist, then they will arrange the appointment time and let you know the name of the specialist and the appointment time and location.

To find a Family Physician in Vancouver, you can visit the College of Physicians and Surgeons website which has an accurate and up to date database of all the physicians in Vancouver. You can search for the physician gender you would prefer, in the neighbourhood where you live and choose doctors who speak Mandarin. Make sure to check the box "accepting new patients", so that it will only show physicians who are able to take on new patients.

如何寻找家庭医生和专科医生

医师搜索https://www.cpsbc.ca/physician_search

家庭医生（也称为普通科医生或全科医生）必须接受过培训，以全面护理模式对待所有年龄的病人。他们治疗每个器官的疾病。通常，每个家庭成员都会在同一个家庭医生的诊所看病。家庭医生办公室可以直接与病人联系；然而，任何与专科医生的联系只能通过家庭医师的推荐转诊。如果您的家庭医生认为您需要看专科医生，他们会安排预约时间，让您知道专家的名字、预约时间和地点。

要在温哥华找家庭医生，您可以访问内外科医生医学会的网站，该网站有准确的和最新的温哥华所有医生的数据库。您可以按照医生性别、您居住的社区以及是否说普通话来搜索您喜欢的医生。一定要确保勾选"接受新病人"的方框，这样就会显示所有能够接收新病人的医生。

March 24   Interesting Facts About Vancouver

3月24日   温哥华趣闻

Greenpeace Began in Vancouver

Greenpeace, one of the world's oldest and most successful international environmental groups started in Vancouver in 1971. The founders met in a little coffeeshop in Gastown and started their campaign to do all they could to be an "independent global campaigning organization that acts to change attitudes and behavior, to protect and conserve the environment and to promote peace." From that small café in Gastown, Greenpeace has grown into one of the largest environmental protection organizations in the world with offices in over 40 countries and an international organizing body in Amsterdam, the Netherlands.

绿色和平组织始于温哥华

　　绿色和平组织是世界上最古老和最成功的环保组织之一，于1971在温哥华成立。创始人在煤气镇的一家咖啡厅会面，开始了他们的运动，他们竭尽全力打造一个"独立的全球运动组织，旨在改变态度和行为，以保护环境，促进和平"。从煤气镇的那间小咖啡馆，到如今，绿色和平已发展成为世界上最大的环保组织之一，并在40多个国家设立办事处，总部设在荷兰阿姆斯特丹。

March 25   Finding Work in Vancouver

3月25日   在温哥华找份工作

Interviews

- ***Paid and Volunteer Job Interviews:*** After you apply for a position (paid or volunteer work), if the employer is interested, they will invite you to an interview. The purpose of the interview is to give the employer a chance to talk to you more about your education, experience and suitability for the job. It is also a time for the job-hunter to ask more questions about the position and find out more about what it is like working at that company. No matter if the interview is for paid work or volunteer work, there are some standard questions that are asked almost every time.

- ***Information Interviews:*** The purpose of information interviews is to explore different careers and learn more about different positions by having an interview with someone already working in the field you are interested in. If you are interested in working in a certain job in Vancouver, then find someone currently doing that job and write them a polite email requesting an information interview. Before the interview, prepare a list of questions you would like to ask them, and after the interview be sure to write a thank you letter to thank them for their time.

面试：有酬的和志愿者工作面试

    有酬的和志愿工作面试：在递交职位申请（有酬的或志愿的）后，如果雇主有兴趣，他们将约您参加面试。 面试的目的是给雇主一个机会，更多地与您谈谈您的教育、经验和适合您的工作。 这也是求职者提出更多关于职位的问题，以及在公司工作的时间。无论面试是有偿工作还是志愿者工作，几乎每次都有一些常见的问题会被问到。

English for Everyday Life
日常生活英语

这里有一些常见的面试问题：

Tell me about yourself.
Why did you leave your last job?
What are your strengths?
Why should we hire you?
What is your attitude towards work?

介绍一下您自己。
您为什么离开您的上一份工作？
您的强项是什么？
我们为什么要聘用您？
您对工作的态度是什么？

他们还会问到您处理问题的能力，他们要求您简述一些职业生涯中的故事：

You completed a task or project successfully - what did you do, how did it work out and so on.
You handled a difficult situation at work - explain what the situation was, how you handled it and the successful result.

您成功完成过那些任务或项目 - 您在其中都做了些什么，您是如何运作的，等等。
您曾在工作中遇到一个困难情况 — 请解释一下是什么情况，您是如何处理它的，结果如何。

Information Interviews（信息访谈）：信息访谈的目的是探索相同职业的不同之处，通过与在您感兴趣的领域工作的人面谈，了解不同职位的更多信息。如果您对温哥华的某项工作感兴趣，那就找一个做这份工作的人访谈一下。在访谈之前，准备一个提纲，您想问他们那些问题，在面谈之后，一定要写一封礼貌的感谢信，感谢他们抽出宝贵的时间。

<table>
<tr><td>**March 26**</td><td># Vancouver Sightseeing</td></tr>
<tr><td>3月26日</td><td>观光</td></tr>
</table>

Boating in the Harbour

Vancouver is a city by the water, and water plays an important part in the daily activities and recreation of the city. One of the best ways to see Vancouver and understand the lifestyle is to take a harbour tour. **Vancouver Harbour Cruises** provides many different length tours and some include a full lunch or dinner as well. If you would rather explore on your own, you can rent a small powerboat from **Boat Rentals Vancouver** at the marina at Granville Island and they will give you a short training session on how to operate the boats and give you information on the best routes to explore. Bring a picnic and enjoy exploring Vancouver from the water.

在海港划船

温哥华港邮轮 https://www.boatcruises.com/
船租 https://www.boatrentalsvancouver.com/

- 温哥华是一座靠海的城市，海水在城市的日常活动和娱乐中起着重要的作用。参观温哥华，了解那里生活方式的最好方法之一就是去海港旅游。温哥华海港游船提供许多不同行程的旅行，其中有的还包括丰盛的午餐或晚餐。
- 如果你想自己探索，你可以在格兰维尔岛的码头温哥华租船公司租一艘小艇，他们将给你一个简短的培训课程，如何驾驶船只，并给你提供最好的巡游路线信息。 带上野餐，享受从水中探索温哥华的乐趣。

Vancouver Transportation

3月27日 温哥华交通运输

Road Closures for Special Events

When there are major events in Vancouver such as the International Marathon or Italian Day, it is common to completely close the roads so that there is enough room for all the people to walk around safely. The roads are closed from four hours to one day. Usually there will be signs posted in the area ahead of time to let people know about upcoming closures.

The new website and app: www.drivebc.ca is an excellent place to check for information about driving all around the province. Any road closures or special information about road conditions will always be updated there. This Drive BC website also has an excellent **"Plan Your Route"** feature that allows you to enter a starting location and an end destination and receive the shortest route (as determined by Google) with step-by-step instructions that you can save on your phone or print out.

遇有重大事件道路关闭

每逢温哥华举办重大活动，如国际马拉松或意大利日，通常完全关闭道路，以便有足够的空间让所有的人安全地走动。 道路关闭从四小时到一天不等。 通常会在该地区提前张贴告示，让人们知道哪些道路即将关闭。

www.drivebc.ca是一个非常棒的路况网站，你可以在那里查找全省各地关于驾驶的详细信息。 所有道路的封闭或各种道路状况的特殊信息都将会那里实时更新。

此网站还有一个优秀的"规划您的路线"功能，输入起点和终点就能获得最短的路线（由Google确定）与分步说明，您可以保存在手机上或 打印出来。

Sports Teams and Special Events

专业体育赛事和活动

Vancouver Whitecaps Team

The Vancouver Whitecaps is Vancouver's professional soccer team. Soccer is not as popular a spectator sport in Vancouver as hockey and football, but it is continuing to grow in popularity as the tickets are much more affordable than the other sports. Also, soccer is a very popular sport for youth to play in Vancouver and they want to watch the professionals play. Vancouver Whitecaps FC (football club) is one of 22 teams that plays in the Major League Soccer (MLS) league in Canada and the US. The Whitecaps play their home matches at BC Place Stadium.

温哥华白帽队 http://www.whitecapsfc.com/

温哥华白帽队是一支职业足球队。 足球在温哥华虽不及曲棍球和橄榄球那样受到热捧，但近年来它的人气持续增长，门票比其他运动项目要便宜得多。 此外，足球运动越来越受到温哥华青少年们的喜爱，他们喜欢看世界足球杯比赛。温哥华白帽FC（足球俱乐部）也是加拿大和美国足球大联盟（MLS）联赛中的22支球队之一。 白帽的主场设在BC广场的体育馆。

March 29   Vancouver Parks

3月29日   温哥华公园

Fraser River Park and Deering Island Park

Located at 8705 Angus Drive at West 75th Ave, the small 91-hectare **Fraser River Park** is a quiet and peaceful area located by the mighty Fraser River. There are large green lawns perfect for picnicking or flying a kite, and beautiful views of the Fraser River are available from the boardwalks that lead between the poplar and alder trees. Crab apple and Nootka Rose lining the pathways are reminders of these plants that farmers of the area once planted along the Fraser River dykes to protect their land from flooding. Tourists usually ignore this simple and pleasant park, but it is much loved by locals who want to picnic with their family and enjoy being outdoors and watching the river flow by.

Nearby the Fraser River Park is the very charming **Deering Island Park**, which is a small island located in the Fraser River. It is another area that is perfect for enjoying the peaceful views of the river and tidal marshes. In late summer, the park is filled with dragonflies and the blackberries.

菲沙河公园和迪尔岛公园

位于8705安古斯大街以西，和西第七十五大道，占地91公顷的小菲沙河公园（Fraser River Park）是位于浩瀚的菲沙河畔的一个安静的地区。有一大片绿色的草坪是野餐或放风筝的理想场所，走在白杨树和赤杨木树之间的木板路上可以欣赏到菲沙河的美丽景色。沿着道路两旁的海棠和努特卡玫瑰提醒人们，当地的农民为了保护他们的土地免受洪水灾害，曾经沿着河堤坝大面积种植这些植物。外来的游客们通常忽略这种看似简单的公园，但它却深受当地人的喜爱，在这种令人愉快的地方与家人野餐，并享受在户外活动的同时观赏流动着的菲沙河。

在菲沙河公园附近有一个非常迷人的迪尔岛公园（Deering Island Park），这是一座很小的岛，位于菲沙河畔。它是另一个完美的享受河流和潮汐沼泽。在夏末，公园里到处长满了黑莓还可以看到很多蜻蜓。

March 30 Stories and Advice for Newcomers

3月30日 移民的故事和建议

Haiying

Done！

史梅芳，新移民，来自东北，就读ESL，给自己取了个洋气的英文名：Francesca（弗朗西斯卡）。

上课期间，老师每完成一件事，总爱习惯性的说：Done（完成的）！她觉得这个词很酷！

那天，在她家做小时工的菲佣结束工作时，问她还需做些什么吗？她说：You are done！然后，菲佣含着泪委屈地离开了梅芳的家，而梅芳更是百思不得其解为何菲佣再也不去她家了。

朋友夫妇来访，谈起我初识他太太的一幕，总让人忍俊不禁。

去年1月9日，上海飞温哥华，巧遇这位吴姓好友，遂上前打招呼："这么巧！您也去温哥华！"吴先生指指身边的女士："我太太要去唱歌，入籍"我无比真诚地伸过手去："很高兴认识您！要录专辑啦？您是唱美声的还是通俗的？"夫妇俩面面相觑……

那天我才明白，因为加入加拿大国籍需宣誓唱国歌，所以在加拿大的华人都将入籍仪式说成去唱歌。

Diverse Vancouver

3月31日 多元文化的温哥华

Celebrating Vancouver's Cherry Trees and Japanese Culture

Every spring there is a large **Vancouver Cherry Blossom Festival (VCBF)** that happens when the beautiful pink cherry blossoms begin to bloom on the streets and parks of Vancouver in the spring. This festival organizes 22 different events throughout the city including **Sakura Day** in VanDusen Gardens with delicious Japanese food, photography contests, blossom-viewing bicycle rides and walks, music and entertainment. The motto of the festival is "there is no stranger under the cherry tree" and they welcome inclusion and participation by all.

庆祝温哥华的樱花树和日本文化http://www.vcbf.ca/

每年春天，当美丽的粉红色的樱花开始在街道两旁和公园里绽放的时候，温哥华市都会举办一场盛大的樱花节Vancouver Cherry Blossom Festival（VCBF）。整个城市一共组织22场以樱花为主题的不同的活动，最著名的是范杜森花园的樱花日，你可以品尝美味的日本料理、参加摄影比赛、樱花观赏、自行车表演、漫步、音乐表演和观看娱乐节目。 节日的口号是"樱花树下没有陌生人"，他们欢迎所有人都来共同庆祝并欣赏樱花的美丽。

April

Weather:	Average temperature: 5°C to 14°C
	Average rainfall days: 18, Average rainfall: 60 mm
Statutory holiday:	Good Friday (schools and gov. offices) and Easter Monday
Other special days:	April Fool's Day

The month of April begins with silly April Fool's Day* on April 1 which is a half day for practical jokes and friendly tricks on people, but only until noon that day.

Later in the month comes the more serious and special holiday of Easter*. While Easter has very deep meaning for Christians, it has also transformed over the years to be more of a special time for families and children to spend time together. Many Vancouverites get together with their family for Easter dinner* and the children eagerly await treats from the Easter Bunny*. Throughout the community, there are egg hunts* and Easter celebrations and activities.

By the time April arrives, everyone is in a happy and joyful spring mood. The beautiful cherry trees that can be found lining many city streets begin to blossom with their beautiful pale pink flowers. The annual Vancouver Cherry Blossom Festival celebrates this yearly event with many community events and activities.

This month the very famous and popular Vancouver Sun Run occurs and more than 50,000 runners and walkers sign up for the 10km charity run and walk*. The route for the Sun Run goes through some of the prettiest parts of Vancouver from downtown, through Stanley Park, along the beaches and over the beautiful Burrard Street Bridge. The organizers make the event extra special by lining the course with live musical acts, water stations and a large gathering at the end in BC Place where all participants get free snacks and the fastest runners receive awards. The name of every person who completes the 10 km course is printed in the Vancouver Sun newspaper the day after the race.

At the end of April, Kerrisdale Village hosts Carnival Days where there are free events for the entire family such as music, clowns, face painting, rides and stores put on sidewalk sales.

4月

气候：平均温度：5°C 至14°C
平均降雨天数：18，平均降雨量：60 毫米
公众节假日：耶稣受难日与复活节（学校和政府办公室）
其他特殊日：愚人节

愚人节定于每年4月1日，这是一个为期半天的恶作剧，人们以各种方式互相欺骗、捉弄和取笑，往往在玩笑的最后，直到当天中午才揭穿并宣告捉弄对象为"愚人"。

复活节是个不固定的节日，一般在本月晚些时候。复活节是一年中除了圣诞节之外最重要的基督教节日。虽然复活节对基督徒来说有着很深远的意义，但多年来它也改变了很多家庭的习惯，人们更愿意在这个特殊的日子和孩子们呆在一起。许多当地民众与他们的家庭在复活节共进晚餐，孩子们则急切地等待着传说中的兔子发送的复活节**彩蛋**。在整个社区，有彩蛋狩猎和各种复活节的庆祝活动。

4月到来的时候，给每个人带来了春天幸福和欢乐的心情。您会发现在许多城市街道两旁长满了美丽的樱桃树，树上长满了淡粉色的樱花。许多社区开始举办一年一度温哥华樱花节的庆祝活动。

这个月最受大众喜欢的活动要数温哥华太阳报举办的**慈善长跑**，有超过5万名长跑爱好者报名参加10公里慈善跑步和健走活动，太阳报长跑的路线将穿过温哥华最漂亮的市区，沿着斯坦利公园的海滩和美丽的布勒桥。终点设在卑诗省广场，主办方在那里提供现场音乐表演，饮水站和一个大型聚会活动，所有参与者均可获得免费的小吃，跑得最快的选手将获得额外的奖品。所有完成10公里长跑者的名字将在比赛后的第二天登在温哥华太阳报上。

4月底，Kerrisdale社区将举办狂欢节，所有的活动对家庭来说都是免费的。如音乐、小丑、画脸谱、游乐设施等等。商家们在人行道上设摊销售他们的商品。

更多的信息：

温哥华樱花节：http://www.vcbf.ca/

温哥华太阳报长跑：http://www.vancouversun.com/sunrun/

Kerrisdale 狂欢节：http://www.kerrisdalevillage.com/news-and-events/

*April Fools' Day愚人节：在每 4 年月 1 日，当日都有恶作剧的习俗。愚人节开的玩笑只能到当天的正午为止。在愚人节上当受骗的人被称作四月的傻瓜。

*Easter复活节：是最重要和最古老的基督教节日。复活节纪念耶稣基督死亡后的复活。复活节在每年北半球春分 （一般在3月21日至4月25日之间）月圆后的第一个星期日举行。

*Easter Bunny复活节兔子：是虚构的。兔子与复活节联系在一起是因为兔子多产，是生命的象征。在复活节用巧克力做成的兔形状的糖果作为小礼物送给孩子们。类似的还有巧克力鸡蛋，因为鸡蛋里蕴藏着新的生命。

*Easter egg hunt复活节彩蛋：是用彩色铝箔纸包裹起来。小孩子们在复活节一早要去寻找彩蛋。彩蛋藏在房子或后院的角落里。有些父母哄孩子说，彩蛋是复活节兔子送来的。

*Easter Foods复活节食品：通常与复活节相关的食物包括羊肉，许多人在复活节的宴席上吃羔羊肉，并称其为"上帝的羔羊"。烤羔羊火腿据说能带来好运。其次是绘有十字的热面包，面包上面的十字架象征着基督。面包是圆形的，加入了葡萄干和肉桂等香料。这种面包既可以用于早餐也可以作为一种小吃，吃之前先热一下，然后切成两半，涂抹黄油。

*Charity run and walk慈善长跑和健走：一种筹款活动，活动中人们把钱捐给某个慈善组织，以支持他们的公益活动。

April 1

4月1日 # Local Customs

当地的习俗

Pregnancy and New Baby Announcements and Celebrations

Generally, it is traditional not to tell anyone about a pregnancy until after three months have passed. After this time, it is customary to let people know. It is popular with younger mothers nowadays to make a special pregnancy announcement photograph to send to friends and family to share the news.

When the baby is born, the family can place a birth announcement in the local paper. There is a birth announcements section of the classified ads section of the paper. Also, many couples email all their friends and family with a birth announcement photograph with the baby's name, date of birth and weight.

It is traditional to send flowers and a card to new parents to congratulate them on the birth of their baby. Either a few weeks before the birth or a few weeks after the birth of the baby, the bride's close friends and family will have a **Baby Shower** which is a party to welcome the baby to the world. The guests bring presents for the baby and enjoy cake and tea together.

In recent years, there is a new tradition of the new father buying the new mother a **Push Present** to thank her for doing the difficult work of being pregnant and going through labour. These presents are usually a piece of jewelry but can sometimes be very generous like a new car!

怀孕公告，新婴儿出生和婴儿庆祝会

一般来说，刚刚怀孕的人不想告诉任何人，过了三个月就慢慢习惯了让别人知道。

English for Everyday Life
日常生活英语

以下是当地人告诉别人她怀孕的两种方式：

"I have some exciting news to share with you. I am pregnant!"
"I want to let you know that I am pregnant and my due date is Sept 23"
"我有一些令人兴奋的消息，与大家分享。 我怀孕了！"
"我想让你们知道我怀孕了，我的预产期是9月23日"

当有人告诉你他们怀孕了，你可以这样说：

"Congratulations! When is the baby due?"
"What great news. I am so happy for you"
"恭喜！ 孩子的预产期是什么时候？
"好消息。 我真为你高兴 "

现在有一种很流行的方法是，年轻的母亲拍一组特殊的怀孕照片发送给亲朋好友们分享。

当婴儿出生的时候，家里可以在当地报纸上刊登出生公告。报社的分类广告部分有一个出生公告栏。此外，许多夫妇会给所有的朋友和家人发送带有出生日期和婴儿体重的出生公告照片。

English for Everyday Life
日常生活英语

如果有人告诉你关于出生的消息时，你应该说：

"Congratulations!" You can also add "I hope mother and baby are doing well"

"恭喜你！" 你还可以补充说 "我希望妈妈和宝宝都表现得很好"

无论是在出生前几周或出生后几周的婴儿，送鲜花和贺卡给新生儿的父母，祝贺他们孩子的诞生这是一种传统。妈妈的好友和家庭成员将办一个新生婴儿的聚会，以欢迎宝宝来到这个世界。客人们给宝宝带来礼物，并一起享用蛋糕和茶。

近年来，又多了一个新的传统，新生儿的父亲会给孩子的母亲买一种叫做生产礼，用来赏赐老婆辛劳生孩子怀孕和分娩艰苦的过程。这些礼物通常是一件首饰，但有时可以很大方，像一辆新车！

Parenting in Vancouver

在温哥华养育子女

School Breaks

Professional Development Days: During the school year, there are a few regularly scheduled breaks from instruction. Every school year, teachers are given approximately one day of professional education every month. These days are called **PD or Pro-D Days**. The children don't go to school and the parents must arrange for their care on that day. The teachers attend a day of administrative meetings and workshops about education.

Winter Break: The schools are usually closed for a two-week period from before Christmas Day until after New Year's Day. As this is usually a time for the family to be together, there are no special education or day camps arranged in the community for the children at this time.

Spring Break: The schools are closed for two weeks in early spring – usually in March. Every community centre offers special spring break day camps for children on a variety of subjects – from academic to the arts to sports. The BC Parent Magazine and website www.bcparent. ca always prepares a list of all the camp options that parents can choose from.

Summer Break: The schools are closed for two months every summer in July and August. Just like during the spring, there are a variety of camps and activities for students to pursue. They can even take additional academic courses in summer schools arranged by each school district. However, in the summer most Vancouver families spend a lot of time doing activities outside together and taking their annual vacation so courses are not the priority. Family fun in the sun is what most families want to enjoy together!

学校假期：专修日（称为PD日），冬季，春季和夏季

专业发展日：在学年期间，有几个定期安排休息的时间。 每个学年，教师每个月大约有一天的专业教育时间。 这些天被称为PD日或Pro-D日。 孩子们不上学，父母必须在那天安排照顾他们。 教师参加一天关于教育的行政会议和讲习班。

寒假：学校通常从圣诞节到新年元旦停课两个星期。 由于这通常是家庭聚在一起的时间，所以在这个时候没有专门为儿童在社区安排特殊教育或日间冬令营。

春假：学校在春季关闭两个星期 – 通常是在每年的三月份。 社区中心为孩子们提供特殊的日间春令营，有各种课程 – 从学术到艺术和体育运动。 BC育儿杂志和网站www.bcparent.ca会为家长们准备一份所有春令营项目的列表，以供他们选择。

暑假：学校每年夏天在七月和八月关闭两个月。如同春假，有各种专为学生们设置的夏令营活动。 他们甚至可以在暑期期间由每个学区安排额外的学术课程。 然而，在温哥华更多的家长会利用他们的年假花更多时间陪孩子在户外活动。所以课程并不是第一选择。 在阳光下一起享受家庭的欢乐才是大多数人想要的！

April 3   # Stories and Advice for Newcomers

4月3日   新移民的故事

Randy

新移民常遇的小问题

初到温哥华的新移民都会遇到不少跟金融理财和税务相关的小麻烦小障碍。以下几个经验和小故事分享给大家以便使初来乍到的新移民更容易克服障碍，尽快适应本地环境。

一元硬币Loonie的故事

刚到温哥华一切都很陌生，甚至连一元硬币都不认识。第一次乘公交车就遇到了麻烦。温哥华的公共汽车停车站都很小，有的甚至只有一个细小的牌子钉在电线杆上很难发现。排队等车的时候从兜里掏出几枚硬币，发现有个黄色圆形的铜板上面没有标明价值。这是什么？是钱吗？询问旁边排队的一位陌生人："请问这是什么？"，那位年轻的男士用诧异的眼光看着我："这是一元钱啊，你们…从月球来的吗？"。后来上了车，却不知道如何下车（错过了好几站），因为下车前都需要拉车窗边的一根绳子提醒司机。还是那位年轻的本地人帮我们拉绳，还下车指引我们如何去到目的地。那是第一次见识到加拿大人的热心助人。

领到医疗卡之前要买旅行保险Travel Insurance

对每个新移民来说，初来乍到控制风险十分重要，比如医疗的风险和保障。加拿大医疗福利保障十分健全，但刚登陆的家庭并未立刻获得本地提供的医疗福利和保险。从申请到领省医疗卡需要等待大约90天。这期间万一发生意外，医疗费用是很高的，比如BC省各医院的急诊挂号费通常每次需要$800加币左右，普通住院费每日几千，重症住院甚至达到每天几万。所以，新移民刚到的这段时间，应该购买90天左右的旅行保险以备不测。一般中年人，每天几块钱就可买到10万左右的旅行医疗险。

April 4 Vancouver Entertainment

4月4日 温哥华娱乐

Car clubs and Legal Car Racing

Exotic and luxury cars have grown in popularity over the past few years. To cater to this growing hobby, there are several car clubs and special auto shows for people to share their interests. There are clubs that offer car related driving and social activities as well. Here is just a small selection of organizations and events for people who get a lot of entertainment out of owning and driving fancy cars:

- **The Vancouver Dynamic Auto Club** has 440 members, 90 per cent of whom are from China, founded by David Dai. To join, a member must have a car that costs more than $100,000.

- **The Vancouver Car Club:**

  The Vancouver Car Club is a new concept in exotic & luxury cars ownership that gives its members access to a changing pool of exceptional cars to drive. The members buy a share in a car they want — from the club's long list. The club then purchases, maintains, stores & insures the car. Each part owner gets four (4) weeks of driving for each ownership unit purchased per year. They also have a selection of Ferrari, Lamborghini, Aston Martin, Porsche, Mercedes, Maserati cars that they will rent out daily, weekly and monthly.

- **Luxury and Supercar Weekend**

  This show takes place on the lawns of the VanDusen Botanical Garden and the large display of exotic supercars and treasured collector cars lets car enthusiasts have a close view at some of the most beautiful examples of automotive design achievement.

- **The Ultimate Supercar Charity Challenge Rally:**

The Diamond Rally is an invitation-only driving rally which takes a selection of truly exclusive luxury and supercars from Vancouver to Whistler via Canada's most scenic route, the Sea to Sky Highway 99.

汽车俱乐部和赛车

近几年国外的豪华汽车越来越受到欢迎。为了迎合人们的兴趣和爱好，一些汽车俱乐部和车展部门提供相关的汽车驾驶体验与社交活动，分享他们驾驶的乐趣。下面简要地介绍几个汽车俱乐部及其组织的活动。让会员们充分享受驾驶豪华汽车的乐趣：

- **温哥华动力汽车俱乐部**
  温哥华动力汽车俱乐部共有440名成员，其中90%是来自中国，由戴伟达创立。要加入的条件是，每个成员必须拥有一辆豪华汽车，且车款必须超过100,000加元。

- **温哥华汽车俱乐部**
  温哥华汽车俱乐部是一个全新的理念，会员们拥有该俱乐部所有进口豪华车的所有权。您可以不停地更换俱乐部中的不同品牌的车辆，也可以和其他会员拼车出游。会员们如果想购车的话可以先从俱乐部提供的长长的车目中挑选出一辆共享的汽车。然后俱乐部负责购买，保养，存放和上汽车保险等等。购买者每年对其所购买的车辆有四周的驾驶时间。他们还可以按天，按周和按月选择租用法拉利、兰宝吉尼、阿斯顿马丁、保时捷、奔驰和玛莎拉蒂等高级轿车。

- **周末超级豪华跑车**
  周末在范渡森植物园的草坪上，通过大屏幕展示各种名贵的国际超级跑车，以方便汽车收藏家们近距离地欣赏。并共享汽车设计的成果。

- **终极超级赛车慈善挑战赛**
  钻石拉力赛仅限于邀请真正驾驶过独特的超级豪华跑车的选手，从温哥华出发，途径加拿大最美的海天99号高速公路至惠斯勒。

4月5日   温哥华著名的小学

St. George's Elementary School (private)

Here is the description of the school from their website: "BUILDING FINE YOUNG MEN. ONE BOY AT A TIMES. St. George's School was founded in 1930 and is located on the west side of Vancouver, British Columbia. At the Junior School campus, over 300 boys from Grade 1 to 7 study in a magnificent heritage building. Junior School students follow a core curriculum including Art, Career and Personal Planning (CAPP), Computer Studies, Drama, English, French, Library Skills, Mathematics, Music, Physical Education, Science, and Social Studies."

圣乔治小学（私立）https://www.stgeorges.bc.ca

下面是学校网站的描述：

"塑造优秀男青年。一个时代的男孩。圣乔治学校创建于1930年，位于不列颠哥伦比亚省温哥华的西边。校舍是一座宏伟的古建筑，有1至7年级300多名男生。初中预备班的核心课程，包括艺术、职业和个人规划（CAPP）、计算机研究、戏剧、英语、法语、图书馆技能、数学、音乐、体育、科学和社会研究。

A Different Way of Thinking

4月6日　　　不同的思维方式

Work-Life balance – a big priority for Westcoast living

Vancouverites believe in the importance of "work – life balance" both for themselves and for their children. They believe that work is important, but they equally value leisure time. They make sure to have enough time to relax, exercise, be out in nature, spend time with friends and family and do many other activities that nourish the heart and soul. Therefore, they try to schedule their days to include work but also plenty of time for life too. The education system puts a high priority on the power of free play time to encourage children to be creative and lead an active lifestyle. The beautiful nature, fresh air, parks, mountains, and beaches of Vancouver make people very motivated to achieve a good work-life balance so they can get outside and enjoy it all!

平衡工作与生活的关系 – 西海岸生活的重中之重

　　温哥华人懂得要为自己和孩子们"平衡工作 – 生活"的重要性。他们认为工作固然重要，但休闲也是必不可少的。他们确保有足够的时间放松身心，锻炼身体，花时间与朋友和家人共度时光，在大自然中，做许多滋养心灵和灵魂的活动。因此，他们设法安排好自己的工作时间，同时留出足够的生活空间。加拿大的教育系统把自由玩耍的时间放在首位，鼓励孩子们勇于创新、积极主动地生活。温哥华自然美丽，空气清新，公园、山脉和海滩使人们非常有活力，要想在实现生活中获得良好的工作与生活的平衡，就要时常走出去，尽情地享受眼前的一切吧！

April 7   Best High Schools

4月7日   温哥华著名的中学

St. Georges Senior School (private)

Here is the description of the school from their website: "St. George's School is an independent university preparatory school for boys located on the west side of Vancouver, British Columbia. At the Senior School campus, over 700 boys study in a newly renovated high school building. In addition to the core curriculum prescribed by the Ministry of Education, our Senior School students have access to an extensive list of academic electives including Business Education, Calculus, Computer Studies and Technology, Consumer Education, Creative Writing, Critical Thinking, Outdoor Education, Geometry and Discrete Math, German, Government and Politics, Information Technology, Japanese, Law, Leadership, Mandarin, Mathematics Principles, Media Arts, Music, Public Speaking. Along with the many academic electives that are available, the School offers a strong co-curricular program that includes over 100 athletic options and over 50 club options. For example, Senior School students have the opportunity to participate in a variety of games that vary from term to term. From Badminton to Rock Climbing, there are games to suit any interest!"

圣乔治中学（私立）https://www.stgeorges.bc.ca

以下是学校网站上的描述：

"圣乔治学校是一所位于不列颠哥伦比亚省温哥华西部的男子独立大学预科学校。在中学校园里，有700多名男孩在新近装修的教学楼上课。除了教育部规定的核心课程外，我们的中学生还可以享有广泛的学术选修课程，包括商业教育、微积分、电脑技术、消费者教育、创意写作、批判性思维、户外教育、几何、离散数学、德语、政府与政治、信息技术、日语、法律、领导、普通话、数学原理、媒体艺术、音乐、公共演讲等等。除了众多的选修课程外，学校还提供强大的课程计划，包括超过100个运动选项，50多个俱乐部的可供选择。例如，高中学生有机会参加各种不同学期的比赛。从羽毛球到攀岩，应有尽有。"

The Homes of Vancouver

4月8日   温哥华住宅

A Mini Castle in the Neighbourhood
老式的迷你城堡

　　在社区散步的时候，你会发现一些像这样的老房子，独特的圆形塔楼建筑造型。

April 9

Best Extracurricular Activities for Kids

4月9日 最佳儿童课外活动

UBC Tennis Centre

The UBC Tennis Centre is the only public tennis centre with 12 new and excellent quality indoor courts. They have a junior tennis program that teaches the fundamental skills and offers further training that continues their development into tournament level. The professional coaching team works with players of all ages and levels of playing ability to improve their tennis skills and help them enjoy playing the game.

UBC网球中心

UBC网球中心是温哥华唯一的公共网球中心，拥有12个新的和高质量的室内球场。 他们有一个初级网球训练计划，教授基本技能，然后提供进一步的培训，继续深造达到锦标赛的水平。 他们为所有年龄和所有水平的人提供所需的设施、 指导和技术服务，来提高他们的网球技能并享受打球的乐趣。

Meeting Locals in Vancouver

与当地人接触

Start Right in Your Own Neighbourhood

One great way to meet local people is to start right in your own neighbourhood! You can introduce yourself to the residents who live right next door to your home. If you visit our website, you can listen to some practice videos of the basic English you need to speak to your neighbours. If you feel shy, you can just start small and simply smile and say hello to people when you go for walks around the area. Get to know the local businesses, the local library and community centre. As you get to know more about your new neighbourhood, you will see the same people more. Neighbours always try to respect each other's privacy and not be too intrusive, but it is common to wave and say hello and, when not in a rush, to have short, polite conversations about things like the weather, garden, children, and things that are happening in the local neighbourhood. If you feel a little shy, you could always write a very short note and give a small present (tea, cookies) to your neighbour to introduce yourself. If you don't want to talk to them, you could just leave it by their front door.

先从您的邻居入手吧

结识当地人有一个很好的方法，那就是从自己身边的邻居开始！您可以向隔壁的邻居介绍自己。如果您访问我们的网站，您可以听到一些与邻居交谈的英语视频。如果您感到害羞，您可以先从简单的小事做起，比如当您在社区周围散步时，微笑着向周围的人说一声，"Hello"（您好）。多了解当地的企业、多去图书馆和社区中心。慢慢地您就会认识更多的新邻居。邻居之间总是尽量尊重彼此的隐私，不要太过打扰，但通常都是挥手示意，并在不太匆忙的情况下，进行简短而有礼貌的谈论当地的天气、花园、孩子和在当地社区中发生的事情。如果您觉得害羞，您可以写一张非常简短的便条，送出一份小小的礼物（茶或饼干）然后介绍您自己。如果您不想和他们交谈，您可以把礼物放在他们的前门。下面是写便条的例子：

English for Everyday Life
日常生活英语

当您第一次搬进来的时候，您可以写给邻居们一张介绍自己的便条，您也可以在新邻居搬进来的时候给他们写一张欢迎的便条。

当您搬进来时，给邻居写的自我介绍的示例：

"Hi, we are new to the area and would like to get to know some of our neighbours, I hope to talk to you in the future. We don't speak much English yet, so thank you for your patience. Your new neighbours: Yan and Yi, 3500 West 33rd Ave"

"您好，我们是新搬来的，想认识一下周围的邻居，我希望将来能和您谈谈。我们目前还不能流利地说英语，所以要感谢您的耐心等待。您的新邻居：严和义，西33大街3500号。"

当新邻居迁入时，给他们写的欢迎便条的示例：

"Hi, welcome to the neighbourhood, we hope you enjoy your time here, if you have any problems, you can speak to us anytime. Looking forward to talking in the future, your neighbours, Yan and Yi, 3500 West 33rd Ave"

"您好，欢迎您的到来，我们希望您在这里过得愉快，如果您有什么问题，可以随时和我们联系。期待着有机会能和您聊一聊，您的邻居，严和义，西33大街3500号。"

April 11   Restaurant Customs and Etiquette

4月11日   餐厅的习俗与礼仪

Table settings

These are two different table settings that you will find in Vancouver Restaurants. The simpler setting is found in a casual or informal restaurant and the more complicated setting is found in an upscale and more formal restaurant.

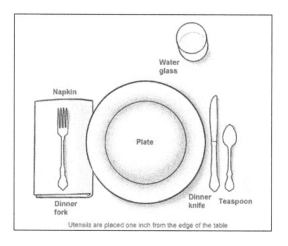

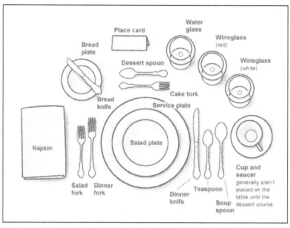

餐桌布置

你会在温哥华餐厅看到这两种不同餐桌形式的布置。普通的或者说是休闲的那种餐馆，餐桌的布置相对比较简单如上图；而高档的或正规的餐厅其餐桌的摆设较为复杂如下图。

April 12　Top English Programs for Adults
4月12日　　成人高级英语课程

MOSAIC

MOSAIC runs Language Instruction for Newcomers to Canada (LINC) classes as well as running an **English Language Institute** that is open to visitors, temporary foreign workers, citizens, and newcomers without Permanent Resident status. Their English Language Institute offers English classes in beginner, intermediate, advanced and workplace English. Their professional and fully certified instructors are experienced at working with adult learners and helping them improve their English language skills. Their classes run for five or six week sessions.

马赛克https://www.mosaicbc.org/

马赛克开设加拿大新移民语言教学（LINC）课程及英语语言学院，向没有永久居民身份的访客、外国临时工、公民和具有永久居民身份的新移民开放。他们的英语学院开设初级、中级、高级和职场英语班。他们专业的和经过认证的讲师都是富有长期教学经验的。每门课程一般为五周或者六周。

April 13	Vancouver Backyard Wildlife
4月13日	温哥华后院的小鸟和动物

Cougars (also known as Mountain Lions)

It is possible to encounter a cougar on the mountain trails up in the mountains close to the city. But it is also possible to have them come in your backyard if you live in the neighbourhoods that are close to the forests such as North and West Vancouver, Port Coquitlam and Port Moody. Cougars have a poor sense of smell, but excellent eyesight and hearing that help them hunt in the early morning and evening hours. They eat mainly deer, but they also eat smaller animals, such as mice and rabbits. Their powerful hind legs enable them to jump as far as 12 to 13 meters. Cougars will quietly stalk their prey and then grab them when the chance arises. They then hide their food under leaves and soil in a "cache" and feed on it over several days.

Sometimes hikers will come across a cache when hiking and that might prompt a cougar attack.

Important Safety information:

- If you come across a cougar, make yourself as big as you can. Spread your jacket, open an umbrella, pick up children, stomp your feet and talk loudly. Sound and look as scary as you can. You want the animal to decide you're a threat, not prey. Don't turn your back. NEVER run. Carry a walking stick when hiking and use it to fight back if the cougar behaves aggressively.

- If you see a cougar in your neighbourhood that is acting aggressively, contact the Conservation Officer Service (COS) Call Centre 1-877-952-7277.

- Do not give food to cougars. It is an offence under the Wildlife Act to feed dangerous wildlife.

美洲狮（又名山狮）

美洲狮，又称山狮，您在城市附近的山间小径上徒步时偶尔可能会碰到一只。有时它们会出没在温哥华西北部的森林地带，如果您居住在靠近高贵林港和穆迪港，它们有时会光顾您的后院。美洲狮的嗅觉很差，但视力和听觉都很出色，能帮助他们在清晨和傍晚时分狩猎。它们吃的主要是鹿，但也吃较小的动物，如老鼠和兔子。美洲狮在跳跃方面有着惊人的"天赋"，它轻轻一跃，便能跳到6、7米开外，更厉害的一跃可长达13米远。美洲狮狩猎时擅长跟踪猎物并埋伏攻击。如果美洲狮捕捉的猎物比较多，它们就会把剩余的食物藏在树上，等以后回来再吃。美洲狮很少攻击人类，但有些人在徒步旅行时会进入到它们的领地，就可能会遭到美洲狮的攻击。

重要的安全信息：

- 如果您遇到了一只美洲狮，尽可能使自己显得很大。 比如展开您的外套，或打开一把伞，抱起孩子，跺脚，大声嚷嚷。 声音大的吓人。 您要让它觉得您对它来说是一个威胁，而不是猎物。 不要背对着它。千万不要逃跑。徒步旅行时随身携带一根手杖，如果美洲狮攻击您，则使用它来反击。
- 如果在您家附近看到一只美洲狮，请联系动物保护（COS）中心，电话：1-877-952-7277。
- 根据 "野生动物法"规定，不得喂食美洲狮。饲养危险野生动物是违法的。

April 14	Support for Newcomers
4月14日	支持新移民

SUCCESS BC

This organization has been helping newcomers to overcome language and cultural barriers since 1973. They are driven by their vision of a "World of Multicultural Harmony". SUCCESS has over 20 locations locally and overseas. SUCCESS offers a variety of programs, classes and services to help newcomers with employment, health, housing, business, insurance and economic, community and social development.

中侨互助会 http://www.successbc.ca/chn/

自 1973 年以来这个组织一直在帮助新移民克服语言和文化障碍。主要目的是协助新移民适应新生活、尽快融入这个多元文化和谐社会。中侨现时在本地和海外拥有29个办事处。中侨互助会提供各种课程和服务，包括就业、住房、卫生、商业、保险、社区和社会经济发展。

Vancouver Neighbourhoods

Yaletown

Fashionable professionals who enjoy the good life make their home in one of the converted warehouse loft apartments or towering condominium towers overlooking False Creek in the high-end neighbourhood of Yaletown. Former industrial buildings and working-class houses are now occupied by professional offices for architects, lawyers, and accountants, upscale eateries, trendy nightspots, and loft-style residences. In the 1900's, this area used to house warehousing companies, truck firms, and small manufacturers as its location near the main Canada Pacific rail lines and shipping dock was very convenient for sending their goods around the world. Since the 1990s, the area has been redeveloped into a vital part of the city with a mixture of art galleries, retail stores, restaurants, offices, and residential towers with the historical details retained to retain its special character. Every evening this neighbourhood comes alive as the restaurants and bars open for business and locals and visitors crowd the area.

耶鲁镇https://yaletowninfo.com/

　　耶鲁镇是温哥华市中心一个高密度住宅小区，该区前身为一个仓库商品集散地和铁路车厂工业区，而如今耶鲁镇的旧货仓成为年轻的艺术家廉价置业的良机，区内的旧工业建筑、货仓陆续被改建成一座座高档住宅、办公大楼、餐厅和夜店。站在塔楼公寓的高处可俯瞰耶鲁镇高端社区及菲沙海湾。经改建后的工业建筑和原工人们的住房现由建筑师、律师、会计师们居住，有的改为高档餐厅、时尚夜总会和商住两用的写字楼。上个世纪初，仓储公司，货车公司和小型制造商集结在这一地区，主要是因为它特殊的地理位置，附近有加拿大太平洋铁路车站和航运码头可以非常方便的将货物发送到世界各地。自上世纪90年代以来，该地区已被重建，融合了艺术画廊，零售商店，餐馆，办公室和住宅大楼，并保留了相当多的历史细节，力求维持其原有的特色。现如今耶鲁镇已经是温哥华最繁华的地方之一了。每天晚上餐馆和酒吧开门迎客，当地人和游客们来这里逛酒吧，吃饭，这里成了朋友们聚会的好地方。

April 16   Basic Everyday English

4月16日   基本日常生活用语

At the Grocery Store

When shopping at the store, it is a good idea to have your phone ready and charged and able to access Google images. When you need help to find a certain food item, find a picture of it in Google images that you can show the store clerk. These images, plus the phrases here and some simple body language will help you be able to successfully complete your shopping.

在商店

在商店购物时，最好事先把手机准备好并充足电，随时准备访问谷歌的图像。当您需要店员帮助查找某个食品时，可以给店员看该食品的谷歌图片。有了这些图片，加上下面的短语和一些简单的肢体语言，可很轻松地帮助您完成购物。

English for Everyday Life
日常生活英语

下面是一些基本的英语短语，您或许听到过， 您可以在商店购物时使用。请访问我们的网站www.mynewlifeinvancouver.com，听一听这些短语的发音并练习会话。

I am looking for this (and point to picture on phone)
Do you have soba noodles?
Where can I find pork floss?
It is in aisle 6.
That'll be $5.00 please
Your total is $5.00
How will you be paying today?
Cash, credit or debit?
Do you have a store points card?
Would you like a receipt?

我在找这个（指图片上的电话）
您有荞麦面吗？
我在哪里可以找到猪肉松？
它在过道 6。
请付5加元。
您的总额是5加元。
今天您将如何付款？
现金、信用卡还是借记卡？
您有商店积分卡吗？
您要收据吗？

April 17   Education

4月17日   教育

Letter Grades and Report Cards

All the letter grades for each course are collected into a Report Card. The students receive a report card three times per year in late fall, early spring and at the end of the school year in June. Two times per year, there is also a chance for parents to meet with the teacher to discuss their child's progress in person at parent-teacher conferences. These happen once in the fall and once in the spring.

If students meet grade level expectations they receive letter grades: A, B, C+, C, C- or I (incomplete). If students are still working toward grade level expectations, there will be an asterisk, star or N/A (not applicable) on their report card.

Students will also receive a work habit mark. Work habit marks are:

G = Good

S = Satisfactory

N = Needs Improvement

Letter grades are only given to students from grades 4 to 12. Students in Kindergarten to Grade 3, students in special programs, and beginner ESL/ELL students do not get letter grades. An additional ESL/ELL Report is often included with elementary report cards. It outlines progress in English listening, speaking, reading and writing.

成绩等级和成绩单

每门课程的所有成绩等级都收集到成绩单中。学校每年有三次颁发正式成绩单：三月，六月和十二月。一般有两次家长会：一次在秋季，一次在春季。家长与老师见面讨论孩子的学习进度，家长会是家长与老师沟通的一个重要良机。

如果学生满足同年级水平要求，便获得成绩等级：A、B、C+、C、C-或I（未完成）。如果学生尚未达到年级水平要求，他们便会得到一个星号或 N/A［不适用］。

他们还会得到一个有关学习习惯的评定： G、S或N。

G = 良好（Good）
S = 满意（Satisfactory）
N = 需要提高（Needs Improvement）

大多数4到12年级的学生及已达到同年级水平要求的学生便可获得有分数的成绩等级。幼儿园到三年级的学生，上特别课程的学生及ESL/ELL初级班的学生没有成绩等级。ESL/ELL小学生除成绩单外另外附有一份 ESL/ELL成绩单。该成绩单概括其英语的听力、口语、阅读和写作的进度。

April 18   Scenes from Daily Life

4月18日   日常生活中的一些镜头

At the Waterpark Playground
在水上乐园游乐场

Best Public Tennis Courts in Vancouver

Vancouver has a wonderful selection of public tennis courts that are open to all members of the public. Here are two of the best:

- **Kits Beach Tennis Club**

  Right beside the ocean at beautiful Kitsilano Beach are 10 outdoor tennis courts and a practice wall. Five of the courts are operated by the Kits Beach Tennis Club which promotes tennis, community and social activities at the site.

- **Stanley Park Tennis Courts**

  Vancouver's favourite park contains 21 tennis courts. During the summer season, six of the courts at the Beach Avenue entrance to Stanley Park are operated as pay courts by "Tennis in Stanley Park". These courses can be booked in advance by calling "Tennis in Stanley Park" or visiting the Pro shop. They also organize lessons and tournaments. All of the other 15 courts are free and open on a first come, first serve basis.

温哥华最佳公共网球场

温哥华有众多公共网球场，向所有公众开放。 其中有两家是最好的：

* **基茨兰诺沙滩网球俱乐部**
  在美丽的基茨兰诺海滩旁边有10个户外网球场和一面练习墙。其中的五个球场由沙滩网球俱乐部经营，该俱乐部在该地区推广网球、社区和社交活动。
* **斯坦利公园网球场**
  斯坦利公园是温哥华人最喜欢的公园，公园内有21个网球场。夏季，斯坦利公园海滨大道入口处由斯坦利公园网球场经营的6间网球场是收费的。这些场地通过拨打"斯坦利公园网球场"电话可以提前预订，或直接前往 Pro 店进行预约。他们还定期举办课程并组织比赛。其他15个球场均以先到先得的方式免费开放。

April 20   Tips to Learning English

4月20日   资深英语老师提供学习英语的小贴士

Use it or Lose it

This is an expression in English that means you must "use" new skills you have learned or you will "lose" them. It can be quite shocking how quickly newly learned material can just fade away if we don't practice it. Every time we practice a new skill, we are making a deeper memory pathway in the brain. Repetition of new vocabulary is very closely linked to memory. So, how can you use your new English? There are many ways, of course, but here are four tips you can try today – yes today! Today is always the best time to do anything.

使用它或失去它

这是英语中的一种表达，意思是您必须"使用"您所学到的新技能，否则您将失去它们。如果我们不去练习它，新学到的东西会很快消失，这可真让人吃惊。每一次我们练习一项新技能，我们都在大脑中形成一个更深层次的记忆路径。新词汇的重复与记忆非常接近。那么，您怎样使用您新学的英语呢？有很多方法，当然，这里有四个提示，您可以今天就可以试试 – 对，就是今天！今天总是做任何事情的最佳时机。

English for Everyday Life
日常生活英语

这里的温馨提示是从图书馆借到附带CD的 ESL读物然后花上15到30分钟练习四种英语的技能：

- Reading: Get an ESL Reader from the library and read one page of the book. ESL Readers are great English novels that have been put in very simplified form. Choose a book that is a low level. Find a comfortable place to sit and enjoy reading one page of the story for five minutes.
  阅读：从图书馆借到一本ESL读物并阅读其中的一页。 ESL读物都是选自著名的英语小说，都是以非常简化的形式改编而成。选择一本初级读物。找到一个舒适的地方坐下，花上五分钟阅读一页的故事。

- Listening: Many of the ESL Readers come with a CD so you can actually listen to the story at the same time you are reading it. This way you can do double the practice in the same amount of time.
  听力：许多ESL书籍均附带一张CD，因此您可以在阅读的同时聆听故事。这样，你可以在同一时间内做双重练习。

- Speaking: Now try to read aloud the page you have just read. If you are not sure of the pronunciation, listen again to the CD. Play a short clip from the CD and then try to say it out loud. Play the clip again, and say it out loud again. Use your smartphone to record yourself. Play the CD clip then play your smartphone clip of you saying the words out loud. This is a very effective way to improve your pronunciation.
  朗读：现在试着朗读你刚刚阅读的页面。如果你不能确定发音是否正确，就再听一遍CD。用CD机播放一段，然后试着大声读出来。再次重复播放，并再次大声读出。用你的智能手机录制自己的发音。播放CD之后，再播放智能手机录制你的声音。这是一个非常有效的提高你发音的学习方式。

- **Writing**: Start an English notebook. Use this notebook to write a few sentences about the reading you just did or how you feel today. It doesn't have to be perfect, it is just a little daily practice to help build your confidence.

  写作：开始做英语笔记。用这个笔记本写几句你刚刚读过的书，或你今天的感受。它不一定是完美的，它只是一个小小的日常练习，以帮助建立你学好英语的信心。

April 21 — A Little Canadian Inspiration

4月21日　　一点点启示

*"I am a Canadian, free to speak without fear, free to worship
in my own way, free to stand for what I think right, free
to oppose what I believe wrong, or free to choose those
who shall govern my country. This heritage of freedom
I pledge to uphold for myself and all mankind."*
-Former Prime Minister of Canada, John Diefenbaker

Freedom is a value that all Canadians treasure deeply. Along with freedom comes a deep acceptance of all the different points of views and beliefs of other people.

"我是加拿大人，我可以自由地发表言论，不用担心什么，我可以自由地以自己的方式来崇拜，可以自由地站在我认为是正确的立场上，自由地反对我认为是错误的东西，或者自由地选择那些统治我们国家的人。"。这就是我为自己和全人类维护的自由遗产。"
——加拿大前总理约翰·德芬贝克

自由是所有加拿大人珍惜的价值。随着自由，人们相互接受对方不同的观点和信仰。

Volunteer in Vancouver

4月22日　　在温哥华做义工

Salvation Army

The Salvation Army's motto is "Giving Hope Today" and all their activities are meant to help encourage, support and bring communities together. Volunteers help them extend the reach of their activities and contributions. They have many ways for volunteers to contribute from being a cashier in their thrift store, to stocking shelves at a food bank or serving a meal to a homeless person.

救世军 http://www.salvationarmy.ca/volunteer/

　　救世军的座右铭是"今天给予希望"，他们召集社区的志愿者，协助他们扩大活动范围，志愿者无私地奉献他们的时间和技能，他们主动去旧货店，食品银行义务工作，向无家可归的人哪怕是提供一顿饭。他们所有的活动都是为了帮助、鼓励和支持需要帮助的人。

Healthcare in Vancouver

4月23日   温哥华的医疗保健

Healthlink BC

When you first arrive in Vancouver, there are so many different things to get organized while you settle in. However, health questions can come up at any time and HealthLink BC is there to help answer any of your questions about health and healthcare in BC. HealthLink BC can help you find health services, check your medical symptoms, and get information about prescription drugs. The helpful HealthLinkBC staff can help you with your non-emergency health issues in more than 130 languages.

BC健康咨询网

用您的手机 — 只需拨打 8-1-1，就可以转到讲普通话的BC省健康咨询网，网址是https://www.healthlinkbc.ca/

当您初到温哥华时，为了把家安顿好，要面临各种问题，身体不适的状况随时都有可能出现。BC省健康咨询公司可以回答您有关健康和医疗保健方面的任何问题。他们可以帮助您找到健康服务机构，检查您的症状，并获取有关处方药的信息。BC省健康咨询公司的员工可以用超过130 种语言帮助您处理非急救的健康问题。

April 24   ## Interesting Facts About Vancouver

4月24日   温哥华趣闻

California Roll Invented in Vancouver

It really should be called the Vancouver Roll! The roll sushi with crab, avocado and cucumber was invented in Vancouver by Chef Hidekazu Tojo. The roll was also unusual as it is "inside out" with the rice on the outside and the seaweed on the inside. His famous restaurant, Tojo, is located at 1133 West Broadway in Vancouver.

加州卷是在温哥华发明的

它真的应该叫温哥华卷！加州寿司卷其实是由温哥华一位寿司厨师Tojo发明的，他使用黄瓜、煮熟的蟹肉和牛油果，再用米反卷的形式隐藏西方人认为卖相不佳的海苔。他所在的著名的餐厅，Tojo，位于温哥华西百老汇1133号。

April 25	Finding Work in Vancouver
4月25日	在温哥华找份工作

LinkedIn: for Making Professional Connections

LinkedIn is a free social networking site that allows members to set up a network of people they know and trust professionally. When you sign up for an account, you enter information in your profile that emphasizes your skills, employment history and education. You can then search the network for other network members called "connections". With basic membership, a member can only establish connections with someone he has worked with, knows professionally (online or offline) or has gone to school with. Premium subscriptions can be purchased to provide members with better access to contacts in the LinkedIn database, but it is not necessary for everyday use.

领英：连接企业和求职者的桥梁https://www.linkedin.com/

　　LinkedIn中文名为领英，是一个免费的社交服务网站，允许其成员们建立他们在商业交往中认识并信任的联系人。当您注册帐户时，输入您的个人资料、技能、工作经历和教育等信息。然后，您可以在网络中搜索名为"人脉"（*Connections*）的其他网络成员。基本会员资格，只能与他合作过的人建立联系，与本专业（在线或离线）或校友建立联系。购买高级订阅可以成为高级会员，以便能够更好地访问LinkedIn数据库中的所有联系人，但对于普通使用者来说是没有必要的。

April 26   # Vancouver Sightseeing

4月26日   观光

The Vancouver Aquarium

The Vancouver Aquarium is Canada's largest aquarium and one of the most visited sites in Stanley Park. It is home to more than 70,000 creatures including dolphins, sea otters, anacondas, three-toed sloths, eels and more. The Vancouver Aquarium is widely respected for its research and marine stewardship, and visitors can learn more about the region's marine life through the numerous exhibits. Adults and kids alike will love the entertaining and educational "encounters" program, which allows visitors to go behind the scenes and get up close and personal with the animals and the people who train them. This includes feeding, helping train and learning about the habitats and lifestyles of dolphins, sea lions, sea otters, sea turtles and other sea creatures.

温哥华水族馆https://www.vanaqua.org/

　　温哥华水族馆是加拿大最大的水族馆，也是史丹利公园最受欢迎的景点之一。 它拥有超过70,000种生物，包括海豚、海獭、蟒蛇、三趾树懒、鳗鱼等。 温哥华水族馆因其研究和海洋管理而受到广泛的尊重，参观者可以通过众多展品了解该地区的海洋生物。成年人和孩子们都会喜欢娱乐和教育的"邂逅"计划，这使得游客可以在幕后与动物和培训人员亲密接触。 这包括喂养，帮助培训和学习有关海豚、海狮、海獭、海龟和其他海洋生物的自然栖息和它们的生活方式。

April 27   # Vancouver Transportation

4月27日   温哥华交通运输

Car Sharing Services

Car Sharing is very popular with Vancouverites and there are four different companies to choose from. Car Sharing is a model of car rental where people rent new and well-maintained cars for short periods of time, often by the hour. Once you are signed up with the system, there is no paperwork needed to rent the cars and the fee includes all gas and insurance costs. These services are very popular in Vancouver as there are many people who only need to use a car occasionally so they don't need to own their own. All the services have an app for your smartphone. Whenever you need a car, the app will tell you the location of the closest car and you can reserve it directly, and then use your app to unlock the door when you arrive at the car. Inside the car there will be the car key and a special card to use to pay for gas purchases. When you are done with the car, you don't need to return it to the original parking spot, just leave it wherever you are. An added feature of the cars is that the city allows you to park them in restricted residential areas which make it easier to save even more money.

汽车共享服务

Car2Go:　　5加元会员费，每公里约0.5加元；
Evo:　　　　35加元会员费，每分钟41分钱；
MODO:　　　500加元 可退还的押金，每小时大约4加元和5加元的月费；
Zip Car:　35加元会员费，每小时 8至10加元。

汽车共享很受温哥华人的欢迎，有四家不同的公司可供选择。汽车共享是一种汽车租赁的模式，人们在短时间内（通常是按小时）租用一辆新的和保养良好的汽车。一旦注册了该系统，您不需要签署纸质文件，租车费用已经包括加满一箱汽油和保险费用。这些服务在温哥华非常受欢迎，因为有许多人只是偶尔用一下汽车，所以他们不需要拥有自己的车辆。所有的服务都包含在您智能手机的一个应用程序中。每当您需要叫一辆车，该应用程序会告诉离您最近车的位置，您可以直接预留，当您抵达该车的时候，使用您的应用程序解锁车门。汽车里面会有一把汽车钥匙和一张用来购买汽油的专用卡。当您用完了汽车，您不需要把车开回原来的停车位，无论您在哪里，只要把它停放在那里就可以了。汽车共享服务的另一个特点是，城市允许您把它们停放在有限制的住宅区，这样可以节省更多的钱。您可以访问上面的网站申请加入。可以只加入其中的一项或全部。 MODO汽车有各种各样的风格和尺寸，EVO汽车有一个用于滑雪板和自行车的车顶行李架，CAR2GO主要是2座智能汽车和Zip Car供车迷朋友选择的。

Sports Teams and Special Events

4月28日　　　专业体育赛事和活动

Vancouver Sun Run

The Vancouver Sun Run is the biggest 10K road race in Canada, running and walking one of the prettiest courses anywhere in the world. Tens of thousands of runners and spectators pack the downtown core every April for the Vancouver Sun Run. A seasonal tradition for Vancouverites, the festive run brings out everyone from world-class athletes to office mates who have been training for weeks, and moms and dads pushing strollers. The race starts downtown and continues through Stanley Park and along English Bay, over the Burrard Street Bridge to south False creek and back over the Cambie Street Bridge to the finish line beside BC Place Stadium. Spectators and even live bands cheer on participants as they walk and run by. Afterwards, the party picks up inside the stadium. Participants, family and friends stream inside for live entertainment and free fruit and bagels.

温哥华太阳报举办的10公里长跑

　　温哥华太阳报（*The Vancouver Sun*）长跑是加拿大规模最大的10公里路跑，跑步和竞走的路线是世界上风景最漂亮的路程之一。每年的四月，数以万计的跑步者和观众聚集在市中心，参加温哥华太阳报举办的长跑。作为温哥华季节性的传统活动，吸引了从世界级的运动员到训练几周的办公室的同事，甚至还有推着婴儿车的爸爸妈妈们参与。比赛的起跑点设在市中心，跑过市区后沿着斯坦利公园和英吉利湾，伯拉德街桥向南至第2大街，然后向东跑回到甘比街桥到卑诗体育馆旁边的终点线。观众们甚至就连现场乐队的乐手们都为跑或者走过来的参与者欢呼加油。之后，人们在体育馆内举行聚会。跑步者与家人和朋友们一起在场内娱乐和享受免费的水果和面包圈。

April 29	Vancouver Parks
4月29日	温哥华公园

Maple Grove Park

Maple Grove Park is a large park located in the heart of Kerrisdale at 6875 Yew Street. It is named after the many tall, graceful Maple trees that cover the park. It is a popular place to go for a stroll and to take children to enjoy the large playground area. There are also soccer and baseball fields for families to enjoy. The park really comes alive in the summer when the large, warm, outdoor wading pool opens and families escape the heat and swim and have picnics by the pool.

枫树林公园

枫树林公园（Maple Grove Park）是以众多高大，优美的枫树命名的，这是一个很大的公园，它位于Kerrisdale中心耀街（Yew Street）6875号。公园里面长满了枫树。人们喜欢在那里散步，大人们带着孩子去大型游乐场玩耍。公园里还有足球场和棒球场。到了夏天，公园里一片生机勃勃，家人可以去那里避暑，有一个大的温暖的室外泳池对外开放，人们在那里嬉水或者在游泳池旁野餐。

April 30   Stories and Advice for Newcomers

4月30日   移民的故事和建议

Kathy

对新移民的一点建议

谈不上建议，是来加拿大的移民朋友的一些亲身体会，希望能对即将来加拿大的新移民有所帮助。

对儿女担保来加拿大的老年新移民的一点体会：第一重要的就是安全问题，1.交通规则不同，过马路一定要走人行道，几乎每个人行道都有交通信号灯，　要按一下过马路的按钮，当过马路的信号（一个白色的小人及伴随的小鸟叫声）出现后才能过马路。个别地方是闪耀的黄灯。总之，跟国内不一样，不能横穿马路；2.来加拿大后一定要立即买一部手机，把亲人的联系方式，您家的地址，周围主要的商场名字都写在纸上，一旦走失，迷路，会立即联系上您的亲人，或获得其他人的帮助，到您熟悉的地方。

对于中青年人，1.一定要学习英语；2.获得一个加拿大的职业证书，找工作相对容易，而且工资也相对高，关于这方面的详情可以咨询新移民服务机构；3.安全问题，中国驾驶证在加拿大公证后可以开车3个月。但我建议不要急于开车，因为交通规则有很多不同于国内。所以先学习理论，了解交通规则，再找教练练习。另外，如果开车违规了，千万别下车，坐在驾驶室内等待交警的指示，不要贿赂交警，不要与交警理论，如果您有异议，过后可以申诉。

May

Weather:	Average temperature: 9°C to 17°C
	Average rainfall days: 15, Average rainfall: 50 mm
Statutory holiday:	Victoria Day (celebrated on the Monday preceding May 25)
Other special days:	Mother's Day (the second Sunday in May)

May is one of the prettiest and most pleasant months in Vancouver. The temperatures are mild and comfortable, the sun is bright and the skies are blue. Everywhere you look flowers are blooming and gardens look beautiful and fresh.

Vancouver's famous International Marathon race happens in the first week of May. This marathon was named a Top 10 Destination Marathon by Forbes.com and one of the world's most "exotic" marathons by CNN Travel. The Marathon takes runners on a 42-kilometre adventure past beaches, through natural parks, and along Vancouver's busy Seawall. Many spectators come out to cheer on the participants who travel to Vancouver from all over the world to join the race.

This month, Dunbar Village celebrates Salmonberry Days which is Dunbar's unique, month-long neighbourhood environment festival. It is organized each year by volunteers and features heritage walks, Dunbar in Bloom garden tours, trail walks, nature walks, and classical music concerts.

Another highlight of the month is Victoria Day which is a statutory holiday across Canada that honours the long life and successful reign of the great British Queen Victoria*. For many families, the long Victoria Day weekend marks the unofficial start of summer and outdoor activities – especially camping trips – but remember that you need to make a reservation using the online provincial campsite reservation site.

If you don't want to leave the city, there are many other outdoor activities right in the city. One of the most popular is the annual Vancouver International Children's Festival on Granville Island that features musicians, acrobats, puppet shows, plays and more.

In May, Canadians also show their appreciation for their mothers on Mother's Day. Children (with the help of Dad) will make their mother cards and give her presents and take her out for a nice meal in a restaurant. They also might make their mom breakfast in bed* as a special treat.

5月

气候： 平均温度：9°C ～ 17°C
平均降雨天数：15，平均降雨量：50 毫米
公众节假日：维多利亚日（5月25日前的星期一庆祝）
其他特殊日：母亲节（5月第二个星期日）

五月是温哥华最漂亮和最令人愉快的月份之一。温暖舒适，阳光明媚，蓝天白云。花园和庭院到处鲜花盛开，漂亮极了。

五月份的第一个星期温哥华将举办著名的国际马拉松比赛。它被福布斯网站评为十大马拉松圣地，美国CNN旅游频道称其为世界上最具"异国情调"的马拉松之旅。马拉松规定的长度是42公里，参赛者沿途要经过海滩，穿过自然公园，并沿着温哥华熙熙攘攘的海堤。许多观众沿途为来自世界各地的参赛选手加油。

鲑莓节是邓巴社区每年5月由志愿者自发组织的为期一个月的由多项室内外活动组成的特色节日，如共赏环保电影、参观百花齐放的私人花园、了解邓巴社区的历史、林荫小道散步和欣赏古典音乐会等，目地在于增强社区内居民的归属感。

　　本月的另一个亮点是维多利亚日，又称为"女王日"，是加拿大的全国公众假日，纪念伟大的英国维多利亚女王的寿辰和统治。维多利亚日当天，全国多个城市举行游行活动，晚上放烟花庆祝，许多家庭安排户外活动，如野营等。对加拿大人来说，维多利亚日加上长周末亦标志着夏季和户外活动的开始。尤其是露营，请记住，您需要在省级营地网站上预订。

　　如果您不打算离开这座城市出游，城里还有许多其他的户外活动。其中最受欢迎的是格兰威尔岛上一年一度的温哥华国际儿童节，那里有著名的音乐、杂技、木偶剧、游戏等等。

　　母亲节是在五月的第二个星期天，加拿大人同样在母亲节那天展示他们对母亲的感激之情。孩子们会在爸爸的帮助下制作母亲卡，并送给她一份礼物，还选一家餐馆带妈妈出去好好享用一顿。他们还可能做一份早餐送到妈妈的床前，作为一份特别的礼物。

更多的信息：

温哥华国际儿童节：http://www.childrensfestival.ca/
卑诗省公园野营预定：
https://secure.camis.com/Discovercamping/
Dunbar社区鲑莓节：www.dunbar-vancouver.org
温哥华国际马拉松：http://bmovanmarathon.ca/
维多利亚女王：1837年即位为大不列颠及爱尔兰联合王国女王。到1901年她统治大英帝国整整60年。这一时期被称为维多利亚时代。英国人民的生活发生了巨大的变化：英国成为世界上最强大的国家，拥有历史上最大的帝国，统治了世界四分之一的人口。
床上的早餐：早上醒来时，有人准备了一份精美的早餐放在一个托盘上，如咖啡、烤面包、果酱和新鲜的水果，吃的时候，坐在床上。

Local Customs

当地的习俗

Classroom Parties

Throughout pre-school and elementary school, it is common for the teacher to organize classroom parties to celebrate special events throughout the year. Usually there will be a Halloween party, Valentine's Day party and so on. They are about one hour long and the children will play some special games related to the event and eat some cake. All the children look forward to these classroom parties. A week or two ahead of the day of the classroom party, the teacher will let the parents know if they need to bring a sweet treat to the classroom for the children. The most popular item to bring is cupcakes! If you attend adult language school, you will also enjoy classroom parties occasionally, especially **Potluck Parties** where every student brings one dish of food to share with the classroom.

Classroom or School Dances

For older children and students in high school, the schools will organize school dances a couple of times per year. They are held in the school gym and are fully supervised by teachers and parent volunteers. They are very popular events with the students who enjoy having a chance to dance with their classmates.

End of School Year Celebrations and Thanking Teachers. Usually there will be some small event in the classroom or school gym to celebrate the end of the school year and the beginning of the summer vacation. At the end of the school year, it is common for the parents to **thank the classroom teacher** by giving their child's classroom teacher a special greeting card thanking them and a small present such as chocolates, tea or flowers. During May and June, many stores such as Purdy's Chocolates will start to sell gifts appropriate for thanking teachers. A long time ago, it was traditional to thank teachers by giving them a shiny red apple. Nowadays we don't do that anymore but some of the gifts for the teacher might be decorated with an apple symbol.

课堂派对

在幼儿园和小学，一年之中每逢遇有重大的事件，比如万圣节，情人节等等，老师都会组织大约一个小时的课堂派对，这很常见。孩子们会玩一些相关的主题游戏，吃一块儿蛋糕。所有的孩子都期待着这种课堂派对。在此之前的一两个星期，老师会告知家长为孩子准备香甜可口的食物带到教室。最受欢迎的食品是纸杯蛋糕！如果您参加成人语言学校，您也将会参加类似的课堂派对，特别是百味餐派对，每个学生各带一份食物到学校，在教室里与大家分享。

课堂或学校舞会

对于高年级的学生，学校每年会在学校健身房组织几次舞会。完全由教师和家长志愿督导。这是非常受孩子们欢迎的活动，喜欢跳舞的学生有机会展示才艺并体验与同学们共舞的乐趣。

学年末校庆活动以及对老师的感恩。

通常在学年的结束和暑期的开始之前，学校教室或体育馆会安排一些小型的庆祝活动。在学年结束时，父母常常要送给班主任一个特别的贺卡和一份小礼物，如巧克力，茶或花以感谢他/她传授给孩子知识和所做的一切。在5月和6月，许多商店如珀迪巧克力店开始销售感谢教师的礼品盒。以往，学生们是送一个色泽鲜艳的红苹果给老师，那是旧时的传统。现在鲜有人这样做，但送老师的一些礼品外包装可能会沿用苹果符号来装饰。

English for Everyday Life
日常生活英语

下面是您可以用来写在卡片或信中感谢老师的话:

Dear Mr. Jones,

Thank you for doing a wonderful job of teaching Benjamin this year. My son learned a lot and enjoyed being in your class. Thank you very much and I hope you have a good summer.

Kind regards,
Karen Peng

尊敬的琼斯先生，

　　谢谢您今年为本杰明所做的一切，非常出色。我儿子学到了很多，他非常喜欢上您的课。非常感谢您，我希望您暑假愉快。

致以亲切的问候，

彭凯伦

May 2   Parenting in Vancouver

5月2日   在温哥华养育子女

Boy Scouts, Girl Guides, and Canadian Cadets

The **Girl Guides and Boy Scouts** have fun adventures and discover new skills and experiences they wouldn't discover elsewhere. Along the way they develop into capable, confident and well-rounded individuals, better prepared for success in the world. Girl Guides and Boy Scouts do rewarding volunteer work and activities that benefit their communities.

The **Cadet Program** is one of the largest federally sponsored youth programs in Canada that includes The Royal Canadian Sea Cadets; The Royal Canadian Army Cadets; and The Royal Canadian Air Cadets. It is a national program for young Canadians aged 12 to 18 who are interested in participating in a variety of fun, challenging and rewarding activities. Cadets are encouraged to become active, responsible members of their communities. They make valuable contributions to Canadian society daily in terms of environmental, citizenship and community activities. Cadets also learn valuable life and work skills such as teamwork, leadership and citizenship. There is no charge for cadet training and the uniform is supplied. There is absolutely no obligation or pressure to join the armed forces at the end of the program.

男童子军，女童军和加拿大军校学员

> **男童子军** http://www.scouts.ca/
> **女童子军** http://www.bc-girlguides.org/web/
> **加拿大军校学生组织** http://www.cadets.ca/

女童子军和男童子军有着冒险的乐趣，他们会发现新的事物和在别处从未有过的经历。透过强调野外实践活动的教育，使他们发展成为有能力，有自信和具有综合素质的青少年，为将来的职业做准备。女童军和男童子军会做一些有益于他们社区的志愿者工作和活动。

学员训练计划是加拿大最大的联邦赞助青年计划之一，包括加拿大皇家海军学员；加拿大皇家陆军军校学员；和加拿大皇家空军军校学员。 这项国家计划是专门为那些有兴趣参加各种具有挑战性和有意义活动的12至18岁的加拿大年轻人设置的。军校鼓励学员们成为社区积极且负责任的成员。他们承担公民责任，每天都在为加拿大社会、环境和社区活动做出有益的贡献。学员们还学习宝贵的生活和工作技能，如团队合作、领导和公民的责任。学员训练是免费的，提供制服。在训练结束时绝对没有加入武装部队的义务或者压力。

May 3 Stories and Advice for Newcomers

5月3日 新移民的故事

Cherry

我在温哥华的第一年

　　有几个朋友问我在温哥华的第一年是否适应了。说实话，当我初来温哥华的时候，还是一个不会讲英语，不了解当地文化的新移民，我确实很难。所有的一切对于我来说都是陌生的。我都快急疯了。最令我沮丧的是我17个月大的儿子发烧了，我拨打了911。在急诊室，我无法向医生解释发生了什么，也听不明白他们在说些什么。我告诫自己，不会说英语的人是无法适应加拿大生活的。

　　我去了一个教堂，虽然我不太了解宗教，但是，那里却是一个练习听和说的好地方。在教堂里，我发现尽管人们来自不同的国家，可是大家都愿意彼此互相帮助，仿佛一个大家庭。

　　我建议新移民多去参加社区中心组织的活动。我从邻居那里得到了许多重要信息，如移民英语课程、个人福利申请等等。

May 4 Vancouver Entertainment

5月4日 温哥华娱乐

Going to the Movies

Going to the movies is the most common indoor form of entertainment for local Vancouverites. Watching a movie in a theatre is a great way to have fun during the very cold and rainy season. Besides seeing movies in theatres, it is also possible to watch movies outside during summer in Stanley Park and to watch a drive-in movie from the comfort of your car all year round. Big Hollywood movies are shown in the large chain of theatres run by Cineplex, but there are a few independent movie theatres that play international films in different languages (with English subtitles) and classic films from the past.

- *Major Hollywood Movies*: shown at many Cineplex theatres around Vancouver

- *Outdoor movies*

  Every Tuesday during the summer, Stanley Park hosts a free movie night where they play popular movies on a large outdoor screen. Bring your friends and a picnic blanket or lawn chair and enjoy the summer evening tradition.

- *Drive-In Movie Theatre*

  Watch a movie from the comfort of your car at the last remaining drive-in movie theatre. It is a classic North American experience to enjoy watching a movie this way. There is also a snack bar where you can buy food and drinks to enjoy in your car.

International and Classic Films in Independent Theatres:

1. ***Vancity International Film Theatre***

   This theatre shows international and film festival movies to the public since 1982. Their goal is to share world and film culture with everyone, and celebrate the best of filmmaking. Every November, they host an annual Asian Film Festival and play the best films made in China and other Asian countries over the previous year.

2. ***Pacific Cinematheque***

   The theatre is dedicated to showing new and classic essential films that inspire and give insight to viewers about important issues.

看电影

去电影是当地温哥华人最常见的室内娱乐形式。 在寒冷和多雨的季节在影院里看电影是最好的娱乐消遣方式。除了在剧院影院内看电影，在温暖的季节还可以去斯坦利公园汽车影城，坐在汽车里舒适的观看电影。Cineplex是温哥华最大的连锁经营的影院。它负责统一管理和放映好莱坞制作的大片，还有几家独立的影院专门放映不同的语言（配有英文字幕）的国际影片和经典老片。

主打好莱坞影片：http://www.cineplex.com/

露天电影

http://www.freshaircinema.ca/summercinema/index.html
夏季的每个周二，斯坦利公园（Stanley Park）都会举办免费的电影之夜，在一个大型的户外屏幕上播放热门的影片。带上野餐毯子或草坪椅子，和您的朋友好好享受夏日的夜晚吧。

汽车电影院 http://twilightdrivein.net/
坐在舒适的车里观看电影，是典型的北美生活方式。影院的旁边有一个小卖铺，您可以在那里买到小吃和饮料。

独立剧院播放的国际和经典的影片：

1. **Vancity 国际电影院** https://www.viff.org
   该剧院自1982年以来多次举办国际电影节，为公众放映国际影片。他们的目标是与观众分享世界影视文化，并庆祝最佳制作的影片。每年11月，他们主办一年一度的亚洲电影节，播放过去一年中在中国和其他亚洲国家的最佳影片。 亚洲电影节网站是http://festival.vaff.org

2. **太平洋电影院** http://www.thecinematheque.ca/
   太平洋电影院以放映新的和经典的影片为主，借以激发观众的洞察力。

Best Elementary Schools
温哥华著名的小学

Kerrisdale Elementary School (public)

Here is the description of the school from their website: "Kerrisdale Elementary is a dual track, English and French Immersion school, enrolling over 650 students from Kindergarten to Grade 7. Our Annex is located one kilometer away at 5901 Balaclava Street and has approximately 100 students in K to Grade 3. Upgrading of our buildings. was completed during the 2006/2007 school year. Our large playground includes an outdoor classroom area, two levels of playing fields, two adventure play-structures, one space net, swings, basketball court, and a landscaped area with benches and picnic tables. Our school has an atmosphere where children have a sense of purpose and direction. Kerrisdale students are well supported and encouraged at home. At school, the staff bring a wide diversity of talents and experiences to support a school-wide commitment to academic, aesthetic, and physical excellence in helping all students strive for and achieve their full potential."

克里斯戴尔小学（公立）http://go.vsb.bc.ca/schools/kerrisdale

下面是学校网站的描述：

"克里斯戴尔小学是一所英语和法语双语浸入式学校，从幼儿园到7年级，共有650多名学生。我们的附属教学楼位于巴拉克拉瓦街5901号一公里处，于2006/2007学年期间建成。从K级到3级大约有100名学生。高年级学生在主楼上课。我们的大操场包括一个室外教学区、两个级别的比赛场地、两个冒险游乐场、一个太空网、秋千、篮球场以及一个带长椅和野餐桌的风景区。我们努力给孩子们营造一个有目标感和方向感的氛围。克里斯戴尔学生在家里得到很好的支持和鼓励。学校拥有众多教学经验丰富的师资，他们在学术、美学和体育方面有着卓越的成就，他们尽最大努力帮助所有学生充分发挥其潜能。

May 6	A Different Way of Thinking
5月6日	不同的思维方式

Saying Sorry – a Lot!

"Once you learn how to properly say "I'm sorry," you will no longer be trying to become Canadian, you will have rewired your brain to such a degree that you will actually be Canadian."

- Karina Schumann, Psychologist, Stanford University
(formerly University of Waterloo)

In many cultures around the world, apologizing can be difficult because it is important to "save face". However, Canadians say "I'm sorry" often and easily to smooth any difficulties over quickly before bad feelings and disagreements get worse. The psychologist, Karina Schumann, has studied this Canadian habit and realized that "saying sorry is not always an apology, it is also a "politeness strategy" – a way to have harmonious interactions". This habit of saying sorry is something that Canadians value and believe is an important feature of polite society. Besides the more serious issues when it is obvious to apologize, Canadians will also say sorry for small things like bumping into someone at the store or when their cell phone rings in a quiet space and so on. Canadians believe that saying sorry when necessary is a way to keep communication polite and positive and strengthen personal connections in everyday life.

很抱歉 – 要多说！

"一旦您学会了如何正确地说"我很抱歉"，您将不必再试图成为加拿大人了，您的大脑已经潜移默化，您已经成为一名真正的加拿大人。"

——卡琳娜·舒曼，斯坦福大学心理学家（原名滑铁卢大学）

在世界各地的许多文化中，道歉很难，因为"面子"很重要。可是加拿大人确经常说"对不起"，因为这样就很容易在分歧和情绪恶化之前迅速平息任何可能失控的行为。心理学家卡拉娜·舒曼研究了加拿大这种习俗，她意识到 所谓的"道歉"并不总是意味着真的道歉，它只是一种"礼貌上的策略"—— 是一种和谐互动方式。这种"道歉"的习惯是加拿大人非常看重的价值观，它是社会讲文明，讲礼貌的重要特征。除了发生较为明显的问题时道歉之外，加拿大人也会对小事情说声对不起，比如在商店撞到某人，或者在安静的环境中手机突然响起等小事表示歉意。加拿大人认为，说对不起是保持礼貌和及时沟通的一种方式，它可以有效地改善日常生活中的人际关系。

Best High Schools

温哥华著名的中学

Point Grey High School (public)

Here is the description of the school from their website: "Honor Ante Honores" "Honor is Greater Than Fame" is the school motto. Their mission: "We are committed to supporting and teaching a diverse group of students to learn, to critically reflect, and to care for themselves and others as they prepare to find their places in the world. With Advanced Placement courses in Biology, Calculus, Chemistry, Computer Science, English, Physics, and Psychology, more than eighty-five per cent of graduates continue with post-secondary education. Point Grey also has a Mini School for academically gifted students."

灰点中学（公立）http://go.vsb.bc.ca/schools/pointgrey

灰点迷你学校：http://pgmini.org/

以下是学校网站上的描述：

"荣誉勋章"、"荣誉大于名"是我们的校训。我们的使命是：致力于支持和教导一批不同的学生学习，批判性地反思，并照顾自己和他人，因为他们正准备在世界上找到自己的位置。学校设有生物、微积分、化学、计算机科学、英语、物理和心理学等高级课程，超过85%的毕业生继续接受高等教育。灰点还为学术上有天赋的学生开设了一个迷你学校。"

May 8   The Homes of Vancouver

5月8日   温哥华住宅

A Waterfront Home
海滨住宅

Best Extracurricular Activities for Kids

5月9日 最佳儿童课外活动

Summer School and Summer Camps

Every July and August, elementary and high school children are off from school for their annual summer vacation. Families use some of the time to take their annual family vacation, but for the rest of the time, many parents like to register their children into some sort of educational program. There are many different programs for parents to choose. The **Vancouver School Board** offers academic programs for students to strengthen weak skills or to study advanced skills and gain extra course credits. All the community centres and other associations offer summer camp programs which aim to develop and strengthen children's hobbies and skills in the arts, computers, science and sports. These programs are well advertised at the end of every school year. In addition, **Westcoast Families** magazine publishes a complete guide to all summer camps every year and posts it on their website.

暑期班和夏令营

温哥华学校教育局暑期学校 https://summer.vsb.bc.ca
西海岸家庭 http://westcoastfamilies.com/

每年的七、八月份，小学生和高中生都要离开学校去过暑假。各家都会抽出一些时间来计划安排家庭度假，在剩余的时间里，许多父母喜欢为他们的子女注册某些教育计划。有许多不同类型的计划可供选择。温哥华学校教育局为学生提供加强薄弱技能或进修高级课程并获得额外学分的学术课程。社区中心和其他协会也都提供暑期夏令营项目，旨在培养和加强儿童在艺术、电脑、科学和体育方面的兴趣爱好和技能。这些课程在每个学年结束时都被广泛宣传。此外，西海岸的家庭杂志每年都会发布一个完整的夏令营指南，并将其发布在他们的网站上。

Meeting Locals in Vancouver

    与当地人接触

Meeting Other Parents

One of the best places to meet new people is through the school that your child goes to. Whenever you drop off and pick up your children from school, there is a chance to have a brief conversation with other parents. Also, the school is always looking for parents to volunteer and help with different events and activities at school. In addition, you can meet other parents at the regular Parent Advisory (PAC) meetings and fundraiser events as well. Another way to meet other parents is when you see them at the various after school classes and activities that your children are involved in. While your children are doing the activity, say hello, and introduce yourself to the other waiting parents. Parents always enjoy talking about their children, so that is always an easy conversation topic! Step by step, one person at a time, you can meet other parents through the years that your children go to school.

认识其他的家长

结交新朋友的最佳场所之一就是您孩子所在的学校。每当您送孩子上学或者接孩子放学，都有机会和其他家长进行简短的交谈。此外，学校总是寻求父母做义工，帮助学校举办不同的活动。您也有机会在定期的家长咨询（PAC）会议和筹款活动中与其他家长见面。认识其他父母的另一种方法是当您在孩子们参加各种课后活动时见到他们。打个招呼，做个自我介绍。父母总是喜欢谈论自己的孩子，所以这总是一个轻松的话题！一次找一个家长聊天。几个星期过去，您就会在温哥华认识很多孩子的父母。

Restaurant Customs and Etiquette

5月11日   餐厅的习俗与礼仪

Ice water

Restaurants automatically serve ice water to their customers all year round – even in the cold and rainy winter months. Even though Vancouver has a large Asian population, some servers are still surprised if you order hot water. If possible, try to request hot water before the waiter automatically brings all the glasses of ice water to the table to prevent him the extra work and irritation of having to replace all the water glasses he just brought over.

Usually the water is provided as a courtesy to guests so that they are comfortable when they first arrive. However, the restaurant owners fully expect the guests to order a drink that costs money. If you only drink hot water, some restaurants will charge a small fee to make up for the difference.

冰水

餐馆常年自动为所有客人提供冰水 – 即便是在寒冷多雨的冬季也不例外。尽管温哥华的亚洲人口众多，但如果您想要一杯热水，有的服务员仍然会感到诧异。如果可能的话，最好是在服务员把装有冰水的杯子带到桌子前就要热水，这样就可以避免她不得不去更换刚刚带过来的所有水杯，额外的工作常常会引起她的不快。

English for Everyday Life
日常生活英语

当迎宾员带您到餐桌坐下来的时候，要马上让服务员知道您想要热水：

"We would like to have hot water, please."
"请先给我们拿一杯热水来。"

如果餐桌上已经摆放了冰水，那么您可以礼貌请求服务员更换热水，你可以这样说：

"I'm sorry, would it be possible to get hot water instead? Thank you"
"真对不起，可以换杯热水吗？ 谢谢"

通常，这些冰水只是出于礼貌为客人提供的，以便他们坐下来用餐的时候感到舒适。不过，餐厅老板完全期待客人还会点一杯付费的饮料。如果您只喝热水，一些餐馆会收取一小笔费用来补偿差价。

Top English Programs for Adults

Langara College

Langara College has two English language programs: **Langara English Proficiency Program (LEPP)** and **Langara English for Academic Purposes (LEAP).** The two programs are designed to meet the different English-learning needs of students for everyday English or for academic English.

- ***LEPP:*** For students who want to feel more comfortable and confident with their English skills, the LEPP program offers flexible part time 6 to 10-week courses scheduled for the evenings and Saturday mornings. Course levels are available for intermediate to advanced learners and are led by qualified instructors who work hard to create an interactive and social environment. In the LEPP courses, students can improve their listening, speaking, writing and pronunciation skills. Also, the more advanced students can improve their business communication and public speaking skills.

- ***LEAP:*** The Langara website describes LEAP as "an intensive ESL program designed to prepare students whose first language is not English for full-time study at English language universities and colleges." The program runs full time during the week and there is a minimum of two hours of homework per evening.

兰加拉学院 https://langara.ca/

兰加拉学院有两类英语课程：兰加拉阶梯英语（LEPP）和兰加拉学术英语（LEAP）。这两门课程是专为满足学生对日常生活英语或学术英语不同需求而设置的。

- **兰加拉阶梯英语**（LEPP）：专为那些兼职的想要提高他们的专业、学术或自我发展语言与扩大其英语技能为目的的学生而设置的，上课的时间是弹性的，每期6至10周的课程。时间安排在晚上和周六的上午。由经过资格认证合格的讲师任教。适合中级到高级英语水平的成人。目标是提供高质量教学的互动、专注学习环境。通过基本技能课程的学习，学生可以发展他们的听力，口语，写作和发音技巧。此外，高年级的学生还可以专注于商务沟通、学术写作与演讲的兴趣。
- **兰加拉学术英语**（LEAP）：兰加拉网站介绍(LEAP)是一种密集的ESL课程计划，旨在培养母语不是英语的全日制大学和学院的学生，每晚不得少于两个小时的家庭作业。

May 13   Vancouver Backyard Wildlife

5月13日   温哥华后院的小鸟和动物

Red Foxes

Red foxes are known for being extremely intelligent and resourceful. They have adapted very well to urban environments. They are solitary hunters who eat rodents, rabbits, birds, and other animals. However, if garbage and pet food are available, they will also eat that. The foxes are not very large but they have a very big, thick and furry tail. They use the tail as a cover in cold weather and they also use it for balance and to signal to other foxes.

赤狐

　　赤狐听觉、嗅觉发达，性狡猾，行动敏捷，适应能力极强。喜欢单独活动。以鼠类、兔子，鸟类和水果为食，有时还吃垃圾和宠物。赤狐个头不大，但是它们的尾巴却非常大而厚实，毛茸茸的尾巴起到了防潮和保暖的作用，冬季用它来护体，还可以用它来保持身体平衡，并向其他赤狐发出信号。

May 14   Support for Newcomers

5月14日   支持新移民

Community Airport Newcomers Network (CANN)

CANN members are there to assist new immigrants and refugees when they arrive to the Vancouver International Airport. Their website also contains helpful information and checklists for newcomers of all the steps they should do before they leave their home country and after they arrive in Vancouver. There are also helpful links to many resources in the city.

新移民机场接待处 (CANN)
http://www.cannyvr.ca/site/info/243/Simplified-Chinese

在抵达温哥华国际机场时，新移民和难民会受到新移民机场接待处（英文简称CANN）的欢迎。CANN网站还提供了一些实用的信息以及抵达温哥华之后应该立刻着手办理的事情清单。还有许多城市资源的链接。

May 15 Vancouver Neighbourhoods

5月15日 温哥华社区

Olympic Village

This wonderful waterfront neighbourhood located on the shoreline of False Creek was created for the 2010 Winter Olympic and 2010 Paralympics to host the athletes for the event. Since that time, it has developed into a thriving and actively growing neighbourhood popular with couples and young families. The False Creek Promenade and bike route connect this neighbourhood with Granville Island and Yaletown and the West End. There is also a wharf where you can catch the small False Creek Ferries, and the Science World and the Olympic Village Skytrain station is a short walk away. Come explore the area and enjoy the attractive village square with its giant bird sculptures. You will also find parks with playgrounds for the children and the interesting giant deck loungers and fun swivel chairs that are public art meant to be played with and used. The area has many great restaurants as well, including a few that specialize in craft beer.

奥运村

奥运村是一片新兴的、美丽的海滨住宅小区，坐落在菲沙海湾上。它是为主办2010年冬季奥运会和2010年残奥会而创立的。至今已逐渐发展成为一个知名的社区，深受年轻夫妇们的热捧。菲沙湾上的步道和自行车道与格兰维尔岛、耶鲁镇和西区相连。奥运村有一个码头，你可以乘坐小型False Creek渡轮摆渡到科学世界。离码头不远的地方就是奥运村轻轨站。村里有公园与儿童游乐场，广场上有巨大的鸟类雕塑，巨型甲板躺椅和转椅。奥运村还有许多有名的餐厅，其中包括一些专门从事手工啤酒的餐厅。

Basic Everyday English

基本日常生活用语

At the Bank

Nowadays, most banks have at least one employee who can speak Mandarin, so it is very rare that you would have to use English for these transactions. However, if you do need some help, the basic phrases below will help you get by.

在银行

如今，大多数银行至少配备一名可以说普通话的员工，所以您基本上不必用英文进行交易。 但是，如果接待您的职员不会讲普通话，下面的基本短语可以帮到您。

English for Everyday Life
日常生活英语

下面是一些基本英语短语，您也许听到过，您可以在银行使用。. 请访问我们的网站*www.mynewlifeinvancouver.com*，听一听这些短语的发音并练习会话。

Hello, I would like to open an account.
Hello, I would like to apply for a credit card
Hello, I would like to make a deposit
Hello, I would like to take money out or make a withdrawal
Hello, I would like to make a payment please

您好，我想开立一个账户。
您好，我想申请一张信用卡。
您好，我想存钱。
您好，我想取钱或取款。
您好，我想付款。

Hello, I have a question.
Can you please tell me more about your savings account?
Can you please tell me more about your line of credit?
Can you please tell me more about your investments?
Thank you for your help

您好，我有个问题。
您能告诉我更多有关您们储蓄账户的事吗？
您能告诉我更多有关信用额度吗的事吗？
您能多告诉我一些您们投资的事情吗？
谢谢您的帮助

Education

5月17日　　教育

Special Programs for Children

The Vancouver Board of Education is committed to providing classrooms that are inclusive and welcoming to all students. However, some students have **"special needs"**, for example a physical disability or a learning disability, need extra support to complete their schoolwork.

In addition, there can also be students who are very bright or **"gifted"** and they need extra resources to enhance the standard curriculum so that they are not bored in the classroom. For both cases, the Vancouver School Board has a Student Support team that works together with school teams, parents and community partners to create classroom environments where all students can be successful and fulfilled. The VSB has a range of programs and services that can support the needs of the students.

有特殊需求或者资优教育方案

> 有特殊需求 https://www.vsb.bc.ca/special-needs
> 资优教育
> http://go.vsb.bc.ca/schools/specialneeds/Programs/gifted/
> Pages/gifted-enrichment.aspx

　　温哥华教育局致力于促进包容性和受所有学生欢迎的教室设置。然而，一些学生有"特殊需求"，例如身体残疾或学习障碍，需要额外的支持来完成标准课程。

　　此外，有的学生非常聪明'天资聪慧'，他们需要额外的资源，以提高其课程标准，使他们不会在课堂上感到无聊。 对于这两种情况，温哥华学校教育局的学生支持团队协同校方、家长和社区的合作伙伴创建所有学生都能成功完成的课堂环境。 VSB拥有一系列的课程和服务，可以支持学生的特殊需求。

May 18   ## Scenes from Daily Life

5月18日   日常生活中的一些镜头

Fun and Games at Picnic
野餐的乐趣与游戏

Outdoor Life in Vancouver

5月19日　　温哥华户外生活

Picnics in the Park

When the weather is nice, Vancouverites like to pack up some food and a blanket or folding chair to sit on and go to one of the many beautiful parks and beaches in the city. The city of Vancouver also has 12 parks that have "designated" picnic sites which have shelters, and some have kitchens, access to electricity and barbecues. These very popular designated picnic sites must be reserved and paid for in advance at the Vancouver parks website. These covered picnic sites are especially good for arranging special outdoor parties because you want to make sure that the picnic tables have shelter in case it rains on the day of your big event!

在公园里的野餐

温哥华市公园野餐信息页面 http://vancouver.ca/parks-recreation-culture/picnics.aspx

当天气晴朗时，温哥华人喜欢带上一些食物、毯子或折叠椅，前往美丽的公园或海滩坐下来，温哥华市有12个公园有"指定的"野餐地点，有棚子、厨房、提供电力和烧烤场地。要预留野餐地点并拿到许可证必须事先完成在线预订和付费。这些地方特别适合安排特殊的户外派对，要确保野餐桌上有棚子，以防在活动的当天下雨！

English for Everyday Life
日常生活英语

一些受欢迎的野餐食品:

Hot dogs and hamburgers (if you have a portable barbecue)
热狗和汉堡包（如果您有便携式烧烤炉）
Sandwiches and wraps
三明治和百味卷
Salads: potato, coleslaw and green salad
沙拉：土豆，凉拌卷心菜和蔬菜沙拉
Fresh fruit - especially watermelon in the summer
新鲜水果 - 特别是夏天以西瓜为主
Potato chips
薯片
Cookies
饼干

Productive Failure

In order to learn, we need to fail. Manu Kapur, a researcher at the Learning Sciences Lab at the National Institute of Education of Singapore, calls this *"productive failure"*. This is the process by which we learn valuable information from our mistakes, especially if we try to figure out the problem on our own first without any outside help. Sometimes in the process of struggling a bit to find the answer, we really come to learn and understand concepts deeply. For example, sometimes English verb tenses can be a little confusing to figure out. However, if you make a mistake with a verb tense, it can be helpful to think about why you think you were wrong before you look up the rules in your grammar book. Be clear about what time period you were writing about, for example, the past. What can you remember about possible verb tenses that are used to write about the past? This is called *"activating prior learning"* which happens when your brain gets stimulated by problem solving. Before you look up the verb rules in your grammar book, try to remind yourself about what you already know. By trying to learn from your mistakes before you look up the rules, you will get your brain into a very good state for learning and remembering.

It is a fact that you are going to make many mistakes on your daily journey towards learning English. However, remember to keep in mind that mistakes are one of the most powerful learning tools there are. By working out on their own what they did wrong, learners regain a sense of control about their own learning which is very important towards building confidence. Successful English learners quickly learn the value of making mistakes and don't let them stop their daily progress.

生产性故障

为了学习，我们需要故障。新加坡国立教育学院学习科学实验室的研究员马努·卡普尔称这是"生产性故障"。这是我们从错误中学到有价值信息的过程，特别是如果我们尝试在没有任何外界帮助的情况下，先自己解决问题。有时在努力寻找答案的过程中，我们真的深入学习和理解概念。例如，有时英语动词时态可能有点混乱，让人费解。然而，如果你用动词时态的时候犯了错误，那么在你查找语法书中的规则之前，想一想你为什么会出错了是很有帮助的。要明确你写的是什么时间段，例如过去。你能记住用来描述过去的可能的动词时态吗？这就是所谓的"激活前先学习"，这种情况会发生在你的大脑获取解决问题的能力受到刺激时。在你的语法书中查找动词规则之前，请尽量提醒自己你已经知道了什么。通过尝试在你查找规则之前从你的错误中学习，你会让自己的大脑进入一个非常好的学习和记忆的状态。

你每天在学习英语的过程中都会犯许多错误，这是一个不可避免的事实。然而，请记住，错误是最强大的学习工具之一。通过找出自己做错了什么，学习者将重新获得了对自己的学习的控制感，这对建立自信心非常重要。成功的英语学习者很快就会懂得学习中犯错误的价值，而且不会让它阻止他们每一天的进步。

May 21   ## A Little Canadian Inspiration

5月21日   一点点启示

*"It's difficult to learn from success. I've
learned more from my mistakes."*

– Louise Penny, Canadian author

Newcomers can feel so nervous about making mistakes, especially with English. However, mistakes are really the best teacher so don't let them get you down.

"从成功中学到东西是很难的。而我从错误中学到了更多的东西。"

— 加拿大作家路易斯·佩妮（Louise Penny）

新移民常常会担心犯错误，尤其是英文。然而，错误真的是最好的老师，所以不要让它把你压垮。

May 22   # Volunteer in Vancouver

5月22日   在温哥华做义工

Vancouver Coastal Health Authority

The Vancouver Coastal Health Authority operates the hospitals and healthcare organizations in the lower mainland. They have many volunteer opportunities at their sites. Here is a list of some of the different volunteer positions they have:

- One-to-one visiting – make friendly conversation with patients
- Retail – sell items in the gift shop, gift cart or thrift shop
- Occupational therapy – support arts and crafts activities, bus outings, gardening programs, breakfast groups, computer sessions and recreation activities

温哥华沿岸卫生局

温哥华沿海卫生局负责在大陆下游的医院和医疗机构。 他们在其网站上给志愿者提供很多的机会。 这里有一些不同岗位的志愿服务列表：

- 一对一访问 – 与患者进行友好的交谈
- 零售 – 在礼品店，礼品购物车或旧货店销售商品
- 职业疗法 – 支持艺术和手工艺活动，巴士郊游，园艺项目，早餐小组，电脑会议和娱乐活动。

May 23   Healthcare in Vancouver

5月23日   温哥华的医疗保健

Medical Emergencies

Always dial **9-1-1** right away if there is a serious medical emergency.

If you need an ambulance to take you to the hospital, call 9-1-1. The ambulance will take you to the nearest hospital. You can also go directly to the emergency department on your own without an appointment and you don't need to arrive in an ambulance. Many people are surprised to learn that they may have to pay a fee for the ambulance service. However, while BC Ambulance Service fees are not an insured benefit under the BC Medical Services Plan (MSP), the fees for this service are heavily subsidized for people with a valid BC Care Card who are covered by MSP. The fee is significantly higher for non-MSP card holders as they do not receive this subsidy. An invoice will be mailed to your home for the ambulance charges.

紧急医疗状况

如果遇到严重的医疗急救情况，请立即拨打9-1-1。

如果您需要一辆救护车送您去医院，请拨打9-1-1。救护车会把您送到最近的医院。您也可以自己直接去急诊室，不用预约，也不用叫救护车。许多人惊讶地发现他们可能要为救护车服务付费。然而，卑诗省救护车服务费不包括在省医疗服务计划（MSP）保险范围之内，但是对于持有BC医疗卡的人来说，这项收费会有相当大的补贴。 而对于没有拿到MSP卡的人来说，这笔费用就很高，因为他们不享受这种补贴。几天后，您会收到一张邮寄到您家里的发票，用以支付救护车的费用。

Interesting Facts About Vancouver

5月24日 温哥华趣闻

The Longest Swimming Pool in Canada

Kitsilano pool is the longest pool in Canada and it is located in Vancouver's Kitsilano neighbourhood. It is almost the length of three Olympic swimming pools, measuring 137.5m in length. The pool is open and heated from May to September each year and is located right beside the popular Kitsilano Beach.

加拿大最长的游泳池

加拿大最长的游泳池位于温哥华基茨兰诺区。总长为137.5米相当于三个奥运会标准的游泳池。游泳池每年五月至九月开放并加热，靠近基茨兰诺海滩。

May 25 Finding Work in Vancouver

5月25日　　在温哥华找份工作

WorkBC

WorkBC is organization funded by the Government of Canada and the Province of British Columbia that run WorkBC Employment Centres. These centres offer a range of services which support job seekers in getting – and keeping – a job as quickly as possible. Their services are available to all unemployed British Columbians who are seeking employment and legally eligible to work in BC. Your WorkBC centre location is based on your home address. You just enter your home address on the WorkBC website and they will tell you the name and address of your centre.

WorkBC（BC就业中心）http://vancouverworkbc.ca/

WorkBC是由加拿大政府和不列颠哥伦比亚省政府资助的组织，WorkBC就业中心提供一系列服务，帮助求职者尽快找到适合和稳定的工作。他们给所有不列颠哥伦比亚省失业的和正在寻找工作的人提供服务，并帮助他们在BC省找到合法的工作。您可以根据家庭住址找到离您家最近的WorkBC就业中心，您只需在WorkBC网站上输入您的家庭住址，他们就会告诉就业中心的名称和地址。

Vancouver Sightseeing

5月26日　　观光

Vancouver's Beautiful Gardens

Vancouverites love their trees and gardens. The city actively plants trees and plants throughout the city streets and parks and the residents also like to maintain gardens at their home. However, for true inspiration, locals love to visit these three beautiful gardens in the city.

- ***VanDusen Gardens*** contains over 22 hectares of beautiful garden landscapes that are organized into different areas representing different ecosystems from the Himalayas to the Mediterranean, from Louisiana swamps to the Pacific Northwest. The Garden's stunning Visitor Centre — with its orchid-inspired design — is one of the city's most lovely buildings. In the Visitor Centre there is a garden's café which is a wonderful place to meet friends and enjoy the view of the gardens. On the garden grounds, there is also a full-service restaurant for dinner and lunch. VanDusen Gardens puts on many community events throughout the year and offers a full program of courses on gardening to landscape painting that are open to everybody.

- The **Bloedel Conservatory** is a domed lush paradise located in Queen Elizabeth Park on top of the City of Vancouver's highest point. On a cold wintery day, it is a wonderful place to experience the colours and scents of the tropics. More than 200 free-flying exotic birds, 500 exotic plants and flowers thrive within its temperature-controlled environment.

- Right in the heart of Vancouver's Chinatown, the **Dr. Sun Yat-Sen Classical Chinese Garden** is the perfect urban oasis. The stunning Garden is an authentic representation of Ming Dynasty-era tradition and the first of its kind outside China. Guests enjoy the winding paths, rocks, plants, water lily covered ponds and the pagoda. Every year, they put on a day of celebrations in honour of the Chinese Spring Festival and New Year which is very popular with locals.

花园：范杜森花园、中山公园、伊丽莎白女王公园

范杜森花园 http://www.vandusengarden.org/
布洛德尔温室 http://vandusengarden.org/explore/bloedel-conservatory/
中山公园 http://vancouverchinesegarden.com/

温哥华人热爱他们的树木和花园。 市府积极在整个城市街道和公园里种植树木和植物，居民们也喜欢在他们的后院养护花园。不过，当地人更愿意访问市里的三座美丽的花园以获取灵感。

- **范杜森花园**拥有超过22公顷美丽的花园景观，分成不同的区域，从喜马拉雅山脉到地中海，从路易斯安那州的沼泽到太平洋西北地区代表着不同的生态系统。 花园的游客中心是温哥华最可爱的建筑之一，它是以兰花风格设计的，令人惊叹。 园里的咖啡馆也是结交朋友，赏花的好地方。Tehre是一家提供全套服务的餐厅，供应午餐和晚餐。 范杜森花园全年举办许多社区活动，提供园艺景观绘画的全套课程。

- **布洛德尔温室**是一个半球形的圆顶，位于伊丽莎白女王公园，温哥华市的最高点。在寒冷的冬季，它依然保有热带的气息，是一个非常奇妙的地方。那里有超过200多只自由飞翔的外来小鸟和500种异国情调植物和花卉在其温度控制的环境中茁壮成长。

- **中山公园**位于温哥华唐人街的中心，简直就是城市的绿洲。它仿效明朝苏州古典花园设计，用料从中国进口，为中国境外首创，你会被公园里的曲径，岩石，植物和美丽的景色所陶醉。你也可以在奇特的岩石、睡莲覆盖的池塘、宝塔和茂密的植物中找到一份宁静。 每年，那里都举行整整一天的庆祝活动，以庆祝非常受当地人欢迎的中国传统的春节和新年。

May 27   Vancouver Transportation

5月27日   温哥华交通运输

Taxis, Town Cars, Limousines, and Uber

All taxis charge $2.50 for the first one sixth of a mile and $2.60 for each mile thereafter (Plus gas surcharge, if applicable). Wait time and traffic delay is $24/hour. There are four major taxi companies in Vancouver and many town car and limousine rental companies as well. At the time of publishing Uber is not allowed to operate in Vancouver as the local taxi companies don't want the competition, but the local people are pushing the government to change the rules and allow Uber to operate in Vancouver.

Town car service (private car and driver) and limousine service (large car and driver for large groups) are available to rent from many companies.

出租车，城市汽车服务，豪华轿车和优步

黄色出租车 http://www.yellowcabonline.com/ （明亮的黄色车身）
黑色出租车 http://btccabs.ca/ （淡黄色的车身配以黑色的车顶）
温哥华出租车 http://www.vancouvertaxi.cab/ （明亮的橙色汽车）
McClures出租车 http://www.maclurescabs.ca/ （蓝车身和白顶汽车）

所有出租车当开到第一个六分之一英里的时候收取2.50加元，此后每跑一英里收费2.60加元（加上燃气附加费，如适用的话）。等待时间和交通阻塞延误费是24加元/小时。

在温哥华有四个主要的出租车公司和许多城市汽车和豪华轿车租赁公司。目前，尚不允许Uber在温哥华经营，因为当地的出租车公司不想与其竞争，但当地人正在推动政府改变规则，以获准Uber在温哥华运营。

还有城市汽车服务（私家车和司机）和豪华轿车服务（大型汽车和大型集团的司机）等许多租赁公司。

English for Everyday Life
日常生活英语

当您坐上出租车的时候，应该事先准备好您要去的地址。如果担心您的英语讲不清楚，可以把完整的地址清楚地写在一张纸上或显示在手机上给司机看。

下面这句话是非常有礼貌的告诉司机您想去哪里：

"Hello, I would like to go to 4587 West 34th Avenue in Dunbar area please"
"您好，我想去邓巴区西第34大街的4587号"

May 28   Sports Teams and Special Events

5月28日   专业体育赛事和活动

Vancouver Canadians Baseball Team

There is no major baseball league team in Vancouver. However, the Vancouver Canadians – a minor league team of the Toronto Blue Jays – are one of the top sports attractions in the summer in Vancouver. They play a very short season from June to late August, and their games are one of the best parts of summer. They play at the Nat Bailey Stadium and the $12 tickets and fun entertainment at the game mean that the games are always sold out. Although the baseball is fun to watch, many fans are there to enjoy the hot sun, the happy crowds, the cold beer, the cheap tickets and the fireworks a few times each season.

温哥华加拿大棒球队

温哥华没有太大的棒球联盟球队。到了夏天，温哥华加拿大人 – 多伦多蓝鸟队的小联盟球队 – 成了温哥华的顶级体育赛事之一。 他们的赛季非常短暂，从每年的6月到8月下旬。赛场设在 Nat Bailey体育场，门票12加元，包含一些有趣的娱乐活动。在观赏棒球比赛的同时，还可以沐浴阳光、沉浸在快乐的人群中、 冰镇啤酒和购买廉价的烟花看台票。比赛中场休息时，球队还安排娱乐性很强的吉祥物比赛。

May 29 Vancouver Parks

5月29日 温哥华公园

Hastings Park

Hastings Park has the usual green features of a park, but this park, located at 2901 East Hastings Street, is much more well known for the many outdoor and entertainment activities that are available for all ages. Some of the highlights include

- Playing soccer on the fields and using the running track at Empire Fields.
- Enjoy the Plateau Sports area and play table tennis, basketball, practice bike skills, beach volleyball, etc.
- Bike and walk the greenways throughout Hastings Park.
- Skateboard at one of two skate parks.

In addition, the **Hastings Park Racecourse** for horse racing has been located at Hastings Park since the 1800s. Live race days (free entrance) take place between April and October. Various restaurants, bars, and a casino gaming floor with 600 slot machines operate year-round.

Hastings Park is also the home of the **Pacific National Exhibition (PNE)** and the **Playland Amusement Park** which hosts shows, exhibits, sporting events, concerts, cultural activities, and the annual summer fair.

黑斯廷斯公园

黑斯廷斯公园 http://vancouver.ca/parks-recreation-culture/hastings-park.aspx
黑斯廷斯赛马场http://www.hastingsracecourse.com/
太平洋国家展览会 http://www.pne.ca/

黑斯廷斯公园(Hastings Park)是位于温哥华市区的一个公园。公园坐落东黑斯廷斯街2901号，公园里有许多户外和娱乐活动，适合于所有年龄段。一些亮点包括：

- 在球场上踢足球，在帝国大道上跑步。
- 享受高原训练、打乒乓球、篮球、练习自行车技巧、打沙滩排球等。
- 骑自行车和步行穿过黑斯廷斯公园的绿道。
- 有两个滑板区。
- 使用帝国操场的跑道

此外，自19世纪以来，温哥华的主要赛马场地黑斯廷斯马场亦位于园内。每年4月至10月期间举行赛马活动（免费入场）。各种餐厅，酒吧和赌场的600台老虎机全年运营。

黑斯廷斯公园也是太平洋国家展览会（PNE）和游乐园的所在地，PNE于园内举办各种展览、体育赛事、音乐会、文化活动和一年一度为期17日的夏季游乐会。

May 30   # Stories and Advice for Newcomers

5月30日   移民的故事和建议

Shine

在温哥华生产的经验，给准妈妈们一些参考

2016年9月在温哥华这个美丽的海滨城市，我迎来了我和先生的第一个宝宝，Benjamin。我想分享一下在温哥华生产的经验，给准妈妈们一些参考。

此行最重要的自然是联系家庭医生和选择生产医院，保证小宝贝顺利出生。朋友推荐是选择家庭医生的一个很好的方式。华人产科医生无论从语言上或是习惯上都是最好的选择，不过因为近年来华人产妇增多，通常需要等候的时间比较长，也有可能档期约不上。所以，没有语言障碍的朋友们也可以联系西人的医生。后来我了解到很多诊所都是可以提供翻译的服务，沟通完全没有障碍。家庭医生可以帮忙预定生产的医院，我选择了Richmond hospital。 这家医院除了设施完善，医护人员都很热情和善，院内也有很多义工可以说中文，考虑到家里老人沟通起来更方便，这的确是一个很好的选择。列治文医院生产中心在YouTube上有详细的介绍视频，包括入院流程、费用等，可以提前了解一下。如果没有朋友给您推荐家庭医生，您可以去一些官方的网站上面查阅，或直接电话到您附近的诊所预约咨询。Kari老师这本书里hospital一章会介绍到一些很有用的网站。提前去医院了解一下环境也是很有必要的，不至于临产的时候慌乱，比如停车，急诊和住院是分开的。急诊的通道是单向的，进去出来两条路等等。 如果是旅游签证过来，全程都需要自费。所以也需要准备足够的现金。有的诊所只收现金，不接受信用卡。我在生产的过程中得到了很好的照顾，特别是助产士非常的专业很有耐心，减少了很多痛苦。家人允许陪同也是给产妇很好的精神支持。

温哥华的医疗的确体现了北美发达国家的先进水平，医生和患者之间彼此也信任、尊重。任何时候，遇到紧急情况，您都可以打911求助，然后放心的把自己交给这些专业的人士。在这里，每一个人都能够得到很好的照顾。

May 31 Diverse Vancouver

5月31日 多元文化的温哥华

Experience Chinese Culture in Vancouver

Vancouver's Chinatown began in the 1890s and is the third largest Chinatown after New York and San Francisco. The main commercial area is about six blocks, bordered by East Pender Street, Gore Avenue, East Georgia Street, and Carrall Street. You can visit many Asian speciality stores, Dim Sum restaurants, Chinese bakeries and the famous Dr Sun Yat Sen Classical Chinese Garden in this area. Every August, there is a large Chinatown Festival that celebrates Chinese culture and its long relationship with Vancouver. The Chinese Benevolent Association of Vancouver organizes the annual **Chinese Lunar New Year** celebrations with a large parade and cultural fair downtown featuring lion dances, cultural dance troupes, marching bands, martial arts performances and much more.

在温哥华体验中国文化

温哥华唐人街艺术节http://www.vancouver-chinatown.com/
中国农历新年庆祝活动http://www.cbavancouver.ca/

温哥华的唐人街开始于1890年，是北美洲继纽约和旧金山之后的第三大唐人街。主要商业区覆盖约有6个街区，毗邻东片打街，戈尔街，东乔治亚街和卡罗尔街。你可以参观许多具有亚洲特色的商店，茶餐厅，中式面包店和餐厅。这个地区最著名的是孙中山古典式中国花园。每年的八月份，唐人街都将举办一次大的活动，庆祝中加长期以来的友好关系。每年的中国农历新年，温哥华中华慈善协会也将组织一次大型的庆祝游行活动，包括舞狮子、舞蹈、乐队、武术表演等等。

June

Weather:	Average temperature: 12°C to 20°C
	Average rainfall days: 15, Average rainfall: 50 mm
Statutory holiday:	none
Other special days:	Father's Day (the third Sunday in June)

The temperature continues to rise in June and many outdoor beach, pool and boating activities become more popular with the locals. The children are excited because June is the last month of school before the summer holidays and they enjoy sports days* and end of the school year celebrations. The grade 12 students celebrate their high school graduation this month with graduation or convocation ceremonies*, proms* and other "grad" activities.

June is also the number one most popular month to get married, and it is common to see bridal parties posing for photographs in the many beautiful parks, gardens, and beaches of Vancouver.

June 20 or 21 is the Summer Solstice* and the official first day of summer. In June Vancouverites enjoy going to see the popular Dragon Boat Festival where they cheer on dragon boat teams from Vancouver and North America as they race in False Creek. The weekend-long event also features music and delicious international food.

The Vancouver International Jazz Festival also begins in June and continues into July. This festival is BC's largest music festival and features almost 2,000 musicians playing more than 400 concerts in 40 venues over 10 days. Many of the concerts are free and are performed in outdoor parks throughout the city. The annual "Bard on the Beach" Shakespeare festival also starts in June and runs to September. Every summer, this festival performs four different Shakespeare plays. The plays are performed in tents that are set up in a waterfront park giving a beautiful ocean and mountain backdrop for the actors.

Father's Day happens in June and on this day children honour their fathers with special gifts, cards and meals out in restaurants.

The South Granville ArtWalk is planned every June. South Granville has the highest number of fine art galleries in Vancouver, and during this special day, visitors can wander up and down South Granville Street and listen to artist talks, enjoy wine and cheese tastings, and attend different art exhibitions.

Italian Day on the Drive is another festival which happens along 13 blocks of Commercial Drive which is in the east side of Vancouver. It is a cultural street festival attracting over 300,000 people that celebrates Vancouver's Italian community. The street comes alive with Italian musical performances, hands-on activities and games, vendors, patios, food and drink tastings, street performers, classic vehicle exhibits and so much more.

Over on Broadway in the west side of the city, Greek Day on Broadway aims to share the rich Greek culture with the City of Vancouver. Broadway is closed to all street traffic for a whole day so that everyone can enjoy the delicious Greek food and drink, market vendors, entertainment, and live music in a happy and relaxed Greek atmosphere.

6月

气候： 平均温度：12°C 到 20°C
　　　平均降雨天数：15，平均降雨量：50毫米
公众节假日：无
其他特殊日：父亲节（6月第三个星期日）

6月份的气温持续上升，海滩，游泳池和划船等许多户外活动越来越受当地人的青睐。孩子们很兴奋，因为六月是学校放暑假前的最后一个月，他们喜欢参加学校的运动会和学年结业庆祝活动，特别是12年级的学生在这个月将庆祝他们高中毕业或举行毕业典礼，班级舞会，和其他与"毕业生"有关的活动。

6月份也是最受新娘欢迎的婚庆月，在许多美丽的公园、花园和海滩上，新娘和新郎们摆着各种姿势在拍婚纱照。

6月20日或21日是夏至，也是夏季正式开始的第一天。6月端午节当地民众去受保护的福溪水域观看国际龙舟比赛并为他们喜爱的龙舟队加油。期间还可以欣赏音乐演奏和品尝国际美食。

温哥华国际爵士音乐节也是在六月份举办，并一直持续到七月。这是BC省最大的音乐节，有近2000名音乐家在40个场馆连续10多天的演奏逾400场音乐会。许多音乐会是免费的，而且是在全市的各大公园里进行。一年一度的"海滩上的游吟诗人"莎士比亚节也从六月开始至九月份结束。每年的夏天，在海滨公园搭建的一个帐篷，为演员们提供了以美丽的海洋和山脉作为背景的舞台，他们会为观众表演四种不同的莎士比亚剧目。

父亲节也是在六月，在这一天，孩子们用特别的礼物、卡片送给他们尊敬的父亲并和父亲一起在餐馆里用餐。

每年的六月南格兰维尔举办艺术漫步。南格兰维尔大街有着温哥华顶级的艺术画廊，在这一天，游客们可以由南至北在南格兰维尔街上漫步，听听艺术家对其艺术品的讲解，品尝葡萄酒和奶酪，参加不同的艺术展览。

在温哥华东边的一条街叫做商业大道，每年的六月份会在这里举行意大利日。这是一个充满活力的意大利文化节，活动范围覆盖了13个街区，热闹非凡，充分展示了温哥华意大利社区的文化。整整一天的活动吸引了超过30万人，街上到处播放意大利音乐，各种表演、手工、游戏、食品、饮料、品酒、街头艺人和经典汽车展览等等。

希腊节则在温哥华西区百老汇西大街上庆祝，其宗旨是与温哥华市民分享丰富的希腊文化。节日期间将封闭5个街区的交通，以腾出足够的地方为市场供应商摆放希腊美味的食物和饮料，现场娱乐表演和音乐烘托着整个热闹的节日气氛。

更多的信息：

温哥华龙舟节：http://dragonboatbc.ca/
温哥华国际爵士音乐节：http://www.coastaljazz.ca/
南格兰维尔街的艺术漫步：
http://www.southgranville.org/artwalk/
海滩上游吟诗人的莎士比亚戏剧节：
http://bardonthebeach.org/
商业大道上的意大利日：http://italianday.ca/
西百老汇街的希腊日：http://greekday.com/

* Summer Solstice夏至：是一种天文现象，北半球白昼最长而夜晚最短。这一天被官方指定为夏季的开始。

* Sports Days学校运动会：所有小学都有一个为期一天的运动会。在校的所有孩子们都在这一天参加各种有趣的体育竞争项目，力争赢得彩旗和奖杯。

* Graduation/Convocation Ceremonies毕业/毕业典礼：学校组织的一种正式的官方的毕业仪式，高中毕业生们头戴高帽身披长袍，接受校方颁发的毕业文凭。

* Proms/ Grad Dances高中生舞会 / 毕业舞会：12年级的毕业生学年末举行的高中生正式的晚宴和舞会。通常男孩子们穿西装而女孩们则穿长裙。

June 1 Local Customs

6月1日   当地的习俗

Celebrating School Graduations

Graduation celebrations have always been an important tradition for high school and university students. High School graduation is probably the biggest celebration of them all and it has a few traditional activities including:

- **High School Graduation ceremony:** This is the formal ceremony where the students wear the cap and gown and walk on stage when their name is announced to receive their high school diploma and shake the hands of the school principal. Special achievement awards are handed out, and one member of the graduating class, called the Valedictorian, is elected by their classmates to give a speech at this ceremony. It is customary to bring a bouquet of flowers to give to female graduates. Also, parents will usually give their children a generous graduation present such as a piece of jewelry or a special vacation and so on. Close friends and family members will also send a special graduation congratulations card to the student. The local stores have special displays of graduation cards from April to June every year.

- **Graduation Photographs:** It is traditional to have a professional photograph taken of the student wearing the official cap and gown to remember this special time.

- **Prom or Dinner Dance:** Schools will organize a formal sit-down dinner attended by the teachers, graduating students and their parents, siblings and other guests. These events are usually held at large hotels downtown and there are some speeches as well as dancing, but are always alcohol-free. It is traditional for the father to dance one dance with his graduating daughter or the mother to dance one dance with her graduating son.

- **Dry Grad:** After these formal events with the parents, schools usually organize a student-only event back at the high school gym that lasts all night long. The purpose of this event is to give the grads a very fun and safe way to celebrate the end of their high school years. There are games, music and dancing. It is called a dry grad because no alcohol is served. The students are always supervised in the school gym by some teachers and other adults.

- **Other Grad Week Activities:** Every year, the graduating students form a Graduation Committee which is responsible for helping organize the formal graduation events. They will usually organize many other events as well such as a party-boat harbour cruise and other fun activities.

College and University Graduation Ceremonies are usually much simpler than for high school graduation. There is one large **Convocation Ceremony** when the student wears the cap and gown to receive their diploma. Traditionally, this will be followed by a small family lunch or dinner celebration and the presentation of flowers and a graduation present to the student. There are also formal photographs taken of the student in the cap and gown as well.

In the last few years, **preschools and elementary schools** have begun holding their own little graduation ceremonies to honour these important times in a student's life. Usually they are just small and fun little events that aren't taken too seriously.

庆祝学校毕业典礼

毕业典礼一直是高中生和大学生的重要传统。最大的庆祝活动应该是高中毕业,一些传统的活动包括:

- **高中毕业典礼**:这是正式的仪式,学生们个个头戴方形帽子,身披长袍,排好队等在台下。当他们的名字被宣布的时候,依次走上舞台,从校长手里接过他们的高中文凭,然后和校长握握手。毕业班里由同学们选出一名公认的优秀毕业生,在典礼上代表毕业生们发表演讲。此外,还颁发特别成就奖。通常给女毕业生送上一束鲜花。父母通常会慷慨的给孩子一份毕业礼物,如一块珠宝或一个特殊的假期等。最亲密的伙伴和家庭成员也会送给该毕业生一张特殊的毕业祝贺卡。此外,每年四月到六月期间,当地的商店都会展销专门的毕业贺卡。
- **毕业照片**:传统上是要拍一张专业的头戴正式的毕业帽身着长袍的毕业照片,以留作美好的记忆。
- **舞会或晚宴**:学校将组织一个正式的(意味着男生穿西装和女生穿很漂亮的裙子),由老师,毕业生和他们的父母,兄弟姐妹以及其他宾客们参加的晚宴。活动通常在市中心的大酒店举行,先是由主持人演讲,然后跳舞。喝一些不含酒精的饮料。传统上,父亲与他即将毕业的女儿跳一支舞,母亲也会与她毕业的儿子跳一支舞。
- **被禁酒的毕业生**:在与父母举行这些正式活动之后,学校通常在高中健身房举办一次仅限学生参加的持续整个晚上的活动。本次活动的目的是给毕业生一个非常有趣和安全的方式来庆祝他们高中毕业的结束。有游戏、音乐和舞蹈。它被称为Dry Grad,是因为不准毕业生喝酒。在健身房的周围会有一些教师和其他成年人在监督此事。
- **其他毕业活动周**:每年,即将毕业的学生都会组成一个毕业委员会,负责协助组织正式的毕业活动。他们通常会举办很多其他活动,如邮轮派对和其他有趣的活动。这些额外活动通常发生在毕业典礼的最后一两个星期。这些项目毕业生是可以选择参加的。

学院和大学毕业典礼:学院和大学举行的毕业仪式。通常要比高中毕业典礼简单得多。毕业生们也是戴上帽子,穿上礼服并接过他们的毕业文凭。毕业典礼过后,传统上,举办小型的家庭午餐或晚餐庆祝一下,送上鲜花和毕业礼物。还要拍一张带着学生帽子和礼服的毕业照片。

近几年来,幼儿园和小学也开始举办小型的毕业仪式,以纪念学习生涯的某些重要的时刻。通常他们不太受到重视,认为可有可无。

June 2   Parenting in Vancouver

6月2日   在温哥华养育子女

Childcare Options for Parents

There are many types of childcare to help "stay-at-home" parents and working parents with their children. Here are the definitions of the different kinds of care:

- **Babysitters:** A babysitter is someone who is paid, usually by the hour, to care for children. Usually parents hire a babysitter to take care of their kids when they go out for an evening event or other short outing. Babysitters are usually teenagers from the neighbourhood that other parents have recommended.

- **Nannies:** A nanny is a professional childcare worker who cares for children full time. The nanny can also help with preparing meals, helping with household chores and driving children to and from activities. Nannies are called "live-in" if they have their own room in your home or "live-out" if they live on their own and just come during the day to help out.

- **Au Pairs or Mother's Helpers:** A young person (foreign or local) who helps the stay-at-home Mom with housework or child care in exchange for room and board. If the Mother's Helper is local, then they just come for a certain number of hours per week and are paid an hourly wage.

- **Daycare Centre:** Supervised full time daytime care for preschool children at a professional, approved center outside the home for a monthly fee.

- **In-Home Daycare:** Supervised full time daytime care for pre-school children at an approved private home with very small groups of children.

家长托儿的选择

有许多儿童保育的类型，以帮助那些"家庭主妇"和上班一族照看他们的孩子。下面是不同护理种类的定义：

- Babysitters小保姆：这种是指按小时付钱，照顾孩子的保姆。通常，当父母出去参加晚上活动或其他短途郊游。他们会雇用小保姆来照顾他们的孩子，Babysitters通常是来自邻居的由其他父母推荐的青少年。
- Nannies保姆：是专业的儿童保育工作者，她们全职照顾儿童。也可以帮助准备饭菜，帮助家务和开车带孩子进出参加活动。 如果给她提供房间，他们就有自己的房间，这种保姆被称为"留宿的"，如果他们有自己的家，只是在白天过来帮忙，那么称为"不留宿的。"
- Au Pair换工或Mother's Helpers母亲的帮手：是一个帮助家庭主妇做家务或者照看孩子的年轻人（外国人或当地人）－以换取食宿。 如果母亲的助手是当地的，那么他们每周按约定的时间来家里帮工，并按小时计酬。
- 日托中心：在家庭以外的专业授权的中心为学龄前儿童提供全日制护理，按月收费。
- 家庭日托：经过认可的私人家庭为学龄前儿童提供全日制白天托儿服务。

June 3 — Stories and Advice for Newcomers

6月3日   新移民的故事

Terry

孩子年龄越小适应环境和学习外语的能力越强

我是Terry一个即将开始12年级的U-Hill学生。大多数新移民刚来的时候在学习新语言和适应新环境的过程里都会经历不少挫折。我很庆幸能够在较小的年龄八岁来到加拿大学习和生活,比较那些12岁以后才来的孩子年龄越小适应环境和学习外语的能力越强。从我的亲身经历来看不管是学习新语言和适应新环境最难的一步总是第一步。在我刚开始学英语的时候很多基础词汇都不懂的我常常只能通过肢体语言来表达我自己的想法。当时的我为此感到非常的恼火。但不久后因为我不断的努力,渐渐地开始对不仅仅是英语还有我的周围的方方面面有新的认识。还记得当终于可以不再用简单的套餐号码而是完整而清晰的流利的英语在麦当劳点餐时我是多么的自豪。第一步往往是最难的一步,但是,一旦你踏出这一步将会发现原来周围的一切是多么的美妙。

June 4	Vancouver Entertainment
6月4日	温哥华娱乐

Shooting Clubs

You can spend a fun afternoon at the indoor **Vancouver Gun Range** while safely and legally practicing your shooting skills without having to complete any special provincial licenses or instructions. The gun range staff will make sure your visit is safe and will provide you with a firearm, safety equipment and an instructor who will stay with you during your visit. The indoor shooting ranges have targets that you can practice aiming and shooting.

If you would like to purchase and own your own firearm, then Canadian federal law requires you to have a **Possession and Acquisition License (PAL).** There are many courses available that will help you prepare and pass the examination required to get this license. The Vancouver Gun Range team can give you more information about the PAL license and training. If it is your first time to get a PAL, then the law requires that you pass the **Canadian Firearms Safety Course (CFSC)**. The course is about 8 hours long. At the end of the CFSC course, you must pass an exam, and then you can get a PAL and buy and own a gun. The PAL license must be renewed every five years. The minimum age to do the CFSC course and apply for a PAL is 18 years old.

射击俱乐部

温哥华射击场http://www.vancouvergunrange.ca/

您可以在温哥华射击俱乐部室内度过一个愉快的下午，在那里您可以安全且合法地练习射击技巧，而无需持有任何特殊的省级许可证及相关的证明。俱乐部的工作人员首先要确保您的打靶是安全的，然后给您提供枪支，和安全设备，射击场教练会陪伴您，让您感到舒适和自信地练习射击。室内射击场有很多供您练习瞄准和射击的靶子。

如果您想购买私人枪支，那么根据加拿大联邦法律的要求，您首先必须通过考试方可获得枪械购买许可证（PAL）。有许多课程可以帮助您。有关PAL牌照和培训的更多信息可以向温哥华射击场咨询，根据法律要求，除了PAL，您还必须通过加拿大枪支安全课程（CFSC）。约8个小时。在CFSC课程结束时，您必须参加考试，一旦考试通过，您就可以获得PAL牌照并购买自己心仪的枪支。 PAL牌照每五年更新一次。参加CFSC课程和申请PAL牌照的最小年龄是18岁。

June 5 # Best Elementary Schools

6月5日　　温哥华著名的小学

Vancouver College Elementary School (private)

Here is the description of the school from their website: "The Elementary School at Vancouver College fosters a love of learning for the students. Students in Kindergarten to Grade 6 are introduced to a variety of teaching styles from grade to grade, while their lessons are still rooted in strong traditional teaching values. The boys are given clear expectations for behaviour and for work expectations. The Elementary years begin the road to learning and it is imperative that parents/guardians and the school work closely in order to promote the growth and development of the spiritual, intellectual, physical, emotional, and social attributes of each individual."

温哥华学院小学（私立）http://www.vc.bc.ca/

下面是学校网站的描述：

"温哥华学院小学专门培养学生对学习的热爱。校内学生从幼儿班至六年级，不同年级有不同的教学风格，教学依然保留传统的价值观。 男孩们对行为和学习有明确的期望。从小学阶段开始走上学习的道路，家长/监护人和学校密切合作，对促进每个学生的精神、智力、身体、情感和社会的成长和发展是非常必要的。

June 6   A Different Way of Thinking

6月6日   不同的思维方式

Coffee culture – in Cafés and at Home

Vancouverites really love coffee. Everywhere you look, you will see coffeeshops. There are big international chains like Starbucks and Tim Hortons and several popular independent cafés, too. The most popular place for locals to meet for everyday socializing is a coffeeshop. Vancouver has a very strong coffee culture which means going to cafés is a typical social activity in Vancouver. In addition to social activities, cafés are a place where people gather to talk, write, read, entertain one another, do their homework, work on their laptop and simply relax. In addition to serving coffee, many cafés also serve tea, sandwiches, pastries and other specially flavoured drinks. Many coffee shops provide free wireless internet access for their customers.

This coffee culture is also present in the home. Having guests over for coffee, tea and cakes is a stress-free way to entertain visitors at home. When Canadians invite people to their home, the purpose is mainly to socialize, not to feast. This is very different from other cultures where it is important to serve guests a big table of special foods so as not to offend the guests. However, this is not the case in Canada, especially when getting to know new friends. Having people over for coffee and finger foods (foods that can be easily eaten with the hands) is a good first step to get to know each other. When making this type of invitation, it is common to have people over for coffee at mid-morning, around 10 am, or in mid-afternoon, around 2 or 3 pm so as not to interfere with mealtimes.

咖啡文化 – 在咖啡馆和在家里

温哥华人喜欢喝咖啡。到处走走，您会看到满大街都是咖啡店。像星巴克和蒂姆·霍顿这样的大型国际连锁店，还有一些受当地人欢迎的独立咖啡馆。对当地人来说，平日的社交活动最受欢迎的场所就是在咖啡馆。温哥华有着很浓厚的咖啡文化，这意味着去咖啡馆是温哥华特有的社会活动。除了社交活动外，咖啡馆也是人们聚在一起聊天、写字、阅读、招待、做家庭作业、用笔记本电脑工作和放松身心的地方。除了提供咖啡，许多咖啡厅还供应茶、三明治、糕点和其他特殊风味的饮料。许多咖啡店也为顾客们提供免费的无线上网服务。

这种咖啡文化同样体现在家中。有客人来访时，请客人在家喝咖啡、喝茶和吃蛋糕是减少压力的一种方式。当加拿大人邀请朋友来家里，其主要目的是要社交，而不是摆宴席请客吃饭。这就是文化的差异，有的族裔会为客人提供一大桌丰盛的饭菜，还生怕招待不周。不过，加拿大情况并非如此，特别是在结识新朋友的时候，顶多邀请他们来家里喝杯咖啡，吃一点手指食品（可以用手抓吃的食物），作为彼此了解的第一步。邀请的时间通常在上午10点左右，或在下午2、3点钟。客人们只是坐下来喝一杯咖啡，尽量避免干扰主人的用餐时间。

English for Everyday Life
日常生活英语

下面是如何邀请某人喝咖啡的方法：

"Would you like to go for coffee?"
"您想出去喝杯咖啡吗？"
"Would you like to come over to our place for coffee and cake this afternoon?"
"今天下午您想来我家喝咖啡，吃蛋糕吗？"

Best High Schools

温哥华著名的中学

Little Flower Academy High School (private)

Here is the description of the school from their website: "Little Flower Academy is one of a kind, here in Vancouver. It is exceptional to be able to offer the very best quality of education, in an all-girls environment, with a Catholic, value-based curriculum. The combination is the only one of its kind in British Columbia. Our academic record reflects our community's steadfast commitment to excellence. Over the past many years, LFA's graduation rate is 100% with more than 90% achieving provincial honours. Not surprisingly, nearly every graduate chooses their preferred post secondary education choice."

小花学院中学（私立）https://www.1fabc.org

以下是学校网站上的描述：

"小花学院中学是温哥华一所女子学校。是不列颠哥伦比亚省唯一以天主教、以价值观为基础的教学，能够提供最好的教育质量。我们学生的学习成绩反映了我们学校坚定不移地追求完美的理念。多年来我们的毕业率一直为100%，90%以上达到了省级荣誉。毫不奇怪，几乎每个毕业生都选择他们喜欢的中学后期教育。"

June 8   # The Homes of Vancouver

6月8日   **温哥华住宅**

A Duplex
双层复式住宅（又称双拼屋）

　　复式住宅分为左右两个对称的单元，每个单元都是独立的住户，每家都分别设有一个入口。

Best Extracurricular Activities for Kids

最佳儿童课外活动

Vancouver Academy of Music

Founded in 1969, the Vancouver Academy of Music (VAM) is a non-profit institution located in Vanier Park by the ocean. The VAM has a spacious facility with teaching studios, large classrooms, a library, and two performance halls, and a beautiful location at Vanier Park. VAM provides private lessons and class instruction to everyone from preschool age to adult students. Their faculty of professional and world-class musicians provide exceptional music instruction in an encouraging and supportive environment. They also organize numerous performance and competition opportunities and have regular masterclasses with world famous visiting artists. VAM also has a well respected Orchestral Training Program which has four levels of orchestra training – including a yearly concert series for the VAM Symphony Orchestra at Vancouver's beautiful Orpheum Theatre.

温哥华音乐学院

温哥华音乐学院（VAM）成立于1969年，是一家卓越的非盈利性机构，位于市中心风景优美的瓦尼埃公园，学院内有宽敞的大教室和教学设施，一个图书馆和两个表演大厅。VAM有一流的教学条件为学前儿童到成人学生提供世界级的私人音乐教育课程。有专业背景很强的老师授课，除了私人课程和课堂教学，还为学员们定期举办世界著名的客座艺术家大师班。他们还组织许多表演和竞争机会， VAM还有一个受人尊敬的管弦乐培训计划，其中有四个级别的管弦乐培训——包括在温哥华最美丽的文化场馆：奥芬剧院举办的VAM交响乐团的年度音乐会系列演出。

Meeting Locals in Vancouver

与当地人接触

Meet People by Volunteering

It is well known that one of the best ways to improve your mood and feelings is by helping people. So, by doing some volunteer work in the community, not only will you help make the community a better place, but you will also benefit by meeting new people and feeling more a part of the city. There are many ways and places to volunteer in the city. In fact, there are so many interesting volunteer opportunities in the city that we have written about one of them in every monthly chapter in this book. There are also many positions that do not require strong English skills. A volunteer position is a good way to meet people because you really get to know them well by working together and feeling like a member of a team. Also, the organizations are always so grateful for their volunteers, so that they are especially patient and make sure their volunteers are happy and comfortable. Check out the many volunteer options in the volunteer entries of this book to find one that is a good fit for you.

做义工：通过帮助他人来结识新朋友

众所周知，改善心情和情绪的最好方法之一就是帮助别人。通过在社区做义工，不仅能使社区变得更加美好，而且还能广交新朋友，从中受益。在这个城市有许多义工活动的场所。事实上，温哥华给义工提供了很多有趣的机会，我们在这本书的每个月都会介绍其中的一个。有许多职位不需要很高的英语水平。之所以说做义工是结交新朋友的最好方法，是因为您是团队中的一员，只有通过在一起共事才能真正地了解他们。这些机构和组织对义工们的付出总会表示感激，他们特别友善，总是希望义工们有一个快乐和舒适的工作环境。查阅本书有关义工的条目，找到适合您的义工岗位。

Restaurant Customs and Etiquette

6月11日　　餐厅的习俗与礼仪

Types of Menus and Specials

When the hostess takes you to your table, she will leave you with a menu to look at until your server arrives to greet you. Sometimes you will also receive other menus for specials, drinks and so on. Here are some of the menus that you might receive:

- **Standard Menu:** This will list their regular selection of food and will be organized into different sections depending on the type of food it is or whether it is meant to be eaten during the first, second or third course.

- **Specials Menu:** "Specials menu" that lists new items that are available in the restaurant for a short period of time. Sometimes the specials are related to a seasonal food such as spot prawns, or sometimes they are related to a special holiday such as Thanksgiving Day. The specials menu can be a printed menu or it can be written up on a blackboard on the wall.

- **Drinks Menu:** There will be a drinks menu left on the table as well. This will list the beer, cocktails, wine, and other alcoholic choices available.

- **Wine List:** If it is a more expensive restaurant, there will also be a separate menu for the wine. This is called a wine list.

- **Children's Menu:** Many restaurants will also have a separate children's menu that has foods that are smaller portions and simpler flavours that children like to eat such as chicken fingers and french fries. You may have to ask for the children's menu.

- **Dessert Menu:** At the end of the meal, your server will ask you if you would like to see the dessert menu. This menu will list the desserts available as well as special coffee beverages and after dinner liqueurs.

菜单的类别及特价菜单

当迎宾员领位到您的餐桌时，她会留下一份菜单，让您先看看，等到负责您桌的服务员过来时，为您点菜。有时您还会同时看到其他特价和酒水等菜单。下面是您可能会拿到的几种菜单：

- **标准菜单**：列出餐厅大体固定的食品，并将具有各种不同口味的食物按一定的程式组合排列，或按照次序分为第一道，第二道或第三道菜，供顾客从中进行挑选。
- **特价菜单**：列出了餐厅在特定的短时间段推出的新品。有时，特价与季节性食物有关，例如：斑点虾或有时与特殊的节日有关，如感恩节。特价菜单可以是打印出来的菜单，也可以写挂在墙上的黑板中。
- **饮料单**：餐桌上还放有一张饮料单。上面列有啤酒、鸡尾酒、葡萄酒和其他含酒精的饮料。
- **餐酒单**：如果是一家比较高档的餐厅，还会有一份单独的葡萄酒单。叫做餐酒单。
- **儿童菜单**：许多餐馆专为小孩子提供儿童菜单，分量不大且口味简单，如炸鸡翅和薯条。您可能得问一下服务员是否有儿童菜单。
- **甜点菜单**： 在用餐结束时，服务员会问您是否想看看甜点菜单。此菜单通常会列出甜点以及咖啡饮料和餐后的甜酒。

Top English Programs for Adults

　　　成人高级英语课程

UBC English Language Institute (ELI)

The **UBC ELI** offers very intensive English language courses that are targeted to the different needs of adult English learners for general English or academic English. The courses take place at the beautiful UBC campus.

- *Intensive English Study (IEP):* These full-time 8 or 16-week courses will help you improve all your English skills (reading, writing, speaking and listening). Class levels include elementary to advanced.

- *English for Academic Purposes (EAP):* These full-time 8 and 16-week courses are for students who need to improve their academic English skills and confidence in order to succeed at university in North America.

不列颠哥伦比亚大学（UBC）英语语言学院（ELI）

　　UBC英语语言学院（ELI）座落在美丽的UBC校园内，提供速成英语课程，针对成年人英语学习的不同需求，可以选择普通英语或学术英语。

- **强化英语学习（IEP）**：是基于技能培训的计划，为期8或16周的全日制课程，旨在提高您的英语阅读、写作、口语和听力的能力。初级到高级共有七个级别

- **学术英语（EAP）**：为期8或16周的全日制课程，为中级到高级英语学生想要发展其学术领域的综合能力，以便在北美大学取得好的成绩。

June 13   # Vancouver Backyard Wildlife

6月13日   温哥华后院的小鸟和动物

Anna's Hummingbirds

In May 2017, residents of the city of Vancouver voted and chose Anna's Hummingbird to be the official bird of Vancouver. It will be used to help raise awareness about bird culture in Vancouver and to show how important birds are to the local ecosystem. These beautiful little birds remain in the Vancouver area all year round. In addition to eating fruit nectar, this type of hummingbird also eats insects and spiders which help them survive the long cold winters. Many residents like to put out special bird feeders with sugar water for these hummingbirds so that they can watch their amazing fast flight and beautiful feather colours.

安娜蜂鸟

蜂鸟体型小，能够以快速拍打翅膀的方式而悬停在空中。2017年5月，温哥华市民投票选出了安娜蜂鸟，作为温哥华的市鸟。 它将被用来帮助提高对温哥华鸟类文化的认识，表明鸟类对当地的生态系统是多么的重要。这些美丽的小鸟一年四季都驻留在温哥华地区。除了吃水果花蜜，也吃昆虫和蜘蛛，借以帮助他们在漫长寒冷的夜晚生存。许多居民喜欢用糖水作为鸟饲料来喂养这些蜂鸟，以观看其漂亮的羽毛，悬停在空中和高超的飞行本领。

June 14   # Support for Newcomers

6月14日   支持新移民

Canadian Immigrant Integration Program (CIIP)

This program aims to give economic class immigrants a very thorough orientation and preparation before they actually arrive in Canada. This preparation is very effective in helping newcomers gain employment in Canada that is appropriate for their skills, credentials and experience. This program has operated since 2007 and is funded by Immigration, Refugees and Citizenship Canada.

加拿大移民融入计划（CIIP）https://www.newcomersuccess.ca/

这个计划的目的是让技术类移民在到达加拿大之前就有一个非常明确的定位和心理准备。这种准备非常有效，它可以帮助新来者能够在加拿大找到适合他们技能、资历和经验的就业机会。该计划自2007年开始运作，由加拿大移民、难民和公民部资助。

Vancouver Neighbourhoods

6月15日   温哥华社区

Dunbar

As I grew up in the Dunbar neighbourhood, and Yi also lives here with his family, we have very fond feelings for this beautiful and peaceful part of town. Dunbar is located on the west side of Vancouver bordered by West16th Ave to the north and West 41st Ave to the south, Pacific Spirit Park to the west and Blenheim Street to the east. It is a quiet and safe neighbourhood full of single family homes, parks, golf courses, and lovely gardens. The Dunbar Residents' Association (DRA) is a group of local volunteers who actively work to keep it a wonderful place to live. They are responsible for organizing the volunteer Dunbar Community Patrol to keep the area safe and the Salmonberry Days Festival to encourage community spirit. Another great organization working in the Dunbar area is the Dunbar Village Business Association (DVBA) which organizes popular special events including the Dunbar Village Harvest Festival and Dunbar Village for the Holidays. Along Dunbar street, there are many great businesses to visit including: restaurants, coffee shops, bookshops, pet supplies, groceries, clothing shops, bakeries, and even a movie theatre!

邓巴

当我在邓巴社区长大，易和他的家人也住在那里，我们对这个美丽而宁静的城镇片区，有着非常喜爱的感觉。邓巴位于温哥华西部，毗邻西十六大街北部，南接西41大街，西面为太平洋精神地区公园，东面为布伦海姆街。它是一个安静且安全的社区，布满了独立屋，公园，高尔夫球场和美丽的花园。该区还有许多优秀的公立和私立学校。邓巴居民协会（DRA）是一群当地志愿者，积极致力于维持居住地的美好。他们负责组织志愿者邓巴社区巡逻队，保持社区安全并以"鲑莓节"节日活动鼓舞社区精神。在邓巴社区的另一个伟大的组织是邓巴村商业协会（DVBA），组织了诸如邓巴村庄丰收节和邓巴村假期等受欢迎的特别活动。DVBA还出版了一本名为"邓巴生活"的日常杂志，借以更新居民们在该社区发生的所有令人兴奋的活动。沿邓巴街，有很多优秀的商业可以参观：包括餐馆，咖啡店，书店，宠物用品，杂货，服装店，面包店甚至电影院！

Basic Everyday English

6月16日 　　基本日常生活用语

Make an Invitation to a New Friend

Perhaps when you saw this category, you thought "No Way!!" I am not going to make any invitations to people or talk to new people until my English is good enough. However, it is difficult to improve English without practicing by talking to people! Remember that Canada, and especially Vancouver, is a city of immigrants and the local people are very used to hearing English spoken in different ways and with different accents and it is completely fine. Also, everyone loves to receive an invitation and know that someone is interested in talking to them. If you make English mistakes when you speak with them – who cares? Just smile and continue! Taking a chance with a new friend can make your life happier in your new country.

> *"Stop being afraid of what could go wrong, and start being excited of what could go right!"*
>
> *-Tony Robbins*

向新朋友发出邀请

当您看到这个类别时，您也许会想 "我做不到！"等我英语足够好的时候，我再向别人发出邀请或者与陌生人交谈。然而，如果不与人交谈，要想提高英语水平是很困难的！请记住，加拿大，特别是温哥华，是一座移民城市，当地人非常习惯于听到以不同的方式和带有不同的口音讲的英语。这根本没有问题。此外，每个人都喜欢收到别人的邀请，并且很高兴得知某人有兴趣与他们交谈。如果您与他们说话时犯了英文错误 – 谁又会在乎呢？笑一笑，然后继续聊下去！在新的国度结交新的朋友会使您的生活更加幸福美满。

"不要害怕出什么问题，即将发生的事情会让人感到无比兴奋！"
——托尼 •罗宾斯

English for Everyday Life
日常生活英语

下面是一些基本英语短语，您也许听到过，您可以用它们来邀请新的朋友。. 请访问我们的网站www.mynewlifeinvancouver.com，听一听这些短语的发音并练习会话。

Would you like to join me for coffee?
Can I take you to lunch?
I would like to treat you to dinner.
I would like to invite you to our home for dinner.
I was wondering if you'd like to get together some time?
I would like to get to know you better

您愿意和我一起喝咖啡吗？
我可以带您去吃午饭吗？
我想请您吃晚饭。
我想邀请您到我们家吃饭。
我想知道您是否愿意在某个时间聚聚？
我想更好地了解您。

Education

教育

Alternative High School Programs

There are three different kinds of alternative high schools available in Vancouver: Mini Schools, International Baccalaureate (IB) and the TREK Outdoor Education Program. All three programs are very popular and many more students apply than can be accepted. Here is a brief description of each of the alternative high school programs available in Vancouver:

- The **Mini School** programs provide opportunities for enrichment for students who are Vancouver residents and consistently achieve B averages or higher, who are highly motivated students and who would benefit from a learning environment with highly motivated peers. Acceptance is based on test marks, Gr. 7 report cards, applications and interviews. Several high schools in Vancouver have Mini Schools.

- The **International Baccalaureate** is a two-year program (grades 11 - 12) with the highly recommended option of a pre-I.B. year in grade 10. The program is open to students with good academic standing and good reading and verbal skills. This program, with a more global outlook, focuses on the enrichment and learning skills necessary for post-secondary success. In recognition of their enhanced content and nature, extra graduation credits are granted for most I.B. courses. Candidates for the I.B. diploma are required to become involved in extra-curricular activities and community service. This program is only offered at two high schools in Vancouver.

- The **TREK** Program combines an enriched education with wilderness adventures and education about environmental sustainability. The students are provided with comprehensive instruction in the safe and proper means of participating in outdoor wilderness activities such as hiking and canoeing, to give students the basis for a lifetime of outdoor adventure. The purpose of the TREK Program is to provide experiences that help students learn about themselves. Their aim is to enable students to make wise choices, take action and take personal responsibility for who they become.

替代高中课程：迷你小学，国际文凭（IB）和TREK户外教育课程

有关这些课程更为详细的信息，请访问温哥华教育局网站：www.vsb.bc.ca

在温哥华有三种不同类型的替代高中课程：迷你学校，国际文凭（IB）和徒步户外教育。 所有三个课程都非常受欢迎，申请这三种类型的人数远远大于被录取的。以下是温哥华可供选择高中课程的简要说明：

- **迷你学校**课程为温哥华居民的子女提供丰富的机会，对于那些积极上进，平均水平一直保持在B或更高的学生，将受益于具有高度积极性的同龄学生的学习环境。 录取是基于考试成绩、7级报告卡、申请和面试。温哥华有几所高中都设有这样的迷你学校。
- **国际文凭**是一个为期两年的课程（11 - 12年级），强烈推荐10年级的学生作为可选的预科IB课程。该课程对那些具有良好的学术水平、阅读和口语表达能力的学生开放。该课程着眼于更广阔的全球视野，包括对语言、人文科学、实验科学和数学的重视。更加侧重于中学后教育并成功掌握必要的学习技巧。为了鼓励该课程强化的内容和性质，授予大多数I.B.培训班额外的毕业学分。要获得IB文凭还需要参加课外活动和社区服务。该课程计划仅限于符合其标准的学生，并且仅限于温哥华的两所中学。
- **TREK长途跋涉计划**将丰富的教育与野外冒险和关于环境可持续性的教育相结合。为学生提供全面的教育，以安全和正确的方式参加野外活动，如远足和划独木舟，给学生未来打下坚实的户外探险的基础。 TREK计划的基本目的是提供经历，帮助学生了解自己。他们的目标是让学生遇到问题的时候可以做出明智的选择，并开始行动，勇于承担个人责任，最终把梦想变成现实，TREK计划仅限于威尔士王子高中。

June 18   ## Scenes from Daily Life

6月18日   日常生活中的一些镜头

Family Bike Ride on Safe Bike Paths
家人在安全的自行车道上骑车

Outdoor Life in Vancouver

6月19日   温哥华户外生活

Play Basketball Outside

"Shooting hoops", the slang expression for playing basketball is very popular in the city, especially with younger people. Most of the community centres have indoor basketball courts with special drop-in times for people who want to come play, but they charge a small fee. As an alternative, there are many excellent basketball courts outside that are free and open to anyone on a first come, first serve basis. Most high schools have outdoor basketball hoops that you can use – just bring your own basketball and play! Also, some of the parks have basketball courts that are open for public play as well. The city of Vancouver maintains a directory of all the outdoor basketball courts in the parks.

室外篮球场

温哥华市公园室外篮球场目录www.vancouver.ca

　　"投篮"这个俚语在城市里很流行，尤其是年轻人。大多数社区中心都有室内篮球场，专门为喜欢打球的人设置的，但要收取少量的费用。除了室内球场，还有许多不错的室外篮球场，都是免费的，本着先到先得的原则。大多数中学都有室外篮球筐，您可以随意使用 – 只要带上您自己的篮球就可以玩了！此外，有些公园也有供公众玩耍的篮球场。温哥华市网站列出了公园所有室外的篮球场。

June 20   Tips to Learning English

6月20日   资深英语老师提供学习英语的小贴士

The Power of Baby Steps

I think the two words that I say the most to my students are **"baby steps"**. I remind them that the best way, in fact the only way, to really learn English is to do mini study or practice sessions every day. That these tiny progress steps – or baby steps as the saying goes in English – are guaranteed to get you to your goal, although probably not at as fast a rate as you would like. In fact, researchers have studied the most successful study techniques and they have discovered that when we're picking up a new skill or learning something entirely new, it is not helpful to spend large periods of time obsessively working on it. The best results come from spreading out learning, also known as **_distributed practice_**. A review of studies in Psychological Science in the Public Interest found that spreading out learning is far more effective than cramming (a slang English expression to describe the process of trying to memorize large amounts of information to prepare for an exam). Distributed practice is an old technique, but it works well for the busy lives most of us lead. Instead of sitting down for hours at a time to learn English, distributed practice is all about shorter, smaller daily sessions where you're stimulating the brain more often throughout time.

婴儿学步的力量

我对我的学生说的最多的就是"婴儿""学步"这两个词。我常提醒他们，这是最好的，也是唯一的学习方式，真正学好英语其实就是每天进行迷您学习或练习。这些微小的进展 － 按照英语俗语的说法就是"baby steps"（蹒跚学步）－ 保证让您实现目标，虽然可能没有您想要的那么快的速度。事实上，研究人员研究出了最成功的学习方法，他们发现，当我们学习一门新的技能或学习某种全新的东西时，花费大量的时间度过地学习效果并不好。正确的方法是采用分散式学习，又称为分布式学习方式。公众利益的心理科学研究结果发现，分散式学习比死记硬背更有效（cramming ，是英语的俚语"临时抱佛脚"，用它来描述那些，为了应付考试而试图记住大量信息的过程）。分布式练习是一种古老的技术，但它很适合我们大多数整天忙忙碌碌生活的人们。分布式学习不是让您一坐下来就学上数个小时，它是利用更短的时间，更频繁地刺激您的大脑。

<table>
<tr><td>**June 21**</td><td># A Little Canadian Inspiration</td></tr>
<tr><td>6月21日</td><td>一点点启示</td></tr>
</table>

"Life is challenging, and I'd say that there is no single guidebook – but there's about a million guidebooks out there. All people have been doing since the dawn of time is trying to figure out how to live this life and be happy."

– Will Arnett, Canadian actor

No one has the answer as to what will make you happy in life except yourself. What is in your guidebook for happiness in Vancouver?

"生活是充满挑战的，我想说的是，虽然没有哪一本书可以解决所有的问题，但是当你读书破万卷的时候，总会找到答案的。黎明到来的时候，人们将会搞明白如何快乐的生活。

——加拿大演员威尔·阿奈特

除了你自己，没有人知道什么会使你快乐。指南给您在温哥华的生活带来那些快乐？

June 22   Volunteer in Vancouver

6月22日   在温哥华做义工

Library Champions Project (LCP)

The Library Champions Project (LCP) is looking for newcomers who are a permanent resident, but not yet a Canadian citizen. You must be 19 years of age or older and enthusiastic about libraries. Once you are trained, you will volunteer to share information about library and settlement resources with other newcomers. They have an excellent orientation and training program for their volunteers.

图书馆支持项目（LCP）http://newtobc.ca/newcomer-resources/

图书馆支持项目（LCP）正在寻找永久居民，但尚未入籍加拿大公民的新移民。 您必须年满19岁，对图书馆充满热情。一旦您接受培训，您将自愿与其他新移民分享有关图书馆和安家资源的信息。他们有很好的指导和培训志愿者的计划。

Healthcare in Vancouver

6月23日   温哥华的医疗保健

Drop-In Clinics

Sometimes family members have a health issue that is not serious enough to go to the emergency department at the hospital, but medical help is still needed right away. In these cases, people visit a walk-in clinic. You don't need an appointment or a family doctor to go to a walk-in clinic. Many are open in the evening and on weekends. To find a walk-in clinic near you, call the Healthlink number. You will need to present a valid BC Services Card at the clinic.

不用预约的诊所

拨打811健康咨询台，找到离您家最近的进去就可以直接看病的诊所（有普通话服务的）。

有时，家庭某个成员出现健康问题，还没有严重到非要去医院看急诊的程度，但仍然需要马上接受治疗，如果正好是晚上或者赶上周末，家庭医生休息，无法预约。在这种情况下，人们会去那种不用预约直接进去就可以看病的诊所。要想找到离您最近的，请拨打健康咨询台。到了诊所您需要出示有效的BC医疗卡。

Stanley Park Bigger than New York City's Central Park

Vancouver's beloved Stanley Park is 10% bigger than New York City's Central Park. The park is over 1,000 acres and is surrounded by the more than 100-year old Vancouver Seawall. The seawall attracts thousands of visitors every day to go running, walking and cycling on the waterfront pathway with very scenic views. In 2014, TripAdvisor named Stanley Park the "top park in the entire world."

Archaeologists have found evidence to show that First Nations people resided in the park dating back more than 3,000 years. The area is the traditional territory of the Coast Salish indigenous people.

温哥华斯坦利公园甚至比纽约市的中央公园还要大

受温哥华人喜爱的斯坦利公园面积比纽约市的中央公园大10%。公园占地1000多英亩，周围的海堤已建有100多年。海堤每天都吸引着成千上万的游客前来跑步、散步、骑车或享受美景。2014年，TripAdvisor把史丹利公园评为"全球最顶级的公园"。

考古学家发现的证据表明，第一批居住在公园里的原住民可以追溯到3000多年前。该地区是萨利希土著族的传统领地。

Finding Work in Vancouver

6月25日   在温哥华找份工作

Immigrant Services Society of BC (ISSBC)

ISSBC provides a variety of support services for immigrants and refugees to help them get settled, find careers and get the information and education they need to start their new life in Canada. They understand that finding work is an important factor in the success of a new immigrant, so they have many programs, courses and career services to help newcomers take that big step into employment.

BC省移民服务协会（ISSBC）https://issbc.org/

BC省移民服务协会为移民和难民提供各种支持服务，帮助他们定居，找工作，并获得他们在加拿大开始新生活所需的信息和教育。他们明白，找工作是新移民成功的一个重要因素，因此他们有许多计划方案、课程和职业服务，帮助新移民迈出就业这关键的一步。

June 26	# Vancouver Sightseeing
6月26日	观光

Whistler, Victoria, and Gulf Islands Daytrips

Even though there are so many sights to see in Vancouver, sometimes it is nice to get out of the city and explore different places.

- Going to visit the capital city of British Columbia, **Victoria**, is a wonderful way to spend a day. The city is not very large, yet there are many historical sites and gardens to visit there including the parliament buildings and Butchart Gardens.

- Visiting the famous mountain town of **Whistler** is also a popular year-round daytrip. Whether you go to Whistler to ski in the winter or go to ride bicycles, hike and swim in the lakes in the summer, it is always a charming place to visit.

- Finally, there are many small **Gulf Islands** close to Vancouver. One of the most popular ones to visit is Saltspring Island which is known for its artistic community and its high-quality food markets and restaurants.

温哥华一日游：惠斯勒，维多利亚，海湾群岛

惠斯勒https://www.whistler.com/
维多利亚 http://www.tourismvictoria.com/
海湾群岛http://gulfislandstourism.com/

即使在温哥华有这么多迷人的景点，有时人们还是愿意离开这个城市，去不同的地方走走看看。

- 不列颠哥伦比亚省首府，维多利亚，是一个值得花上一天游玩的好地方。 这座城市不是很大，但却拥有许多历史遗址和花园，包括议会大厦和布查德花园，又名宝翠花园。
- 惠斯勒是著名的山镇，同时它也是闻名世界的滑雪胜地。一年四季都可以去那里一日游。 无论您是在冬天去滑雪，还是在夏天骑自行车，徒步旅行或者在湖里游泳，它总是能给人留下美好回忆的地方。
- 最后，温哥华附近有许多小的海湾群岛。 其中最受欢迎的是盐泉海岛，岛上有著名的艺术社区和高品质食品市场和餐馆。

June 27   Vancouver Transportation

6月27日   温哥华交通运输

Small Ferries in False Creek

The most enjoyable and easy way to commute to all destinations around False Creek such as the Olympic Village, Yaletown, Granville Island, West End, South False Creek, Science World and so on is to take one of the cute little ferries that have regular routes throughout the harbour. They provide frequent, daily passenger ferry service to all major destinations in False Creek and all boats are wheelchair, bicycle, pet and stroller friendly.

You can pay for a single ticket ($3.25), buy a book of tickets or a monthly pass ($60). Their websites show the full details of the routes and schedules.

福溪小渡轮

格兰威尔岛渡轮 http://www.granvilleislandferries.bc.ca/
水上巴士 http://theaquabus.com/

通往福溪周围的所有目的地，如奥林匹克村、耶鲁镇、格兰维尔岛、西区、南弗斯克里克和科学世界等地，最方便和最快捷的方式是在该港口乘坐一条固定航线可爱的小渡轮。它们每天为从福溪港口开往所有主要目的地，提供频繁的客运渡轮服务，所有船只都允许轮椅，自行车，宠物和婴儿车随行。

您可以购买单程票（＄3.25）、本票或月票（$60）。他们的网站列出了航线和时间表等全部细节

Sports Teams and Special Events

6月28日　　　专业体育赛事和活动

BMO Vancouver International Marathon

The BMO Vancouver Marathon is an annual race held on the first Sunday of May each year in Vancouver. It is the largest international marathon event in Canada and includes a wheelchair division, half-marathon, an 8k run, and a kids' 1k run, as well as a family-friendly street festival for runners and spectators. Canadian Running Magazine called the marathon one of the best "anywhere in the world" for its beautiful course, which takes in "...the most spectacular of Vancouver's running routes — through UBC campus, Point Grey and the most beautiful final 10K of any marathon, along Stanley Park's Seawall."

*BMO 温哥华国际马拉松赛*http://bmovanmarathon.ca/

　　一年一度的BMO温哥华马拉松竞赛是每年5月的第一个星期天在加拿大不列颠哥伦比亚省的温哥华举行。 它是加拿大最大的国际马拉松赛事，还包括轮椅、半程马拉松、8公里赛跑和儿童1公里赛跑，以及为运动员和观众举办的家庭友好街道节。 加拿大跑步杂志称BMO温哥华马拉松是"世界上最美也是最壮观的长跑路线"，它途经UBC校园和灰点，最后的10公里路线是沿着史丹利公园的海堤奔跑，这也许是任何马拉松赛都无法比拟的。

　　# Vancouver Parks

6月29日　　温哥华公园

Pacific Spirit Regional Park

Pacific Spirit Regional Park is a hiker's paradise located in the western part of the city by the University of British Columbia. There's over 54 kilometres (34 miles) of walking/hiking trails, with a mix of forest and waterfront trails. There are large areas of forest in the park, and an easy loop trail will allow you to take a three-hour hike through much of it. However, there are many smaller trails for those looking for a shorter hike. In addition, 38 kilometers of the park's trails are open to multi-use so they are available for cycling and horseback riding.

For those who dare, there is a clothing-optional beach (nude beach) called Wreck Beach located on the western edge of the park!

太平洋精神公园

　　太平洋精神公园是徒步旅行者的天堂。它位于城市西部的英属哥伦比亚大学。有超过54公里（34英里）的森林和海滨相混合的步道。园内有超过750公顷的原始森林，和一个简单的循环步道，要想徒步走遍大部分路径，你至少需要花上三个小时。当然，园内还有许多较短的小径可供选择。此外，38公里的公园步道是多用途的，除了健走以外还可用于骑车和骑马。

　　对于那些喜欢裸晒的人来说，位于公园西部尽头，有一个可选择不穿衣物的沉船沙滩（裸体沙滩）

Stories and Advice for Newcomers

移民的故事和建议

Bob

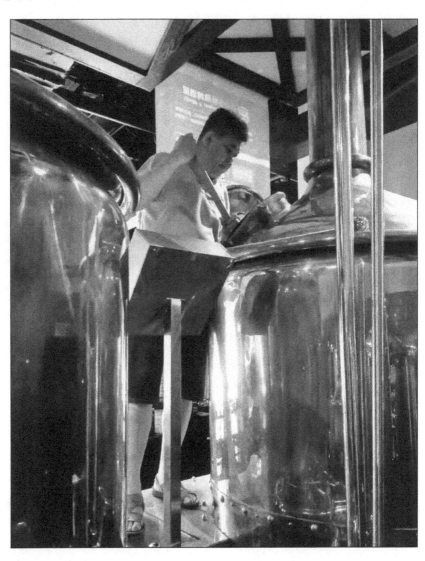

发挥自己已有优势，敢于尝试，就会有成功的机会！

我叫杨波，英文名字Bob，2014年我携妻子，女儿移民加拿大。我的故乡哈尔滨坐落于中国的北方，是中国屈指可数的一座时尚浪漫的国际都市。它的气候特点是四季分明。也许由于哈尔滨独特历史和气候的因素，哈尔滨人也以豪爽、纯朴、耿直和好客的性格而闻名于全中国。我从小生于此处，长于此处，自然也传承了此种性格特点。1993年大学毕业我就开始从事对俄贸易，从而积累了丰富的经验，2000年初到俄销售啤酒设备，成为中国在俄销售啤酒设备的第一人，2003首家中俄合资的啤酒厂在海参崴成立，现在俄全境已销售35家啤酒设备。基于以上经验，2014年由我全程设计并投资的"马迭尔精酿啤酒屋"在中国哈尔滨最著名的中央大街开业，正式营业至今，啤酒一直好评如潮且销量非常好，甚至在旺季出现供不应求的现象。移民加拿大后，我一度也困惑，该如何融入这个崭新的国度，该如何在这里实现我的价值，最后通过对这里的调查和了解，在一些志同道合的朋友的帮助下，我得知BC省是整个加拿大精酿啤酒的发源地，精酿啤酒需求量很大，正在蓬勃发展，所以通过多方的考证和努力我决定在温哥华开设小型自酿啤酒厂，命名为Vancouver B Brewing，截止到发稿的时候，我们的厂址已选定，并且工厂的设计图纸已完成，届时我会动用我国内和美国的安装技术，打造一个全新的自酿啤酒厂，奉献给我的第二故乡－温哥华的市民！

我给新移民的心得体会是：发挥自己已有优势，敢于尝试，就会有成功的机会！

July

Weather:	Average temperature: 14°C to 23°C
	Average rainfall days: 10, Average rainfall: 20 mm
Statutory holiday:	Canada Day July 1
Other special days:	USA birthday July 4

The month of July begins joyfully with a long weekend, parties and fireworks to celebrate Canada's birthday. Big outdoor celebrations with concerts and fireworks happen at Canada Place, Granville Island in Vancouver and in Richmond at the Steveston Salmon Fest and Canada Day celebration.

Many Canadians also enjoy going south of the border on July 4 to join in all the amazing celebrations and fireworks organized by Americans to celebrate their country's birthday.

Doing business and work is the last thing on Vancouverites' mind in July and the pace of life slows down to match the high temperatures. The children are all on vacation from school, the days are long and bright and hot and many employees take their annual vacation now. The beaches, parks, outdoor pools and restaurant and café patios are full as people spend as much time outdoors as they can. Backyard barbecue parties are very popular where people invite their friends over to enjoy typical summer foods such as grilled hot dogs, hamburgers, potato salad, BC corn on the cob and fresh watermelon slices.

The Celebration of Light fireworks show lights up the sky over English Bay for three nights in July and August. This international show features fireworks companies from different countries competing with amazing firework shows set to music. The best viewing sites are from the beaches and parks surrounding English Bay or from a Fireworks boat cruise.

The colourful rainbow pride flag flies high during the Vancouver Pride Parade and Festival that takes place every July/August. The very popular parade features colourful floats*, bands, community groups, politicians, and dancers and goes along downtown streets lined with hundreds of thousands of people that come out to celebrate and support Vancouver's lesbian, gay, bisexual and transgender (LGBT) community.

On the west side of Vancouver, in the Southlands* neighbourhood, another way to spend a sunny July day is to witness the sport of kings and watch the Pacific Polo* Cup matches in an elegant setting. The well-dressed crowds to this event are served the best champagne and the finest food as they enjoy this very special event at the Southlands Riding Club.

For a more casual mood, the Marpole neighbourhood celebrates summer in July with their annual Marpole Summerfest event with sidewalk sales and store promotions, musicians and balloon artists, face painters and juggling shows, street chalk murals, and a classic car Show 'n Shine.

7月

> 气候： 平均气温：14°C 到23°C
> 平均降雨天数：10，平均降雨量：20毫米
>
> 公众节假日： 加拿大国庆日7月1日
>
> 其他特殊日： 美国独立日7月4日

七月始于一个快乐的长周末，每年的七月一日是加拿大的国庆节，这一天大家聚集到加拿大广场共同庆祝加拿大的生日，广场上举行大型户外音乐会，傍晚燃放烟花。庆祝模式随地区而异，温哥华的格兰威尔岛和里士满的渔人码头分别举办三文鱼节等庆祝活动。

许多加拿大人也喜欢在7月4日这一天南下到美加边境去参加各项热闹的庆祝活动，观看由美国人放的烟火来庆祝他们的独立日。

七月份当地民众心里最不想做的事情就是做生意和工作。他们会放慢生活节奏以适应高温天气。孩子们都在度假，白天很长，天气很热，很多员工会把他们的年度假期用在这个时候。在海滩、公园、室外游泳池、餐厅和咖啡馆外面到处都挤满了打发时间的人群。邀请朋友们在自家后院烧烤聚会也是常见的。每年的这个时候邀请朋友到家里享受典型的夏季食品如烤热狗、汉堡包、土豆沙拉、BC省玉米和新鲜的西瓜。

每年七月底至八月初的三个晚上，在英吉利海湾举办国际烟花表演，由来自三个不同国家的烟花代表队同台竞技。在欣赏令人眼花缭乱的烟花表演的同时还可以听到悦耳的背景音乐。最佳观赏地点是英吉利海湾周围的海滩和公园或乘小船在烟花船附近观看。

每年七、八月份温哥华都会举行同性恋大游行。多彩的彩虹旗高高的飘荡在温哥华的上空，同志们装扮着五颜六色的花车沿着繁华的街道巡游、有乐队、社区团体、政客、演员助兴，街道两边挤满了成千上万的人住脚观看，并为他们支持的女同性恋、男同性恋、双性恋和变性(LGBT)群体呐喊。

在阳光明媚的七月，温哥华西区，南部地区马术俱乐部也是一个度假的好去处。在那个环境优雅的地方观看并见证"国王"的运动 – 争夺太平洋马球杯，共有两场赛事。凡来这里的人，个个衣冠楚楚，他们品着最好的香槟酒和美味的食物。

马珀尔社区每年七月举办的夏日狂欢活动似乎更加随意，商贩们直接在人行道上销售他们的商品，店内搞促销活动。音乐家、气球艺术家、杂耍表演、脸谱画家和街头粉笔画家各展绝技，闪闪发光的老爷车展，烘托着暖暖的夏日。

更多的信息：

加拿大国庆日官方网站：www.canadaday.gc.ca

加拿大广场国庆日：

https://www.canadaplace.ca/events/canada-day/

格兰维尔岛加拿大国庆日：

http://granvilleisland.com/canada-day

渔人码头三文鱼节和加拿大国庆日的庆祝活动：

http://stevestonsalmonfest.ca/

国际烟花爆竹比赛庆祝活动：

http://hondacelebrationoflight.com/

太平洋马球杯：http://www.pacificpolocup.com/

温哥华同性恋大游行：http://www.vancouverpride.ca/

马珀尔夏日狂欢节：www.marpoleonline.com/summerfest/

*Southlands南国马术俱乐部：位于温哥华西南海滨地区，有许多驯马，养马的基地（马厩、马术俱乐部、河流等等），还有供游人散步，骑马的小径，感觉就像是"城市里的乡村"。

*Polo马球比赛：马球是由两只球队，各队4人，骑在马上挥动马球杆击球，以攻球入对方球门为目的的团体竞赛活动.

*Parade Float游行花车：是把一辆卡车装饰成一个平台或卡车后面拖挂一个装饰的平台，这是许多节日游行的一部分。

July 1   Local Customs

7月1日   当地的习俗

Celebration of Happy News

The four most common ways for locals to express their congratulations about happy news are:

1. Saying a simple "congratulations" and shaking hands with them
2. Giving them a special greeting card with the appropriate message
3. Giving them a bouquet of flowers
4. Taking them out for a celebration dinner

Depending on how close our relationship with the person is, we decide whether we simply say congratulations, or we give them a card, or flowers or take them out to dinner to celebrate. We only take people out for a celebratory dinner if they are close friends. We choose the restaurant, make the invitation, make a small toast of congratulations at dinner and pay the bill.

Greeting Cards

Dollar stores, stationary stores, and pharmacies all have big greeting card displays. The card racks are divided up into many different sections: Birthday cards, get well cards, thank you cards, congratulation on new job/home/baby cards, wedding cards, sympathy cards and so on. They have nice messages printed in the inside. Most people will also write an additional small personal message and sign their name on the bottom of the card, but it is also acceptable to just sign your name at the bottom.

欢庆喜讯（第一份工作，开业，晋升等）

当得知某人取得成就时，当地人有四种表达祝贺的方式。这四种方式是：

> 1. 简单的说一声 "恭喜" 并与他/她握握手；
> 2. 送给他/她一张特别的贺卡，上面附有适当的贺词；
> 3. 送一束鲜花；
> 4. 约出去吃庆祝晚宴。

根据我们与这个人关系的密切程度，来决定我们是否只是说声恭喜、送卡、送花还是约他/她出去吃饭。如果我们和他/她的关系非同一般，那么我们不仅仅一起去吃饭。我们还会做东、选择餐厅、发出邀请、在晚宴上发表祝酒词，最后支付账单。

English for Everyday Life
日常生活英语

下面是一句简单的举杯敬酒祝贺的例子:

"Here is a toast to Susan - congratulations on your new job/business/promotion"
"这是为苏珊干杯 - 祝贺您获得新的工作/生意/晋升"
然后所有的客人一起碰杯并说
"To Susan" （为苏珊干杯）。

贺卡

一元店、文具店和药房都有大量贺卡展示。卡架按类别分为许多不同的区域：有生日贺卡、康复卡、感谢卡、婚礼卡、同情卡和祝贺新工作/新家庭/新生婴儿卡等等。里面印有许多温馨的祝福语。大多数人还会额外添上几句个人的祝语，并在卡的底部签上他们的名字，当然，只是简单的在卡的底部签上您的名字也是可以的。

Parenting in Vancouver

在温哥华养育子女

Household Chores and Allowances

When children are old enough, they are expected to do some small tasks in the home to help the family. Some examples of these household chores include: Taking out the garbage, feeding the pets and tidying up their own bedroom. Some parents give their children a small amount of money called **an allowance** each week in exchange for helping. The children can use their allowance money any way they want. They can spend it on candy or a toy or they can save it. The amount of money a child gets depends on how old they are, for example 5 yr. old children might get $2 per week and teenagers might get $20 or more per week. However, allowances are a controversial issue. Some parents don't believe that children should be paid for household chores as it should be part of their duty to the family. Each family makes their own decision about allowances.

家务劳动和津贴

大一点儿的孩子会在家里帮助大人做一些小工。这些家务包括：倒垃圾，喂养宠物和整理他们自己的卧室。有些家长每周给孩子一小笔钱称为津贴，以换取帮助家务。孩子们可以支配自己的津贴。可以购买糖果或玩具，或者把它们存起来。孩子得到的钱数取决于他们的年龄，例如5岁每周可能得到2美元，而青少年每周可能得到20美元或更多。然而，津贴是一个有争议的问题。有些家长不认为儿童做家务就应该得到津贴，因为这是他们对家庭责任的一部分。当然，至于津贴的多少由每个家庭自己来决定。

Stories and Advice for Newcomers

新移民的故事

Karen

我在温哥华的第一年

时间过得真快，一转眼来到这个多元文化的城市已经3年了。回想起温哥华的第一年，有时觉得应该享受当下的生活，因为这里的自然环境好，既有雪山、森林、又有蓝天、碧海，春日有美丽的樱花，夏天有蔚蓝的大海，秋天有火红的枫叶，冬天银白的雪山，温哥华的风景美轮美奂。每天晚上出去散散步，吸着新鲜的空气。出门大概走20分钟即可到达海边，沿海边行走，海水在夕阳的映照下显得格外的美！站在沙滩上眺望远处的雪山，顿觉得天地辽阔，风光无限。偶尔又觉得自己像海里的浮木，随波逐流，找不到属于自己的目标和方向。此时的心情又特别忧愁，不是为了自己，而是为了我的宝贝女儿们，就怕她们来到这个陌生的国度一切都不习惯！没有想到优秀的她们来到了温哥华后依然很优秀，我和我老公豪不怀疑她们将来会进入加拿大最好的大学，读她们喜欢的专业。

生活在温哥我还是比较幸运的，第一次通过驾照考试，很快也收到去VCC读语言的通知。虽然我是比较幸运的，但是我也有很多担忧，放弃在国内的优越生活，到一个几乎完全陌生的国家生活对我来说语言确实是一大障碍。进入学校读书是学习语言的一个最好的途径，也是加拿大政府给新移民一次免费上学的机会，在学语言的同时也可以去做义工或工作，这样就会有一个语言环境，逼着自己去开口讲英语，熟悉当地的语言习惯，口音，表达方式和文化，另外去各部门办事，比如到银行办理业务，借此增加语言实战的机会，尽快提高自己的英语水平。融入到这个多元文化的移民国家，可以展现自我！

Vancouver Entertainment

温哥华娱乐

Exclusive and Private Member Clubs

Vancouver has several private clubs that are for the exclusive use of members and their guests. These high-end members-only clubs are in beautiful buildings with meeting rooms, banquet rooms and private lounges and areas for the members to enjoy and entertain their clients and friends. To join these clubs, you must pay an initial entrance fee of several thousand dollars as well as a monthly fee to maintain the membership. Individuals, families or businesses can purchase these memberships. There is usually a long waiting list of applicants to join these clubs, and not all applicants are accepted for membership. They must be approved by a membership committee. Once you are a member, however, these clubs can feel like a second home and the club staff will make every effort to take care of you and your guests with the best possible service and in very luxurious surroundings.

The **Vancouver Club** and the **Terminal City Club** are both located in the business district and cater to the needs and entertainment of working professionals and their guests. Members can start their day at the fitness centre, meet their clients in the private meeting rooms and then relax in the evening with a drink in the lounge. Weddings and other large special events can also be accommodated in these beautiful heritage buildings.

The **University Women's Club of Vancouver at Hycroft Manor**. This private member club is only for professional, educated women. The club is in a beautiful Edwardian mansion in Shaughnessy. The club provides a warm and welcoming space for women to connect offline, engage in stimulating activities, and continue the club's legacy of promoting women's rights and education.

Vancouver has two premium private clubs that focus on recreation and entertainment for families. The **Arbutus Club** is in the West side of Vancouver and the **Hollyburn Country Club** is high up on the mountainside in West Vancouver. These exclusive clubs are like a home away from home for families where they can use the private pool, tennis courts, fitness rooms, and many other facilities and then enjoy first class food and beverages in the fine dining restaurants and lounges. These clubs offer their members a place to entertain their friends and families in style. The clubs can also host weddings and other special events for the members.

Private Member Sports Clubs are another very popular category of exclusive private members' clubs which are based around popular sports. The members have exclusive access to world class sporting facilities. In addition to offering top-notch sporting facilities, these private clubs have fine dining restaurants, lounges, meeting rooms and banquet and conference rooms for weddings and other special events.

高档私人俱乐部

温哥华有几家私人俱乐部，专供会员和其客人使用。这些高端俱乐部一般位于漂亮的建筑内，有会议室，宴会厅和私人休息室。会员除了可以自己享用外，还可以招待他们的客户和朋友。 要加入这种俱乐部，您必须支付几千加元的初始入会费以及月费用来维持会员的资格。个人、家庭或企业均可以购买这种会员资格。通常是先把申请人列入等候加入俱乐部的名单，并不是所有申请者都能被接纳为会员。他们必须经过会员委员会的批准。一旦您通过了，您会发现俱乐部就像是您的第二个家，俱乐部将竭尽一切努力为您和您的客人提供最好的服务和最豪华的环境。

温哥华俱乐部和城市码头俱乐部一般都设在商务区，以方便商务人士和客人们的需求和娱乐。会员们可以在健身中心开始他们新的一天工作。白天在私人会议室里会客，晚上放松一下，在休息室里喝一杯咖啡。在这种豪华的建筑物里面还可以安排婚礼和其他大型的活动。

温哥华大学女子俱乐部设在Hycroft庄园，是肖内西社区里面的一个漂亮的爱德华豪宅。 这个私人俱乐部只接纳职业和受过良好教育的女性。该俱乐部为女性提供了一个温馨的空间，经常组织各种令人兴奋的活动，以促进妇女的权利和教育。

　　温哥华还有两个高级私人俱乐部，专注于家庭娱乐。一个是在温哥华西侧的**杨梅俱乐部**，另一个地处西温哥华山上**霍莉本乡村俱乐部**。这些高级俱乐部就像在自己家里一样，有私人游泳池，网球场，健身室等设施，运动之后在高级餐厅和休息室享用一流的美食。俱乐部为其会员按照家庭的风格提供一个款待亲朋好友的地方。俱乐部还可以为会员举办婚礼和其他特别的活动。申请者必须得到批准才能成为会员，然后他们必须缴纳入会费以及入会以后的月费。

　　私人会员体育俱乐部是另一类非常受欢迎的俱乐部，是为那些酷爱某项体育运动的人开设的。会员们可以享用世界一流的体育设施。除了提供顶级的体育设施，这些私人俱乐部设有高级餐厅，休息室，宴会厅和会议室，可以在这里安排婚礼或者其他特别活动。申请者必须支付入会费才能成为会员，并按月缴纳会费。

- 海滨高尔夫俱乐部 http://www.marine-drive.com/welcome
- 肖内西高尔夫乡村俱乐部 http://www.shaughnessy.org/
- 灰点高尔夫乡村俱乐部 http://www.pointgreygolf.com/
- 温哥华高尔夫俱乐部 http://www.vancouvergolfclub.com/
- 西摩高尔夫乡村俱乐部 http://www.seymourgolf.com/
- 卡皮拉诺高尔夫乡村俱乐部 http://capilanogolf.com/
- 杰里科网球俱乐部 https://jerichotennisclub.com/
- 温哥华草地网球和羽毛球俱乐部 http://www.vanlawn.com/
- 温哥华皇家游艇俱乐部 http://www.royalvan.com/
- 菲沙溪谷游艇俱乐部 http://fcyc.com/
- 西温哥华游艇俱乐部 https://www.wvyc.ca/
- 温哥华划船俱乐部https://www.vancouverrowingclub.ca/
- 南地马术俱乐部http://www.southlandsridingclub.com/

Best Elementary Schools

7月5日   温哥华著名的小学

Cedardale Elementary School (public)

Here is the description of the school from their website: "École Cedardale is an authorized International Baccalaureate (IB) World School offering the Primary Years Programme in a French Immersion format. These are schools that share a common philosophy—a commitment to high quality, challenging, international education that École Cedardale believes is important for our students."

Cedardale 小学（公立）

下面是学校网站的描述：

"École Cedardale是经过授权的有国际文凭（IB）国际学校，提供法语浸入式小学课程。学校有着共同的理念 – 致力于高质量、具有挑战性的国际教育的承诺，这对我们的学生说是很重要的。"

A Different Way of Thinking

不同的思维方式

Modesty is Important: Tall Poppy Syndrome

Wikipedia defines Tall Poppy Syndrome as a situation where people of high status or success are criticized because they have been labelled as being better than other people. The name of this syndrome comes from the image of a tall red poppy standing high above all the regular white flowers. It sticks out and is an easy target for envious thoughts or a belief that everything should be equal and fair and so the red flower must be cut down. Sometimes Canadian businesses that are very successful will find that their every move is examined and criticized instead of supported. Some say that the reason for this attitude is due to the Tall Poppy Syndrome. Also, in a workplace or school setting, if people are very successful and loudly boast about their success, then they could face quiet criticism and be disliked. However, if someone is very successful but very humble and discrete about it, while also continuing to be helpful and polite to others, then that person will receive a lot of support and encouragement. Some people claim that Canadians have this attitude as a way of proving they are different than Americans who can be quite loud about their many successes

高大罂粟花综合征

　　维基百科把高大罂粟综合症定义为一种地位高或成功的人时常受到批评，因为他们被贴上了比其他人更好的标签。这个综合症的名称来自于形象高大的红色罂粟花，它高高耸立在所有的白花之上。它很显眼，很容易成为被嫉妒的目标。持平等态度的人认为，一切都应该是平等和公平的，所以必须将粟米的红色顶部切去。比如，当加拿大的某个企业在生意场上获得巨大成功的时候，反倒会发现，他们的一举一动都会受到审查和批评，而不是支持。有人说，这种态度的原因是由于高罂粟花综合症。此外，在工作场所或学校，如果有人取得成功，大声地显摆，那么他们可能会被人讨厌和不受欢迎。但是，如果一个人非常成功，且非常谦虚和低调，同时乐于助人和彬彬有礼，那么这个人会得到大量的支持和鼓励。有些人认为这才是加拿大人特有的态度，与美国人完全不同，他们以自夸，标榜自己而闻名。

Best High Schools

　　温哥华著名的中学

Prince of Wales High School (public)

Here is the description of the school from their website: "Prince of Wales motto is "Ich Dien" (meaning "I Serve"). The Mission of Prince of Wales Secondary School is to provide a safe, supportive learning environment within a diverse school community. This community will foster self-esteem, co-operation, and mutual respect, and will allow students and staff to pursue self-discovery and excellence. Prince of Wales also offers a very well-respected Prince of Wales Mini School which is a district enrichment program. The PW Mini school was established in 1973 in order to meet the academic and social needs of highly motivated students. Prince of Wales Mini School consists of 150 students from Grade 8 to 12 (30 students in each grade). The purpose of Prince of Wales Mini School is to create a positive learning environment where students are challenged to excel in a broad range of subjects. PW also hosts the outdoor education program called TREK"

威尔士王子中学（公立）

以下是学校网站上的描述：

"威尔士王子中学的座右铭是"Ich Dien（意思是"我服务"）。我们的使命是在多元化的学校社区内提供一个安全，相互支持的学习环境。这个社区将培养自尊、合作、互助和尊重，并允许学生和员工追求自我、 追求完美。威尔士王子还提供了一个非常受人尊敬的威尔士王子迷你学校，这是一个浓缩的挑战计划。因为，那些优秀的学生需要面对更大的挑战。PW迷你学校成立于1973年，它是为了满足极有天赋的学生在学术和社会方面的需求。威尔士王子迷你学校由8至12年级的150名学生组成，每年级有30名学生。威尔士王子迷你学校的目的是创造一个积极的学习环境，让学生在广泛的学科中出类拔萃。PW还举办了名为TREK "长途跋涉"的户外教育项目。

July 8   The Homes of Vancouver

7月8日   温哥华住宅

A Modern Look with Clean Lines
线条简洁外观现代

Best Extracurricular Activities for Kids

最佳儿童课外活动

Split Second Basketball

This is the top basketball training organization in Vancouver for children and teens in Vancouver who are passionate about basketball and want to improve their skills and competitive abilities. Led by a team of coaches who are former professional players, the students learn the specific details of how to execute the fundamental skills needed to be a successful player. The Split Second team is committed to building the competence, confidence and character of their students. Previously their instruction was only available in private clubs and private schools like St. Georges and Crofton House, but now they have expanded their programs so that others can join in their Prince of Wales and Lord Byng gyms. In addition to weekly instruction, they also offer special events, tournaments, and camps.

二次分解篮球培训http://splitsecondbasketball.com/

　　这是温哥华顶尖的篮球训练机构，为那些热衷于篮球的儿童和青少年培训，希望提高他们的技能和竞争力。由前职业球员的教练执教，学生们学习如何成为一名成功球员的基本技能。二次分解团队致力于培养学生的能力、信心和素质。以前，他们的教学仅在私人俱乐部和私立学校，如圣乔治和克罗夫顿之家，现在他们扩大了他们的培训计划，以便其他人也可以在威尔士王子和劳宾健身房。除了每周的指导，他们还提供特别活动，赛事和营地。

July 10   Meeting Locals in Vancouver

7月10日   与当地人接触

How to Meet Other Single People

If you are a single newcomer to Vancouver, there are many ways that you can meet new people for dating purposes. Of course, single people are everywhere, and it is possible to meet them in your English classroom, or at the grocery store or at the park. Most nightclubs are aimed at very young people in their early twenties, so it is not common for older single people to go to nightclubs. However, if you want to be more focussed in your search for a relationship, the most popular way is to use online services that allow you to search very large databases of single people in Vancouver and contact them through the service. You can search by age, hobbies, education, and so on. When you find some people that you are interested in, then you send them a note through the service. By sending the messages through the web services, your identity and private contact information are protected and never shared. If they are interested, then the next step is to meet in a safe public place like a coffee shop. If you like each other and would like to meet again, then you can give them your personal contact information. There are many different online dating services including one for singles over 50 years old.

如何结交其他单身人士

　　如果您是单身一人来到温哥华，您可以通过各种约会方式结识新朋友。当然，单身人士随处可见，可以和他们约在英语教室，杂货店或公园见面。大多数夜总会服务的对象大多是针对二十多岁的年轻人，所以老年单身去夜总会并不常见。但是，如果您想更加专注于寻找您所希望的朋友，最受流行的方式是使用在线服务，您可以在温哥华搜索单身人士的大型数据库，并通过在线服务与他们取得联系。您可以根据年龄、爱好、教育等进行搜索。当您找到意中人时，您可通过服务站向他/她发送一则消息。通过Web服务器发送消息，您的身份和私人联系信息将受到保护，而不是全部共享。如果对方感兴趣的话，下一步就是选在一个安全的公共场所见面，比如咖啡店。如果您们喜欢彼此并且想再次见面，您可以给他/她留下您的个人联系信息。这里有两个在线约会服务网站，您可以试试，一个是标准的，另一个适用于50 岁以上的单身人士。

- www.match.com从在线约会数据库里找到兴趣相同的单身的人士
- www.ourtime.com 是50岁以上人士的在线约会数据库

Restaurant Customs and Etiquette

7月11日 餐厅的习俗与礼仪

Three Course Meal

The common way to order meals in a restaurant is in courses. Although there can be more courses during very, very special celebrations, usually there are three courses. These courses are:

The first course (also known as starters, appetizers): The first course of the meal is a small portion of warm food such as hot wings or calamari. The first course can also be a small salad or a bowl of soup.

The second course (also known as main course, entrée): The second course is the main part of the meal and will be a larger size than the first course. This course can be many different food choices, but a very common combination is for each guest to order a dish for themselves that includes one serving of meat (fish, meat, chicken), one serving of starch (potatoes, rice or pasta) and one serving of vegetables. Other entrée choices can be a large serving of pasta or a burger and french fries and so on.

The third course (desserts): This course is for sweet desserts. However, sometimes people are too full to order this course and just have a cup of coffee or tea instead. In expensive restaurants, they will also have a "cheese plate" instead of dessert.

三道菜

在餐馆里点菜的常见方法是依照上菜的顺序。除了在某些大型的庆祝活动日子里可以点很多道菜式，通常只点三道菜。上菜顺序是：

第一道菜（也称头盘，开胃菜）：第一道菜是一小盘暖胃的开胃菜，数量少，口感好，如热鸡翅或鱿鱼。 第一道菜也可以是一小份沙拉或一碗汤。

第二道菜（称为主菜，entrée）： 第二道菜是这顿饭的主要部分，比第一道菜分量大。这道菜可以有许多不同的食物组合，每个客人都可以点自己喜欢的，包括一份肉（鱼、肉、鸡），一份淀粉（土豆、米饭或意大利面），再搭配一份蔬菜。其他entrée的选择可以是一大份意大利面或汉堡包加炸薯条等等。

第三道菜（甜点）：甜品是安排在主菜之后。然而，许多人在吃完前两道菜之后就饱了，于是就点上一杯咖啡或茶来代替甜点。在高档的餐馆里，会用 "奶酪拼盘"来代替甜点。

Top English Programs for Adults

7月12日　　成人高级英语课程

Douglas College

The English Language Learning and Acquisition (ELLA) programs at Douglas College are aimed at the adult learners who would like to improve their academic English language skills to transfer into college level programs. Starting in 2017, they offer a new program of study called **Academic College English (ACE).** Their website states that the courses in this program "will improve students' ability to participate in university-level conversations, understand academic texts and discussion, and write effectively in a college environment." The ACE program has three levels with four courses in each level. Each level focuses on either "Culture and Community", "Academic Issues" or "Global issues" themes.

道格拉斯大学英语学习与习得（ELLA）

　　道格拉斯学院的英语课程是针对想要提高他们的学术英语语言能力后转入大学课程的成年学者。从2017年开始，他们提供一个新的学习计划，叫做学术英语（ACE）。该网站声明，这个计划"将提高学生参与大学阶段对话的能力，理解学术文章和讨论，并有效地在大学环境中进行写作。"ACE计划按难易程度分三个级别，每个级别都有四门课程。共有三大主题，分别是"文化和社区"、"学术问题"和"全球问题"。

July 13	Vancouver Backyard Wildlife
7月13日	温哥华后院的小鸟和动物

Black Bears

The black bear is the smallest and most common species of bear. Unlike the very dangerous Grizzly Bear found in wilderness areas far from the city, the black bear is not very aggressive and will usually retreat when it hears people. Black bears are omnivores, with their diets varying greatly depending on where they live and the time of year. They are attracted to fallen fruit and berries in back yards and will also be attracted to garbage. Black bears usually walk along quite slowly, but they can run at a surprisingly fast speed of up to 40 km/h and can climb trees very effectively. They may stand up on both legs to see farther, but this is not a sign of aggression or attack. Attacks by black bears are very, very rare. In the rare event of a black bear attack, the best thing to do is to fight back as hard as you can. The advice of "playing dead" is not a good strategy with black bears.

Black bears are more common in the backyards of houses in North and West Vancouver and in Port Coquitlam and Port Moody.

Important Safety Information:

- Remember that bears and coyotes are attracted to fruit as it has a high calorie value. Try to pick fruit as soon as it is ripe on the tree and don't let fallen fruit gather around the foot of the tree.

- If bears and coyotes get in the habit of eating fruit and garbage from your backyard, they will become more of a danger to you and your family.

黑熊

黑熊是熊科中最小和最常见的物种。与远离城市荒野地区发现的非常危险的灰熊不同，黑熊很少会无故攻击其他生物。当它听到人类的声音时通常会躲开。黑熊是杂食性动物，食物范围广泛，他们的饮食多半取决于它们的居住地和季节的变化。它们常常被居民后院掉下来的水果，浆果和垃圾所吸引。黑熊脚底扁平，行走缓慢，可是，一旦它们奔跑起来，速度惊人，每小时高达40公里。当它们遇到危险时会爬到树上。黑熊能用后肢站立和行走。不像棕熊，黑熊较喜欢吃死了的生物，因此在被黑熊攻击时，不能"装死"。最好的办法是尽可能地反击。黑熊在温哥华西北部地区以及高贵林港和穆迪港的居民后院时常可以见到。

重要的安全信息：

- 请记住，黑熊和郊狼喜欢吃水果，因为它含有很高的卡路里值。尽量在树熟的时候采摘水果，不要让它们落在树脚下。
- 如果熊和郊狼养成了在后院吃水果和垃圾的习惯，它们会对您和您的家人构成很大的威胁。

Moving Ahead Program (MAP)

Immigrating to a new country is not easy, and sometimes newcomers have many extra challenges and barriers to success. This Moving Ahead Program (MAP) provides specialized services to immigrant and refugee families (adults and youth) to help them succeed and integrate into the community. With a case-management approach, the newcomers are matched with one Case Worker who will work with them one on one.

发展计划（MAP）http://map.successbc.ca/

　　移民到一个新的国家并不容易，有时候新移民需要面临许多额外的挑战和障碍之后才会获得成功。这项发展计划通过案例管理，以客户为中心的方式，为移民和难民家庭（成人和青年）提供专项服务，以帮助他们成功地融入社会。通过案例管理方法，新移民与一名个案工作者合作，共同完成发展计划。

Vancouver Neighbourhoods

Lonsdale

Hop on the Seabus and take the short 20-minute trip over to Lower Lonsdale which is North Vancouver's oldest neighbourhood. The area extends four blocks up Lonsdale Avenue and two blocks east and west, but its heart is at Lonsdale Quay. The Lonsdale Quay Market has more than 80 unique shops and services selling everything from fresh West Coast seafood to handmade chocolates. You can also walk along the pathway to the west to find the kid-friendly Waterfront Park. In addition, you can enjoy the public art and great views of the city from the market. The Pier is another lovely venue located on the City's historic old shipyards site. The Pier offers spectacular 360-degree views of the North Shore and Vancouver skylines. The beautiful Pinnacle Hotel at The Pier is located near the Pier and the Lonsdale Quay Market. The area surrounding the Quay is full of little shops and restaurants to explore and enjoy on your daytrip.

朗斯代尔http://www.lowerlonsdale.ca/

　　乘坐海上巴士经20分钟的短途旅行，就到达了温哥华北部最古老的街区下朗斯代尔。该地区一直往北延伸到上朗斯代尔大街的四个街区，东西有两个街区，但其中心则位于朗斯代尔码头（Lonsdale Quay）。码头市场有80多家商铺，销售各种新鲜的西海岸海鲜和手工制作的巧克力。沿着通往西部的小路走走，您会看到一个适合小朋友们玩耍的海滨公园。此外，您还可以欣赏到市场上的公共艺术和城市的美景。码头还保留了一个历史悠久的多功能造船厂遗址。站在码头上，可以360度的观赏北岸和温哥华壮观的天际线美景。美丽顶峰酒店距离码头和朗斯代尔码头市场仅几步之遥。码头周边地区还有一些小商店和餐馆，您可以和亲朋好友们分享您的旅途见闻。

Basic Everyday English

At the Doctor

Vancouver has many doctors who can speak Mandarin, so this is another area where you don't need to worry too much. If you need to speak English to describe your health concerns, this is a good time to use a Mandarin/English dictionary because usually the translations of medical terms are very accurate and helpful. You can also use body language to demonstrate your symptoms.

看医生

温哥华有很多会讲普通话的医生，所以这是另一个您不必太担心的地方。如果您需要用英语讲述您的健康问题，这是使用汉英词典一个很好的机会，因为通常医学术语的翻译是非常准确的。您还可以使用肢体语言来补充说明您的症状。

English for Everyday Life
日常生活英语

下面是一些基本英语短语，您也许听到过， 在您看医生时可以用到它们。 请访问我们的网站www.mynewlifeinvancouver.com，听一听这些短语的发音并练习会话。

I need an appointment to see the doctor.
I have pain in my _____
I need medicine for _____

我需要预约看医生。
我的_____很痛
我需要治疗_____的药

July 17　　　　Education

7月17日　　教育

Getting Learning Assistance for Your Children

If your child is struggling with their homework, there is a lot of help available. The best place to start is to read the excellent advice in the Vancouver School Board's **Guide for Parents to Help Children Succeed**. It has a lot of information in Chinese on this topic as well.

Also, the **Vancouver Public Library** has prepared websites specifically for children and teens that contain information they can use to successfully complete their homework assignments.

If these self-help resources are not enough, then other options are hiring a private tutor or going to a commercial Learning Centre. The **Teachers' Tutoring Service (TTS)** is a non-profit organization started in 1983 that is run entirely by certified BC teachers who are knowledgeable about the BC curriculum and tutor all subjects at a reasonable rate. Because TTS tutors are qualified teachers, the student gets a tutor who is a trained teacher with experience teaching the BC Curriculum. As well, all TTS tutors have passed a Criminal Record Check, and follow the TTS Code of Ethics in addition to the BC Teachers Federation Code of Ethics.

为孩子获得学习帮助和辅导

VSB的家长指南帮助孩子们成功 http://vsb.bc.ca/
温哥华公共图书馆儿童帮助页面http://guides.vpl.ca/kids
温哥华公共图书馆青少年帮助页面http://guides.vpl.ca/teens
教师补习服务https://tutor.bc.ca/

如果你的孩子正在努力做家庭作业，上述网站有很多帮助。最好的开始是阅读温哥华教育局关于帮助孩子成功的指南。它有很多关于这个话题的中文信息。

此外，温哥华公共图书馆还专门为儿童和青少年准备了网页，其中包含了他们成功完成家庭作业所需的全部信息。

如果这些资源还不够的话，那么就聘请一名家教或去商业学习中心都是不错的选择。注册教师补习服务（TTS）是一个非营利性的组织，始于1983年，完全都是经过认证的BC省教师，他们了解BC省的课程，可以按照合理的节奏辅导所有科目。由于TTS提供的都是合格的教师，他们训练有素，具有教授BC课程的经验。此外，所有TTS辅导员都通过了犯罪记录检查，他们都符合BCTF道德规范和TTS伦理道德规范。

Scenes from Daily Life

7月18日　　日常生活中的一些镜头

Coffee with Friends
和朋友们一起喝咖啡

Outdoor Life in Vancouver

温哥华户外生活

Beach Volleyball

Volleyball is a popular outdoor sport to play. All it requires is a net and a ball. You can play volleyball at most beach areas, parks, and fields in Vancouver with your own equipment. However, there are many parks in Vancouver that already have permanent sand volleyball courts installed with the support poles already set up. You only need to borrow the net (free of charge) from the lifeguard when you provide a piece of identification as a deposit. However, you must bring your own ball.

Volleyball play areas are available on a first come, first served basis. Courts don't require a reservation unless you are organizing a league practice or tournament. There is no time limit for volleyball court use. From May to September, the Volleyball Court Times are from 11:30am to 8:30pm. Spanish Banks Beach and Kitsilano Beach are the most popular places to play as they both have several permanent volleyball courts.

沙滩排球

　　排球是一项非常受欢迎的户外运动。它所需要的只是一个网子和一个排球。您可以带上自己的设备在温哥华大部分海滩、公园和球场打排球。实际上，有很多公园都已经安装好了永久性的沙滩排球场，支撑网杆也已经立在那里。您只需要提供一张身份证件作为押金，就可以从救生员那里借到网子（免费的）。但是，您必须带上自己的球。

　　排球场地不需要预约，先到先得。除非您组织球队练习或打一场锦标赛，排球场使用没有时间限制。每年从5月到9月，排球场开放的时间是从上午11:30到下午8:30。西班牙海滩和基茨兰诺海滩是两个最热闹的地方，那里有好几个永久性的排球场。

Tips to Learning English

7月20日   资深英语老师提供学习英语的小贴士

Make it Fun

Many adults think that learning new skills should be done in the same way that they learned things in school when they were younger. However, you need to remember that you are now an adult and free to choose to learn English any way you want to! So, why not make it fun? There are many ways that you can make your daily mini study sessions fun and enjoyable so that you actually look forward to them instead of feeling stressed or worried about them.

让它变得有趣

许多人认为学习新的技术应该和他们年轻时在学校里学到的东西一样。然而，您需要记住，您现在是一个成年人，可以自由地选择任何您想要的学习英语的方式！那么，为什么不让它变得更加有趣呢？有很多方法，可以让您每天的迷你学习课程充满乐趣和享受，让您真正的期待他们，而不是感到压力或担心他们。

English for Everyday Life
日常生活英语

这里有一些建议，您可以尝试一下，以使学习英语更加愉快：

- *Reward Yourself*奖励自己：每次学习时都给自己一个很好的奖励。也许是一顿香甜可口的饭菜，或者花时间给朋友打个电话或只是坐在沙发上放松一下，听听您最喜欢的音乐。
- *Nice Study Area*良好的学习环境：为您的英语学习准备非常漂亮的笔和纸，让您感觉有一个非常舒适的学习区域，
- *Take Breaks*休息一下：与奖励一样重要的是休息。记住，短而频繁的学习要比长时间马拉松式的学习要好得多。所以记得休息和放松。您的学习时间不应该超过30分钟，而且至少要有10分钟的休息。

- *Use Music* 借助音乐：听，唱一首英语歌曲歌。您可以在YouTube上搜索有"英语歌词"的音乐视频，以便了解要演唱的内容。如果您不知道这些歌词是什么意思，也没关系，这是一个强大的练习发音的方式，很有乐趣！

- *Try New Foods*品尝新的食物：去一家西餐厅，饶有兴趣地点菜然后品尝新的食物。这也许将是您从错误中发现并学到您不喜欢该食物的另一个机会！

- *Enjoy Library Story Time* 享受图书馆故事时间：到公共图书馆去听听图书馆员给孩子们讲的故事，欣赏他们活泼的阅读技能，和特别推荐好的书籍。这些故事通常是非常有趣的，对所有年龄段的读者都适合。

- *Try New Local Recipes*尝试新的当地食谱：尝试在YouTube上一步一步完成烹饪的视频，并学习新的食谱。这是一个有趣同时学习新的食物和技术词汇的方式。当您完成的时候，您还可以吃到一些美味的食物，！

- *Keep it Fun and Light*让它充满乐趣时光：记住学习英语不要太认真。您会有顺心的日子和郁闷的日子。有时您会觉得英语太难了，学不进去，那么此刻，您最好停下来去做另外一件事情。学习英语最好的方法就是尽可能保持轻松和愉快。

- *You are the Boss of Your Own Learning* 你是自己学习的老板：记住您现在是老板！没有老师来烦您或惩罚您。您可以用您想要的任何有趣的或者疯狂的方式学习英语。无论您选择什么途径让您达到目标，这完全取决于您自己。感受自由，让自己充分享受这个冒险吧。

July 21 A Little Canadian Inspiration

7月21日 一点点启示

"It took cancer to realize that being self-centered is not the way to live. The answer is to try and help others."

-Terry Fox, Canadian hero*

Terry Fox inspired Canada with his Marathon of Hope where he attempted to run across Canada to raise money for cancer research. Unfortunately, he passed away from lung cancer before he could complete the run. The Marathon of Hope cancer fundraising continues to this day and $700 million dollars has been raised in his name.

"癌症让我意识到，以自我为中心不是生活的方式。 答案是要尽力去帮助他人。"

——加拿大英雄泰瑞 • 福克斯

泰瑞 • 福克斯以他的希望马拉松的方式激励国人，他计划是横跨加拿大，跑遍十个省，决心为癌症的治疗和研究筹集资金。不幸的是，他未能跑完全程，因为癌症扩散, 身体情况恶化, 被迫退出。希望马拉松癌症筹款一直持续到今天，以他的名字已经筹集到了7亿加元。

July 22   Volunteer in Vancouver

7月22日   在温哥华做义工

Keep Vancouver Spectacular Volunteer Program

Keep Vancouver Spectacular is a series of programs that help to reduce litter and support a healthy and clean Vancouver. Individuals and groups that want to help keep their community clean can sign up for neighbourhood cleanup events all year long. Throughout the year, registered cleanup teams work in their own communities to remove litter from public spaces. Teams receive:

- Garbage bags

- Gloves and other cleanup tools

- Free pickup of litter collected

You can join a neighbourhood cleanup team and help and meet your neighbours. Just sign up at the website and they will help you find a cleaning team in a neighbourhood near you. You can also create your own volunteer position and volunteer to be a **Block Captain** and organize a group of your friends to do a cleanup of your own block. The program will give you all the information you need to do that task.

保持温哥华壮美景观的志愿者计划

保持温哥华壮美景观有助于减少垃圾、支持健康、充满活力和清洁的温哥华一揽子计划。个人、企业和组织都可以报名参加为期一年的附近社区清洁运动。在自己的社区注册清理小组工作，清除公共场所的垃圾。清理小组将获得：

- 垃圾袋
- 手套和其他清理工具
- 收集垃圾的免费皮卡

您可以加入一个社区清理小组，帮助和熟悉您的邻居。只需在网站上注册报名，他们会帮您在附近的社区找一个清洁队。您也可以创建自己的志愿者职位，自愿做一个队长，并组织一群朋友来清理自己的街区。网上会为您提供完成该任务所需的所有信息。

Healthcare in Vancouver

温哥华的医疗保健

How to Find a Dentist

The BC Dental Association maintains an accurate and up-to-date database of all the dentists in Vancouver. The website has a feature where you can search for the type of dentist you would like, in the neighbourhood where you live and whether they speak Chinese. Fortunately, there are many dentists in Vancouver who speak Mandarin. The database is kept up to date and you can feel confident that the dentists are fully certified and approved to practice dentistry.

The Provincial Medical Services plan does not cover dental care, so the cost must be paid entirely by the patient. However, it is possible to purchase "extended health and dental care" plans for the family where you pay a monthly fee in exchange for only having to pay a percentage of the total cost of the dental work you have done during the year, including cleaning appointments and check-ups.

如何找牙医

卑诗省牙科协会有一个温哥华所有牙医准确的和最新的数据库。该网站有一个搜索功能，您可以搜索您喜欢的牙医类型，居住地区以及他们是否会说中文。幸运的是，温哥华有很多牙医会讲普通话。该数据库是最新的，您可以完全放心，该网上所列的牙医都是获得执业牙医认证的。

省级医疗服务计划不包括牙齿护理，因此费用必须完全由患者支付。但是，您可以为您的家庭购买全年牙科"扩展保健"计划，按月支付，包括牙清洁预约和检查。

Interesting Facts About Vancouver

7月24日 **温哥华趣闻**

Destroyed by the Great Vancouver Fire

In 1886, when Vancouver was only 2 months old, it was almost completed destroyed by the Great Fire of Vancouver. Many dozens of people died in the fire and almost all the structures were destroyed. One of the only structures to survive was the Hastings Mill. After the Great Fire, the building was used as a hospital and a morgue for the fire's victims. You can still visit this building today as it was moved to its waterfront location in Point Grey and converted into the Old Hastings Mill Store Museum. The museum features artifacts and objects from Vancouver's past, along with First Nations art. It is an interesting place to visit.

被大火烧毁的温哥华

1886年6月13日在温哥华发生过一场大火灾，这场大火几乎烧毁了这座刚刚成立只有2个月的城市。大火夺去了数十人的性命，几乎所有的建筑物都被烧毁了。而唯一幸免于难的建筑物是位于西区的一间锯木厂，大火之后，这座建筑物被用作医院和火灾遇难者的停尸房。今天您仍然可以去参观这座建筑物，它被迁址到灰点的滨水区，并改建成了旧的黑斯廷斯锯木厂博物馆。目前该博物馆展出温哥华的历史文物，以及第一民族的艺术品，值得一看。

Finding Work in Vancouver

在温哥华找份工作

MOSAIC

MOSAIC is one of the largest and most well-known settlement organizations in Canada. MOSAIC provides more employment supports and programs than any other immigrant serving organization in B.C. They offer very innovative programs to help get newcomers into the workforce. One of their well-known programs is called **Pathways to Employment** which is a free 11-week program designed for newcomers who are interested in working in retail or office occupations. Participants learn effective job search strategies and workplace communication skills, gain training related to the retail or office field and have an opportunity for a 4-week work experience placement. Recently they introduced a new **Fast-track to IT (FIT) Program** which is a 20-week program designed for newcomers interested in working in the Information Technology industry. Participants will receive 10 weeks of skills training in Information Systems Analysis and Software Quality Management, one week work experience preparation, seven weeks of work experience, and two weeks of job search and follow-up support.

MOSAIC马赛克https://www.mosaicbc.org/

  MOSAIC是加拿大最大和最知名的解决移民定居的组织之一。在BC省，和任何其他移民服务组织相比，MOSAIC提供更多的就业支持、项目和创新计划。它帮助新员工快速融入劳务市场。他们的一个著名的策划被称为就业途径，这是一个为期11周的免费项目，专为有兴趣从事零售或办公职业工作的新移民设计的。参与者学习有效的求职策略和工作场所沟通技能，获得与零售或办公领域相关的培训，并有机会进行为期4周的工作实习的机会。最近，他们为有兴趣在信息技术行业工作的新人推出了一个新的IT（FIT）快速通道计划，这是一个为期20周的计划。参加者将获得10周的信息系统分析和软件质量管理方面的技能培训，一周的工作经验准备，七周的工作实践，以及两周的寻找工作以及后续支持。

July 26   Vancouver Sightseeing

7月26日   观光

Banff, Okanagan, Seattle Short Trips

Vancouverites love to visit the wine country of the **Okanagan Valley** in the summer as it is one of the warmest regions in all of Canada. The Okanagan includes the cities of Kelowna, Penticton, Vernon and Osoyoos. During the summer months, visitors enjoy sandy lake beaches, hot sun, and a variety of outdoor and water activities. Okanagan Lake provides the valley not only with excellent swimming but also has many golf courses, wineries and popular ski resorts.

Banff & Lake Louise. Just over the border in the province of Alberta is the famous Banff National Park where you can feel truly immersed in nature with the impressive Rocky Mountain chain providing beautiful mountain scenery. Lake Louise's clear blue water is an unforgettable sight. After exploring the natural surroundings, visitors can enjoy the world class restaurants, hotels and stores of Banff.

Seattle, in Washington USA, is surrounded by water, mountains, and evergreen forests, and contains thousands of acres of parkland. Seattle is home to a large tech industry, with Microsoft and Amazon headquartered in its metropolitan area. The futuristic Space Needle, a 1962 World's Fair legacy, is its most recognizable landmark. Visitors to Seattle enjoy visiting the loud and lively Pike Street Market and enjoying the many restaurants, shopping areas and music and theatre performances.

温哥华周边游：班芙，奥肯那根，西雅图

温哥华人喜欢参观奥肯那根谷的葡萄酒之乡，它是加拿大最温暖的地区之一。奥肯那根包括基隆拿、彭蒂克顿、弗农和奥索尤斯等城市。在夏季，游客们可以在那里享受沙滩，明媚的阳光，以及各种户外和水上活动。 奥肯那根湖不仅有优良的游泳场所，而且还有以壮观的绵延起伏的山丘为背景的高尔夫球场、奥肯那根酒厂以及位于这个葡萄酒谷的极受欢迎的滑雪胜地。

班夫和路易斯湖坐落于艾伯塔省西南靠近卑诗省的落基山脉中，是著名的度假胜地，拥有悠久的历史。在班夫国家公园，你能真正感受到大自然的魅力，令人印象深刻的落基山脉美丽的山峦，路易斯湖清澈蓝色的湖水让人流连忘返。在探索自然环境后，游客可以回到班夫市享受世界一流的餐厅，酒店和商店。

西雅图在美国华盛顿州，四周被山水和森林环绕着，有常绿之城的美誉，并包含数千英亩的公园。西雅图是华盛顿州最大的城市，有一个大型的科技产业区，微软和亚马逊总部都设在其中。西雅图最特别的地标就是太空针塔，它是为1962年的21世纪博览会修建的，其周围的博览会会址被更名为西雅图中心，至今依然是许多重要的民间和艺术活动的场地。游客们可以参观派克农贸市场或称派克市场，它位于西雅图市中心的派克街，是全美国最老的农贸市场。那里有许多餐馆，购物区和音乐剧院表演。

Vancouver Transportation

温哥华交通运输

The Skytrain Network

The elevated Skytrain Network is the longest fully automated driverless train system in the world. The SkyTrain Network has 57 stations on three lines:

- **The Expo Line** connects Waterfront Station in Vancouver to King George Station in Surrey. It now has 24 stations. The stations have a very simple design compared to the Millennium Line.

- The **Millennium Line and Evergreen Extension** operates between VCC–Clark Station in Vancouver and Lafarge Lake–Douglas station in Coquitlam. The Millennium Line has 17 stations, three of which are transfer stations with the Expo Line (Commercial–Broadway, Production Way–University, and Lougheed Town Centre) and two which connect with the West Coast Express commuter train (Moody Centre and Coquitlam Central). The interesting and unique Millennium Line's stations were designed by British Columbia's top architects.

- The **Canada Line** begins at the Waterfront Station hub, then continues south to the City of Richmond and Sea Island. From Bridgeport Station, the Canada Line splits into two branches, one heading west to the YVR–Airport Station at Vancouver International Airport and the other continuing south to the Richmond–Brighouse Station in Richmond's city centre. Waterfront Station is the only station where the Canada Line connects with the Expo Line and Millennium Line.

温哥华架空列车：分博览线，千禧线，长青线和加拿大线

高架的天车网络是世界上最长的全自动无人驾驶列车系统。整个系统中目前共有53个车站，分博览线、千禧线和加拿大线三条路线和长青延伸线运行。

- **博览线**从温哥华市滨海站起至素里市的乔治王站为终点站它现在有20个车站。与千禧线相比，这些车站设计非常简单。

- **千禧线和长青线**在温哥华的VCC-Clark站和高贵林的拉法基湖－道格拉斯站之间运行。千禧线一共有17个车站，其中有3个与博览线交汇的换乘站（商业百老汇，生产方式大学和卢吉德镇中心站），其中两个（穆迪中心和高贵林中心）与西海岸快线通勤列车衔接。千禧线(温哥华至本那比段)的车站皆由卑诗省最顶级的建筑师设计，这些车站的风格亦因此与博览线和长青延线的车站大相径庭。

- **加拿大线**从海滨站中心开始，然后继续南行到里士满和海岛。在Bridgeport站，加拿大线分成两个分支，一个向西到温哥华国际机场的YVR-机场站，另一个继续南行到里士满市中心的布里格豪斯站。海滨站是加拿大线唯一与博览线和千禧线相连的车站。

English for Everyday Life
日常生活英语

Oddly enough, you don't really need English for the SkyTrain routes as it is not common for people to talk on the trains. Usually the commuters are reading their phone, listening to music or just looking outside and enjoying the view. It is not an easy place to begin a conversation, no matter what your English level!!

奇怪的是，当你乘坐架空列车的时候，你不需要讲英语。你很快就会发现车上的乘客很少讲英语。 通常，大部分通勤者都在看他们的手机，有的人在听音乐还有的人只是看着并享受着车窗外面的风景。这不是一个容易找话题开始聊天的地方，无论你的英语水平如何！

Sports Teams and Special Events

专业体育赛事和活动

The Subaru 5i50 Vancouver Triathlon

The Subaru 5i50 Vancouver Triathlon starts and finishes in downtown Vancouver with stunning views of the North Shore Mountains, sparkling oceans, and the rain forest of Stanley Park. This race is the Canadian Triathlon Championship race. The Subaru 5i50 Vancouver Triathlon features a 1.5-kilometer swim, 40-kilometer bike and 10-kilometer run. The race starts with a swim in Coal Harbour. Athletes then bike through Stanley Park and along Beach Avenue with views across English Bay before returning to Harbour Green Park. From there they run along the seawall around Stanley Park before finishing in downtown Vancouver. The name 5i50 or 5150 comes from the total distance of the race equaling 51.5 kilometers (1.5km swim, 40km bike and 10km run.

斯巴鲁5i50温哥华铁人三项

斯巴鲁5i50温哥华铁人三项赛的起点和终点是在温哥华市中心，整个赛程将沿着北海岸山脉，波光粼粼的海洋和景色秀美的斯坦利公园。 这是加拿大铁人三项赛的冠军争夺战。斯巴鲁5150温哥华铁人三项包括一个1.5公里的游泳，40公里的自行车和10公里跑。比赛始于在煤港湾游泳。然后运动员们骑上自行车通过斯坦利公园和海滩大道，沿线可以看到英吉利湾，然后返回海港绿色公园。接下来从那里，赛跑者将沿着风景秀丽的斯坦利公园的海堤跑完最后的赛程，最终返回温哥华市中心。斯巴鲁5i50名字就来自比赛总距离51公里（1.5公里游泳，40公里自行车和10公里跑）。

Vancouver Parks

7月29日　温哥华公园

John Hendry (Trout Lake) Park

This East Vancouver park is named after one of the founding pioneer families in Vancouver. It is a popular neighbourhood park famous for being one of the only parks with a large lake. The park is located at 3300 Victoria Drive at East 15th Avenue. In addition to the lovely lake, there are green lawns, shady trees, playgrounds and picnic tables. There is a beach area and a wildlife habitat area that is perfect for birdwatching during any season. The walking trails, basketball courts, tennis courts and baseball and soccer fields provide recreation activities for everyone. This park is also a common location for large community celebrations and gatherings.

约翰·亨德利（鳟鱼湖）公园

这个东温哥华公园是以温哥华的一个创始先驱家族约翰·亨德利命名的。公园里有一个很大的湖泊叫做鳟鱼湖(Trout Lake)。公园位于东第十五大街和维多利亚大道3300号。园内有一个海滩和一个野生动物栖息地，任何季节都适合观赏鸟类野生动物。除了可爱的湖泊，周围还有绿色的草坪、遮荫树、儿童游乐场和野餐桌子。公园提供娱乐活动设施齐全，有步行道，篮球场，网球场，棒球和足球场这个公园也是大型社区组织庆祝活动和聚会的常见地点。

July 30 Stories and Advice for Newcomers

7月30日 移民的故事和建议

Sabrina

我们移民到底为了什么？

不同的人会有不同的答案，加拿大提供全民免费医疗与教育，这是绝大多数华人移民的主要原因。

我的孩子回答："非常感谢父母把我带到多元文化的加拿大，学位不是光环和目的，而是我有了一个自己可以改变自己命运的机会，一个我想要拥有的生活方式。"我非常感恩，也为孩子骄傲！感谢在这和谐的社会里，培养了孩子诚实自信、勇敢坚强、责任能力、互助包容等优良品德，更指引了人生的方向和意义，这是何其珍贵的精神财富啊！

我与大家分享的是学会了给予。我一直认为自己是个善良的人，当我遇到许多志愿者，无私地奉献自己宝贵的时间和财富，帮助弱势群体，我才明白什么是真正意义的善良。捐助是加拿大的文化传统之一，我孩子很小的时候，就参加基督教会的慈善活动，每逢圣诞佳节，用自己攒的钱买食物、玩具和书籍，包装成精美的礼品，送给有需要的儿童。学校也会教孩子如何帮助，"水资源长跑"项目就是让孩子亲自筹款，我孩子才一年级，就挨家敲门请捐，卖废品破烂儿和车库摆摊儿赚钱，所有捐款都用于改善援助非洲水生态，孩子的微薄之力，能帮助干旱疾苦人民，是何等的幸福啊！

绝大多数慈善捐助，如乳腺癌路跑、前列腺癌骑车和痴呆症健行等，都是为防治疾病和提升医疗系统的专项研究筹助资金。还有少部分援助，是孩子为孤寡老人唱歌、跳舞和演奏；义工组织大型慈善晚宴，款待难民……无论哪里有灾难，加拿大人都尽可能伸出援手，贡献金钱、时间和人力。如果每个人都付出一点援助，世界将变得更美好，我们都可以做到！

如果现在有人问我，来加拿大收获了什么？我会毫不犹豫地告诉你们：最重要的不全是教育和医疗，而是我明白了生活的意义，是一种简单平淡的心态和无私地帮助给予，这足以让我受益终身。

Little India in Vancouver

There is a neighbourhood in Vancouver known as Little India. It is located along six blocks of Main St near 49th Ave. There are many authentic Indian restaurants and shops along this part of Main street. It is a wonderful place to buy colourful silk fabric and fine gold jewelry. Of course, you can also enjoy delicious Indian food such as spicy samosas, butter chicken and Indian desserts. The area comes alive with music, dancing, and parades two times a year to celebrate important Indian festivals. The five-day **Diwali Festival** celebrates the Indian New Year in November and in April there is the **Vaisakhi Day Parade** which celebrates the start of harvest time. This parade attracts more than 50,000 spectators to the district to watch the parade and enjoy lots of free food and live music.

温哥华的小印度

在温哥华有一个社区叫作小印度。 它位于主街和第49街占有附近的六个街区。沿主街两旁分布了许多地道的印度餐馆和商店。这是一个奇妙的地方，可以买到彩色丝织物和精美的黄金首饰。当然，你也可以享用美味的印度食品，如辣萨摩萨，黄油鸡和印度甜点。该社区每年举办两次游行活动，伴有音乐和跳舞来庆祝重要的印度节日。印度的新年是在11月份，有为期五天的排灯节，四月份有一个Vaisakhi日游行活动是来庆祝收获季节的开始。这个游行吸引了超过50,000观众到现场观看，同时还可以享用很多免费食物的同时聆听美妙的现场音乐。

August

Weather:	Average temperature: 14°C to 23°C
	Average rainfall days: 10, Average rainfall: 20 mm
Statutory holiday:	BC Day (first Monday of August)
Other special days:	The Fair at the PNE (last two weeks of summer before school starts)

For the locals, August is a very relaxed and laid-back month. Most activities take place outside and so the beaches, parks, pools and sightseeing attractions continue to be busy. Many people also use this month to travel and go overseas to visit relatives or take long trips abroad. Going on a road trip* to many of the beautiful small towns, lakes and islands close to Vancouver is also a common type of vacation for the locals. The more adventurous take longer driving trips to the Rocky Mountains in Alberta or down to California to visit Disneyland.

The Cambie Village neighbourhood and the Kitsilano neighbourhoods hold their annual summer fairs now. In both events, the major road is closed and the street is taken over with entertainment and food stalls and lots of fun activities and games for everyone to enjoy.

A modern activity that takes place in Vancouver during this month is the Dîner en Blanc, meaning "dinner in white" which is an exclusive, worldwide event (on six continents!) in which people gather in a public space and set up a temporary, elegant dining area where everything

– tables, chairs, tablecloths – is white. All the attendees must come dressed formally in white clothes and everyone enjoys quality food, wine, and good company. The location for the event is always kept secret until the actual day of the event when all registered guests are sent a message about where to go.

August only has one big festival called The Fair at the PNE. Residents from the small towns of BC like to make the journey to Vancouver to attend this traditional event that has been a Vancouver tradition for more than 100 years. At the Fair at the PNE, you can enjoy free nightly concerts, agricultural* events, and the whole fair is packed with more than 50 thrilling rides and much more. Families take their children to the PNE to see and touch the farm animals, watch the entertainment, and go on the rides. Older adults enjoy going to the PNE to eat the wide variety of food and watch the many shows and entertainment that goes on during the fair. Some local favourites of the PNE are the Superdogs show where you can see many cute dogs perform and compete in fun events, and eating a bag of warm, fresh mini donuts – small circles made of dough that are fried in oil and covered in cinnamon and sugar.

8月•

气候： 平均气温： 14°C 到 23°C
平均降雨天数：10，平均降雨量： 20毫米
公众节假日：BC省日（八月第一个星期一）
其他特殊日：PNE交易会（暑假开学前的最后两个星期）

对当地人来说，八月是是一个非常轻松和悠闲的月份。大多数人都会到户外活动，海滩、公园、游泳池、景点观光忙得不亦乐乎。许多人也利用这个月外出度假，出国探亲或在国外观光。温哥华周边有许多美丽的小城镇。湖泊和岛屿也是当地人常去度假的好去处。喜欢开车探险的人会驱车去更远的阿尔伯塔省的落基山脉或者南下去加利福尼亚参观迪斯尼乐园。

每年的这个时候甘比村和基茨兰诺附近地区都会举行年度夏季博览会。在这两个事件中，主要道路将关闭，街道两旁全是娱乐消遣、食品摊位、有趣的活动和游戏，每个人都可以参加。

这个月在温哥华会发生一种相当奇特的现代的新式用餐方式，叫做恩布兰克晚餐，意思是独家的"白色晚餐"， 它涉及全球范围内的六大洲！所有用餐者聚集在一个公共的空间，搭建一个临时的、时尚的和典雅别致的用餐区，这里的一切：桌子、椅子、桌布全都是白色的。所有的与会者都必须穿着正式的白色服装，每个人都享有高品质的食品和葡萄酒，结识志趣相投的伙伴。用餐的位置总是保密的，直到最终确定下来，所有注册的客人都会收到去哪里用餐的消息。

八月只有一个大的节日叫做PNE交易会。BC省的小城镇的居民们最喜欢来温哥华参加这项已有100多年历史的传统活动，在交易会上，您可以享受免费的晚间音乐会，观看农场动物比赛，整个交易会设置了50多个惊险刺激的游乐设施，大人带小孩子去看并触摸农场的动物、观赏或亲身乘坐游乐园里的过山车或其他的飞车项目。岁数大的人喜欢去PNE，除了参加娱乐，观看各种节目，更重要的是因为那里可以品尝各种美食。在交易会期间，最受欢迎的要数超级狗狗秀，许多可爱的小狗同台竞技表演。再吃上一袋热乎的，新鲜的迷你甜甜圈 – 一种小圆面团制成的，在油里炸，外面裹着肉桂和糖。

更多的信息：•

基茨兰诺节：http://kitsfest.com/
甘比村夏季酷暑日：www.cambievillage.com
PNE交易会：www.pne.ca
恩布兰科晚餐：http://vancouver.dinerenblanc.info/
*Road Trip自驾游：就是自己驾驶汽车进行漫长的出游，以自驾车为主要交通手段的旅游形式。沿途会寻找一些小旅馆小住。
*Agricultural events农场竞技活动：这类活动给农民一个竞争的机会，他们带上自己农场里的动物参加竞赛，赢取奖品，同时也证明了他们饲养的动物是最健康、最具吸引力的。

Local Customs

　　　当地的习俗

Housewarming Parties

To fill their new home with the positive feelings of family and friends, people host a Housewarming Party whenever they move into a new house or apartment. They invite their closest friends or family members to enjoy drinks and appetizers and give them a tour of the new home. The guests will traditionally bring a bottle of wine, flowers, or a gift for the home.

乔迁之喜

当人们搬进新的房子或公寓时，为了让他们的新家增添喜庆。都会请亲朋好友来搞一个乔迁聚会。主人提供饮料和开胃菜，并带他们参观新家。传统上客人们会带一瓶葡萄酒、鲜花或礼物送给主人。

English for Everyday Life
日常生活英语

这里为了表达你对他们的新家的美好祝愿，分享他们的快乐你可以说：

"*We wish you much happiness in your new home*"

"*祝你们乔迁之喜，幸福快乐*"

Parenting in Vancouver

8月2日   在温哥华养育子女

Parent Involvement at Schools

Parents have many opportunities to do volunteer work with schools. In elementary schools, there are classroom parent volunteers who help with activities in the classroom, in the lunchroom, on field trips and with fundraising. At the high school level, most parent volunteer work is fundraising work. If you would like to volunteer with your child's school, the best place to start is to contact the Parent Advisory Committee (PAC) at your child's school. Each elementary and high school has a committee of parents who volunteer to serve on the committee and organize parent involvement at the school.

家长参与学校活动•

家长们在学校有很多做志愿服务的机会。在小学，有教室志愿者，他们协助组织教室里的各种活动，还有午餐室的志愿者和课外实习志愿者以及筹款志愿者。在高中阶段，大多数家长志愿者的工作是筹款。 如果你想得到孩子学校志愿者工作的机会，最好是先与家长咨询委员会（PAC）取得联系。每个小学和高中都有一个PAC委员会，委员会的成员是由志愿者们组成的，委员会定期组织家长参与学校的活动。

August 3   Stories and Advice for Newcomers

8月3日   新移民的故事

Grass

说说课堂之外的教育·

绝大多数家庭移民的重要原因之一，就是为了孩子。很多家长们都毫不吝啬地为孩子支付各种课外补习的学费，文化课的内容自不必说，音乐，美术，运动等等都不曾忽略，但是，孩子的成长，素质的全面提高，还有一些"功夫在诗外"的东西。

记得我儿子在小学的时候，就参加过一个西餐礼仪的培训。培训的方式非常简单直接：老师直接把孩子们带到正规的西餐厅，从餐具的摆放开始说明，到如何看菜单，如何点菜，如何使用各种餐具，这样现场教学，使得孩子们记忆深刻，还丝毫不觉得枯燥无趣。这样一次培训，使我儿子收益匪浅。

而真正在各方面帮助我儿子全面提升的训练是"青年领袖培训"和"模拟联合国"。如今，模联在国内也比较流行，就不多说了。我儿子当年参加了"爱丁堡公爵青年领袖培训计划"的铜章和银章培训。据说，在私校里，学校会组织学生几乎全员参加铜章培训，而公校的孩子就需要家长自己安排了。这个计划涵盖了许多方面，要求孩子在不同的领域提升自己的能力。篇幅有限，只举一个例子。迄今为止，我们作为父母，从来没有带孩子去野外露营过。但是，在培训过程中，老师带领着孩子们，从铜章的三天两夜，到银章的五天四夜，从普通的camping营地，到人迹罕至的高山峻岭，背着几十磅的背囊，爬山涉水，露宿山间，没有厕所，不能洗澡，自己做饭，等等，孩子仿佛一下子成长了许多。

August 4	# Vancouver Entertainment
8月4日	温哥华娱乐

Wine Tasting in Vancouver

One of the best places to learn about and taste wine is at one of the **Liberty Wine Merchant** locations around Vancouver. They are the largest chain of private wine retailers in Western Canada and they carry over 5,000 types of wine. Their staff are passionate and knowledgeable about wine and often lead small events where customers can learn more about different wines.

A wine bar is a bar that focusses on selling wine instead of liquor or beer and many wines are available to order by a single glass. It is also possible to order a specially selected collection of wine samples that focus on wines from a certain area of the world or a certain wine variety. These are called *tasting flights.* In a wine bar, the usual practice is to order a tasting flight of wine and a few appetizers to eat while enjoying the wine. The food provides a balance to the different wine tastes. In Vancouver, some restaurants have a wine bar area, but some bars have wine as their only focus. The Wine Bar is a quietly elegant and comfortable place to enjoy their wine list which focusses on French wines with some other choices from Mediterranean countries and BC. UVA Vancouver is a high-end downtown wine and cocktail bar that has won awards for its fine selection of wines, cocktails, and imported beers. UVA also offers some very creative wine tasting flights with interesting themes like "Pretty Things", with exotic fruit flavours and "Italian Tourist" which is a trio of red wines.

温哥华品酒会

了解和品尝葡萄酒的最佳场所之一是温哥华周边的**自由葡萄酒商店**之一。它们是加拿大西部最大的私人葡萄酒零售连锁店，经营着5000多种葡萄酒。他们的员工对葡萄酒充满激情和知识，经常举办小型的品酒活动，让顾客更多地了解不同的葡萄酒。这是他们的网站http://libertywinemerchants.com/

葡萄酒吧顾名思义就是专门出售葡萄酒的酒吧，它不卖白酒或是啤酒，您可以按杯来点想喝的葡萄酒，许多牌子的葡萄酒均可以先品尝，满意了再购买。商家有时会精心挑选来自世界某一地区的名酒或者某一年份陈酿的好酒供客人们品尝，酒单上还有一些怪异的酒水的名字，比如弗莱特飞飞。酒吧通常在品酒的同时，还会给客人们提供一些开胃小菜，为不同的葡萄酒口味提供很好平衡。在温哥华，有些餐馆专门设有葡萄酒吧区，每个酒吧又有它们各自不同的卖点：

- Wine Bar：http://www.thewinebar.ca/wp/ 这个葡萄酒吧位于僻静舒适的地方，他们的葡萄酒单主要是法国葡萄酒，还有来自地中海国家和卑诗省的葡萄酒。
- UVA：https://www.uvavancouver.com/ 这是一个高端的位于市中心的葡萄酒兼鸡尾酒酒吧。它曾赢得过精选葡萄酒、鸡尾酒和进口啤酒等多个奖项。Uva精选的葡萄酒单非常有创意，比如把某个酒水起名为弗莱特飞飞，主题也很有趣，如"心动"，酒盘上装饰着异国情调的花卉和水果，名字各有不同，如"雨影"，红色三重奏和"意大利旅游"专机等等。

English for Everyday Life
日常生活英语

- *A Flight* 飞飞：是葡萄酒品尝师用来描述葡萄酒的一个术语，通常在三到八杯之间，但有时多达五十种，用于抽样和比较。
- *Wine list* 酒单：包含所有葡萄酒品种的酒单名称。在酒水单上，您将看到大体被分为白葡萄酒、红葡萄酒或起泡的葡萄酒。 葡萄酒名称将包括产地和装瓶的年份。葡萄酒一般是按杯或按瓶来出售的。

这是一个客人在葡萄酒吧点酒时的对话：

Server: *Can I get you started with anything?*
Customer: I would like to order something from your wine list.
Server: *Here it is. You can select from this menu.*
Customer: I'd like to order a bottle of red wine. I'll have the 2008 Bordeaux.
Server: *Good choice. I'll be right back with your wine.*
Customer: Thank you.

酒吧服务员：可以开始点酒了吗？
客人：我想从您的酒单上点一些。
酒吧服务员：这是酒单。 您可以从酒单中选择。
客人：我想来一瓶红酒。 我要2008年产的波尔多。
酒吧服务员：不错的选择。 我马上去拿给您。
客人：谢谢。

West Point Grey Elementary School (private)

Here is the description of the school from their website: "Founded in 1996, West Point Grey Academy is an independent coeducational day school in Vancouver, British Columbia. Set on 18 acres, with sweeping views of English Bay and the North Shore mountains, we offer future-focused programs to 940 students in junior kindergarten to grade 12. Central to our mission, *Shaping Lives of Inquiry, Action and Joy*, is our educational philosophy to develop the whole child, who, guided by creative, dedicated teachers and supported by our inclusive, vibrant community, is nurtured to achieve his or her full potential – academically, emotionally, physically and socially."

西点小学（私立）•https://www.wpga.ca•

  下面是学校网站的描述：

  "西点小学成立于1996年，是不列颠哥伦比亚省温哥华一所独立的男女同校的学校。占地18英亩，可饱览英吉利海湾和北海岸山脉的美景，我们为幼儿园至12年级940名学生提供着眼于未来、行动和快乐体验式的课程，我们有优秀的教师团队和社区的支持。我们的使命是培养每个学生在学业上、情感上、身体上和社交上最大的潜能"

August 6	A Different Way of Thinking
8月6日	不同的思维方式

Changing Attitudes to Smoking

Canada has run one of the most effective anti-smoking campaigns in the world. In fact, the very steep decline in smoking is very dramatic and continues to this day. The biggest change is the very negative attitude towards smoking and smokers. Nowadays it is considered very socially unacceptable to smoke, especially for successful professionals and highly educated people. There are very few areas that people can still smoke in public. It is forbidden to smoke in: All bars and restaurants, in the workplace, in front of buildings, in schools, in apartment buildings and parks. These restrictions were made because of all the research that shows how dangerous second-hand smoke is to health. There are still a few designated smoking areas outside but they are usually in ugly dark locations in the back of buildings. Smoking is a behaviour that is looked down on and is considered a very dirty and embarrassing habit. The sale and advertising of cigarettes is strictly controlled, highly taxed and restricted. Cigarettes are never given as gifts and are considered a wasteful way to spend money. In the continually shrinking number of smokers in Canada, there are equal amounts of male and female smokers. The government is continuing to strengthen the rules and restrictions around smoking and the Canadian public fully supports these actions as it is proven how dangerous smoking is to the health and safety of the public.

改变对吸烟的态度•

　　加拿大是世界上最有效的禁烟运动的国家之一。事实上，吸烟的人数急剧下降是非常有戏剧性的，并一直持续到今日。最大的变化是对吸烟者的态度非常冷漠。现在，吸烟者是不被大众所接受的，特别是对于成功的专业人士和受过良好教育的人来说。他们很少有人在公共场所吸烟。

　　禁止吸烟的场所：所有酒吧、餐馆，工作场所、楼前、学校、公寓楼和公园内。这些限制是因为所有的研究显示二手烟对身体伤害比一手烟更为严重。室外僻出一些指定的吸烟区，但它们通常位于建筑物后面丑陋阴暗的角落。吸烟是一种被人瞧不起的行为，是一种非常肮脏和令人难堪的习惯。卷烟的销售受到高税收，其广告受到严格的控制。香烟不会作为礼物赠送，被认为是浪费金钱。在加拿大吸烟人数不断减少的情况下，男性和女性烟民在数量上相等。政府正在继续完善吸烟的规则和限制，加拿大公众完全支持政府的这些行动，因为证据表明吸烟对公众的健康和安全有太大的危险。

Best High Schools

温哥华著名的中学

West Point Grey Academy (private)

Here is the description of the school from their website: "The Senior School offers a truly personalized, dynamic educational experience, preparing students to successfully pursue their postsecondary path of choice. As the only Canadian member school in Global Online Academy, and with our signature Global Studies Diploma, International Outreach and Outdoor Environmental Education programs, students have the opportunity to become citizens of the world and stewards of their local communities."

西灰点学院附中（私立）https://www.wpga.ca

以下是学校网站上的描述：

"西灰点学院附中提供真正个性化和动态的教育，帮助学生为追求他们中学后高等教育的选择作好准备。作为加拿大唯一的全球在线学院，我们有国际推广和户外环境教育计划，我们可以签发国际学习文凭、学生们有机会成为世界公民及当地社区的管理者。"

August 8   The Homes of Vancouver

8月8日   温哥华住宅

A Bungalow in the Snow
雪中的平房•

　　Bungalow为一层的小房子，或许还有一个地下室。往往适合人口不多的家庭居住，前后院与其住宅相比会留有更多的空间。

August 9   # Best Extracurricular
                      Activities for Kids

8月9日   **最佳儿童课外活动**

Vancouver Fine Art Atelier

This school is run by a group of classically trained artists who love to teach fine art. They offer classes for kids, teens and adults in classes, private lessons and special summer camps. Students can sign up for art, drawing or craft courses. The teachers share their knowledge of European fine art with their students in a creative and encouraging environment using the best materials. Every year the school hosts exhibitions of the students' inspirational creations.

温哥华美术工作室•http://www.vancouveratelier.com/

这所学校由一群训练有素的古典艺术家组成，他们爱教美术。他们为孩子，青少年和成年人开班，提供私人课程或特殊的夏令营课程。 学生可以注册参加艺术、绘画或工艺课程。他们乐于使用最好的材料，在创造性和令人鼓舞的环境中与他们的学生分享对欧洲美术创作的知识。激发学员们的艺术创造力，学校每年都会举办鼓舞人心的学生作品展览会。

Get Active Together

Even if you can't have long conversations with others in English, it is still possible to communicate through play and activity, so consider joining a fun activity or sports group to meet people and get some exercise at the same time. Two suggestions for gentle exercises that you can do at any age or fitness level are walking and lawn bowling.

The Running Room might have "running" in their name, but they are also involved in organizing walking groups and training. The Running Room is a chain of stores that sell sports clothing, but they are also one of the best organizers of walking and running groups in the city. They have training classes for every skill level – from beginner walker to marathon runner. In addition, they have training classes that can help participants prepare for annual walks and runs in Vancouver such as the Vancouver Sun Run and the Vancouver International Marathon. Joining a walking club is a great way to meet people as the walking and fresh air will make you feel more relaxed and comfortable.

Dunbar and Kerrisdale Lawn Bowling Clubs provide one of the best ways to meet people while enjoying easy exercise in a peaceful outdoor setting. You can lawn bowl afternoons, evenings or weekends -- whatever time suits your schedule. All you need to start is an inexpensive pair of smooth-soled shoes. Use the club bowls and you're all set to start learning. In addition to the bowling, there are social activities throughout the season where you can meet and get to know new people.

一起做运动•

> 健走和跑步团体（所有等级）www.runningroom.com
> 邓巴草坪保龄球 www.dunbarlawnbowling.com
> 卡里斯道尔草坪保龄球 http://kerrisdalebowlsclub.webs.com/

即使您不能长时间的与他人用英语进行交谈，您仍然可以通过游戏和各种活动进行交流，所以考虑加入运动一个团体或参加一项有趣的活动，以此来认识新的朋友，同时也锻炼了体魄。这里我们推荐两项适合任何年龄或者身体状况且不是很剧烈的运动：健走和草地保龄球。

- **跑步室**可能是以"跑步"冠名的，他们也参与组织步行团体和训练。跑步室是一家销售运动服装的连锁店，但也是城市健走和跑步团队的最佳组织者之一。他们有各种技能水平的训练班，从初学到马拉松运动员。此外，他们还有培训班，可以帮助参加者准备在温哥华举行一年一度的健走和跑步活动，如温哥华太阳长跑和温哥华国际马拉松赛。加入健走俱乐部是认识新朋友的一个很好方式。与他人在新鲜的空气中散步会让您感到更加愉悦和放松。
- **邓巴和卡里斯道尔草坪滚球**是一项充分享受安静的户外阳光、空气、绿草的休闲健身运动，同时也是认识新朋友的最佳方式。您可以选择下午，晚上或者周末，无论什么时间去玩都可以。所有您需要的只是一种廉价的平底鞋子。俱乐部提供滚球。除了打球之外，俱乐部还经常组织社交活动，在那里您可以结识很多新的朋友。

August 11   Restaurant Customs and Etiquette

8月11日   餐厅的习俗与礼仪

Sharing Meals

In the past, it was considered very unusual to share food at a restaurant. It would only happen with parents of very young children sharing their food with them or a couple of friends sharing one dessert. However, this custom is quickly changing and more people are enjoying the idea of sharing dishes at the table both to save money and to be able to try many different foods. When people share food here, usually they will divide the food onto individual plates instead of sharing from one plate. Sometimes a restaurant will take the dish and divide it onto separate plates for you in the kitchen before they bring it out. It is always polite to mention to the server that you plan to share the dishes.

共享食物•

过去，在餐馆里共享食物是很罕见的。只有非常年幼的孩子与他们的父母共享食物，或者是两个朋友共享一份甜点。然而，这种习俗正在迅速的改变，越来越多的人愿意在餐桌上共享菜肴的新理念，这样既省钱又能品尝到更多不同的食物。当地人在共享食物时，通常他们会把食物按人数分装到不同的盘子，而不是在同一个盘子里共享。有时候，餐馆会在后厨先把它们分好装盘，然后再把它们端出来。如果您打算共享菜肴，一定要事前告诉服务员。

English for Everyday Life
日常生活英语

以下是您打算与同桌朋友共享食物与服务员对话的例子：

Server: Are you ready to order?
Customer: Yes, we are. We would like to share a couple of appetizer dishes.
Server: Certainly. What would you like?
Customer: We would like to order the ravioli pasta and the garden salad with oil and vinegar dressing.
Server: Great, and I will bring you some extra plates for dividing up the food.
Customer: Thank you.

服务员：您准备点菜了吗？
顾客：是的，我们想一起享用几个开胃菜。
服务员：当然可以。您想要点什么？
顾客：我们想订的意大利式小方饺与田园沙拉配上油和醋的调味汁。
服务员：真好，我这就去给您拿些额外的盘子来把食物分开。
顾客：谢谢。

Top English Language Programs for Newcomers

8月12日   成人高级英语课程

Kwantlen Polytechnic University (KPU)

KPU offers two tracks of English classes. The first is the **Diploma in English Language Studies** which enables you to develop your English language skills needed from beginner level to advanced. The second program is **Customized English Language Studies** which is a combination of classroom instruction, individual guided learning, small group seminars and the development of an online portfolio. This option is a full-time program that runs for 7 weeks. This option is ideal for students who want to improve their English ability and confidence to successfully complete university level courses.

昆特仑理工大学（KPU）www.kpu.ca

昆特仑理工大学提供两套英语学习计划。第一个是英语语言学习文凭，从初级到高级逐步发展你的英语语言能力。第二个是定制的英语语言学习课程，以课堂教学、个别指导、小组研讨并结合电子档案。为期7周的全日制课程，它对于希望提高英语能力和有信心成功完成大学课程的学生来说是非常理想的选择。

August 13   Vancouver Backyard Wildlife

8月13日   温哥华后院的小鸟和动物

Barred Owls

These large beautiful birds fly silently through the trees and rest high in the tree branches quietly during the day. At night they hunt small animals, especially rats and mice. They hunt by sitting and waiting on a high branch while using their very good eyesight and hearing to watch for prey. They swallow small prey whole and large prey in pieces, eating the head first and then the body. You might hear their very distinctive bird call which sounds like: "Who cooks for you?". It is believed that the pairs probably mate for life, raising one batch of babies each year. They can live for over twenty years.

猫头鹰·

猫头鹰悄无声息地在树间飞翔，白天在树枝上静静地休息，晚上它们捕猎小动物，特别是小型哺乳动物如鼠类。它们隐匿于树丛中不易被猎物察觉到，它们的视觉和听觉都极佳。对于体积稍小的猎物可以整个吞下去，您可能会听到他们非常独特的叫声，听起来像："Who cooks for you?"（谁煮给你吃？）猫头鹰通常一雄一雌配对，每年产卵数量不定，猫头鹰一般可以存活二十年以上。

August 14   Support for Newcomers

8月14日   支持新移民

Settlement Online Pre-arrival (SOPA)

SOPA is another program run by Immigration, Refugees and Citizenship Canada (IRCC) to help approved immigrants arrive prepared for the Canadian workplace. They offer courses on how to work with others, on job search strategies and on Canadian workplace integration.

到达前在线解决方案(SOPA)•http://arriveprepared.ca/•

　　SOPA是由加拿大移民、难民和公民部（IRCC）管理的另一项计划，旨在帮助已经批准的移民到达之前做好在加拿大职场工作的准备。他们提供以下课程：

- *与他人合作：*学习实用的沟通技巧，您可以即刻把它们运用到实际的职场中去。
- *求职策略：*学习和实践你需要在加拿大劳动市场上的职位更具竞争力的技能。
- *加拿大工作场所整合：*学习沟通方式，如何适应加拿大工作场所的劳务机制。

August 15   Vancouver Neighbourhoods

8月15日   温哥华社区

Main District

Main street, the shopping and restaurant area of the Mount Pleasant area, was called one of the top 15 "coolest streets" in North America. The area has a strong independent feeling and is home to the city's hippest trendsetter people and artists – over 50 percent of the population is between 30 and 50 years old. Many of the shops and restaurants are small and specialized and serve the trendiest food and drinks. They cherish their individuality and discourage large chain stores and restaurants from moving into the area. Main Street is also home to most of the city's antique furniture stores, and many hours can be spent exploring the fine goods from the past. Main Street's unique combination of history and modern trends makes it a fascinating place to spend an afternoon.

主街·http://mountpleasantbia.com/·

　　主街是南北走向，贯通整个温哥华市，其中芒特普莱森特地区最热闹的餐饮和购物区被称为北美十五个最酷的街道之一。该地区非常独特，是温哥华那些最时尚且引领潮流的艺术家们所在的地方。其中半数以上的人年龄都在30至50岁之间。许多商店和餐馆不大，但都很有特色，专门供应最前卫的食物和饮料。他们非常珍惜和维护当地的传统，阻止大型连锁店和餐馆迁入该地区。主街上还有很多旧的古董家具店，花上几个小时，说不定可以淘到精美的东西。融合了独特的历史和现代潮流使得主街成为当今温哥华最迷人的地方。

August 16   # Basic Everyday English

8月16日   基本日常生活用语

At the Coffee shop

Vancouverites love to meet their friends and business colleagues at coffee shops. Usually coffee shops serve coffee, tea, frozen fruit and cream mixed drinks and simple snacks like muffins, cookies and sandwiches. Some coffee shops chains like Starbucks and Tim Hortons almost have their own language with their unusual names for their drinks and drink sizes!

在咖啡馆·

温哥华人喜欢约上朋友和同事在咖啡馆见面。 通常咖啡馆供应咖啡、茶、冷冻水果、奶油混合饮料和简单的小吃，如松饼、饼干、 三明治。大型咖啡馆连锁店如星巴克和蒂姆·霍顿都有各自的语言，他们的饮料和不同饮料杯尺寸都有不同寻常的名字！

English for Everyday Life
日常生活英语

下面是一些基本英语短语，您也许听到过，在咖啡馆可能会用到。 请访问我们的网站 www.mynewlifeinvancouver.com，听一听这些短语的发音并练习会话。

How can I help you?
I would like a large black coffee
I would like a medium coffee with 2 milk and 2 sugar
I would like a small coffee with 1 milk and 1 sugar
Would you like anything else?
I would like a muffin please
Would you like that heated up?
I would like a muffin heated up please

我能帮您什么忙吗？
我想要一份大杯的不加奶的清咖啡。
我要一份中杯的咖啡，加2份牛奶和2份糖。
我要一份小杯的咖啡，加1份牛奶和1份糖。
您还要点别的吗？
我想要一块松饼。
您想把它加热吗？
我想要一块松饼，请热一下。

August 17   Education

8月17日　　教育

French immersion and Mandarin Immersion School Programs

French Immersion is a program that can offer your child a fun, effective and challenging way to learn French at an early age. Generally, the curriculum is instructed in French from Kindergarten to the end of Grade 3. From Grades 4-7, 50-80% of the curriculum is taught in French. In Secondary School, from Grades 8-10, 50% of the curriculum is taught in French, in Grade 11, 25% of the curriculum is taught in French, and in Grade 12, at least 12.5% of the curriculum is taught in French. Students enrolled in French immersion study the same BC curriculum as students in the English-language program.

The **Early Mandarin Program** is in Norquay Elementary School. The program is a language instruction program where children learn the language and study in the language for part of the day. The day is structured to allow 50% of the time to be in Mandarin: Mandarin Language Arts, Music, Physical Education, and Career and Personal Planning. The program is intended for children who have fluency in English.

沉浸式法语和普通话课程·

　　沉浸式法语课程是一个可以为您的孩子提供的学习计划：一个有趣，有效和具有挑战性的方法来在幼年学习法语。一般来说，BC课程是从幼儿园到3年级的法语教学。在4-7年级，BC省的50-80％的课程是用法语授课的。在中学，8-10年级，BC省50％的课程采用法语授课，11年级，25％的课程采用法语授课，12年级至少12.5％的课程授课法语。参加法语沉浸的学生与英语语言课程中的学生一样学习同样内容的BC课程。

　　早期普通话双语课程设在诺奎小学。该计划是一个教学计划，让孩子在一天中花一部分时间学习汉语。允许50％的时间说普通话：普通话语言艺术，音乐，体育，职业和个人规划。该计划面向英语流利的儿童。

August 18 # Scenes from Daily Life

8月18日　　　日常生活中的一些镜头

Going for a Walk on the Seawall
在海堤上散步·

Outdoor Life in Vancouver

温哥华户外生活

Outdoor Swimming Pools

There are many public swimming pools in Vancouver, but the most beloved ones are the five outdoor swimming pools that are only open from May to September each year. Visiting the outdoor pools is a popular summer tradition. They are very large, heated and child-friendly pools located in beautiful locations — three in oceanfront locations and two in in beautiful treed parks. There is a small admission fee to enter, but it is possible to stay all day and enjoy a picnic and family time in between swims in the pool. The Kitsilano Beach and at Stanley Park outdoor pools are the largest ones and most popular. When the outdoor summer pools open, everyone knows for sure that summer has arrived!

室外游泳池·

　　温哥华有许多公共游泳池，其中有五个室外游泳池最受欢迎，其中三个位于海滨，两个设在美丽的绿树浓荫的公园内。每年仅在5月至9月开放。到了夏季人们喜欢前往室外游泳池玩耍，泳池都很大、可加热的，还有儿童游泳池。入场费很便宜，如果您愿意的话，可以一整天泡在那里，在泳池旁可以和家人享受野餐和分享快乐时光。基茨兰诺海滩和斯坦利公园室外游泳池是最大的，也是最热闹的。当室外夏季游泳池开放时，大家就知道夏天已经到了！

Tips to Learning English

资深英语老师提供学习英语的小贴士

Start with Vocabulary for Your Own Life

One tremendous advantage of being an adult English learner is that you are in full control of **WHAT** you learn and **HOW** you learn it. This is especially important for vocabulary. We all know that the larger your English vocabulary, the easier it will be for you to understand and use English. However, if the vocabulary words that you have are from categories that you never need in daily life – such as the English words for farm animals – then that is not going to be much help. So, focus your vocabulary studies on the categories of vocabulary that you need right now. Perhaps the words for foods for your grocery shopping, or the words for golf or tennis for your hobbies, or the words for banking and so on. Choose a category and learn the basic words for that one group and practice them daily, then focus on words for another category and practice them and before long, you will have mastered the key vocabulary you need for your daily life. These words could be different for everyone, depending on their lifestyle and hobbies. Write your vocabulary divided by categories in your English notebook, for example one page for food, one page for weather and so on. It is easier to learn and remember words in groups like this. It is even better if you can include pictures. Also, you can put post-it notes around your home with the English word for the various objects and items in your home. After a couple of weeks, you will have memorized many new words with this method.

从您自己生活所需的词汇开始·

　　成人学习英语最大的优势是，您完全可以控制您所学的东西以及如何学习它。词汇特别重要。我们都知道，您的英语词汇量越大，您就越容易理解和使用英语。然而，如果您所拥有的词汇来自于日常生活中不常用到的类别，比如农场动物，那就不会有太大的帮助了。因此，把您的词汇学习集中在您目前需要的词汇类别上。也许您需要去超市购买食品的词汇，或为您所爱好的高尔夫或网球运动的词汇，以及有关银行的词汇等等。选择一个类别，学习这一组词汇，每天勤加练习，然后再专注于另一个类别的词汇，并继续练习，不久之后，您就掌握了日常生活所需要的关键词汇。这些词汇对每个人来说都是不同的，这取决于他们的生活方式和爱好。在英语记事本上写下词汇分类，比如，一页为食物，一页为天气等等。像这样的分类学习和记忆单词相对比较容易。如果您可以附上图片则效果会更好。此外，您可以把家中所有物品贴上英语单词的便利贴。用这种方法，几个星期后，您会记住许多新的词汇。

　　　A Little Canadian Inspiration

8月21日　　　一点点启示

*"Medicine, as we are practising it, is a luxury trade. We are selling
bread at the price of jewels... Let us take the profit, the private
economic profit, out of medicine, and purify our profession of
rapacious individualism... Let us say to the people not "How
much have you got?" but "How best can we serve you?"*

– Norman Bethune, Canadian Physician

Although it is difficult to believe, Norman Bethune was completely
unknown in Canada during his lifetime. He only became famous in
Canada and around the world when Chairman Mao Zedong of the
People's Republic of China published his essay entitled In Memory of
Norman Bethune which documented the final months of the doctor's
life in China.

> 正如我们正在经历的那样，医学是一种奢侈品交易。我们正以珠
> 宝价格出售面包 – 它让我们获利，获得私营经济的利润，如何才能净
> 化我们贪婪的医学职业。我们不能对患者说：“你们有多少钱？”而
> 是“我们该怎样才能更好地为您服务？”
>
> 　　　　　　　　　　——加拿大医生诺尔曼·白求恩

　　很难想象，诺尔曼　·　白求恩生前在加拿大完全不为人知。直到
1939年11月12日，白求恩在医治伤员时被感染，在河北唐县不幸逝
世；中华人民共和国毛泽东主席发表题为《纪念白求恩》的文章，高
度赞扬了白求恩的共产主义、国际主义精神，才广为世人所知。

Vancouver Farmers Markets

Do you love healthy, organic and delicious food? Do you love the exciting environment of a busy food market? If so, volunteering at one of the seven outdoor Farmers' Markets will interest you. Here are some of the volunteer jobs that you can find with the markets:

- Create a welcoming atmosphere at the market

- Help the food vendors when they need a break

- Help manage pedestrian traffic around the market

- Promote special events

- Accept donations to local food programs

温哥华农贸市场 http://eatlocal.org/volunteer/

　　您喜欢健康，美味的有机食物吗？ 您喜欢繁忙的令人兴奋的食品市场吗？ 如果是这样，7个不同的户外农贸市场会对您感兴趣。以下是您可以在市场上找到的一些志愿服务工作：

- 在市场上创造友好的气氛；
- 在食品供应商需要休息时帮助他们；
- 帮助管理市场周边的行人交通安全；
- 特别促销活动；
- 接受捐赠给当地的食物。

Healthcare in Vancouver

8月23日　　温哥华的医疗保健

Registered Massage Therapist

In British Columbia, a Registered Massage Therapist is a highly trained health professional who must complete a challenging 3000-hour program before becoming registered. Massage Therapists must be licensed by the RMT Association of BC before they can work with clients. Registered Massage Therapists work to treat your symptoms of pain and dysfunction caused by many different underlying health conditions. They are responsible for:

1. Assessing and diagnosing soft tissue and joints of the body

2. Treating and preventing injury, pain and physical disorders

One hour of therapeutic massage by a licensed RMT will cost between $120 and $180, and the Medical Services Plan will not cover these costs. However, many extended health plans will cover a percentage of the cost of massage, but only if the massages are done by licensed RMTs. The professional RMT Association of BC has a search screen that helps you find a licensed RMT in a convenient location. You do not need a doctor's referral to see an RMT.

注册按摩师•

BC省注册按摩治疗协会 https://www.rmtbc.ca/find-rmt

在不列颠哥伦比亚省，注册按摩治疗师都是受过高度训练的健康专业人士，他们必须在行医前完成具有挑战性的3000小时课程。按摩治疗师必须获得BC省RMT协会许可，才能为客户服务。注册按摩治疗师主要治疗由许多不同健康状况引起的疼痛和功能障碍的症状。他们负责：

1. 评估和诊断身体软组织和关节。
2. 治疗和预防损伤、疼痛和身体障碍。

有RMT执照的按摩师一小时治疗按摩费用在120加元到180加元之间，而医疗服务计划将不包括这些费用。然而，许多扩展的健康计划将包括按摩项目。但必须由授权RMT的按摩师来做。BC省注册按摩治疗协会网站有一个搜索界面，可方便地帮助您在附近找到一个有执照的RMT。您不需要其他医生的推荐。

Interesting Facts About Vancouver

8月24日　　温哥华趣闻

The Five Sister Cities

Sister cities are a form of legal or social agreement between different cities around the world to promote cultural and commercial ties. The purpose of making sister city agreements is to promote friendship and understanding between different cultures and to encourage trade and tourism. The idea came after World War II as a way to prevent such a terrible event ever happening again.

Vancouver has five sister cities around the world:

1. Guangzhou, China

2. Los Angeles, USA.

3. Yokohama, Japan

4. Edinburgh, UK

5. Odessa, Ukraine

温哥华的五个姊妹城市·

　　姐妹城市（是指友好城市）是世界不同城市之间促进文化和商业联系的一种法律或社会协议。建立姐妹城市协议的目的是增进不同文化之间的友谊和理解，并鼓励贸易和旅游业。姊妹城市这个概念是在第二次世界大战之后发展出来的。

　　温哥华在世界各地共有五个姐妹城市：

　　1.　中国广州
　　2.　美国洛杉矶
　　3.　日本横滨
　　4.　英国爱丁堡
　　5.　乌克兰敖德萨

August 25   Finding Work in Vancouver

8月25日   在温哥华找份工作

SUCCESS

S.U.C.C.E.S.S. is one of the largest social service agencies in British Columbia and it offers many services to support newcomers to the city. One of the biggest programs is S.U.C.C.E.S.S. Employment Services (SES) which was started to assist job seekers to overcome employment barriers in 1984. SES is a culturally diverse service team providing career development guidance services for all job seekers. They also have a virtual resource website to give job seekers easy access to online resources and run an online job board. Their advisors are available to provide free one-on-one appointments to answer your questions about employment, government services and benefits as well as immigration and work permits.

SUCCESS 中侨互助会 https://www.successbc.ca/

中侨互助会（简称中侨）是加拿大卑诗省最大的社会服务团体之一，始于1984年，服务对象是省内的各族裔新旧移民和居民，最大的课程之一是S.U.C.C.E.S.S. 就业服务。主要目的是协助新移民适应新生活，克服就业障碍，协助新旧移民尽快融入社会。中侨互助会也是一个文化多元化的服务团队，为所有求职者提供职业发展指导服务。他们还有一个虚拟资源网站，使求职者能够轻松地访问在线资源，并查看在线工作招聘广告。他们的顾问可以提供免费的一对一指导，回答您有关就业、政府服务、福利以及移民和工作许可证等问题。

August 26   Vancouver Sightseeing

8月26日   观光

Science World

The large silver dome of Science World is a well-known site by False Creek. It is home to many displays that will excite your mind and help you discover the wonders of science. Their displays are interactive and their live science demonstrations and films in the OMNIMAX Theatre will entertain the family for a whole afternoon. The exhibitions change regularly, so there is always something new and interesting to see at Science World.

科学世界·https://www.scienceworld.ca/

　　科学世界是一座位于福溪东端的球型屋顶建筑，是温哥华的一个知名的景点。众多的展品将激发您的灵感，帮助您发现科学的奇迹。展品是互动的，现场提供科学演示，OMNIMAX影院整个下午都在循环放映科技节目。展品定期更新，所以您总可以在科学世界看到一些新的和有趣的东西。

August 27　　　Vancouver Transportation

8月27日　　　温哥华交通运输

The Bus Network – on Land and Sea

There is a large network of buses, trolleys and community shuttle buses that run throughout the city and connect to the Skytrain stations. The buses run from early morning to late evening. Late in the night, there are 12 Nightbus routes that cover the city until approximately 3 am. There is also a Seabus passenger ferry that connects downtown Vancouver (Waterfront Station) with the North Shore (Lonsdale Quay Exchange). It can seat up to 400 passengers at a time and departs every 15 to 30 minutes during the day and evening. From Lonsdale Quay Exchange, it is possible to connect with the large network of North Shore buses, including the buses that go up to the local ski mountains.

Although the bus system is very good, it is not always able to handle all the people who want to ride during the rush hours (7:30 to 9:00 am and 3:30 to 6:00 pm). The buses are packed during these times and if there is no more space for another passenger, and if no one is getting off at the bus stop, the driver won't stop and will just keep driving. Sometimes this can happen two or three times before a bus comes along that has room for passengers, and it can be very frustrating. On the positive side, this situation usually encourages all the people at the bus stop to talk to each other, and so is a chance for more English practice!

巴士网络· ·陆地的和海上的·

Translink旅行计划http://tripplanning.translink.ca/
Translink手机程序 – 下一班车提醒http://m.translink.ca/
海上巴士信息www.translink.ca

温哥华有一个大型的交通枢纽：公交车、电车和社区穿梭巴士遍及整个城市并与天车相连。公共汽车从清晨一直运营到深夜。晚间有12条巴士路线，覆盖整个城市，末班车大约在凌晨3点左右。还有一个海上巴士客运渡轮，连接温哥华市中心（海滨站）与北岸（朗斯代尔码头交换站）。它一次可以容纳多达400名乘客，每天早晚每间隔15到30分钟开一班。朗斯代尔码头也是北温哥华大型的交通中转站，在那里您可以换乘去不同目的地的公交车，其中包括抵达当地滑雪山的巴士。

公交系统是非常好的，但是，在高峰时间（上午7:30至9:00和下午3:30至6:00），它无法满足所有的乘客的需求。在这两个时间段里，公共汽车都挤满了，如果没有更多的空间再容纳另一名乘客，或者如果没有人在中途的公共汽车站下车，司机是不会停车的，他/她将继续开往下一站。有时这种情况可能会发生两到三次，这是非常令人沮丧的。不过，也有它积极的一面，这种情况通常鼓励所有等车的人在公共汽车站互相交谈，以便有更多机会来练习英语对话！

English for Everyday Life
日常生活英语

请记住，靠近车门的座位是提供给残疾人和老年人的，也包括那些抱着非常年幼的儿童以及推着婴儿车的父母。这些人真的很感谢您为他们让出座位。在这种情况下您可以说：

"Excuse me, would you like a seat?"

"对不起，您要座位吗？" "

有时候，他们会喜欢站着，会回答说

"no thank you",

"不啦，谢谢"，或者他们会说

"thank you and sit down in your seat".

"谢谢您，不要起来"。

August 28   # Sports Teams and Special Events

8月28日   专业体育赛事和活动

Vancouver Giants Team

The Vancouver Giants are a junior ice hockey team playing in the Western Hockey League (WHL). The junior major league is where young players practice their skills and improve until they are recruited into the major Canadian Hockey Leagues at the yearly draft pick. Although not professional players, the level of play is very competitive and the games are very family friendly and affordable. The Giants always make an effort to make the game nights a fun time for every-one. Their home rink is the Langley Events Centre in the Township of Langley which is a suburb of Vancouver.

温哥华巨人队•http://vancouvergiants.com/•

　　温哥华巨人在西部冰球联盟（WHL)是一支重要的少年冰球队。 初级大联盟是年轻球员练习和提高他们的技能，直到每年在选秀的时候被招募到加拿大主要冰球联赛中去。虽然他们不是职业球员，但其比赛的水平非常有竞争力，比赛总是在友好的气氛中进行的，门票很便宜。巨人们总是努力让比赛之夜成为每个人的快乐时光。他们的主场设在温哥华的郊区兰利镇上的活动中心。

Vancouver Parks

8月29日 温哥华公园

Central Park

This is one of Burnaby's most popular parks and it is easily accessible just off Boundary Road and Kingsway with easy access to Skytrain. This park stands out by having so many towering trees. The large park is covered with Douglas fir, Western Hemlock, Cedar, Poplar and Maple groves. Central Park is also known for its excellent sports and recreation facilities. Tennis courts, outdoor swimming pool, horseshoe pitch and a pitch-and-putt golf course are all popular attractions. Swangard Stadium is located in the park and it hosts many sporting events such as track and field competitions, soccer matches and charity fundraising sports events. In addition, it hosts cultural events like the Annual Korean Cultural Heritage Festival.

中央公园•

中央公园是本拿比市最受欢迎的公园，去那里很方便，乘坐轻轨在金斯韦街毗邻的边界路站下车即是。超过85公顷的园区面积矗立着许多参天大树，有道格拉斯冷杉、西铁杉、雪松、白杨树和枫树林。中央公园的体育和娱乐设施都是一流的。网球场，室外游泳池，马蹄形球场和一个迷你高尔夫球场都是受当地人欢迎的。斯万加德体育场也坐落在公园里，那里举办许多体育赛事，如田径比赛、足球比赛和慈善筹款体育赛事。此外，它还举办各种文化活动，如一年一度的韩国文化遗产节。

August 30　Stories and Advice for Newcomers

8月30日　　移民的故事和建议

Joel

新移民可以彼此学到很多东西·

　　在我的家人、朋友、英语老师以及我在温哥华遇到的所有人那里学会了如何成功地在这座新城市创造一个新的生活。新移民可以彼此学到很多东西。我们老师和学生之间的关系是上帝赐予的。我们应该敞开心扉，在这个新的世界中创造出更加美好的生活。此外，由于文化是一门世界性的语言，我们必须养成学习新文化的习惯。Kari是新移民最好的英语良师和传播加拿大文化的益友。我从未见过像她这样热心肠的老师，一旦她成为您的老师，那您就已经成功了。

August 31	Diverse Vancouver
8月31日	多元文化的温哥华

Experience Persian Culture in North Vancouver

The upper Lonsdale area of North Vancouver from 15th Avenue onward is where many of Vancouver's immigrants from Iran live and operate businesses and restaurants. To experience a taste of Iranian culture, you can eat at some famous Persian restaurants like the Cazba and Zeytoon, or enjoy some sweet treats at the Golestan and Laleh bakeries, or choose from a very large selection of nuts and dried fruits at Ayoub's beautifully decorated store. A great time to visit the area is during the Persian New Year celebration called **Nowruz** in March when you can enjoy many small celebrations with live music, shopping and special food for sale.

在北温哥华体验波斯文化•

北温哥华北部朗斯代尔地区从第15大道起，许多从伊朗来温哥华的移民在那里的居住并经营企业，开餐馆。要体验伊朗的饮食文化，你不妨去一些有名的波斯餐厅用餐，比如Cazba和Zeytoon，或者在Golestan和Laleh面包店品尝一些甜点，或者从装饰精美品种齐全的Ayoub 商店的中选择你喜欢的坚果和干果。访问该地区的最佳的时间是在每年三月份波斯新年的庆祝活动称为Nowruz。届时你可以在北温哥华享受许多小型庆祝活动，现场音乐，购物，还可以买到特别的食品。

September

Weather:	Average temperature: 11°C to 20°C
	Average rainfall days: 11, Average rainfall: 22 mm
Statutory holiday:	Labour Day (the first Monday in September)
Other special days:	First day of school!
	First day of Autumn and the Chinese Mid-Autumn Moon Festival

Even though the first day of Fall is in September, this month feels like another summer month in Vancouver. The weather continues to be sunny and fairly dry, yet the locals continue to be outside as much as possible to enjoy the long days and good weather. After a two-month summer vacation, the children go back to school at the beginning of September and most after-school activities and sports also resume in September. From late August to mid-September all the shopping malls are busy with people preparing for the "Back to School" rush. Life really gets fast again for everyone. Many businesses and offices start working on new projects and working longer hours again after the slow days of summer. However, despite the busy work and school schedules, there are many events that happen in September, some of which celebrate the coming of fall on the Fall Equinox* (Sept 20 or 21).

The beautiful Dr. Sun Yat-Sen Classical Chinese Garden hosts the Mid-Autumn Moon Festival to celebrate the second biggest holiday in the Chinese calendar. At this annual family festival, there is music, storytelling, games, kids' crafts; the creation of a community lantern; and of course, Moon cakes.

The Southlands neighbourhood hosts a Country Fair in September which has pony rides, petting farm, games, horse entertainment, silent auction*, used book/toy sale, food, free activities, and more.

The west side neighbourhood of Kerrisdale also hosts Kerrisdale Days which feature live music, clowns, face painting, rides and amazing sidewalk sales at all the boutiques along West 41st Avenue. Also in the west side, Dunbar Village holds its annual Harvest Festival during this month with live music, activities for adults and kids plus games and giveaways from the local stores. The Wesbrook neighbourhood at UBC holds their Wesbrook Village Festival every September with a free barbecue, live music, rock-climbing wall and kids' zone.

The Mount Pleasant neighbourhood hosts the Autumn Shift Festival which brings live entertainment, shopping, food and fun to the streets – they even close Main street to vehicles so that there is more room for the celebration.

West Vancouver holds its annual Coho Festival on the second Sunday in September and it features their famous Coho Salmon Barbecue, pancake breakfast, the Coho Garden, Kids Park, Main Stage, and the Squamish Nation Village.

Another popular event is the Luxury & Supercar Weekend which takes place in VanDusen Gardens and showcases the very best in rare, classic and modern supercars, high fashion, watches and jewelry and is accompanied by the best specialty foods, wines and spirits.

For those feeling homesick for movies from their home country, the Vancouver International Film Festival (VIFF) is a great way to see over 400 films from more than 70 countries screened over 16 days in late September and early October. The international movies are shown in the original languages with English subtitles.

Finally, the GranFondo Bicycle race takes place every September. This race is Canada's premier cycling event and hundreds of competitors ride 122 km from Sea to Sky on a dedicated highway lane from downtown Vancouver to Whistler.

9月

> 气候： 平均温度：11°C 到 20°C
> 平均降雨天数：11，平均降雨量： 22 毫米
> 公众节假日： 劳动节 （9月的第一个星期一）
> 其他特殊日：开学的第一天
> 秋天的第一天和中国的中秋节

即使秋季的第一天是在九月，可是这个月温哥华的气温让人感觉起来仿佛还未脱离夏季。天气依旧晴朗、相当干燥，当地人尽可能多的留在户外晒晒太阳，同时享受爽朗的天气。经过两个月的暑假，九月初孩子们回到学校，大多数的课外活动和体育活动经过暑期的停顿之后也陆续恢复了正常。从8月底到九月中旬，所有购物商场都会为那些准备"返校"的孩子们忙碌着。每个人的生活节奏又开始变得快了起来。经过漫长的夏季，许多企业和办公室又开始着手研究新的项目。然而尽管繁忙的工作和学校的教学日程，九月份仍然会发生许多事件。最主要的是庆祝即将到来的秋分（9月20日或21日），不同的社区和街区庆祝的方式会略有不同。

在美丽的中山公园里举办一年一度的大型庆祝活动，庆祝中国第二大传统节日 – 中秋节。有音乐、讲故事、玩游戏；有孩子们制作的工艺品；还有社区制作的灯笼；当然少不了月饼。

南国马术俱乐部9月份举办一个集市，可骑小马、抚摸宠物、马术娱乐；无声拍卖会、旧书和玩具销售；饮食、各种免费的活动等等。

克里斯戴尔西部地区举办克里斯戴尔日，当天有现场音乐、小丑表演、画脸谱、还有游乐设施，沿西 41街人行道上所有的精品店都有惊人的销售量。此外，在西边的邓巴社区9月也举办一年一度的丰收节，有现场音乐演奏，当地的商店特意为大人和孩子们准备了游戏和赠品。于此同时，在哥伦比亚大学附近的维斯布鲁克社区每年9月有免费的烧烤、现场音乐、攀岩和儿童活动区。

芒特•普莱森特社区举办金秋节，主要项目有现场娱乐表演、购物、食品和趣味街道 – 他们甚至关闭Main大道，禁止车辆通行，以便为庆祝活动腾出更多的空间。

西温哥华在9月的第二个星期天举办其年度的银大麻哈节，最引人注目是它著名的银大麻哈鱼烧烤配有煎饼的早餐。节日特别安排了银大麻哈鱼花园、儿童乐园、主舞台表演和斯夸米什民族村上演的节目。

另一个受欢迎的活动是周末发生在范杜森花园奢华跑车和展示最罕见的古典与现代超级跑车，还有高级时装，手表和珠宝，配有最好的特色食品，葡萄酒和烈性酒。

对于那些思乡的人来说，能看一场本国的电影也是一个不错的方法，温哥华国际电影电影节（VIFF）从九月下旬一直持续到十月上旬历时16天，有来自超过70个国家的400多部影片上映。所有的影片均保持原始语言对白，配上英文字幕。

最后是每年9月举行GranFondo 自行车赛。它是加拿大首屈一指的自行车赛事。从温哥华市中心到惠斯勒的海天公路上有一条专用的车道，全程122公里，它吸引了数百名参赛者。

更多的信息：

周末奢华的超级跑车：http://www.luxurysupercar.com/

中秋月饼节：http://vancouverchinesegarden.com/things-to-do/public-programs/

南国马术俱乐部：
http://www.southlandsridingclub.com/country-fair/

芒特·普莱森特金秋节：http://mountpleasantbia.com/bia-events/autumn-shift-festival/

克里斯戴尔日：http://www.kerrisdalevillage.com/

韦斯布鲁克村节：http://discoverwesbrook.com/

银大马哈鱼节：http://www.cohosociety.com/coho-festival/

邓巴丰收节：
http://www.dunbarvillage.ca/component/rseventspro/event/6-harvest-festival-2016

温哥华国际电影节：https://www.viff.org

温哥华到惠斯勒的GranFondo海天公路自行车赛：
http://granfondowhistler.com/

Fall Equinox （秋分）：秋天的第一天。

Fall or Autumn （秋天或秋季）：这个季节有两个名字！Fall是美式英语秋天的说法，Autumn是英式英语秋天的说法！在加拿大这两个单词都可以使用。

silent auction（无声拍卖会）：捐赠的奖品放在显示器上，人们可以写下他们愿意购买的价钱，悄悄地、秘密地写一张纸上。在活动结束时，主办方将查看所有的文件和把它送给写的最高价格的人。

September 1   Local Customs

9月1日   当地的习俗

Customs for Responding to Bad News

"Get Well" Customs When Someone is Ill or Injured

We express our concern when we hear bad news about people who are ill or injured in a few ways, depending on how well we know them. If someone that we are close to becomes sick or injured, we send them a special greeting card or a bouquet of flowers. In addition, if they are seriously sick or inactive for a long time, we will also drop off some cooked meals or snacks so that they don't need to worry about cooking. Also, we might offer to help them with difficult physical tasks such as cutting the grass or shovelling the snow.

Responding to General Bad News

The custom for responding to hearing bad news is to show sympathy and then offer support. It can be very difficult to know what to say in these situations, but you can simply express that you are sorry to hear about their bad news and ask if you can help.

如何面对坏消息

当得知某人生病或受伤时，习惯上说"您会好起来的"

当我们得知某人生病或受伤的消息时，我们在表达对其关注有一下几种方法，这取决于我们对这个人的了解程度。

English for Everyday Life

日常生活英语

我们可以简单地说一些安慰的话，例如：

"I am very sorry to hear that you are not feeling well"
"I am sorry that you are injured. Is there anything I can do to help?"

"我很抱歉听到您感觉不舒服"
"我很遗憾您受伤了。有什么我可以帮忙的吗？"

如果人们对您说这些话时，您可以回答说：

"Thank you for your concern"
"Thank you for your offer of help, but so far I am doing ok"
"谢谢您的关心"
"谢谢您的帮助，我目前的状况还好。"

如果我们亲密的朋友生病或受伤，我们寄一张特别的卡片或一束鲜花。如果他们患有严重疾病或者是行动不便，我们会煮一些菜肴，如炖锅菜、烤宽面条（浇上肉末番茄汁），或小吃如松饼，直接送过去，使他们不必担心做饭的问题。此外，我们可能会提供其他需要体力的帮助，如割草或铲雪等等。

回应一般的坏消息

当我们听到坏消息的时候，首先是表示同情，然后提供帮助。也许我们很难知道在这些情况下该说些什么，尽管如此，我们还是提供一些常用的表达方式。

English for Everyday Life

日常生活英语

当您听到坏消息，想要表达您对此关切的时候，有这样一句短语，您可以在任何情况下使用：

"I am very sorry to hear that. If there is anything I can do to help, please let me know."

"听到这个消息我很难过。如果有什么我能帮忙的，请告诉我。"

Parenting in Vancouver

在温哥华养育子女

Playdates and sleepovers

For young children, parents play a role in helping them make friends. One way that parents can help is by making **playdates** for their children. When parents see that their child likes to play with a certain child at school, they can contact the child's parent and invite them over for a playdate. A playdate is an appointment that parents make for their children to play together. As children today have very busy schedules, this can be a way that parents can make sure there is also time for friends and practicing social skills.

Older children like to have **sleepovers**. This involves inviting some close friends to dinner and then to sleep overnight in their home – usually in sleeping bags in the living rooms so they can stay up late and have fun. The next morning everyone shares a big breakfast together, plays some more and then the guests go home. Sleepovers are special events that only happen on the weekend or during school holidays and sometimes as part of a birthday party.

玩耍约会和在同学家过夜

对于年幼的孩子，在帮助他们交朋友方面父母将发挥很大的作用。 其中的一种方法就是帮孩子安排玩耍约会。当父母看到自己的孩子喜欢在学校和某个孩子玩耍时，他们可以联系那个孩子的父母，约个时间邀请他们过来一起玩耍。playdate(是由几个家长安排的)玩耍约会。由于今天的孩子有非常繁忙的日程安排，这可能是一种非常有效的方式，父母可以确保孩子有时间与其他小朋友练习社交技能。

岁数大一些的孩子，喜欢在别人家过夜。这包括邀请一些亲密的朋友共进晚餐，然后在朋友家里睡一会儿 – 通常是在客厅的睡袋里，所以他们可以晚上呆在一起熬夜，开开心心的玩。第二天早上，大家在一起共享一顿丰盛的早餐，再玩一会，然后各自回家休息。在别人家过夜属于特殊的事件，通常只发生在周末或者学校的假期，有时也作为生日聚会的一部分。

September 3   Stories and Advice for Newcomers

9月3日   新移民的故事

Keri

在温哥华成功的培养孩子成长的心得

我10年前移民加拿大温哥华，当时儿子10岁，现在儿子上大学三年级。很高兴有机会分享一下培养孩子成长的心得。

首先要陪伴孩子一同成长。陪伴孩子成长不仅是煮饭接送他，也要与他一起学习和上进。例如努力学英文，一个榜样的示范力量强大。我从ESL 1级开始，直到完成Law 12 and English 12.

其次，一起去做义工，参与接触社会并回馈社会。我和儿子一起做了上千个小时的义工，双双获得2013 年度UNA 社区优秀义工奖。例如创建了社区青年乐队，乐队去老人院演出并为Food bank 筹集善款。

创建Lord Byng secondary 华人家长委员会，担任四年义工主席，组织华人家人，支持学校的多项活动；做义工参与了解支持政治选举。

最后也是最重要的一点，就是带儿子去教会，接触基督教信仰并成为基督的门徒。我们一起读圣经祷告，经历上帝的大能和大爱，使我们生命得以更新，更有爱心，喜乐，和平和盼望。谢谢！

Classical Music and Dance

There are many small classical music and dance societies and groups that organize concerts in small venues around the city. However, there are only three major classical music and dance organizations in Vancouver: a symphony orchestra, an opera company, and a professional dance company. All of them produce a yearly calendar of events. You can buy tickets to individual concerts or you can become a season ticket holder and receive a package of tickets to several of the concerts in the season.

古典音乐与舞蹈

温哥华有许多民间小型的音乐和舞蹈团体经常在城市周边的小场地上举办免费的音乐会。此外，温哥华有三大古典音乐和舞蹈组织，他们分别是：温哥华交响乐团、温哥华歌剧院和BC芭蕾舞团。他们每年会预告演出活动的日程安排。您可以购买单次门票，季票，或者是几场音乐会的套票。

September 5 # Best Elementary Schools

9月5日　　温哥华著名的小学

Norma Rose Point Elementary School (public)

Here is the description of the school from their website: "Norma Rose Point School is located on Musqueam land, within the University Endowment Lands, neighbour to the University of British Columbia (UBC) and part of the University Hill Secondary and Elementary Family of Schools. The staff and Parent Advisory Council are committed to working with our community in helping each child enjoy a positive and challenging educational experience. We look forward to serving this school community well!"

诺玛玫瑰点小学（公立）
http://go.vsb.bc.ca/schools/normarosepoint

下面是学校网站的描述：

"诺玛玫瑰点学校位于马斯魁地区，是UBC大学捐赠的土地，临近UBC大学，是其附属中学和小学的一部分，工作人员和家长咨询委员会尽最大的努力与我们的校区合作，帮助每一个儿童享有积极的和具有挑战性的教育经验。我们期待着为这所学校服务！"

Expressing Yourself

Canadians consider their country a place where all are considered equal and there is not a strict hierarchy of different classes and status that need to be respected. Instead, everyone is considered to have the same right to expressing their opinions as anyone else. Hierarchy and different status levels is not something that Canadians think are important. Canadians consider themselves strong individualists who can take care of themselves while also taking care of their community. Therefore, if they see something that needs to be changed to make things better, then they will feel comfortable to express themselves. This right also extends to children. Canadian children today can speak their thoughts and feelings, even to adults and parents, in the same open way that they would do with their friends. Also, in the workplace, employees can express their thoughts, opinions, and ideas openly to their employers. It is also possible for citizens to share their opinions and ideas with the local, provincial, and federal government officials. However, all this communication must be done in a very polite, quiet, and respectful way. Everyone can share their thoughts, but if it is done in a violent or aggressive manner then Canadians don't like that as it disturbs the peaceful quality of everyday life.

表达自己的观点

加拿大人认为自己的国家处处都是平等的，不存在严格的等级制度，人人都需要得到尊重。相反，每个人都拥有与其他人一样表达自己观点的权利。加拿大人认为社会地位并不重要。他们十分强调个人的独立，他们在照顾好自己的同时也去照顾他们的社区。因此如果他们看到有任何改变可以使事情变得更好，那么他们会毫无顾虑地说出自己的想法。这项权利也适用于儿童。今天加拿大的孩子们可以同样开诚布公说出自己的想法和感受，即便是对大人和父母直言。此外，在工作场所，员工可以向雇主公开表达自己的意见和想法。公民也可以直接与地方，省，联邦政府官员分享自己的意见和想法。然而，所有这些沟通都必须以礼貌、安静和尊重的方式进行。每个人都可以分享他们的想法，但如果是以暴力或侵犯的方式去做，则不受加拿大人的欢迎，因为它打扰了人们平静的生活。

Best High Schools

温哥华著名的中学

Magee High School (public)

Here is the description of the school from their website: "Magee Secondary is committed to: Developing capable young people, promoting creative minds, healthy bodies, ethical values and providing a rigorous academic program leading students to take responsibility for learning, community and the joy of learning. The MAGEE LEADERSHIP PROGRAM fosters the responsibilities of citizenship and individual potential to effect positive change in our society. The cohort consists of curious, compassionate and committed grade 8 and 9 students looking for academic enrichment, and leadership and community service opportunities. The SPARTS program is an educational program to students competing in "High Performance Athletics" at the provincial, national or international levels, and students performing in an area of the "Arts" at an extremely high level of excellence. The SPARTS program offers students in grades 8 through 12 the opportunity to complete their academic requirements at Magee in preparation for secondary school graduation and post-secondary entrance, while allowing them to maintain their rigorous training and competition schedule outside of school. Magee's SPARTS program is open to "high performance" artistic or athletic performers who are seriously committed to their education, training and competition."

玛吉中学 （公立）http://go.vsb.bc.ca/schools/magee

以下是学校网站上的描述：

"玛吉中学致力于培养有能力的年轻人，开发创造性思维、健康的身体和道德价值观，提供严谨的学术课程，引导学生学习的乐趣并承担社区的责任。玛吉领导计划强化公民的责任和提高个人的潜能，使我们的社会发生积极的变化。该计划小组由好奇、富有同情心和有决心的8，9年级的学生组成，他们希望获得学术上的成就，以及领导和服务社区的机会。SPARTS计划是针对在省级，国家或国际层面参加"高性能竞技运动"学生的教育计划，以及在"艺术"领域表现过人的学生。SPARTS计划为8至12年级的学生提供机会，要求他们完成在玛吉的学业，做好中学毕业和升学的准备，同时允许他们在校外保持严格的训练和竞赛日程。玛吉的SPARTS计划对"高绩效"艺术或体育天赋的同学开放，学生们认真接受教育、培训和参与竞争。"

September 8   The Homes of Vancouver

9月8日   温哥华住宅

A Townhouse
排屋

　排屋是一种居住房屋的式样，由多幢相连的双层或三层房屋组成，一排排屋之内相邻的房屋共用同一堵山墙。每户都有一个可直接进出的外门。

September 9 # Best Extracurricular Activities for Kids

9月9日   最佳儿童课外活动

Phoenix Gymnastics Club

Phoenix Gymnastics is one of the largest and most highly respected gymnastics clubs in Western Canada. Since 1969, their professional team has provided instruction and coaching from preschool to teenage children. Their programs are based on the "Fun, Fitness and Fundamentals" philosophy. They make sure children have fun while being active and learning and practicing their gymnastics skills. Their new Millennium Gym is a 15,500 square foot training facility equipped with full size competitive and recreational equipment. They also have a Tree House Gym which is a 1,100 square foot gym with specialized preschool gymnastics equipment. In addition they have a 3.600 square foot gym on West 10th that is designed specifically for preschool and pre-competitive training with a sprung floor, foam pit and trampoline.

凤凰体操俱乐部 http://www.phoenixgymnastics.com/

凤凰体操是加拿大西部最大和最受尊敬的体操俱乐部之一。自1969年以来，其专业团队提供了从学龄前到少年儿童的教学和辅导。他们的计划是基于"乐趣、健身和基本原理"。他们确保孩子们在积极进取的同时学习和练习体操技巧。他们全新的千年健身房是一个15,500平方英尺的培训设施，配备了全尺寸竞争地板、杆底、转筒式轨道，地板上铺有蹦床、泡沫坑、全套男女竞技和娱乐设备。他们还有一个树屋健身房，它是一个1100平方英尺的健身房，位于千年体育中心的夹层楼，配有专门的学龄前体操设备。他们在体育馆西10号也有一个3.600平方英尺的健身房，专门为学龄前和竞争前训练而设计的，配有弹簧地板，泡沫坑和蹦床。

September 10 Meeting Locals in Vancouver

9月10日   与当地人接触

Help Your Children Meet New People

It is always easy for newcomer children and teens to meet local people and other newcomers through school. However, another great way that you can help your children meet new people and improve their skills is by signing them up for a variety of activities outside of class time. There are many choices in Vancouver and there is a new online database called **Classtop** that makes it much easier for parents to know which activities are the best ones for their child. You can choose the categories of arts, sport and language and then read about the different groups and classes your children can join, as well as read ratings and reviews of the services by other parents.

通过课外活动帮助孩子认识新朋友

用中/英文提供的儿童课外活动单位的目录www.classtop.com

新移民的子女通过学校认识当地人和其他新移民总是比较容易的。其实，还有另一种更好的方式，可以帮助孩子结交新的朋友，那就是通过参加各种课外活动。在温哥华，有一个新的在线数据库，称为Classtop，便于家长知道哪些活动最适合提高孩子的技能。您可以选择感兴趣的艺术、体育和语言等类别，然后阅读其他家长的评分和点评。

September 11   Restaurant Customs and Etiquette

9月11日   餐厅的习俗与礼仪

Pairing Alcohol and Wine with Food

Many people just order one type of drink, say a glass of wine, and that is what they have during their whole meal at the restaurant. However, others like to order different alcoholic beverages to match different courses of their meal. Alcoholic drinks can be ordered with the different courses usually like this:

1. When you first arrive and during the **first appetizer course**: Enjoy beer or cocktails. Sometimes people prefer to enjoy a few of these drinks and small dishes before they order the main course because they want to take their time and enjoy the company and conversation. If the dinner is for a special celebration then champagne is ordered and served during this first course.

2. During the **second or main course**: Enjoy wine that goes well with your dinner. Traditionally, white wine is drunk with chicken and fish dishes and red wine with beef and pork dishes. However, these old rules are changing. Wine can be ordered by the glass or by the bottle.

3. During the **third or dessert course**: Enjoy coffee and after-dinner liqueurs like Cointreau or Grand Marnier with your dessert or cheese plate. Ice Wine, Sherry or Port are also some very sweet drinks that are enjoyed during the dessert course. Finally, there are special coffees like Spanish Coffee which combine coffee and strong liqueurs in a very delicious, yet powerful drink.

与食物搭配的酒精饮料和葡萄酒

许多人他们在餐厅用餐的整个过程，只是点一种饮料，比如说一杯红酒。不过，有的人则很讲究，他们会点不同的酒精饮料来搭配不同的菜肴。如何搭配请看下面的介绍：

1. 当您开口点菜的时候，可以让服务员在上第一道开胃菜的同时来一杯啤酒或鸡尾酒。有的人喜欢在上主菜之前就着小菜先喝着，因为他们想要花一点儿时间和朋友们聊聊天。如果是为特殊庆祝活动而举办的晚宴活动的话，则随第一道菜会送上香槟。

2. 在上第二道菜也就是主菜的时候，要搭配葡萄酒。传统上，白葡萄酒是用来搭配鸡肉和鱼之类的菜肴，而红葡萄酒则与牛肉和猪肉搭配。葡萄酒可以按杯或瓶来点要。

3. 在上第三道甜点的时候，您可以要一杯咖啡，和一杯甜酒，如君度或是金万利。您可以细细地品味。冰酒、雪利酒或普特酒都是非常甜的饮料。还有各种特殊口味的咖啡，像西班牙咖啡，它将咖啡和烈性酒兑在一起，非常好喝，当然后劲也不小。

September 12   Top English Programs for Adults

9月12日　　　成人高级英语课程

Vancouver School Board (VSB)

In addition to running all the elementary and high schools in Vancouver, the VSB also offers "upgrading" courses for adults. They provide English instruction for adults in their popular **English Foundation** courses. There are seven Foundation level courses and they are divided up into two skill groups: Speaking and Listening, Reading and Writing. After completing English Foundations level 7, students can continue taking adult education courses at the grade 10, 11 and 12 level. The Foundation courses are offered in the morning, afternoon, and evening.

温哥华教育局（VSB）　http://go.vsb.bc.ca

　　在温哥华除了所有的小学和中学，温哥华教育局也提供成人进修课程。为成人提供口语、听力、阅读和写作的基础英语指导。共有七级。达到7级水平的学生可以继续参加10、11和12年级的成人教育课程。 基础课程安排在早上，下午和晚上。

September 13　Vancouver Backyard Wildlife

9月13日　　温哥华后院的小鸟和动物

Coyotes

Coyotes are another animal that has learned how to survive in an urban environment. Cities provide many food opportunities for coyotes from garbage, pets, fruit/berries, compost, and bird seed. Coyotes are the most common wild dog species in BC. In urban areas, coyotes tend to more active during dusk, dawn and through the night. However, out in the mountain trails, you can see them at any time. They eat small mammals such as mice, voles, ground squirrels, rabbits and hares. They will also eat young birds, fish, insects, plant matter and berries.

Important Safety Information

- It is rare that there are human-coyote conflicts, but there have been records of coyotes becoming interested in and/or pursuing children during periods of low food availability or if they have become too used to being fed illegally by people.

- If you do come across a coyote who seems aggressive, pick up small children and slowly back away carrying them.

- Coyotes that lack fear of humans and/or display aggression towards humans should be reported to the Conservation Officer Service (COS) at 1-877-952-7277.

郊狼

郊狼是另一种在城市环境中学会生存的动物，与狼是近亲。城市中的垃圾、宠物、水果、浆果、堆肥和鸟蛋为郊狼提供了许多食物机会。郊狼是卑诗省最常见的野生动种。郊狼往往在黄昏、黎明和夜晚较为活跃。在山路上，您也可能随时看到它们。它们吃小型哺乳动物，如老鼠、田鼠、松鼠、家兔和野兔。他们还会吃小鸟、鱼、昆虫、植物和浆果。平均寿命为6-10年。

重要的安全信息

▸ 郊狼很少与人发生冲突，但有记录表明，在食物供应不足或他们习惯于被人非法喂养时，会袭击儿童。

▸ 如果您遇见一只看起来有攻击性的郊狼，把小孩抱起来，慢慢地走开。

▸ 当遇到不惧怕您或企图攻击您的郊狼，应该立刻拨打动物保护部门（COS）1-877-952-7277。

September 14   Support for Newcomers

9月14日   支持新移民

Immigrant Settlement & Integration Program (ISIP)

S.U.C.C.E.S.S. Immigrant Settlement & Integration Program (ISIP) assists immigrants, refugees and their families to learn about Canada's systems and services to settle successfully into their local B.C. communities. They offer the programs in many different languages. They help newcomers develop English language skills, learn about Canada's labour market, network, and develop professional and social networks.

移民安置和融入计划（ISIP）https://isiponline.ca/

中侨互助会移民安置和融入计划（ISIP）协助移民、难民及其家属了解加拿大的制度和服务，并成功地融入当地社区。他们提供多语种课程。帮助新学员提高英语技能，了解加拿大劳务市场、网络、拓展专业和社交网络。

September 15 ## Vancouver Neighbourhoods

9月15日　　温哥华社区

The Drive

The neighbourhood located around Commercial Drive is more fondly known as the Drive. This neighbourhood repeatedly receives the Georgia Straight Reader's Choice award as the best neighbourhood in the City. In addition, it has been ranked as one of the 10 hippest neighbourhoods in North America by Utne Reader. It is a fun area to explore as it has all the bohemian and artistic charm of Greenwich Village in New York. This area used to be the home of Italian immigrants to the city so there are many signs of Italian heritage from sidewalk cafes serving the best gelato, baked goods and espresso to delicatessens serving the best meats and cheeses. Explore the many hip and trendy stores, boutiques and art galleries in the area to find a selection of unique products you won't find anywhere else in the city. Explore the surrounding tree-lined streets to enjoy the lovely heritage homes and gardens that are more than 100 years old and have been carefully restored to their former glory.

商业大道 http://www.thedrive.ca/

　　商业大道被当地居民亲切地称为大道。作为城市最好的社区，它曾多次获得佐治亚读者评选奖，被北美洲最时尚的乌托内读者杂志列为北美10个最古老的街区之一。它具有波希米亚的传统和纽约的格林威治村的艺术魅力。这个地区曾经是意大利移民的聚居地，保留了很多意大利的传统文化，被称作小意大利。街道两旁有意大利式的露天咖啡馆可以品尝到浓浓的意大利咖啡和风味独特的意大利冰淇淋。有各种肉类和奶酪熟食店，嘻哈和时髦的商店，精品店和艺术画廊，非常独特，许多有个性的物品在其他任何城市都很难找到。漫步在绿树成荫的街道，欣赏身边百年珍贵的古迹、住宅和花园，仿佛看到了他们昔日的荣耀。

September 16　Basic Everyday English

9月16日　　基本日常生活用语

At the Restaurant

Some newcomers prefer to eat at Chinese restaurants when they first arrive in Vancouver because they feel worried about their English skills in a western-style restaurant. One way to help you to feel more comfortable before eating in a new restaurant is to go look at their online menu. This way you can take your time to look at the photos and the description of the choices before you go. You could even write down the names of your choices on paper to show the server if you want to be sure you get the food you want. Remember, the restaurants are very happy to welcome you to their restaurant and will do whatever they can to help. The restaurant customs entries in this book will also give you a lot of information about restaurants that will help you feel better prepared.

在餐厅

一些刚到温哥华的移民宁愿选择在中餐馆吃饭，他们不敢去西餐厅因为他们担心自己的英语水平。有一种方法可以帮助您解决去西餐厅点菜的问题，那就是事先到网站上去查看他们的在线菜单，临行前花点时间看看菜品图片及其描述。如果您想确保得到想要的食物，您甚至可以在纸上写下您选择的菜品名称，拿给服务员看。请记住，餐厅非常期待您的光顾，并将尽其所能为您提供帮助。这本书的餐厅部分也会给您提供很多关于餐馆的信息，这些信息可以帮助您建立起信心。下面是一些基本的餐厅用语。

English for Everyday Life
日常生活英语

下面是一些基本英语短语，您也许听到过，在餐厅会用得到。请访问我们的网站www.mynewlifeinvancouver.com，听一听这些短语的发音并练习会话。

Are you ready to order?
Yes, I would like to have soup to start and steak for my main course
您准备好点菜了吗？
是的，我想先喝汤，主菜要牛排。

How is your food?
It is really good, thank you.
您点的食物怎么样？
真的很好吃，谢谢。

Can I please have hot water?
Can I have some more hot water?
请给我拿杯热水好吗？
我能续些热水吗？

Are you finished?
I would like to take the leftover food home please
I would like the bill please
I will pay with a credit card please
您吃完了吗？
我想把剩饭剩菜打包带回家。
请给我账单。
我会用信用卡结账。

Education

9月17日   教育

Summer School

Elementary and High School students have no classes in the month of June and July. During this period, the Vancouver School Board runs Summer School. There are six kinds of summer school classes:

1. **English Language Learning:** This program is designed to help ELL students who will be attending school in the upcoming school year so that they will be able to transfer to non-ELL courses.

2. **Preview:** These courses are designed to provide a preview of the course that the students plan to take in the upcoming school year.

3. **Remedial:** The objective of this program is to help those students who have took a course in the regular school year, but were not successful or received a low "Pass" and need to improve.

4. **Secondary Skills Development:** These courses provide an opportunity for students to experience a course that may not be available in the regular school year and are open to students who are currently in Grades 7-9.

5. **Completion:** These classes are intended for students who have not yet graduated and who are 18 years or younger and:

   - Wish to obtain a credit toward secondary completion

   - Wish to improve their mark or who have never taken the subject and wish the opportunity to complete a course during the summer.

6. **Elementary:** Elementary students are permitted to register in a maximum of one summer school course at their current grade level.

暑期学校

温哥华教育局暑期学校 https://summer.vsb.bc.ca/

小学和中学生在7、8月不上课。在此期间，温哥华教育局开办暑期班。一共有六种：

1. **英语学习**：该计划旨在帮助ELL学生将参加即将到来的下一个学年的课程，以便他们能够转到非ELL课程。
2. **预览**：这些课程旨在提供学生计划在即将到来的学年采取的课程的预览。
3. **补课**：这个计划的目的是帮助那些在正常学年修成了一门课程，但不及格或勉强通过，仍需要提高的学生。
4. **第二技能发展**：这些课程为目前在7至9年级的学生提供一个机会，可以体验到在正常学年可能没有涵盖的另外一个课程。
5. **结业**：课程适用于尚未毕业并且年满18岁或以下的学生：
   - 希望获得第二技能的学分
   - 希望提高自己的成绩，或者从未接触过该课程，并希望有机会在暑假完成一门课程。
6. **小学**：小学生最多可以根据他们目前的年级水平注册一门暑期课程。

September 18   Scenes from Daily Life

9月18日   日常生活中的一些镜头

Picking up Kids from School
放学接孩子回家

Outdoor Life in Vancouver

9月19日   温哥华户外生活

Let's Go Biking!

The City of Vancouver encourages Vancouverites to leave their cars at home and enjoy riding bicycles for fun and fitness. Over the last ten years, the city has built many separated bike paths that allow cyclists to safely ride their bike and be protected from traffic. In addition, many of these bike paths connect to many of the seawall paths along the waterfront. Riding a bike is a great way to enjoy the fresh air and scenery of Vancouver. The website **Let's Go Biking** provides all the information you need to find easy bike routes in the lower mainland for cyclists of all ages and abilities. You can find printable route maps and photos for each route on their website. Take the family and enjoy Vancouver on two wheels!

Please remember: there is a law that requires all cyclists to wear a helmet when riding a bicycle in the city of Vancouver.

我们骑自行车吧！ http://www.letsgobiking.net/

温哥华市鼓励市民把车停在家里，骑上自行车，享受健身的乐趣。在过去的十年里，市里修建了许多独立的自行车道，让骑自行车的人能够安全地骑自行车，避免交通堵塞。许多自行车道与海滨的步道和车道是连通的。骑自行车是享受温哥华新鲜空气和风景的绝佳方式。网站Let's Go Biking提供了您所需要的一切信息，您可以找到适合所有年龄和能力的骑车路线，您可以将其网站上的自行车路线图和照片打印下来随车携带备用。好好和家人一起享受在两个轮子上的快乐吧！

请记住：有一条法律是要求所有在温哥华市骑自行车的人，骑车的时候必须戴上头盔。

September 20 Tips to Learning English

9月20日　　　资深英语老师提供学习英语的小贴士

Be Like a Language Researcher:
Look, Listen and Learn

When you are new to a city and new to a language, it can be intimidating to know where to start your explorations and your learning. I suggest that you gently begin the process by just listening and learning first. Go to a café and be like a language researcher and write down in your English notebook any words or cultural differences that interest you. Enjoy your coffee while you "watch the world go by" as we say in English. Look and listen to how people greet each other. Do they use the standard "how are you?" or do they usually say something different? Listen to the intonation of people speaking. Can you hear how the language goes up and down – almost like singing? Intonation is a way that we can add more information and emotion to our words to make ourselves understood better. Again, it doesn't matter if you don't understand what they are saying – never mind the content – just listen to the way that people speak. It will be helpful for you to get your ear trained to hear for the common vocal ups-and-downs of English pronunciation. Don't feel worried that you don't understand, just think about the biggest purpose for communicating – being able to share information, opinions and feelings. Listening to people speak English and getting your ear used to hearing the sounds and pronunciation of English will really help your pronunciation later.

成为一名语言研究人员：观察、倾听和学习

当您来到一个新的城市，接触到新的语言环境，往往令人生畏，不知道从何处入手开始您的学习。我建议，您先从听开始，然后再逐步展开。先去一家咖啡馆，像语言研究人员那样，在英语笔记本上写下任何让您感兴趣的语言或文化差异。在享受咖啡的同时，坐在那里静静地欣赏眼前这个匆忙的世界，周围的人都在说英语。看看，听听他们是如何彼此打招呼的。他们会使用标准的"how are you?""您好吗？"还是他们说些不同的对话？倾听他们说话的语调。您能分辨出像唱歌似的高低起伏吗？语调是一种表达方式，用它可以添加更多的信息和情感，可以使对方更好地理解说话者的意思。同样，如果您听不懂他们在说什么，也没有关系，不要太在意谈话的内容，只是听听别人说话的方式就行了。这将有助于耳朵得到训练，听到正常声音起伏的英语发音。您听不明白不用担心，作为一名语言研究人员，您应该着眼于更大的目标 – 分享信息和情感沟通。我敢肯定，您肯定会惊奇地发现，有那么多的沟通是来自说话者的肢体语言和语调。您至少可以明白他们是否喜欢对方或此刻心情的好坏。多听别人说英语，让您的耳朵习惯英语的发音，这对您以后的发音会有帮助。当您来到温哥华，为了您的新生活，有很多事情要做，有时唯一的语言学习，就是婴儿学步，而第一步就是听。

September 21   A Little Canadian Inspiration

9月21日   一点点启示

*"The tiniest dream that you make happen is worth more
than the biggest dream that you never attempt."*

-Shane Koyczan, Canadian Poet

Consistent "baby steps" of progress all add up to build your new life in Vancouver. Set one tiny dream, achieve it, and then set another and before you know it, you will have achieved more than you ever could imagine.

"您所去实现的哪怕是最微小的梦，要比您从未尝试过的最大梦想更有价值。"

——*加拿大诗人沙恩·科济赞*

在温哥华建立新的生活需要时间，先按照婴儿学步的方法，先设定一个小小的梦想，去实现它，然后再设定另一个，慢慢地、逐步地、日积月累地，您就会发现您得到的比您想要的更多。

Volunteer with the YMCA of Greater Vancouver

The YMCA is another organization that really works hard to connect members of the community through health, fitness, recreations, employment, and new immigrant programs. There are activities at the YMCA for all ages and for all members of the family. They have a very well organized and respected volunteer program and are known for their excellent volunteer training and recognition programs. They have many volunteer positions available in many different areas – from physical fitness, to producing special events to fundraising. As a YMCA volunteer you will make a big difference in the lives of people in your community.

大温基督教青年会与志愿服务 https://gv.ymca.ca/Volunteer

　　基督教青年会是一个真正努力通过健康、健身、娱乐、就业和新移民计划连接社区成员的组织。基督教青年会为所有年龄和家庭成员举办一系列活动。他们有一个很好的组织和受人尊敬的志愿者计划，并以其出色的志愿者培训和表彰计划而闻名。他们在许多不同的领域—— 从健身班、 青少年工作到特殊筹款活动，有很多志愿者的职位空缺。作为YMCA的志愿者，无论您做什么，对改善社区人们的生活都将产生重大的影响。

Healthcare in Vancouver

9月23日   温哥华的医疗保健

Physiotherapist

Physiotherapy is a type of treatment that focuses on the movement of the body and helps people to regain, maintain and improve their physical strength and function so that they can be physically active and mobile. A physiotherapist will use their in-depth knowledge of how the body works, combined with hands-on clinical skills, to assess, diagnose and treat your symptoms. They help patients recover from sports injuries and other painful health conditions that limit movement. Physiotherapists are highly educated and must complete a minimum of five years of applied clinical experience and several clinical practice hours before they can be licensed.

A physiotherapy session will cost between $75 and $100. The Medical Services Plan will cover the cost of treatment in certain circumstances such as treatments giving during a hospital stay. However, many extended health plans will cover a percentage of the cost of physiotherapy. The Physiotherapy Association of BC website has a search screen that helps you find a physiotherapist in a convenient location.

物理治疗师

卑诗省物理治疗协会 https://bcphysio.org/find-a-physio

物理治疗是一种专注于身体运动的治疗方法，可帮助人们恢复，维持和改善他们的体力和机能，有助于提高身体的灵活和平衡。物理治疗师将运用其对身体如何运作的深入了解，结合实际的临床技能评估，诊断和治疗您的症状。他们帮助病人从运动损伤和其他限制运动的痛苦状况中恢复过来。物理治疗师都受过高等教育，他们至少要完成五年的临床经验和若干个小时的临床实践，才能获得行医执照。

一次物理治疗费需花费75加元到100加元。这项医疗服务计划在某些情况下是可以包括的，比如住院期间的治疗费用。不过，许多扩展的健康计划已经涵盖了物理治疗的一部分费用。BC省物理治疗师协会网站上有一个搜索界面，可以帮助您快速地找到离您最近的物理治疗师的位置。

9月24日   温哥华趣闻

BC Place's Retractable Roof and Light Show Downtown

BC Place Stadium has the largest retractable roof in the world. Depending on the weather, the roof can be open to the sky. Also, BC Place is lit up every evening in colours that are suited to the event that is happening in the stadium. If the BC Lions are playing football, then the stadium is lit with orange lights to match their uniform. If the Whitecaps are playing soccer, then it will be lit in blue to match their colours. The lights also change depending on special festivals and cultural events: Red and green at Christmas and bright red for Chinese New Year. The colourful light show on the BC Place roof really brightens up the downtown area.

卑诗体育馆开合式屋顶和灯光秀

卑诗体育馆有世界上最大的可开合式屋顶。根据天气情况，屋顶可以完全敞开。每天晚上卑诗体育馆的灯都会点亮，并配合体育馆内举行活动的颜色。如果卑诗雄狮队在踢足球，那么体育馆就用橙色的灯光来配他们的制服。如果是白帽足球俱乐部在踢主场，它将点亮蓝色的灯搭配其颜色。灯光的颜色还根据特殊节日和文化活动而变化：圣诞节是红色和绿色，而中国的春节，则是大红色。五颜六色的灯光秀照亮了周围市中心的街区。

September 25   Finding Work in Vancouver

9月25日   在温哥华找工作

Skills Connect BC

The Skills Connect for Immigrants Program is part of the Welcome BC umbrella of services, made possible through funding from the Government of Canada and the Province of British Columbia. The Skills Connect Program helps immigrants in British Columbia move into careers that match their experience and background. They specialize in helping immigrants prepare for and obtain employment in every sector of the B.C. economy including construction, transportation, manufacturing, tourism, and healthcare to name a few. Their program is a free service that connects employers with qualified individuals in their industry.

BC省技术移民联盟计划 http://www.skillsconnect.ca/

技术移民联盟计划是BC省一种伞状连接服务的一部分，它是由加拿大政府和不列颠哥伦比亚省资助的。技能连接计划旨在帮助不列颠哥伦比亚移民从事符合他们经验和背景的职业。 他们专注于帮助移民准备和获得在BC省的不同行业的就业。包括建筑、交通、制造、旅游和医疗保健等等。总之技术移民联盟计划是将雇主与符合其行业资格的个人联系起来，而且他们的服务计划是免费的，

September 26 Vancouver Sightseeing

9月26日　　观光

Sightseeing about Nature

For those interested in sightseeing and learning more about the natural world, there are three great attractions to see in Vancouver:

The **George C. Reifel Migratory Bird Sanctuary** consists of nearly 300 hectares (850 acres) of managed wetlands, natural marshes and low dykes in the heart of the Fraser River Estuary. For the millions of birds seeking feeding and resting areas during their annual migrations along the Pacific Coast, the Sanctuary is ideally located. It is a place where wildlife and their habitats are protected from harm, and visitors and birdwatchers can walk along the trails and enjoy this very popular natural viewing area. It is ranked as one of the top ten birdwatching sites in Canada.

Inside Stanley Park, there is the **Stanley Park Ecology Centre and Nature House** beside Lost Lagoon. Every year, their educators connect thousands of people with nature through school and public programs while their conservation team engages community volunteers in habitat restoration and wildlife monitoring. Learn about all the many animals that live within Stanley Park from the helpful staff.

The **Beaty Biodiversity Museum** is Vancouver's natural history museum. Its beautiful, compelling exhibits work to make the research conducted at UBC more accessible to the public. Explore the university's spectacular biological collections, with 20,000 square feet of exhibits showcasing over 500 permanent exhibits. Among their two million treasured specimens are a 26-metre-long blue whale skeleton suspended in the atrium, the third-largest fish collection in Canada, and myriad fossils, shells, insects, fungi, mammals, birds, reptiles, amphibians, and plants from around BC and across the world. Through dynamic exhibits, interactive activities and rotating temporary gallery exhibitions visitors can increase their knowledge and understanding of the interconnectedness of all life on Earth.

自然：斯坦利公园生态中心和贝蒂生物博物馆

瑞菲尔鸟类保护区 http://www.reifelbirdsanctuary.com/
斯坦利公园生态中心 http://stanleyparkecology.ca/
贝蒂生物博物馆 http://beatymuseum.ubc.ca/

对于那些对大自然感兴趣的人来说，有三大著名的景点，可以看到和了解更多自然世界：

- **乔治·C·瑞菲尔迁徙鸟类保护区**由弗雷泽河口中心地区近300公顷（850英亩）的托管湿地、天然沼泽和低堤坝组成。对于以百万计的鸟类每年在太平洋沿岸迁徙期间寻求喂养和休息区，鸟类保护区的地理位置非常理想。它是一个野生动物及其栖息地受到保护免受伤害的地方，游客们可以沿着步道漫步，近距离的观赏各种鸟类。它被列为加拿大十大观鸟景点之一。
- **斯坦利公园**，在迷失的泻湖旁边有斯坦利公园生态中心和自然之家。每年，那里的教育工作者通过学校和公共项目将人与自然联系起来，而他们的保护团队则与社区志愿者一道参与栖息地恢复和野生动物的监测。以了解所有栖息在斯坦利公园的各种动物的生活习性。
- **贝蒂生物博物馆**是温哥华的自然历史博物馆。位于UBC大学。馆内有20,000平方英尺的展区，200万珍贵的标本其中有一个26米长的蓝鲸骨架悬挂在中庭，它是加拿大第三大鱼类收藏，以及来自北极和世界各地的无数的化石、贝壳、昆虫、真菌、哺乳动物、鸟类、爬行动物、两栖动物和植物。通过动态展览，互动活动和旋转画廊，使游客增长知识，加深对地球上所有生命相互联系的理解。

September 27   Vancouver Transportation

9月27日   温哥华交通运输

The Westcoast Express Train (WCE)

West Coast Express is a commuter railway that links Mission, Maple Ridge, Pitt Meadows, Port Coquitlam, Coquitlam and Port Moody with downtown Vancouver. It operates Monday to Friday during peak morning and evening periods. The trains are very comfortable and every car is equipped with a washroom and each train has a coffee bar located onboard. Most WCE stations have Park & Ride parking lots where you can leave your car and take the train in to the city. Bicycles are also welcomed aboard. The single fare to Mission is about $13 and a monthly pass is around $340.

西海岸快线

　　西海岸快线属于通勤铁路，它将枫树岭、匹特草原、高贵林港、高贵林和满地宝等5个主要的市镇与温哥华市中心连接起来。在星期一至星期五早晚的高峰时段运营。列车很舒适，每节车厢都配有一个洗手间，火车上有一个咖啡吧。大多数西岸快车车站都有停车场，您可以把车存放在那里，并乘火车进城。自行车也可以推进车厢。单程票价约为13加元，月票约为340加元。

September 28   Sports Teams and Special Events
9月28日   专业体育赛事和活动

Terry Fox Run

This annual fundraising run for cancer research is more than just an athletic event, it is a deeply emotional and personal event for Canadians. The Terry Fox Run is a non-competitive event where people get together as individuals, families, and groups to raise money for cancer research in Terry's name. This running event is a day of celebrating Terry's legacy and helping to keep alive his dream of finding a cure for cancer.

Terry Fox was only 18 years old when he was diagnosed with osteogenic sarcoma (bone cancer) and forced to have his right leg amputated 15 centimetres (six inches) above the knee in 1977. While in hospital, Terry was so upset by the suffering of other cancer patients, many of them young children, that he decided to run across Canada to raise money for cancer research. He would call his journey the Marathon of Hope. Terry started his run quietly in St. John's, Newfoundland on April 12, 1980 and enthusiasm soon grew, and the money collected along his route began to mount. He ran close to 42 kilometres (26 miles) a day through Canada's eastern provinces. However, on September 1st, after 143 days and 5,373 kilometres (3,339 miles), Terry was forced to stop running outside of Thunder Bay, Ontario because cancer had appeared in his lungs. An entire nation was stunned and saddened. Terry passed away on June 28, 1981 at the age 22. The heroic Canadian was gone, but his legacy was just beginning. To date, over $650 million has been raised worldwide for cancer research in Terry's name through the annual Terry Fox Run, held across Canada and around the world.

泰瑞·福克斯长跑 http://www.terryfox.org/Run/

一年一度的癌症研究筹款活动不仅仅是一个体育赛事，它凝聚着加拿大人深深的个人情感。这种跑步活动是以加拿大人特有的方式进行，以实现泰瑞福克斯找到治愈癌症方法的美丽梦想。泰瑞福克斯跑是一个非竞争性的活动，人们聚集在一起，作为个人，家庭和团体以泰瑞的名字筹集资金用于癌症研究。这是一个纪念泰瑞，并帮助实现他的梦想找到治愈癌症的一天。

泰瑞福克斯年仅18岁时，就被诊断出患有骨源性肉瘤（骨癌），1977年右腿膝盖以上15厘米（6英寸）处被截肢，住院期间，泰瑞看到了其他癌症患者的痛苦，其中许多是幼儿，因此他决定长跑横穿加拿大为癌症研究筹集资金。他将他的旅程命名为希望马拉松。泰瑞于1980年4月12日以纽芬兰岛圣约翰市为起点，悄悄地开始了他的长跑，而后关注的人越来越多，人们的热情越来越高，沿途收集的捐款数额也开始上升。他每天跑过加拿大东部省份近42公里（26英里）。然而，9月1日，在经过了143天和5,373公里（3,339英里）之后，在安大略省桑德贝，泰瑞不得不终止了他的步伐，因为癌症已经扩散到了他的肺部。整个国家都处在震惊和悲痛之中。泰瑞于1981年6月28日去世，享年22岁。英勇的加拿大人走了，但他的遗志才刚刚开始。迄今为止，已经通过在加拿大和世界各地举办的年度泰瑞·福克斯希望马拉松长跑（Terry Fox Run）在全球范围内以泰瑞的名字筹集了超过6.5亿加元的癌症研究费用。

Vancouver Parks

9月29日   温哥华公园

New Brighton Park

Although this park is located near the large grain elevators and industrial harbour area, it stands out by its waterfront location and memorable view of the North Shore mountains, Burrard Inlet, Iron Workers' Bridge and the tall Cascadia Terminals grain elevators. There is a walking trail along the water, large grass lawns for picnics and a very large and popular heated outdoor pool that opens in the summer. It is one of the secret favourites of Vancouver locals and is a busy place for family picnics and get-togethers.

新布莱顿公园

新布莱顿公园位于大粮仓和工业港口附近，地处北海岸的海滨，周围有铁工人大桥和高大的卡斯卡迪亚终端谷物升降机，沿着海滨的步行道散步，遥望对面的北岸山脉令人难以忘怀。家人们在大草坪上坐下来野餐。园内有一个非常大的可以加热的室外游泳池每逢夏季对外开放。新布莱顿公园人气很旺，是野餐，家庭聚会理想的好地方。当地人对它情有独钟，

September 30   Stories and Advice for Newcomers

9月30日   移民的故事和建议

Lorraine

　　如何一毕业就能找到工作？大学期间是最佳充实简历的机会。不要盲目地追求以最短时间内毕业。建议多支配1-2年的时间去做实习，参加学生社团，充分锻炼领导才能和表达能力。这些要比学历和成绩单更有价值。（SFU工商管理研究生）

October

Weather:	Average temperature: 7°C to 14°C
	Average rainfall days: 20, Average rainfall: 120 mm
Statutory holiday:	Thanksgiving (second Monday in October)
Other special days:	Halloween (October 31)

The leaves begin to turn a beautiful golden red in October and the air becomes cold and crisp. October is also the first month of the rainy season in Vancouver so the popular activities begin to move indoors. October is a time for families to celebrate Thanksgiving Day and for children to get very excited for the costumes, jack-o-lanterns and trick-or-treating of Halloween.

In fact, Halloween is considered a major event for children and they usually spend quite a lot of time and energy during the month thinking and talking about their costumes and counting the days until they can go trick or treating on Halloween evening*. It is a popular topic to speak about and most schools will have a Halloween party in the classroom. Most homes in the neighbourhood will put carved pumpkins out on their front porch and buy lots of candy to hand out on October 31. Some families also put up big displays of Halloween decorations in their front yards using witches, skeletons, and other scary items. A wonderful traditional family outing is to go out to the Pumpkin Patch at the Richmond Country Market and choose a pumpkin to carve for home. Thousands of people visit this pumpkin patch each year and enjoy the music played by their farm band. You can also take a ride on their hay wagon and enjoy all the Halloween decorations on the farm.

In the Kerrisdale Village skating rink, you and the family can get dressed up in costumes and enjoy a free family skate to live music and try the free sugar cookies. The Dunbar Village businesses put on a free trick-or-treat event where the kids wear a costume and go from store to store to get a Halloween treat.

The Stanley Park Ghost Train is another popular Halloween activity as it goes on a journey through a scary and magical Halloween world. The famous Kids Market at Granville Islands hosts a Halloweenie event which includes a Halloween balloon hunt, crafts, games, and a free hotdog and drink for kids who come in their costumes. The most popular Vancouver Halloween attraction for teenagers and adults is Fright Nights at the PNE. During Fright Nights, the PNE's Playland amusement park becomes a thrill park, with themed rides, creepy attractions, and seven seriously haunted houses. However, Fright Nights is only for older teenagers and adults as it is very, very scary – young children and nervous adults SHOULD NOT go to this event.

If you get tired of pumpkins, the UBC Botanical Garden has its Apple Festival every October. Some highlights of the festival are the taste tests of 60 different types of apples, plus family entertainment, games, and storytelling for children.

In the middle of the month, the Thanksgiving long weekend is a very important event for families. Families gather together to eat the traditional meal of roast turkey with pumpkin pie for dessert. It is a holiday where everyone takes some time to feel gratitude for all that they have in life. If you don't want to cook a big Thanksgiving meal*, most Vancouver restaurants will be open on Thanksgiving or you can order Thanksgiving meals-to-go from grocery stores like Whole Foods.

For a change from turkey and Halloween candy, The EAT! Vancouver Food + Cooking Festival also takes place in October. This event is the premier food event in Canada with celebrity chefs, popular local restaurants, wineries, food and beverage manufacturers, cookbook authors and retailers put on displays and cooking demonstrations. You can sample different kinds of food, beer, wine and spirits from all over the globe.

Finally, if reading and writing is more your interest, then you will like the Vancouver Writers Fest which attracts local and internationally acclaimed writers. Book lovers can enjoy readings, interviews, panel discussions and workshops.

10⊠

气候： 平均温度：7°C 至 14°C
平均降雨天数：20，平均降雨量： 120 毫米
公众节假日：感恩节（在10月的第二个星期一）
其他特殊日：万圣节（10月31 日）

十月，树叶开始变成美丽的金红色，空气逐渐变冷而清爽起来。十月也是温哥华雨季的第一个月，所以各种户外活动转入了室内。十月是一家人庆祝感恩节的日子，这一天，孩子们穿上派对的服装，激动不已，万圣节用南瓜制作各种怪异的"杰克灯"，孩子们挨家挨户敲门，喊着"不给糖，就捣蛋！"

事实上，万圣节对儿童们来讲是一个非常重大的事件，他们通常在这个月要花上相当多的时间和精力去思考和谈论他们的服装，并计算着到万圣节的天数，他们可以在万圣节晚上去玩不给糖就捣蛋的恶作剧。这是一个热门话题，大多数学校在教室里会组织一个万圣节派对。大多数家庭会把雕刻的南瓜灯放在他们前门的廊上，并购买很多糖果，在10月31日晚上分发。一些家庭还在他们的院子里摆放女巫、骷髅和其他可怕的东西来装饰万圣节。大人会带着孩子到里士满乡下的南瓜市场，挑选一个南瓜带回家雕刻。每年都有成千上万的人参观访问这个南瓜市场，欣赏农场乐队演奏的音乐。您也可以乘坐他们的干草车，欣赏农场上所有万圣节的装饰品。

在克里斯戴尔社区溜冰场，您和家人可以穿着节日的盛装，聆听现场音乐，品尝无糖饼干并享受免费的家庭滑冰。邓巴社区的各个商铺提供免费的"不给糖就捣蛋"的活动，孩子们穿上特殊的服装，挨门挨户地去讨要免费糖果。

斯坦利公园幽灵火车会带您经历一次可怕而神奇的万圣节之旅。在格兰维尔岛著名的儿童市场举办的万圣节活动，包括万圣节气球狩猎、工艺品和游戏，每个身穿万圣节服装的孩子都可以领到一份免费的热狗和一杯饮料。青少年和成人则最喜欢去的地方是温哥华PNE游乐场，去感受万圣节惊悚之夜。在这个夜晚，PNE游乐园变得即兴奋又令人毛骨悚然，有七间闹鬼的房子，非常恐怖。因此，幼儿和容易引起紧张的成年人都不适合观看。

如果您不喜欢南瓜，哥伦比亚大学植物园每年十月举办苹果节。节日的亮点是有60个不同品种的苹果的口味测试，还有家庭娱乐、游戏和给孩子们讲故事。

10月中旬，感恩节的长周末是家庭最非常重要的事件，一家人聚在一起吃传统的烤火鸡，餐后甜点是南瓜派。这个节日的特点是，每个人都需要一些时间来感恩他们所得到的一切。如果您不想在家做一顿感恩节大餐，大部分温哥华餐馆都会在感恩节开放，您也可以从食品店，比如Whole Foods天然食品店订购感恩节套餐。

如果说从感恩节火鸡到万圣节糖果有什么变化，那就是一个字"吃"！温哥华十月美食烹饪节也是加拿大最大的厨艺事件，各路名厨尽展其拿手绝活，当地著名的餐馆、酒厂、食品饮料制造商和零售商纷纷加入，烹饪书籍的作者和零售商们将烹饪过程通过显示屏展现出来。您可以品尝来自世界各地不同的食物、啤酒、葡萄酒和烈性酒。

最后，如果阅读和写作是您的兴趣所在，那么您一定会喜欢温哥华作家节，它是作家们的盛宴，每年都吸引了当地和国际知名作家欢聚一堂，爱书人可以尽情享受阅读、访谈、小组讨论和研讨会。

更多的信息：

吃在温哥华：http://eat-vancouver.com/
苹果节：http://botanicalgarden.ubc.ca/events/event/apple-festival-2016/
Kerrisdale万圣节免费滑冰：www.kerrisdalevillage.com
邓巴社区万圣节：www.dunbarvillage.ca/events/trick-or-treat-in-dunbar-village
斯坦利公园万圣节的幽灵列车：http://vancouver.ca/parks-recreation-culture/ghost-train.aspx
PNE游乐园惊恐之夜：http://frightnights.ca/
里士满南瓜农场：www.countryfarms.ca/the-nursery
格兰维尔岛上的孩子乐园 Halloweenie：www.kidsmarket.ca/#events
温哥华作家节：www.writersfest.bc.ca/

* Halloween evening**万圣节之夜：**10月31日天黑前，家家都把前门廊的灯打开，把杰克灯笼里的蜡烛点亮摆在门前，准备一个装满糖果的大碗，准备发给那些"小捣蛋鬼们"。听到邻居的孩子们敲门说"不给糖就捣蛋！"，您就发给他们每人一颗或两颗糖果。最小的刚学会走步，大的都上中学了。

* Halloween costumes**万圣节服装：**仅在10月31日穿的特别服装。深受儿童喜爱的服装有超级英雄蜘蛛侠、超人、公主、巫婆、口袋妖怪、动物等等。

* jack-o-lanterns**杰克南瓜灯：**在南瓜上挖出人面形窟窿的灯笼，里面点上一盏小灯或蜡烛

* trick or treating**不给糖果就捣蛋！：**这是一句儿童们身着万圣节服装挨家挨户敲门时说的一句话。

*Thanksgiving meal**感恩节大餐：**传统的烤火鸡塞满面包和香料（填料），配肉汁，酸果曼沙司，土豆泥和甘蓝。甜点通常是南瓜派。

Local Customs

当地的习俗

Customs When People Die

Death is a difficult topic to think or speak about in any culture. The English language has many words and expressions for dying and some commonly used phrases that we say during the uncomfortable time when we find out about a death.

If someone's family member has died, we will send them a sympathy greeting card, or we will send them flowers if we know them well. If we are very close to the grieving family, we might also bring over cooked food so that they don't need to cook when they are so sad. If we know them very well, we might offer to help with other tasks such as helping with the children and so on.

When someone dies, the family may choose to have the body placed in a **coffin** and buried in a **cemetery** at a **gravesite** marked with a **headstone**. It is customary to visit the headstone every year on the anniversary of the death to place flowers on the grave.

The family may choose to have the body **cremated** and the ashes will be put in an **urn**. Then they choose to bury the urn and mark the spot with a headstone or spread the ashes in a location that had special meaning to the person who died.

There are two types of gatherings that a family might choose to hold in honour of someone who has died: a **funeral** or a **memorial service**. The first kind of event is called a funeral. It is held in the first week or two after someone has died. A funeral can be held in a church or in a **Funeral Home**. If the funeral is in a church, the church minister will lead the ceremony. If it is held in a Funeral Home, then the family members will organize who does the speaking at the ceremony or service. The family will also choose the music to be played at the service, the photographs to be on display, the flowers to decorate the church or funeral home and the food to serve at the reception after the service.

The second type of event is a **"memorial service" or a "celebration of life" service**. This type of service can happen anywhere from a month to a year after the person dies. They don't usually happen in a church as the purpose of the event is to celebrate the wonderful life of the person who died. There can be home movies shown, photograph displays, the person's favourite music played and many speeches by the people who were close to the deceased person. Many of them share personal memories and stories in their speeches.

Finally, when a person dies, the **next-of-kin** must request a **Death Certificate** from the government. They need this document to legally cancel their cell phone accounts, bank accounts etc. Everyone should have a **Last Will and Testament** which is a legal document that lets your next-of-kin know your wishes for their money and belongings. If someone dies without a Will, then the government of BC will make the decisions about what to do with your savings and belongings.

The daily newspapers have a daily section of the newspaper called the **Obituaries**. This is the section of the newspaper where families post a notice that their loved one has died. Usually the format is a photograph of the person with their birth and death dates, as well as a brief description of the family members who are left and how the person will be missed. The newspaper provides the family with sample texts that they can use to help them write the **Obituary Notice** that will be published in the paper. There is a small fee to publish the notice.

当人们死了的时候

死亡在任何文化中，都是人们不愿意去思考或者谈论的话题。英语中有许多表达死亡的单词和一些常用的短语，当我们身边有人过世了，总是让活着的人感到难过。

English for Everyday Life
日常生活英语

以下是一些常见的对死亡的英语表达方式：

He/she died
He/she passed away
We lost him or her

他/她死了
他/她去世了
我们失去了他或她

当某人失去了心爱的人的时候，我们可以这样安慰说：

"I am very sorry for your loss."
"Please accept my condolences for your loss" *(this is very formal)*
"It is hard to believe that he is gone. He was a very special person" *- (if you were close to the person who died and their family).*

"对您的损失我很遗憾"。
"请接受我的哀悼"（这是非常正式的）
"很难相信他已经走了。他是一个非常特殊的人" *- （如果您和逝者以及他/她的家人关系密切的话）。*

如果某人去世了，我们会寄给他的家人一张同情安慰卡；如果我们非常了解这个人我们会送出鲜花；如果和逝者的家人关系非常密切的话，我们还会送去熟食，以免在他们最伤心的时候还要煮饭。我们还会提供其他帮助，如帮助他们照看孩子等等。

当某人过世了，家人通常的选择是把尸体放进一口棺材，埋在标有墓碑的墓地之中。每年的忌日家人们会去扫墓，将鲜花放在坟上。

家人还可以选择对尸体进行火化，将骨灰放在一个骨灰盒里。然后将它埋在葬缸，用墓石标记该地点，或将骨灰分撒在对死者有特殊意义的地点。

为纪念已故的人，有两种类型的聚会供人们选择：第一种被称为葬礼或追悼会。它是在人死后的第一个星期或者第二个星期举行。葬礼可以在教堂或殡仪馆举行。如果葬礼在教堂举行，将由教堂里的牧师主持仪式。如果是在殡仪馆举行，那么将由家庭成员组织并决定由谁在仪式上做演讲，由谁提供招待服务。现场还将有选择的播放音乐，展示死者生前的照片，用鲜花来装饰殡仪馆以及仪式结束以后的食品招待服务。

第二种类型的活动属于"纪念仪式"或"追忆生活"的庆祝活动。这种类型的活动可以从死者死亡的一个月到一年之内在任何地方举办。他们通常不只限于在一个教堂里举办，因为活动的目的是为了追忆死者生前曾经历过的美好生活。可以放映家庭录像，展示照片，播放其最喜欢的音乐以及与死者关系密切的人发言。通过演讲分享美好的回忆和故事。

最后一点是，当一个人死亡的时候，亲属必须向政府申请死亡证明。他们需要这份文件以便合法地取消他们的手机和银行帐户。每个人都应该留有一份遗嘱和遗愿，这是一份法律文件，它可以让您的亲人知道您是打算如何处置您身后的金钱和财物。如果死者没有立遗嘱，那么BC省政府将做出关于如何处置您的储蓄和财产的决定。

每天的报纸都有一栏叫做讣告，它是报纸的一部分，由家人刊登告示，他们的亲属已经死亡。通常的格式是死者的姓名，照片和他/她的出生年月和死亡日期，并简要地介绍死者，以及对死者的怀念。报社提供范本，可以用它来帮助撰写讣告，费用不多。

Parenting in Vancouver

1月2日   在温哥华养育子女

Local free parenting magazines:

Urban Baby and Toddler and Westcoast Families are two free full colour parenting magazines that are published regularly and can be picked up all over the city – especially in libraries and in the free newspaper section of supermarkets. They contain current information about raising children of all ages, as well as ideas to keep children busy, healthy, and happy. The magazines also contain the newest information about products and services for children in Vancouver.

当地免费育儿杂志：

城市婴儿与儿童杂志http://www.urbanbaby.ca/
西岸家庭杂志http://westcoastfamilies.com/

这两本免费的全彩色杂志定期出版，遍及整个城市 – 特别是可以在图书馆和超市门前的免费报纸架上拿取。内容包含关于养育所有年龄段的儿童最新的信息，以及如何想办法让儿童把时间利用起来，健康和快乐的成长。杂志还包含有关温哥华儿童产品和服务的最新信息。

October 3   Stories and Advice for Newcomers

10月3日   新移民的故事

Qi

温哥华的医疗急救

初到温哥华最担心的就是生病，习惯了找熟人，托关系。在这里不知所措，再加上语言问题，很怕对病情描述不清，有一天我先生胆结石病发，让我紧张到了极点，我们来到急诊室，做了登记，旁边的病人安慰我们别急，护士会按病情安排先后，果然很快就轮到了我们。躺在检查室里，开始做不同的检查。我发现这里没有嘈杂声，没有跑来跑去的人。医生护士各司其职，井然有序。心情一下就轻松了许多。检查以后，医生说我可以回家了，病人就交给他们。我问"不用家属陪吗？"医生很耐心的给我写了一张字条，让我再来时出示给护士。

当我第二次来到病房时，看到护士正在精心的照顾病人，我先生说医生已经和他讨论过手术方案，已经签完字了。没有那种吓得病人及家属面临两难选择签字的感觉。不一会儿，营养师来和我先生谈话，根据他的饮食习惯和病情配送饮食。

我第三次去医院时，就通知我接病人出院了，这让我很吃惊，没有输液，而且伤口处也没有贴纱布，在我的要求下医生才勉强给开了两片止痛药，后来听我先生说整个手术过程都很轻松，医护人员的态度和蔼可亲，让你一点都不紧张。

这件事后，我再也不担心生病了。我开始喜欢上温哥华了。

Vancouver Entertainment

温哥华娱乐

Cigar Lounges and Whiskey Bars

Vancouver's very strict anti-smoking laws make it impossible to find one location where you can enjoy both cigars and whiskey at the same time in a comfortable lounge setting. However, there are some fantastic places where you can enjoy drinking whiskey and stores where you can buy premium cigars:

Whiskey Bars

Fets Whiskey House: Fets has the largest whisky selection in the country with nearly 800 different whiskies. They also serve excellent Southern United States inspired meals.

Prohibition: Located in downtown Vancouver, in the Rosewood Hotel Georgia, Prohibition is a world class, 3,000 square foot bar that is luxuriously decorated to create a rich and inviting atmosphere. The bar serves wine, cocktails and has an extensive selection of whiskeys.

Hopscotch Whiskey Festival: This festival is a premium whiskey tasting event that happens in Vancouver every November. Their Great Tasting Hall offers festival-goers a chance to try the very best brands of whiskey from around the world.

Cigar Stores and Lounges

City Cigar Emporium: City Cigar is the premiere cigar store in Vancouver with over 12 years of bringing the largest and finest selection of Cuban cigars and cigars from other countries to locals and celebrities.

Cigar Connoisseurs: The shop is located in the heart of historic Gastown with a large selection of Cuban cigars, lighters, cutters, pipes, cigar accessories and much more. After 5pm they have a smoking lounge where you may enjoy a cigar purchased at the store.

雪茄店和威士忌酒吧

　　温哥华有着非常严格的禁烟令，您很难找到一个舒适的既能抽雪茄又能喝威士忌的地方。为此，我们特别介绍几个可以喝威士忌的酒屋，以及在什么地方可以买到优质雪茄的商店：

威士忌酒吧

Fets威士忌酒屋 http://www.whiskykitchen.ca/
Fets是加国最大的威士忌酒屋，它拥有近800种不同的威士忌。并且还提供美国南部地道的美食。

Prohibition 禁 https://www.rosewoodhotels.com/en/hotel-georgia-vancouver/dining/prohibition
禁位于温哥华市中心的乔治亚红木酒店，禁称得上是世界级的酒吧，占地3000平方英尺，装饰豪华且温馨。酒吧供应葡萄酒，鸡尾酒和各种威士忌。

Hopscotch 威士忌节 http://www.hopscotchfestival.com/
这个是每年11月份在温哥华举行的威士忌品尝活动的盛大节日。品酒大厅为来宾提供了品尝世界上最好的威士忌名酒的机会。

雪茄店和抽烟室

城市雪茄店 http://www.citycigarcompany.com
城市雪茄店是卑诗省温哥华首家开办的雪茄店，至今已有12年的经营历史，其规模最大。它给当地人和名流们提供了上等的古巴雪茄和来自其他国家的雪茄。

雪茄鉴赏家 http://www.cubanbest.com/
该店位于历史悠久的煤气镇中心，拥有多种古巴雪茄、打火机、切割刀具、烟管和雪茄配件等等。下午5点以后，吸烟厅开门营业，您可以在那里好好享受雪茄的味道。

English for Everyday Life
日常生活英语

不同类型的威士忌:

- Scotch苏格兰威士忌（拼写上没有"e"），必须在苏格兰生产，主要原料是大麦麦芽，在橡木桶中陈酿三年以上。
- Bourbon波旁酒是美国威士忌，由玉米制成，必须储存在烧焦的橡木容器中，并且不能添加任何香料。
- Rye黑麦是由黑麦籽粒制成的，可以指美国威士忌或加拿大威士忌（其生产过程中可能包含也可能并不包含黑麦）。

相关术语:

A dram一杯: 用来描述一小杯威士忌的术语。

Neat不加冰的: 购买威士忌时，您必须让服务员知道您是否想要它配水或冰或什么都不放。通常不加冰(without ice)的苏格兰威士忌叫做"Neat。"

on the rocks加冰的: 如果您想要在酒等饮料中加一点冰，那么您要说"on the rocks"

举例来说:

I'll have a Johnnie Walker whiskey neat.
我要一杯不加冰的尊尼获加威士忌。
I'll have a Johnnie Walker whiskey on the rocks
我要一杯加冰的尊尼获加威士忌。

Best Elementary Schools

　　温哥华著名的小学

York House Junior School (private)

Here is the description of the school from their website: "Bright, engaging learning spaces. Colourful classrooms brimming with boundless energy. It's fun to learn here. The Junior School is a safe and supportive environment that embraces the curious mind. Girls are eager to learn and are enthusiastic about sharing their ideas. They learn independence and build self-confidence as teachers focus on exploration, critical thinking, and teamwork in the classroom. The curriculum is enhanced with field trips, visiting instructors who are experts in their field, as well as resource teachers who help support the diverse learning needs of our students."

约克屋小学（私立）https://www.yorkhouse.ca

下面是学校网站的描述：

"明亮迷人的学习空间。五彩缤纷的教室，洋溢着无限的活力。在这里学习是很有趣味的。校区的环境安全且受到支持。女孩们有好奇心，勤奋好学，热衷于分享她们的想法。她们在这里学会了独立和建立自信，教师们则专注于在教室里探索，批判性思维和团队精神。通过实地考察、聘请客座教师帮助和支持我们学生多样化的学习需求。"

October 6 A Different Way of Thinking

10月6日 不同的思维方式

Household Work Equally Shared (Almost!)

Statistics Canada's 2015 survey of all households in Canada showed that Canadian fathers do an increasing share of the household tasks like cleaning, cooking, and taking care of the children. It is very common, especially for highly educated professional Vancouver couples, to share the tasks in the home. Partly this is because it is very expensive to hire people to help with household tasks and partly it is due to Canadian fathers wanting to be much more involved with home life nowadays. Canada's excellent paid parental leave program – which can be used by both the mothers and fathers to stay home with their newborn baby has resulted in fathers becoming much more involved in the care of children and the running of the home. Some fathers even choose to become a stay-at-home father who takes care of the children while the mother goes back to work. The Statistics Canada survey showed that preparing meals is the household task that has seen the highest increase in involvement by fathers. The proportion of fathers who participated in meal preparation, over the course of a day, has practically doubled in the last three decades. Women still do more of the cleaning, laundry, and daily care of the children, but this is rapidly changing as men are much more interested in contributing to making a happy and harmonious home.

共同负担家务劳动

加拿大统计局2015年对加拿大所有家庭的调查显示，加拿大父亲在家务活，如清洁、做饭和照顾孩子方面所占的比例越来越大。这是非常普遍的现象，特别是对于受过高等教育的温哥华职业夫妇来说，在家里分担家务，部分原因是因为雇人来帮忙做家务非常昂贵，另一部分原因是因为加拿大的父亲们现在想更多地参与家庭生活。加拿大推出优秀的带薪育儿假计划 —— 母亲和父亲都可以在家里陪伴新生婴儿，这使得父亲越来越多地参与到孩子的照料和家庭的运转中。甚至一些父亲选择成为一名全职父亲居家照顾孩子，让母亲回单位上班。加拿大统计局的调查显示，做饭是父亲参与率最高的家庭工作。在过去的三十年里，参与准备饭菜的父亲的比例几乎翻了一番。当然妇女仍然要做许多清洁、洗衣和日常照顾孩子的事情，但随着男性对家务更感兴趣，将有助于建立一个更加幸福和谐的家庭。

English for Everyday Life
日常生活英语

随着时间的推移，用来描述负担家务角色的词汇正在发生变化：

描述一位呆在家里，照顾家庭和孩子的全职母亲是：

Homemaker家庭主妇（而不是以往的家庭妇女）
Stay-at-home Mom 呆在家里的妈妈

描述一位呆在家里，照顾家庭和孩子的全职父亲如下：

Stay-at-home Dad 呆在家里的爸爸
Househusband 家庭主夫

October 7 Best High Schools

10月7日 温哥华著名的中学

Crofton House Senior School (private)

Here is the description of the school from their website: "Crofton House Senior School provides an enriched and accelerated curriculum which meets or exceeds the BC Ministry of Education graduation requirements. Exposure to fine arts and applied skills complements a rigorous academic program that prepares young women for successful post-secondary studies and/or opportunities. Physical education is compulsory to the end of grade 10, and students have a variety of opportunities to be physically active, both in scheduled classes and in the extensive athletics and intramural programs. While all curricular areas provide depth in learning, various curricular areas provide different levels of defined enrichment and acceleration. In several curricular areas, students can take Advanced Placement courses as offered by the College Board in Princeton, New Jersey. Beyond Ministry requirements, all students in the school: complete their grade 12 English in their eleventh year (thus allowing them to pursue an enriched English course in their final year); complete French up to and including grade 11; complete a comprehensive planning and graduation transitions program; and complete a program that has an included balance of Fine Arts and Applied Skills. Students are assigned to teacher advisors who play an integral role in the lives of the students. Advisors act as advocates for students as well as liaisons with parents and other teachers. Students meet with their advisors each morning and remain with their advisors and fellow students in grades 8-9, and then are assigned a new advisor and student group for grades 10-12."

罗夫顿豪斯中学（私立） http://www.croftonhouse.ca/

以下是学校网站上的描述：

"罗夫顿豪斯中学提供一种非同寻常的速成课程，可提前达到或超过省教育部的毕业要求。接受额外的美术和应用技能是一项严格的学术计划，为每个女孩子获得中学后教育的成功研究和/或机会提供了条件。在10年级结束时，体育课是必修的，无论是在预定的课程，还是在田径或校内其他体育活动，学生们都有很多机会参加各种体育活动。虽然所有课程和领域都提供了深入的学习，但不同的课程提供了不同程度的加速。在一些科目，学生可以选修由新泽西普林斯顿大学教育部提供的高级课程。除了校方要求之外，所有的在校学生在第11年级可以完成12年级的英语课程（从而允许他们在最后一年进修更加丰富的高级英语课程）；包括11年级修完法语课，完成全面规划和毕业过渡方案；并完成包含美术和应用技能平衡的课程。教师顾问在学生生活中起着不可或缺的作用，他们是学生、父母和其他教师的联络员。8-9年级的学生每天早上与顾问会面，然后是10-12年级的学生。"

October 8   The Homes of Vancouver

10月8日   **温哥华住宅**

Low-rise Condominiums
低层公寓

低层公寓的高度有限。 这种类型的公寓在温哥华的许多地区都很受欢迎，从而避免遮挡了山脉的景色。

Best Extracurricular Activities for Kids

10月9日   最佳儿童课外活动

Musquem Golf and Learning Academy

Musqueam Golf and Learning Academy has a variety of junior golf programs for beginners to advanced level players which will help build great athletic and social skills.

Musquem高尔夫学校http://www.musqueamgolf.com/junior-academy/

Musqueam高尔夫学校有适合各种水平的高尔夫课程，无论您的孩子是初学还是高级的玩家，他们都有相应的高尔夫球课。这将有助于发展特定的以及进一步提高高尔夫运动的技能。

October 10   Meeting Locals in Vancouver

10月10日   与当地人接触

Meetup.com

Meetup is a global online social networking site that members can use to find and join groups that have been formed around common interests like hiking, wine tasting, cooking, pets, health, languages and so on. It is a very helpful service that makes it easier for you to find people that like the same things that you do. Also, Meet-up has many groups for newcomers who want to learn and practice English and learn more about Vancouver. Some of those groups combine English practice with fun outings and adventures around Vancouver. To find these groups, just search for "ESL" and many choices of groups will be displayed.

All you must do is sign up for a free Meet-up account. Then, you can search all the different groups that are going on in Vancouver. If you see one you like, then check for the date of their next meeting and register online that you will attend. This is called an RSVP.

The Meet-up events are always in a safe public area like a coffeeshop. On the day of the event, there will be a small sign on the table in the coffeeshop so you can find the group. The meetings are usually free or a very low cost, unless there is food or wine for tasting. The meetings last about 1 ½ to 2 hours. If you don't like the group, you don't have to go again, but if you enjoy it, then you can RSVP to future meetings. It is very low pressure and low commitment so you can easily try out many different groups that match your different interests.

在Meetup.com 网上找到乐于分享您兴趣和爱好的人
https://www.meetup.com/

Meetup是一个全球性的在线社交网站，会员们可以查找和加入志趣相投的兴趣小组，如徒步旅行、品酒、烹饪、养宠物、健康、语言等等。这是一个非常有用的网站，通过它很容易找到志同道合的人。有许多小组是专门为那些想通过学习和练习英语，同时还想了解更多关于温哥华见闻的新移民组建的。其中的一些团体将英语练习与温哥华附近的郊游结合起来。要找到这些小组，我们只需要输入"ESL"，就会有很多选择。

您所要做的就是注册一个免费的账户。然后，您可以搜索到温哥华所有不同的小组。如果看到一个您喜欢的，然后查看下一次碰面的日期，并在网上登记您将会参加。这就是所谓的RSVP。

见面活动总是选在一个安全的公共场所，如咖啡馆。在活动当天，咖啡厅的桌子上会摆放一个小号牌，这样您就可以找到这个小组。聚会通常是免费的或非常低的费用，除非有食物或葡萄酒品尝。会议时间一般为1个半至2个小时。如果您不喜欢这个小组，您就不必再去了，要是您喜欢的话，您可以回复参加下一次的聚会。不必有什么顾虑，也不用承诺什么，您可以随意尝试许多不同的群体，看看哪些小组真正适合您。

October 11　　　Restaurant Customs and Etiquette

10月11日　　　餐厅的习俗与礼仪

Table manners

Having good table manners shows a person has been brought up well. It is also a sign of politeness to your fellow tablemates and to the other guests in the restaurant. Even children and teenagers are expected to follow these rules when dining in restaurants with their families. Teaching your children these manners is an important way to help prepare them for future success when they will need to go out to restaurants with their business clients and so on. Here are the seven most important table manners that locals try to follow when eating in a restaurant in Vancouver:

1. Do not talk with food in your mouth and always chew with your mouth closed as it is not very pleasant for your tablemates to watch.

2. Loud eating noises such as slurping and burping are very impolite. These are considered extremely offensive and rude.

3. Unfold your napkin and place it on your lap when you sit at the table to dine. When you are finished with your dinner, place the napkin loosely on the table, not on the plate and never on your chair.

4. Keep your elbows off the table.

5. Do not blow your nose at the dinner table. Excuse yourself to visit the restroom. Wash your hands before returning to the dining room. If you cough, cover your mouth with your napkin to stop the spread of germs and muffle the noise

6. Do not use a toothpick or apply makeup at the table.

7. Say "Excuse me," or "I'll be right back," before leaving the table. Do not say that you are going to the restroom.

餐桌礼仪

良好的餐桌礼仪表明一个人很有教养。这也是您对待同桌以及餐馆里其他客人的一种尊重。即使是儿童和青少年，与家人一起在餐馆用餐时也应遵守这些礼仪。从小教会他们这些礼仪有助于帮助他们健康成长。他们未来也许少不了要和其业务客户去餐馆用餐。以下是在温哥华饭馆就餐时要遵守的七个十分重要的餐桌礼仪：

1. 不要嘴里含着食物说话，这是非常粗鲁和难看的！总是闭着嘴嚼东西！等您吞下了口中的食物再说；
2. 大声地吃东西发出的噪声，打嗝都是很不礼貌的。这些被认为是极为粗鲁和无礼的；
3. 坐在餐桌上用餐前，用1分钟不到的时间打开餐巾，放在您的腿上。当您用餐完毕，再把餐巾松散地放回桌面上，但不要放在盘子里，也不要放在椅子上；
4. 不要将肘部支在餐桌上；
5. 不要在餐桌上擤鼻子。请他人原谅自己去洗手间。回到餐桌前要洗手。如果您要咳嗽，请用餐巾捂住嘴巴，以阻止细菌的传播，减少噪音；
6. 不要使用牙签或在餐桌上涂化妆品；
7. 在离开餐桌前先说声"对不起"或"我马上回来"。不要说，"我要去洗手间。"

Top English Programs for Adults

10月12日　　成人高级英语课程

Burnaby English Language Centre

This organization has centres in Burnaby, New Westminster, and Surrey. Their mission is to "effectively assist new immigrants in their adaptation to life in Canada by providing English language training, cultural orientation & labour market integration". They offer Language Instruction for Newcomers to Canada (LINC)English classes from levels 1 to 8 in a friendly and welcoming environment with professional instructors.

伯纳比英语语言中心 http://www.englishcentres.ca/

　　伯纳比英语语言中心在伯纳比，新西敏和萨里都设有学习中心。他们的使命是通过"提供英语语言培训、文化取向和劳动力市场一体化"，有效地协助新移民适应加拿大生活。 他们开设从1级 到 8级的加拿大新移民英语（LINC）课程，由专业英语教师在友好热情的气氛中授课。

October 13   Vancouver Backyard Wildlife

10月13日   温哥华后院的小鸟和动物

Harbour Seals

If you are lucky enough to live in an oceanfront property in Vancouver, then Harbour Seals will be one type of animal that you will see often frolicking in the water and on the beach. You will see them diving down to search for fish to feed on. They can dive up to 300 metres and an adult Harbour Seal can hold its breath up to 25 minutes. They use nerves on their whiskers to detect their prey. They also have big eyes that allow them to see well underwater. They are preyed on by Killer Whales.

Important Note about Baby Harbour Seals:

- Harbour Seals have their pups in the spring each year. The mother seal will nurse them on the beach.

- People regularly assume that seal pups are orphaned or abandoned when they see them alone on beaches and will take them away from the beach to the Aquarium or to a vet. However, the pups are only left alone so the mother can get food and she will be returning. If the pup is removed and touched by humans, it is almost impossible to reunite the pup with the mother. So, the pups must be left alone on the beach.

港海豹

如果您在温哥华的港湾附近置业，那么您会经常看到一种在海水里和沙滩上嬉戏的港海豹。您会看到它们潜下去寻找鱼吃。它们可以下潜到300米深的地方，成年海豹可以屏住呼吸达25分钟。他们用触须上的神经来探测猎物。他们有一双大眼睛，能让它们看清水下的情况。它们的天敌是虎鲸。

有关港海豹幼崽重要提示：

- 每年春天，海豹都会生下幼崽。海豹妈妈会在海滩上守护他们。
- 人们通常认为独自呆在海滩上的小海豹是失去了母亲或是被遗弃的，他们往往会把它们从海滩带到水族馆或兽医那里。其实，它们的妈妈是下海觅食去了，因此不得不把幼崽暂时留在海滩上，她会返回的。和狗不同，如果是狗崽被人抱走，几乎不可能再让它回到妈妈的怀抱。因此，不要好心挪走港海豹的幼崽，一定要让它独自留在海滩上等它的妈妈。

October 14 ## Support for Newcomers

10月14日　　支持新移民

Language Instruction for Newcomers (LINC)

The LINC program is funded by Immigration, Refugees, and Citizenship Canada (IRCC). You do not have to pay to for LINC classes. LINC provides basic language skills. If you need specific language skills, you may want to consider a program that better fits your educational or career goals. LINC offers both full- and part-time classes, and some centres have free child-minding while you attend classes. Every adult in your family can take LINC classes if they are eligible. LINC goes from level 1 (low beginner) to level 8 (high intermediate).

After you apply for LINC, you will be given an appointment for an English assessment (test). There are LINC classes in many different schools throughout Greater Vancouver. After your assessment, the assessment office can show you where the classes are in your area, the class levels, class types, class times and waitlist information. You can choose which school to attend, depending on availability.

新移民语言指导（LINC）

LINC计划由加拿大移民，难民和公民部（IRCC）资助。 您不必为LINC课程付费。 LINC提供基本的语言技能。 如果您需要特定的语言技能，您可能需要考虑一个更适合您的教育或职业目标的计划。 LINC分全日制和兼职课程，一些中心在上课的过程中可以免费照看您的孩子。凡是符合条件的成年人都有资格参加LINC课程。 LINC从1级（初学者）一直到8级（中高级）。

申请LINC后，您将等候英语评估预约（测试）。大温哥华的许多学校都有LINC课程。 评估后，评估办公室将告诉离您家最近的学校，上课时间和排队等候等信息。您可以根据自己的情况选择任意一所学校参加学习。

对于居住在温哥华、北温哥华、西温哥华、里士满、南三角洲、本拿比或新威斯敏的新移民，语言评估中心的地址和联系电话如下：

Western ESL Services
LINC Assessment and Referral Centre
#208 - 2525 Commercial Drive
Vancouver, BC V5N 4C1
Tel (604) 876-5756 Fax (604) 876-0134

October 15   # Vancouver Neighbourhoods

10月15日   温哥华社区

Chinatown

Vancouver's Chinatown is the one of largest in the Western Hemisphere, and, no matter the weather, it's always packed with people and bustling with energy. It's one of the most vibrant areas of the city, home to a wide range of shops, restaurants, and historic attractions. Chinatown is one of the city's earliest commercial and residential districts, containing a remarkable collection of buildings from Vancouver's boom years at the turn of the 1900s. Chinatown has always been popular with local residents who travelled there with the enthusiasm of tourists – sampling foods, buying curios, and enjoying the district's Chinese distinctiveness. There are some very famous attractions to see in Chinatown: the Millennium Gate, West Han Dynasty Bell, Dr Sun Yat Sen Classical Chinese Garden and the Monument of Canadian Chinese in Vancouver. Whether you go there for fresh fruits or dried seafood, Chinese imports, fabulous Dim Sum, or summer concerts, if you live in Vancouver, Chinatown is always a special place to visit.

唐人街 http://www.vancouver-chinatown.com/

　　温哥华的唐人街是西半球面积最大的一个，不管天气如何，那里总是挤满了过往的人群。它是温哥华最活跃的地区之一，有林林总总的商店、餐馆和历史名胜。唐人街是温哥华最早的商业区和住宅区之一，很多令人惊叹建筑物都是20世纪20年代温哥华繁荣时期建造的。唐人街一直深受当地居民和游客们的喜爱。人们可以品尝到中国的美食，买到古玩字画，唐人街有一些非常知名的景点：像千年门，西汉钟，孙中山古典园林和加拿大华人在温哥华的纪念碑。唐人街上店铺密布，随处可以卖到新鲜水果、海鲜、干货、中国进口和口味奇特的点心。每逢夏季，这里都会举办夏季音乐会。唐人街是值得你花一整天逛逛的。

October 16   Basic Everyday English

10月16日   基本日常生活用语

At the Community Centre

Community centres are the heart of every neighbourhood. They are a place to go for exercise, classes, different community group activities and meeting new people. Here are some phrases you can use at the community centre to register for classes or get information about different programs.

在社区中心

社区中心是每个社区的核心。 那里是健身、上课、参加社区活动和结识新朋友的好地方。下面是一些您可以在社区中心使用的短语，用于注册课程或者获得关于不同课程的信息。

English for Everyday Life
日常生活英语

下面是一些基本英语短语，您也许听到过， 您会在社区中心用到它们。请访问我们的网站 <u>www.mynewlifeinvancouver.com</u>，听一听这些短语的发音并练习会话。

Can you tell me about the dance course?
When is the course?
How much is the course?
Where is the classroom?
When does the fitness centre open?
How much does the fitness centre cost?
Do you have classes in Mandarin?
Do you have English Conversation classes?

您能告诉我有关舞蹈的课程吗？
课程什么时候开始？
这门课要付多少钱？
教室在哪里？
健身中心什么时候开门？
健身中心要多少钱？
您这儿有国语课吗？
您这儿有英语口语课吗？

Education

10月17日   教育

English Language Learners

The Vancouver School Board has prepared a very detailed website with all the information that newcomers need to know about their eligibility and assessment for education in the system. All of the information is available in Chinese; just select language near the top of the page. Every effort has been made to help newcomers feel safe and welcome and to make the process of school and class registration as easy as possible.

英语学习

温哥华教育局给新移民提供的信息
https://www.vsb.bc.ca/new-canadians

温哥华学校教育局为新移民准备了一个内容非常详细的网站，其中包含需要了解的关于其教育系统、资格评估的所有信息。 附有中文页面，您只需选择页面顶部的中文语言。教育局尽一切努力使新移民感到安全和受到欢迎，并使学校和班级注册的过程尽可能简便。

October 18　Scenes from Daily Life

10月18日　　日常生活中的一些镜头

Commuting Downtown on the Seabus
乘海上巴士往返市区

Outdoor Life in Vancouver

10月19日   *温哥华户外生活*

Horseback Riding in the City

You can experience the joys of horseback riding right in the city with these three top equestrian centres in Vancouver, Richmond and North Vancouver:

Southlands Riding Club (Vancouver) This private member club, founded in 1943, is in North America's only officially designated urban equestrian neighbourhood – Southlands. The club provides top quality riding facilities, instruction and events and competitions. They also host the Annual Pacific Polo Cup and the Southlands Country Fair.

Riverside Stables (Richmond) These stables offer a full range of services including beginner level riding lessons and summer camps and competitive coaching to the national level of competition. Riverside Equestrian Centre has a large indoor riding arena and outdoor riding facilities and is one of the largest equestrian complexes' in the Lower Mainland.

North Shore Equestrian Centre (North Vancouver). This riding centre provides services for English Discipline riders. They offer instruction from beginner to advanced with professional instructors. In addition, they offer full boarding and riding programs.

在城市里骑马

您可以在温哥华、里士满和北温哥华的三个马术中心体验骑马的乐趣：

南地马术俱乐部（温哥华）http://www.southlandsridingclub.com/
这是一个私人会员俱乐部，成立于1943年，是北美地区唯一的官方指定城市马术社区 – 南地社区。俱乐部提供优质骑乘设施、指导、活动和比赛，他们还举办一年一度的太平洋马球杯和南地乡村博览会。

滨江马厩（里士满）（Richmond）http://www.riversidestables.ca
这些马厩提供全方位的服务，包括初级骑马课程、夏令营、和国家级竞赛教练。马术中心有一个大型的室内骑马场地和室外骑马场设施，是低陆平原最大的马术馆之一。

北岸马术中心（北温哥华）http://www.wecreateriders.com. 这个骑马中心专门培养英式骑手。他们提供从初级到高级的专业指导。此外，他们还提供全面的寄宿和马术训练计划。

Tips to Learning English

资深英语老师提供学习英语的小贴士

Keep Your Eye on the Prize

This English expression means always remember your goal – the prize – that you are working towards in life. When we set a goal for ourselves, we usually must overcome many barriers and these can distract us from the beauty of our original goal. When you are a newcomer learning English, there will be good days and bad days, perhaps even good weeks, and bad weeks. But, through it all, if you stubbornly **"keep your eye on the prize"** of being able to comfortably use English in daily life, then the glory of the goal will keep you motivated to keep going and persist. Olympic athletes use affirmations (a positive statement that something is true) to remind them of their goal. They write a simple statement that explains what they want to be reality and they repeat it frequently, especially when feeling frustrated. An athlete might have an affirmation like "I am now a gold medal winner for boxing". An affirmation can also work for language learners too. Why not try it? Repeat this phrase every day, and especially when you are having a difficult day: ***"I can now speak and understand everyday English."*** This simple statement can help you remind you of the prize at the end of your hard work.

坚持就是胜利

　　这个英语表达意味着永远记住您的目标 – 奖杯得主 – 您在生活中努力使自己保持一种工作状态，当我们为自己设定一个目标时，通常必须克服许多障碍，这些障碍会分散我们对最初美好的目标的注意力。作为新移民您在学习英语时，往往会有顺心和烦躁的日子，也许这种好与坏的日子会持续好几个星期。但是，经历了这一切之后，如果您依然坚持，不放弃自己的目标。您就能够自在地在日常生活中使用英语，正所谓坚持就是胜利。奥运健儿们时时刻刻都在提醒给自己制定的目标。他们先写一句简单的豪言壮举，使用肯定的（积极的陈述，某事是真的），并详述他们只要通过努力就能把它变成为现实，他们经常重复这句话，特别是当感到沮丧的时候。运动员会有一个心理暗示，比如"我现在是拳击的金牌得主"。这种暗示也可以用在语言学习上。比如"我现在可以说和听懂日常英语。"为什么不试试呢？每天都重复这句话，尤其是当您遇到困难的时刻来安慰自己：像这样简短有力的一句话，可以起到意想不到的效果。努力之后就是获得奖杯之时。

October 21　A Little Canadian Inspiration

10月21日　　一点点启示

*I like a lot of food. I like Taiwanese food, of course. I
like baguettes, especially the ones that my dad buys.
Vancouver has a lot of variety, with pizza, hot dogs, Italian,
Indian, seafood - a great combination of culture.*

-Godfrey Gao, Vancouver Model and Actor

Godfrey Gao was born in Taiwan, but raised in North Vancouver.
He returned to Taiwan to model in 2004 and since that time he has
become a world-famous model and actor featuring in many popular
Asian movies.

*"我喜欢各种食物。我喜欢台湾菜，当然， 我更喜欢法式长棍面
包，特别是爸爸买的那种。温哥华有很多品种，有比萨饼、热狗、意
大利菜、印度菜、海鲜，这是饮食文化极好的融合。"*

——温哥华模特和演员高以翔

　　高以翔出生在台湾台北市，但却是在北温哥华念书长大。 2004年
回到台湾做模特，自那以后，他出席许多时尚派对，出演了许多部亚
洲电影。多次受到新闻媒体、杂志的报导，非常惹人注目。

Volunteer in Vancouver

10月22日   在温哥华做义工

Volunteer in the Neighbourhood

Volunteer opportunities can be found everywhere – even in your own neighbourhood. Usually schools, churches and community centres have many responsibilities to do on a very limited budget, so volunteers make a tremendous difference in their success. If you visit the main office of these organizations, they will find ways for you to be able to contribute your time and effort to their organizations.

社区义工

　　到处都可以找到志愿服务的机会，即使是在自己的社区。通常，学校、教堂和社区中心在预算非常有限的情况下仍然承担着许多责任，所以社区的成功与义工们付出的时间和精力是分不开的。如果您去访问这些单位，他们一定会给您提供机会的。

English for Everyday Life
日常生活英语

以下是您如何询问志愿服务的机会：

"Hello, I have some free time and would like to help"
"Do you have any volunteer work that I could do?"

"您好，我有一些空闲时间，愿意提供帮助。"
"您有我能做的志愿者工作吗？"

Healthcare in Vancouver

10月23日 温哥华的医疗保健

Chiropractor

Chiropractic medicine is a type of treatment based on the diagnosis and manipulative treatment of misalignments of the joints, especially those of the spinal column. These misalignments can cause other disorders by affecting the nerves, muscles, and organs. The chiropractor will move the body in certain ways to correct misalignments in the body. For many conditions, such as lower back pain, chiropractic care is frequently the primary method of treatment.

A chiropractic session will cost between $50 and $80. The Medical Services Plan does not cover the cost of treatment. However, many extended health plans will cover a percentage of the cost of chiropractic sessions. The College of Chiropractors of BC website has a search screen that helps you find a Chiropractor in a convenient location.

脊椎指压理疗师

卑诗省脊椎医学院　http://www.chirobc.com/

整脊医学是基于对关节错位诊断和手术治疗的方法，特别是对脊柱的治疗。这些错位可能通过影响神经，肌肉和器官而引起其他疾病。脊医将以某些方式移动身体，以纠正身体的不正。对于许多症状，如腰痛，背痛，脊椎按摩治疗常常是主要的治疗手段。

脊椎治疗费用一次在50加元到80加元之间。 医疗服务计划不包括脊椎指压治疗费用。不过，许多扩展的健康计划可以涵盖部分整脊疗法的费用。BC省脊椎医学院网站有一个搜索界面，可以帮助您快速地找到离您最近的脊椎指压治疗师的位置。

October 24   # Interesting Facts About Vancouver

10月24日   **温哥华趣闻**

Seawall Walking Paradise

There are three seawalls in Vancouver: Stanley Park, Kitsilano and West Vancouver. These paved walkways go along the ocean and give walkers a peaceful and safe place to walk without traffic and noise. Depending on the seawall you choose, you will see entirely different and beautiful views of the city.

海堤 – 散步者的天堂

温哥华有三个海堤： 斯坦利公园、基茨兰诺和西温哥华。沿着太平洋铺着人行道的路径行走，给人一种安静舒适的感觉，没有交通，没有噪音，从不同的角度欣赏美丽的城市景观，是理想的步行场所。

Finding Work in Vancouver

10月25日　　在温哥华找工作

Resources for Job Hunters

The Vancouver Public Library (VPL) has many job search resources. The librarians are an excellent source of information and can show you how to find the information you need. In addition, the VPL has created an excellent **"Chinese immigrants' guide to living, studying and working in BC"** website that lists all their resources that are available in the Chinese language, as well as many links to resources that are explained in Chinese.

The VPL has information for job searchers of every age. In addition, the major colleges and universities in Vancouver all provide career planning and job search centres that specifically help college age students looking for work during and after their studies. These school centres help students with their job search by providing resume writing, interview practice and job boards that list jobs that are suitable for students. Their services are free for students to use.

温哥华公共图书馆和大学/学院就业中心

温哥华公共图书馆（VPL）有很多求职资源。图书馆理员本身就是一个很好的信息来源，他/她可以告诉您如何找到所需的信息。此外，VPL创建了一个优秀的网站"华人移民在BC省的生活、学习和工作的指南"。

http://guides.vpl.ca/Chinese-immigrants-guide

这个中文网站用中文列出了所有可用的资源，以及许多以中文注解的资源链接。

VPL为不同年龄的求职者提供相应的信息。此外，温哥华的主要高校都提供职业规划和求职中心，专门帮助在校生在学习期间和毕业后寻找工作。这些学校的求职中心通过提供简历写作、面试练习和招聘会，列出适合学生的工作，从而帮助学生找到工作。他们的服务都是免费供学生使用的。

Vancouver Sightseeing

10月26日   观光

Vancouver Museum and HR McMillan Space Centre

At Vanier Park, on a beautiful piece of land by the water, are two important Vancouver cultural institutions. The first one, the **Vancouver Museum**, has a mission to inspire a deeper understanding of Vancouver through stories, objects and shared experiences. They really focus on trying to teach Vancouverites about themselves and how Vancouver connects to the world with their programs, exhibitions, and collections. Their vision is to inspire a socially connected, civically engaged city. The **H.R. MacMillan Space Centre** is located in the very distinctive white circular building above the Vancouver Museum. The building holds an auditorium with a curved ceiling and special projector that allows visitors to experience space from the comfort of their seats. They have interesting programs, exhibits, and activities that educate, inspire and evoke a sense of wonder about the Universe, our planet and space exploration.

温哥华博物馆和 HR 麦克米兰太空中心

HR 麦克米兰太空中心 http://www.spacecentre.ca/
温哥华博物馆 http://www.museumofvancouver.ca/

凡尼尔公园建在一片美丽的水上土地，有两个重要的温哥华文化机构。第一个，是温哥华博物馆，它是以教育为主题，通过讲故事，实物和分享经验，来激发人们对温哥华更深入的了解。他们是通过节目，展览和收藏让人们了解温哥华是如何与世界联系的。他们的目标是促进社会的紧密关系，使居民们热爱自己的城市。

第二个是麦克米兰空间中心，它位于温哥华博物馆上方非常独特的白色圆形建筑物中。该建筑有一个带有弯曲的天花板和特殊投影的观众席，让观众在舒适的座位上体验太空。 他们借助大屏幕讲解有趣的节目，游客们可以尽情感受太空的神秘，唤起对我们的地球、太空和宇宙的好奇心，充分领略天空的神秘。

October 27   Vancouver Transportation

10月27日   温哥华交通运输

Free and Low-Cost Shuttle buses in Vancouver

There are many free or low cost, privately run shuttle buses that take people to and from parts of the city that are difficult to access by public transportation. The local mountains Grouse, Seymour, and Cypress Mountain all operate shuttle buses to help people get up the mountains. Also, popular sightseeing locations like Capilano Bridge and Stanley Park have shuttle buses to help tourists and locals reach these beautiful places. Finally, the casinos and the horse racing track have free shuttle buses to transport their customers from public transportation sites to their locations conveniently. Many of the shuttle buses change their schedules and routes depending on the season so it is best to check their websites before planning to take the shuttles.

温哥华免费和低成本的巴士

有许多免费或低成本私人经营的穿梭巴士，帮助人们往返于城市的公共交通网络难以到达的地方。如温哥华的山区，松鸡山、西摩山和赛普拉斯山都有专营的穿梭巴士，给爬山和滑雪的人们提供方便。此外，像吊桥公园和斯坦利公园等热门旅游景点也设有穿梭巴士服务。赌场和赛马场也都有免费穿梭巴士，以方便他们的客户从公交站点直接拉到指定位置。许多班车是根据季节来调整他们的时间表和路线的，所以最好是在计划乘坐班车前上他们的网站查看一下。

抵达山区的穿梭巴士：

- 免费松鸡山穿梭巴士（季节性）
  https://www.grousemountain.com/shuttle
- 西摩山穿梭巴士（季节性/收费）
  http://www.mountseymour.com/shuttle-bus
- 赛普拉斯山穿梭巴士（季节性/收费）
  http://cypresscoachlines.com/

观光巴士：

- 免费卡普兰诺吊桥公园接送巴士
  https://www.capbridge.com/visit/shuttle-service/
- 斯坦利公园穿梭巴士（季节性/收费）
  http://www.vancouvertrolley.com/tour/stanley-park-shuttle

赌博和赛马巴士：

- 免费水滨赌场娱乐场穿梭巴士
  http://www.edgewatercasino.ca/transportation/shuttle-bus
- 免费黑斯廷斯赛马场穿梭巴士（季节性）
  http://www.hastingsracecourse.com/free-shuttle-service/
- 免费豪华别墅赌场穿梭巴士
  http://www.grandvillacasino.com/promotions/free-shuttle/

October 28 ## Sports Teams and Special Events

10月28日　　专业体育赛事和活动

HSBC World Rugby Sevens Series Vancouver

BC Place Stadium hosts one of the Annual HSBC World Rugby Sevens Series every year. This event is one of the most dynamic global sporting events in the world show-casing the fast- paced sevens rugby with fun entertainment and fan engagement and costumes that are always so fun to see. In the Sevens series there are ten tournaments held around in the world. Vancouver joins Hong Kong, Dubai and London as one of the host cities for the series. There are 15 "core" teams who participate at each round of the Series. The 2016-17 core includes: Argentina, Australia, Canada, England, Fiji, France, Japan, Kenya, New Zealand, Russia, Samoa, Scotland, South Africa, USA, and Wales. The tickets for the games sell out quickly and it is the new popular sporting event to watch in Vancouver.

温哥华汇丰杯世界七人制橄榄球系列赛
http://www. canadasevens. com/mens/

　　每年三月，由汇丰银行冠名的七人制世界橄榄球系列赛在卑诗体育馆举行。这项活动是最具活力的全球性体育赛事之一。它融合了七人制橄榄球的快节奏，娱乐，与身着滑稽服装的球迷互动。看上去总是令人捧腹大笑。七人制橄榄球在世界各地共举行十场比赛。温哥华、香港、迪拜和伦敦均作为该系列赛的主办城市。共有15支球队入围。参加2016-2017年比赛的球队有：阿根廷、澳大利亚、加拿大、英国、斐济、法国、日本、肯尼亚、新西兰、俄罗斯、萨摩亚、苏格兰、南非、美国和威尔士。门票很抢手，这是温哥华最受欢迎的体育赛事。

Vancouver Parks

10月29日　　温哥华公园

Lynn Canyon Park and Suspension Bridge

This park, located in the forests of Lynn Canyon in North Vancouver, is over 617 acres and a popular destination with tourists and residents for family picnics, leisurely hikes and refreshing swims in one of the many popular swimming holes. There is also the famous Lynn Canyon Suspension Bridge that swings 50 meters above the canyon. Unlike the Capilano Suspension Bridge, it is free for anyone to use the Lynn Canyon Bridge. Another popular feature is the Lynn Canyon Ecology Centre that highlights historical information about the park and even has a popular educational puppet show for children in the theatre.

林恩峡谷公园和悬索桥 http://lynncanyon.ca/

　　这个公园位于北温哥华的林恩峡谷的森林中，面积超过617英亩，是游客和当地居民的热门去处，公园为家庭提供了野餐桌。人们可以悠闲的远足，或者在许多清爽的游泳池洞中游泳。著名的林恩峡谷悬索桥，在峡谷上方50米处摆动。与卡皮拉诺吊桥不同之处是，它是免费的。林恩峡谷生态中心是另一个受欢迎的地方，它特别介绍了公园的历史，还有流行的受儿童欢迎的木偶教育节目。

October 30　　Stories and Advice for Newcomers

10月30日　　**移民的故事和建议**

Victor

几点建议

我叫Victor，作为移民，像每个人一样经历新鲜期、漫长的适应期和逐步生活融入期。

首先，思想上要稳定下来，树立"既来之，则安之"，不要有任何放弃的想法，要时刻有信心面对自己在新的环境下适应人生。

其次，需要不断的学习英语和找工作需要的专业知识，给自己定一个可实现的学习计划和方案，每天坚持，3个月后就会有很好效果；

第三，广交朋友，多交流和参加各种活动，特别多做志愿者工作，从中感受到移民的乐趣和帮助别人的快乐

最后，通过网络、自学和外围帮助，做足充分找工作前的准备，机会是留给有准备的人，相信自己一定行。

Diverse Vancouver

    多元文化的温哥华

Korean Cultural Heritage Festival

There is not a "Korea Town" in Vancouver, although parts of the West End and a large part of Coquitlam both have large and growing Korean communities. In addition to enjoying the many excellent Korean restaurants and stores in these two neighbourhoods, you can also experience Korean culture at their annual festival. Every year in August, The Korean Cultural Heritage Society (KCHS) hosts an annual **Korean Cultural Heritage Festival**. This free day long event is full of special Korean pop (K-POP music) and Tae Kwan Do performances, authentic Korean dishes, and many fun activities for the whole family.

韩国文化遗产节

温哥华有两个韩国社区，一个位于温哥华西区，而另一个更大，在高贵林，那里有很多韩国移民。不过，到目前为止温哥华还没有形成"韩国城"。在这两个社区有许多知名的韩国餐馆和商店，每年的8月份，韩国文化遗产协会（KCHS）都会举办一年一度的韩国文化遗产节。你可以去那里体验一下整整一天的韩国传统的文化。欣赏一下韩国流行音乐（K-POP）和跆拳道表演，品尝正宗的韩国饭菜，和许多有趣的为整个家庭安排的活动。

November

Weather:	Average temperature: 3°C to 10°C
	Average rainfall days: 22, Average rainfall: 225 mm
Statutory holiday:	Remembrance Day (November 11)
Other special days:	Thanksgiving (USA), Black Friday (USA)
	Time Change to Pacific Standard time (PST)

November is the month when newcomers to Vancouver really start to get tired of the dark and rainy days. Vancouverites spend a lot of time indoors in November because it is often too early to go up to the mountains and enjoy the snow and skiing, and it is too wet to enjoy the parks in the city.

However, this month there is a very special statutory holiday called Remembrance Day when the whole country takes a day to honour all the members of the military who have fought in wars and to remember the many soldiers who lost their lives fighting. Locals wear a bright red poppy pin* on their left lapels (as that side is closest to the heart) from November 1 until Remembrance Day on November 11. The poppies can be bought by donation at many locations around the city. The City of Vancouver organizes a very respectful and moving Remembrance Day Ceremony and Parade at Victory Square in downtown Vancouver. This park contains a large monument called the Cenotaph. This statue was built in remembrance of the men who died in the war. The Remembrance Day program begins with a performance by the Vancouver Bach Youth Choir and then a large parade of military marching units, bands and flag bearers that ends up at Victory Square. It ends with a formal ceremony including two minutes of silence, followed by a 21-gun salute and ending with the Royal Canadian Air Force conducting a military jet fly-by overhead.

After the somber Remembrance Day event, Vancouverites start to turn their attention to the very busy work of preparing for the Christmas season. Two popular events provide many opportunities to shop for presents and decorations for Christmas. The first event is the very popular Circle Craft Christmas Market which features hundreds of artisans and artists from coast to coast selling very high-end pottery, wood, glass, metal, fibre, fashion, jewellery, and crafts. Second is the Eastside Culture Crawl which provides another excellent opportunity to purchase art from more than 300 up-and-coming or already well-known artists. This event takes place in a very artistic east side neighbourhood in Vancouver where you wander the neighbourhood to meet the artists and view or purchase art right in their studios.

Finally, to really start to feel the Christmas spirit, a wonderful event is called Christmas at Hycroft where you can experience the magic of live music, local artisans, kitchen creations, door prizes, Santa and much more — all inside the traditional Edwardian mansion located in the luxurious Shaughnessy neighbourhood. All three floors of the gorgeous Hycroft manor are decorated and are sure to inspire the holiday season in you.

In November, the time moves back one hour to Pacific Standard Time (PST)* and all appreciate the extra hour of sleep for that one day! There is a popular saying to help us remember the time changes and whether to move the time forwards or backwards. It is *"In Spring we spring forward and in Fall we fall back"*.

11月

气候： 平均温度：3°C 到10°C
平均降雨天数： 22，平均降雨量： 225 毫米
公众节假日： 阵亡将士纪念日(11月 11日)
其他特殊日： 感恩节 （美国），黑色星期五 （美国）
更改太平洋时区 （PST）

十一月是阴雨天气。如果新移民是在这个月登陆温哥华，可能会有些不适应。由于天亮的晚的缘故，爬山、赏雪和滑雪都太早了，市里面的公园又太潮湿。此时，温哥华人都习惯了呆在室内，

不过，本月有一个非常特殊的公众节假日，于每年的11月11日，为一个纪念所有在战争中牺牲的军人与平民，当地人从11月1日起直到11日在他们的左边翻领戴上一朵鲜艳的红色罂粟（靠近心脏一侧）。罂粟花以捐赠的形式在城市的很多地方可以买到。市府组织民众在温哥华市中心的胜利广场英雄纪念碑前游行然后举办一场非常隆重的悼念仪式。首先，由温哥华巴赫青年合唱团表演，然后进行大的阅兵仪式，护旗手和游行乐队走在前面，最后回到胜利广场，广场上的所有人默哀两分钟，随后是21 响礼炮，加拿大皇家空军进行低空飞行表演后结束。

忧郁的纪念日过后，当地民众开始把他们的注意力转移到繁忙的圣诞季节，他们将为圣诞节做大量的准备工作。有两次重大的活动提供了最佳购买圣诞节礼物和装饰品的机会。第一个是非常流行的Circle 手工艺品圣诞市场，从东海岸到西海岸数以百计的工匠和艺术家们制作的非常高端的陶瓷、玻璃、木材、纤维、金属、珠宝、服装和手工艺品。第二是东区文化艺术街，提供了另一个极好的购物机会，有300多知名艺术家——包括陶工、玻璃吹制工、摄影师和家具制造商，向公众开放他们的私人工作室。地点就位于温哥华东区的艺术社区，您在附近走走逛逛，直接与艺术家们见面聊一聊或许可以在他们的艺术工作室买到称心艺术品。

最后，真正开始感受到圣诞节的精神，一个最美妙、最精彩的是在Hycroft庄园里举行的圣诞节活动，在那里您可以体验神奇的现场音乐，当地的工匠制作的手工艺品，厨房的创意设计，抽奖活动，圣诞老人，还有更多——所有传统的活动都在肖尼西社区豪华的爱德华大厦内进行。所有楼层都是经过超豪华的装饰，Hycroft庄园是激发您灵感的好地方。

　　每年11月的第一个星期日，就是夏令时结束之日，恢复到正常时间，或者我们叫冬令时。时间拨回一小时至太平洋时区（PST）这一天可以多睡一个小时！究竟向前拨快一个小时还是向后拨慢一个小时。记住下面这个口诀可以帮助我们记住时间的变化。它就是人们常说的"春前秋回" 即 "春天，我们向前拨一个小时，秋天，我们往回拨一个小时"。或者记住这四个字：夏少东多。意思是夏天少睡一小时，而冬天则多睡了一小时。

更多的信息：

东区文化艺术品：http://culturecrawl.ca/
Circle工艺品市场：www.circlecraft.net/
在胜利广场公园的阅兵式和悼念仪式：
Hycroft 庄园圣诞节：www.christmasathycroft.com

* red poppy pin红罂粟胸针：我们佩戴红色的罂粟，因为它主要野生在法国和比利时北部的许多地方，第一次世界大战（1914-1918）在那里曾发生过惨烈的战斗，数千名士兵阵亡。罂粟花具有顽强的生命力，它可以在任何地方生长，看上去很娇艳。人们认为它最适合纪念死亡的士兵。加拿大著名的军医诗人用罂粟花描写 "在佛兰德斯的战场" 上的士兵。红罂粟象征着回忆和希望。

* Pacific Standard Time (PST)太平洋时区：向后拨一个小时

November 1 Local Customs

11月1日 当地的习俗

Retirement and Goodbye parties

The average retirement age in Canada is 65 years old. Usually retirement is mainly celebrated with work colleagues with some cake and coffee or going out for dinner together. The colleagues will usually each contribute some money towards a present for the retiree and all sign a happy retirement greeting card. The presents are usually related to activities the person will be able to do when they are retired for example a gift certificate to a gardening centre and so on. Some newly retired people plan a big retirement party for their friends and family as well, but it is not common.

When a colleague leaves a company to go work at a different company, their colleagues will plan a goodbye party for them. The activities are similar to the ones for a retiring colleague, the colleagues sign a goodbye and good luck card and collect money for a goodbye present.

When someone close to us goes away on a long trip, we might give them a **Bon Voyage** (French for good trip) card or small party. We usually will do this only if the trip is a very special and long one that the person has been planning for a long time.

When someone close to us is going to move away, we will sometimes host a **Goodbye and Good Luck** party to wish them well if they are our close friends.

退休派对与告别派对

在加拿大的平均退休年龄为65岁。退休派对主要是为了退休前再一次与共事多年的同事们搞一个庆祝活动，分享蛋糕、咖啡或走出去与大家一起共进晚餐。同事们通常会凑钱为退休人员买一份礼物，并附上一张签名的快乐的退休贺卡。礼物通常适合退休后能够参加的活动，如园艺中心的礼品卡等。近年来有的退休人员会为他们的朋友和家人筹办更大的退休派对，但这并不常见。

当同事离开公司去在另外一家公司工作时，临别时，他/她的同事们也会为其筹办一个告别晚会。这与退休聚会有一点儿相似，同事们共同签署一张祝他/她好运的告别卡，并凑钱购买送别礼物。

当某人准备远行或者搬走，临行前的告别

当我们的好友即将离开我们去很远的地方旅行，我们会送给他们一张Bon Voyage（法语为旅行愉快）卡或小型聚会。我们通常会这样做，特别是当他/她为此已经准备了很长的时间。

当某人要搬走的时候，如果是我们要好的朋友，我们有时会举办一个告别会，祝他们好运。

November 2   ## Parenting in Vancouver

11月2日   在温哥华养育子女

Extracurricular Activities for Kids

It is very common for children to be involved in some extra activities outside of their activities in school. These activities are usually sports, music or dance related. Some Canadian parents try to limit the extracurricular activities so that there is still time to play and time to "just be a kid". There are often discussions about how many activities are healthy for a child's development. Many parents try to have a balance of activities so that some are sports-related and active like swimming lessons or soccer and the other activity requires deeper thinking like piano or chess.

儿童课外活动（校外活动）

儿童在课外参与一些其他额外的活动是很常见的。 这些活动通常有运动、音乐或者舞蹈。 一些加拿大父母限制课外活动，以便孩子有更多的时间玩耍，因为他/她还是个孩子。经常有人讨论这个问题，究竟参加多少课外活动对儿童的发展才是健康的。许多家长试图寻找一个平衡点，比如他们安排孩子参加一些与运动相关的活动像游泳课或踢足球，而其他活动则需要更深层次的思考像弹钢琴或下象棋。

November 3 Stories and Advice for Newcomers

11月3日 新移民的故事

Emma and Jason

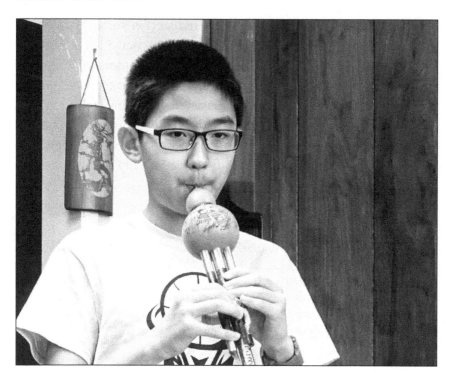

有一些建议和大家分享

2015年8月6日是我生命中最重要的一天——我们一家三口登陆温哥华，成为加拿大永久居民。

然而一开始我们便被困难和疑虑包围，尤其是遇到中西教育理念的碰撞。当儿子从学校拿回一张复印纸，说这就是课本时；当儿子告诉我上课就是讲故事、做游戏时；当儿子因为语言生涩而没有朋友时……再想到国内孩子每天争分夺秒学习，我们更加焦虑不已，甚至萌生出打道回府的念头。

后来通过多方了解，和老移民朋友深入沟通，尤其是温哥华教育局派驻学校的移民安顿工作者及家校协调员的帮助，使我们逐渐了解并适应了北美的教育理念。

现在，孩子越来越快乐，我也从开始的不适，到现在知足、感恩，并爱上这个友善的城市，有一些建议和大家分享：

1、积极调整家长的焦虑心态，从正规渠道收集正确资讯，汲取正能量、好方法。

2、给孩子时间，让孩子从最擅长、喜爱的活动开始，在运动中建立自信，在集体活动中找到朋友。

3、鼓励孩子多参加户外活动，可以尽快融入当地生活，并磨练意志。

4、充分运用温哥华分馆众多的图书资源。

如今，每天目送儿子背着书包、迎着朝阳走向学校时，我发现他的背影越来越自信，而我也品味出这段历练给予我的独特味道。祝愿所有新移民家庭能尽快融入新环境，开始美好新生活！

November 4   # Vancouver Entertainment

11月4日   温哥华娱乐

Live Music Concerts

All throughout the city you will find small restaurants and bars that offer live music. Vancouverites really enjoy watching musical events. In addition, many famous musical acts come to Vancouver to put on big concerts. The famous musical acts will play in the bigger venues: Roger's Arena and BC Place Stadium. The smaller shows will be at the medium sized venues which are the Orpheum and the Commodore Ballroom in downtown Vancouver, and in the big showrooms located in the major casinos. The concert schedule is often known many months ahead of time. You can find out the upcoming concerts by searching on the most popular event listing websites: Ticketmaster and Concert Fix Vancouver.

现场音乐演唱会

您也许会感到奇怪，温哥华整个城市，甚至就连小餐馆和酒吧都会提供舞池和音乐演奏场地。温哥华人太喜欢观看音乐表演了。除了国际爵士音乐节，民间音乐等小型活动和音乐节以外，许多世界著名的音乐剧团也常常到温哥华来举办大型的音乐演唱会。知名度高的音乐剧团会选择在更大的场馆中演出：像罗杰体育场和卑诗广场体育馆。普通的将在中等规模的场地，像温哥华市中心的奥芬剧院和舰队舞厅，或在赌场的大展厅里面演出。音乐会演出的时间表通常会提前几个月公布。通过搜索相关的活动网站，您可以快速地查找到即将举行的音乐会。您也可以在下面的网站上直接购买演唱会的门票：

温哥华演唱会 http://concertfix.com/concerts/vancouver-bc
票务 https://www.ticketmaster.ca/

Best Elementary Schools

11月5日 温哥华著名的小学

Dr. Annie Jamieson Elementary School (public)

Here is the description of the school from their website: "Dr. Annie B. Jamieson Elementary School is located just south of Oakridge, on the west side of Vancouver. Currently, program offerings at Jamieson include the largest elementary Strings Program, as well as the only intermediate Mandarin Bilingual Program in the district. Approximately 260 intermediate students participate in the Strings Program. Also, approximately 145 students participate in the intermediate Mandarin Bilingual Program. Jamieson School offers a range of sports and extra-curricular activities. In addition to two regular physical education classes per week, extra-curricular sporting activities for intermediate students often includes: Cross Country, Volleyball, Basketball, Track and Field and sometimes Badminton and Ultimate Frisbee."

安妮·贾米森博士小学（公立）
http://go.vsb.bc.ca/schools/jamieson

下面是学校网站的描述：

"安妮贾米森博士小学位于温哥华西侧奥克里奇的南部。目前，贾米森提供的课程包括最大的管弦乐基础课程，以及该地区唯一的中级普通话双语课程。大约有260名学生参加了管弦乐课程。此外，另有145名学生参加中级普通话双语课程。贾米森学校提供各种体育和课外活动。除了每周定期上两次体育课以外，中高年级学生的课外体育活动通常包括：越野、排球、篮球、田径、羽毛球和极限飞盘等。

11月6日   不同的思维方式

Helping Attitude

Canada is a country that values individualism as a basic cultural trait; however, Canadians are also tolerant, polite, and very determined to maintain an accepting and helpful community. Therefore, it is considered very important to feel a sense of responsibility for maintaining the community by being helpful whenever possible. Residents who are helpful to other people and to the community are very respected and valued. Also, in Canadian society, senior citizens and people with obvious handicaps and physical disabilities are treated with compassion and understanding and an extra effort is made to be helpful to them. Maintaining a balance between taking care of one's personal goals and being helpful to others and the community are considered very important to ensure that Canada maintains a very high quality of life and a pleasant atmosphere.

对待帮助的态度

加拿大是一个将个人主义视为基本文化特征的国家。然而，加拿大人又是宽容的，有礼貌的，并且非常坚定地接受和维护乐于助人的社区。因此，只要有可能就去帮助他人，保持社会责任感是很重要的。对社区有帮助的居民非常受大家的尊崇和爱戴。还有，在加拿大社会，老年人、有明显残疾和智障的人士会受到大家的同情和理解，人们为此做出了额外的努力，为他们提供帮助。在兼顾个人目标、帮助他人和社区三者之间保持平衡是确保加拿大非常高的生活质量和愉快的气氛。

English for Everyday Life
日常生活英语

以下是您提供帮助时想要说的话:

"Is there anything I can do to help?"
"有什么我可以帮忙的吗？"

"Please let me know if I can help"
"如果我能帮忙，请告诉我"

Best High Schools

温哥华著名的中学

Vancouver Technical High School (public)

Here is the description of the school from their website: "Vancouver Technical School provides a safe, nurturing and stimulating environment in which students are given the opportunity to develop their intellectual, social, ethical, aesthetic, physical and emotional intelligences; to respect the individual, embrace diversity, and participate in the human community. In addition, there is a Flex Humanities Mini School where students will study integrated curricula of Humanities, Fine Arts, and Modern Languages. Flex Humanities has been designed to meet the needs of above average ability students in grades 8, 9, and 10 who are interested in working with other self-motivated students. The Flex Humanities program encourages students to pursue topics which have personal and social relevance."

温哥华技校（公立） http://go.vsb.bc.ca/schools/vantech

以下是学校网站上的描述：

"温哥华技术学校提供了一个安全，刺激和受欢迎的环境，学生有机会发展其智力、社会、伦理、审美、身体和情感智慧；尊重他人、拥抱多样性、参与社区活动、促进发展的社会意识和责任感。 另设有一个福莱克斯迷你人文学校，学生将会学习人文、美术和现代语言等综合课程。学校将致力于满足8、 9 和 10 年级有兴趣且有上进心学生的需求。福莱克斯人文课程鼓励学生追求具有个人和社会关联性的课题。"

November 8   # The Homes of Vancouver

11月8日   **温哥华住宅**

The Famous "Vancouver Special" Design House
著名的温哥华"特别"屋

  这种设计是八十年代建造的最流行的住宅风格。它非常宽敞，顶部和底部有两个大的生活区。由于这种款式在温哥华很受欢迎，所以被人们亲切地称作"温哥华特别"屋。

November 9   # Best Extracurricular
                     Activities for Kids

11月9日   最佳儿童课外活动

League sports: baseball, soccer, and football

Vancouver parents can be found at the local parks in the early evening and on the weekends standing on the sidelines and watching their children play team sports like baseball and soccer. They believe that team sports teach their children very important communication and leadership skills that are needed in life. Also, many universities look favourably on team involvement on university application forms as well. In western culture, the relationships and connections built during team play can often last a lifetime. Also, the games and practices give parents an opportunity to meet and socialize with each other. Each sport has their own association that takes care of registration and arranging the yearly practice and game schedule. Each neighbourhood has their own sports league and children can only register in the league of the neighbourhood they belong to. Both boys and girls play on the same baseball and soccer teams when they are young, but later they will split into girls and boys' leagues.

小联盟：棒球，足球和橄榄球

克里斯戴尔小联盟 http://www.kerrisdalebaseball.com/
邓巴小联盟 http://dunbarbaseball.ca/
小山棒球小联盟 http://www.eteamz.com/lmbll/
温哥华联合足球俱乐部 （足球）http://www.vanufc.com

周末傍晚时分，父母们站在公园操场的旁边，看着孩子们玩棒球和足球等运动。他们相信球队运动能教会孩子们生活中所需要的非常重要的沟通和领导技巧。此外，许多大学也看好球队队员们的大学申请。在西方文化中，团队合作中建立起来的关系和友谊往往可以维持一生。此外，球队活动也给父母提供了一个相互认识和交往的机会。每项运动都有属于自己的协会，负责登记和安排年度训练和比赛日程。每个社区都有自己的运动联盟，孩子只能在他们所属的社区联盟注册。男孩和女孩在年轻时都会在同一个棒球队和足球队玩耍，但大了以后他们将会分为女孩和男孩的联赛。

November 10　　Meeting Locals in Vancouver

11月10日　　与当地人接触

Community Service Clubs

A service club or service organization is defined as a voluntary non-profit organization where members meet regularly to perform charitable works either by direct hands-on efforts or by raising money for other organizations. Service clubs also arrange social occasions, networking, and personal growth opportunities for their members. These clubs provide a great opportunity to meet new people and contribute to the community. There are numerous service clubs in Vancouver. Here is a just a sample of them:

Lions Clubs International

Lions Clubs International is the largest service club organization in the world with 1.4 million members who perform valuable service in 210 countries and geographic areas around the globe. Lions are friends, family and neighbors who share a belief that our community is what we make it. There are more than 30 Lions Club branches in Vancouver so you can find a group that has a location, meeting time and membership that is suitable to you.

Rotary International

The world's first service club, the Rotary Club of Chicago, was formed in 1905 by Paul P. Harris, an attorney who wanted to create a club with the same friendly spirit he had felt in the small towns of his youth. The Rotary Club is a global network of 1.2 million neighbors, friends, leaders, and problem-solvers who come together to make positive, lasting change in communities at home and abroad. For more than 100 years, Rotary members have used their passion, energy, and intelligence to take action on projects from literacy and peace to water and health.

The Canadian Club of Vancouver

The Canadian Club recently celebrated its 110th birthday. Their goals are to foster fellowship among people encouraging the celebration of Canadian identity, as well as to educate and stimulate thought around issues of national significance. Focusing primarily on organizing events featuring guest speakers who share their knowledge and insight, the Club also remains involved in unique initiatives including citizenship ceremonies for "new Canadians" and the BC-resident Order of Canada recipients luncheon.

社区服务俱乐部

社区服务俱乐部被定义为一个自发的非营利组织，会员们定期举办慈善公益活动，为其他组织筹措资金。社区服务俱乐部还为其成员安排社交活动，网络和个人发展的机会。在这些俱乐部您不仅可以结识新朋友，还能为社区做出应有的贡献。温哥华有许多这样的服务俱乐部。这里只简要介绍其中的三个：

国际狮子会 http://www.lionsclubs.org

国际狮子会是世界上最大的服务组织，拥有140万名成员，在全球210个国家和地区提供有益的服务。狮友是指朋友，家人和邻居们，狮子会的座右铭是（我们服务社区）强调"我们"而非个人。温哥华有超过30家分会，您可以选择一个适合您的分会，聚会的时间和会员资格。

国际扶轮社 https://www.rotary.org

全球第一个扶轮社是由律师保罗·哈里斯于1905年创立于美国芝加哥。他希望以他在青年时期的小镇上所感受到的友好精神创建俱乐部。目前，国际扶轮在全球有超过120万来自各种不同的职业的社员，它已成为共同努力解决问题的全世界社团组织。他们携手共同为国内外社区做出积极和持久的贡献。100多年来，扶轮社成员利用他们的激情、精力和智慧，对扫盲、和平、水资源和健康等项目采取了有效的行动。

温哥华加拿大俱乐部 https://www.canadianclubvancouver.com/

加拿大俱乐部最近庆祝加拿大150岁的生日。俱乐部一直致力于促进加拿大身份，并推动在人口高度多样化的爱国情操。同时鼓励了解加拿大的历史知识，艺术、科学、商业和公共事务，并通过各种举措举行客座嘉宾演讲分享他们的知识和洞察力，俱乐部还为"新加拿大人"举行公民入籍宣誓仪式以及为不列颠哥伦比亚省居民提供特色午餐。

November 11 # Restaurant Customs and Etiquette

11月11日　　餐厅的习俗与礼仪

Cheers and Giving Toasts

Sharing a meal and drinks together with friends is one of the most enjoyable activities we can do together. It is always nice to raise and click our glasses together to show our happiness about being together. When doing this simple movement, we simply say **"Cheers!"**. Sometimes, it is a nice thing to do to make a "toast" at the meal. A toast is a very short speech made to honour the reason for the gathering such as a birthday, or a work promotion or celebrating seeing each other again after a long way apart. Anyone can make the toast; however, it is usually customary that the person who planned the get-together at the restaurant would do it. After a toast or cheers is said, it is customary for everyone to take a drink from their glass before continuing with the conversation.

干杯和祝酒

与朋友一起喝酒进餐是人与人之间交往中最愉快的事情。席间人们端起酒杯，轻轻地互碰以表示大家在一起是多么的幸福。在碰杯的时候，我们会说"干杯！"。在饮酒时，通常还要讲一些祝愿、祝福之类的话甚至主人还要讲几句祝酒词，英文称作'toast吐司'；吐司是一个非常简短的演讲，说明聚会的原因，比如生日或升职，或经过长途跋涉后再次相遇。任何人都可以吐司；然而，习惯上，是由筹划聚会的主宾来主持。经过一番吐司之后会提议众人干杯，接着每个人都喝一口杯中的酒，然后开始闲谈。

English for Everyday Life
日常生活英语

下面是两句非常典型的祝酒词的例子：

- 当您祝酒时，先端起手中的酒杯，说一句话:提醒大家注意：

  "I would like to make a toast"
  "我想给大家敬酒"

- 宾客们也会像您一样拿起酒杯，表示他们愿意听您讲话。.

  "Thank you all for joining us tonight. We want to wish our guest a very happy birthday"
  "谢谢大家出席我们今晚的活动。我们希望我们的嘉宾生日快乐"

- 客人们此刻都会说

  "happy birthday" *"生日快乐"* 或
  "cheers" *"干杯"*，大家一起碰杯，然后抿上一口。

November 12 Top English Programs for Adults

11月12日 成人高级英语课程

Community English Education

Most neighbourhoods have a community centre or a neighbourhood house and at least one church. These organizations are very interested in promoting the health, education, and connections between residents in the area. Therefore, many provide some type of English as a Second Language classes or conversation clubs for adults who live in the area. Usually these language groups are more informal than other activities and are only offered once or twice per week. For example, many community centres have a weekly **"Conversation Corner"** where newcomers can meet and practice speaking English with each other and with a volunteer leader.

社区中心、 邻里协会和教堂

大多数社区都有一个社区中心，一个邻里协会和一座教堂。这些组织对促进该地区居民的健康、教育和邻里间的关系起到了相当重要的作用。他们为该地区的成年人提供英语作为第二语言课程或对话俱乐部。通常这些活动不那么正规，每周仅提供一次或两次。例如，许多社区中心每周都有一个"英语角"，新来的人可以在那里见面，练习说英语，由志愿者负责组织。

November 13   Vancouver Backyard Wildlife

11月13日   温哥华后院的小鸟和动物

Robins

When Vancouverites see the orange-breasted robin in their backyard, they know that spring has finally arrived! Their lovely birdsong can be heard when the sun rises in the spring. Robins build nests of grass and mud in shrubs and trees. Their food is mostly insects, earthworms, and fruit. Another special fact about these birds is the beautiful blue colour of their eggs. In fact, the name of that colour is known as "robin-egg blue". It is the same colour of blue used by the famous Tiffany & Co. Jewelry store for their beautiful blue boxes and packaging of their products.

知更鸟

当温哥华人在他们的后院看到橙色胸脯的知更鸟时，就知道春天终于来临了！春天当太阳升起的时候，可以听到可爱的鸟鸣声。知更鸟在灌木和树上用草和泥筑巢。它们以昆虫、蚯蚓和水果为食。产下的蛋很特别，外壳是蓝色的。被称作"知更鸟蓝蛋"。您可能会联想到，著名的蒂凡尼珠宝专卖店漂亮的产品包装盒也是蓝色的。

November 14　　## Support for Newcomers

11月14日　　　**支持新移民**

New To BC

New To BC is a free online resource centre that helps newcomers find the information they need to get a job or explore careers in Vancouver. The Vancouver Public Library manages this website.

New To BC（图书馆为新移民提供的链接）http://newtobc.ca/

　　初到BC省（New To BC）是一个免费的在线资源中心，它帮助新移民在温哥华找工作或探索其职业生涯等信息。该网站由温哥华公共图书馆负责运营。

November 15   Vancouver Neighbourhoods

11月15日   温哥华社区

The West End

The West End includes all the best aspects of the Vancouver lifestyle. The West End lies west of Downtown, and bodies of water surround it on three sides: English Bay, Coal Harbour, and Lost Lagoon in the world-famous Stanley Park. Recreational facilities are within walking distance for residents of this high-density area of condominium towers. Stanley Park (and its long seawall) is like the backyard for West End residents. English Bay makes the Pacific Ocean easy to reach for everyone. Downtown Vancouver is right at the doorstep of the West End. The West End is an example of "West Coast living" at its best. In addition to the natural beauty of this district, Davie, Denman and Robson streets are famous for their world-class shopping and tremendous selection of restaurants.

西端 http://westendbia.com/

　　西端区是温哥华市一个高档住宅小区，它是有钱人喜欢居住的地区。西端区位于市中心以西，三面环水：英吉利湾、煤港和世界著名的斯坦利公园里的失落的泻湖。居住在这个高密度多层公寓大厦里的居民健身很方便，周围有各种康乐设施。举世闻名的斯坦利公园（它那长长的海堤）就像是西端区居民的后院。美丽壮观的太平洋英吉利湾是温哥华观看日落最好的地点。简单地说，西端是温哥华最有代表性的街区，它是"西海岸生活"最好的地方。除了自然美景，戴维、登曼和罗布森的街道都是世界上一流的购物和餐饮的好去处。

Basic Everyday English

11月16日   基本日常生活用语

On the Bus

It is a good idea to have the address written down for the location you are trying to get to. This way you can always show the paper to the bus driver so he can help give you information about how to get there. Also, the Translink website gives detailed step by step instructions on how to get to your destination. These phrases will help you for your bus adventures.

在公交车上

将您想要去的地址写下来是一个不错的主意。您可以随时出示给公交车司机看，这样，他/她就会告诉您在哪一站下车，以及如何到达那里的信息。此外，交通局网站也详细提供了如何到达目的地的步骤。以下短语也将帮助您体验乘公交车的乐趣。

English for Everyday Life
日常生活英语

下面是一些基本英语短语，您也许听到过，您可以在乘车时使用。 请访问我们的网站www.mynewlifeinvancouver.com，听一听这些短语的发音并练习会话。

Does this bus go to UBC?
How much is the ticket?
How much is it?
Is this seat taken?
Would you like my seat?

这车是去 UBC 吗？
车票多少钱？
多少钱？
这个座位有人吗？
您想要坐我的座位吗？

November 17 Education

11月17日　教育

Education Savings Plans

Paying the tuition fees at colleges and universities in Canada is very expensive. Both the federal and provincial governments have designed education savings plans to assist parents with this cost.

A **Registered Education Savings Plan (RESP)** is a smart way to maximize education savings. The government allows you to save up to $50,000 in an RESP sheltered from tax. No income tax is paid on investment returns as long as money remains in the plan. When money is withdrawn to pay for a child's education, the withdrawals are taxable in the child's hands but, because the child will likely have a low income and low tax rate while attending school, taxes should be minimal. In addition, the government will match 20% of the annual RESP contributions to a maximum of $500 per year and $7,200 over a child's lifetime.

Families in British Columbia are encouraged to start planning and saving early for their children's post-secondary education or training programs. To help, the B.C. Government will contribute $1,200 to eligible children through **the B.C. Training and Education Savings Grant (BCTESG).** To receive this money, the child must be born in 2006 or later and have a registered RESP set up with a participating financial institution.

教育储蓄计划

在加拿大，高校学费支付是非常昂贵的。 联邦和省政府都设计了教育储蓄计划，以帮助父母解决这笔费用。

- 注册教育储蓄计划（RESP）是最大限度地提高教育储蓄的聪明方式。政府允许您在免税的RESP中节省高达50,000加元。只要资金留在计划中，就不会支付所得税。当钱被取出来支付孩子的教育费用，提款的时候是以孩子的名义纳税，但因为孩子在上学期间会有较低的税率，税收应该是最低的。此外，政府将把 20%的年度RESP款项，每年最多500加元和7,200加元的儿童寿险用在一个孩子身上。
- 在不列颠哥伦比亚省，政府鼓励每个家庭尽早规划和为子女的中学后的高等教育或培训存钱。为此，省政府会通过培训和教育储蓄补助金（BCTESG）为符合条件的儿童提供1,200 加元。要收到这笔钱，孩子必须在2006年或以后出生，并且与参与该计划的金融机构注册RESP。

November 18   Scenes from Daily Life

11月18日   日常生活中的一些镜头

Patiently Lining Up for the Bus
耐心地排队等候公共汽车

Outdoor Life in Vancouver

11月19日 温哥华户外生活

Mountain Fun

There are three major mountains just a short drive away from downtown Vancouver: Grouse Mountain, Seymour Mountain, and Cyprus Mountain. All three offer facilities for guests to enjoy outdoor activities all year round. In the summer, you can go for a long hike and enjoy lunch in their restaurants. In the winter, you can ski, snowboard, or take a long hike in snowshoes and enjoy warm chocolate fondue afterwards.

In addition to the regular hiking and skiing activities on the mountains, Grouse Mountain and Seymour Mountain also have two very special and popular activities:

The Grouse Grind – a famous hiking challenge! If you enjoy challenging hikes through nature, then you will love the Grouse Grind. The Grouse Grind is a 2.9-kilometre trail up the face of Grouse Mountain, and it is known as "Mother Nature's Stairmaster." (an exercise machine that duplicates the exercise of going up stairs). The trail is very challenging and will take about two hours to complete. Many Vancouverites go up the Grouse Grind two or three times per week to maintain their fitness and enjoy nature.

Snow Tubing at Mount Seymour! Your kids will love sliding down the mountain in a specially designed inner tube. When you get to the bottom, you can just attach your inner tube to a towline and be pulled back up to the top of the hill and slide back down again. It is fun, safe, and exciting for the whole family.

山地乐趣：

Grouse Mountain松鸡山　https://www.grousemountain.com/
Seymour Mountain 西摩山 http://mtseymour.ca/
Cyprus Mountain 塞浦路斯山 http://www.cypressmountain.com/

　　距离温哥华市中心不远处有三座大山：松鸡山，西摩山和塞浦路斯山。他们均提供完备的设施，让客人们全年享受户外活动。夏天，您可以徒步旅行，在餐厅享用午餐。冬天，您可以滑雪和雪地行走，然后来一杯热巧克力。

　　除了山上的常规徒步旅行和滑雪活动之外，松鸡山和西摩山还有两项非常特殊的广受欢迎的活动：

- **松鸡山登山道 – 一条著名徒步挑战山道！** 如果您喜欢挑战高难度的天然徒步健身，那么您肯定会喜欢松鸡山的。松鸡山登山道是一条长达2.9公里的小道，被誉为"天然踏步机"（一种可以模拟重复爬楼锻炼的机器）这条路非常具有挑战性，全程大约需要两个小时。许多温哥华人每周去松鸡山爬两到三次，在享受大自然美的同时保持健康的体魄。
- **西摩山的滑雪胎！** 您的孩子肯定会喜欢坐在特制的内胎中滑下山的。当您滑到山底时，您就可以拽着胎上附加的拖绳将其拉回到山顶，并再次滑下来。这很有趣，也很安全，是一种令全家人着迷的活动。

Tips to Learning English

11月20日　　资深英语老师提供学习英语的小贴士

Be Brave – Real Life is Not a Test

Without doubt, my students who have learned English the fastest have been the ones who are fearless. As soon as they learn a word, they try to use it, they talk to anyone they see, they get volunteer work and, most importantly, they do not care at all if they make a mistake. They simply smile, shrug their shoulders, fix the mistake, and continue. Of course, only a small percentage of students do not care at all about making mistakes. At the other end of the scale, there are students who become paralyzed with fear of making mistakes. They are so worried about making a mistake that they don't even try in the first place. I think that many newcomers come from cultures that have more of a test-culture than Canada. So, they put this extra pressure on themselves and worry about "failing" or not being good enough. As a teacher, I must remind them that ***"real life is not a test"***! We are all doing the best that we can and sometimes we don't do very well at all! However, no one is going to give us a bad report card. The most important reason for learning English is to be able to share thoughts, information, feelings, and emotions with each other. Getting to know each other and feeling like you are part of the community are the main reasons to learn a language. These things do not need to be done perfectly to be effective. So, please, be brave, have fun and remember that mistakes are the best teacher!

要勇敢 – 现实生活不是考试

毫无疑问，我的那些学习英语进步最快的学生都是勇敢的。一旦他们学习一个新的单词，他们就会尝试使用它，他们会与任何人交谈，他们去找一份志愿者工作，最重要的是，他们根本不在乎他们是否犯了一个句法错误。他们只是笑笑，耸耸肩，纠正错误，然后继续交谈下去。当然，只有少数学生根本不在乎出错。而相反的，有的学生因害怕出错而不知所措。他们很担心口误，他们甚至没有先去尝试一下。我认为许多新移民来自本民族的文化，更多的是一种考试文化，而不同于加拿大的文化。所以，他们给自己增加了额外的压力，担心"失败"或不够优秀。作为老师，我必须提醒他们，*"real life is not a test"* 现实生活不是考试"！我们都在尽我们最大的努力，有时我们做得不是很好！然而，没有人会给我们一个差的成绩单。学习英语的最重要的原因是能够彼此分享想法、信息、感觉和情绪。去了解彼此，感觉你就是这个社会的一部分，这就是学习一门语言的最主要原因。有些事情不需要做完美才会有效。所以，请勇敢起来！享受生活，记住，错误是最好的老师！

November 21   A Little Canadian Inspiration

11月21日　　一点点启示

"I believe the world needs more Canada"
—*Bono, singer from internationally famous U2 rock band*

Bono is known for his humanitarian work around the world. He has met with Canadian government officials to talk about issues such as poverty relief and environmental protection.

"我相信这个世界需要更多的加拿大"

——*来自国际著名的 U2 摇滚乐队的主唱歌手博诺*

博诺是一位出色的社会活动家，以他在世界各地的人道主义工作而闻名。 他曾经与加拿大政府官员会晤，讨论扶贫，环境保护等问题。

Volunteer in Vancouver

11月22日　　在温哥华做义工

Volunteer with Senior Citizens

The Health and Home Care Society of BC offers many services to seniors and other people in need. By volunteering with them for just a couple of hours a week, you can make a big difference in the lives of lonely senior citizens. One program run by this organization is called **Meals on Wheels** and this program delivered over 111,000 meals to over 1000 clients last year. They write on their website that "each delivery is more than a hot meal; it's a chance for volunteers to make a meaningful impact in a senior's life. With each delivery, volunteers are helping seniors live independently in their own homes, are reducing their loneliness, and are actively improving the community". The other volunteer program they run is at the **Family Respite Centre** where volunteers help ensure that clients truly feel like they are in a "home away from home". During the volunteer visits with the residents, volunteers will sit down with coffee or tea with the clients, or help them with their exercise class or play Mahjong or other games together. The volunteers help create a warm and welcoming environment for the senior citizens.

为老年人提供服务

卑诗省卫生和家庭护理学会
https://www.carebc.ca/volunteering.html

卑诗省的健康和家庭护理协会为老年人和其他有需要帮助的人提供许多服务。通过每周自愿做几个小时的服务工作，您可以在孤独老人的生活中起到重要的作用。该组织运营的一个项目叫做"轮子"志愿者上门送餐服务。这个项目仅去年就为1000多个客户提供了超过111,000热腾腾的饭菜。他们在其网站上写道："每一次递送的不仅仅是一顿热饭，而是志愿者有机会对老年人的生活产生有意义的影响。志愿者们正在帮助老年人在自己的家中独立生活，减少孤独感，并积极改善社区生活。" 另一个志愿者项目是家庭休养中心。在志愿者帮助下，客户有一种"宾至如归"的感觉。通过看似不起眼的行为，如打麻将，坐下来喝一杯咖啡或茶，或帮助客户上健身课，为老年人创造一个热情友好的环境。

November 23   Healthcare in Vancouver

11月23日   温哥华的医疗保健

Private Medical and Surgical Clinics

The public healthcare system is a tremendous benefit of living in Canada. Knowing that you and your family members' healthcare costs are covered relieves stress for many people. However, the downside to this wonderful system is that sometimes there are long waiting lists for certain procedures and diagnostic tests- especially for common, non-life-threatening surgeries like knee and hip replacement surgeries. If they are financially able to afford it, some people would rather pay private medical clinics to receive this care immediately than wait months, or even years, to feel better again.

The **Specialist Referral Clinic** is a service that will help you receive rapid access to world class medical specialists and treatments. There two main locations are in Vancouver and New Westminster. They can also arrange surgery at the most state of art facility in Canada, the Cambie Surgery Centre.

The **Copeman Healthcare Centre** is another private healthcare alternative. The Copeman team of physicians and specialized healthcare professionals offer annual assessments, ongoing care programs and a wide selection of supporting healthcare services to individuals, corporate clients and families in Vancouver and West Vancouver on an annual membership basis. As they state on their website, they offer "a strong focus on disease prevention and early detection through the use of diagnostic technologies and health monitoring tools to help ensure the best health outcomes possible." Copeman offers 12 month health programs for an annual fee. The fees for the annual program range from $500 per year for children, to $2500 for young adults (18 to 24) and between $3500 to $4500 for adults. In addition to the 12 months of care, the fee includes an annual comprehensive health prevention screening test.

私人医疗和外科手术诊所

专家推荐的转诊诊所 http://www.specialistclinic.ca/
科普曼医疗中心 https://www.copemanhealthcare.com/

公共医疗体系是生活在加拿大一个巨大的福利。知道您和您的家庭成员的医疗保健费用都包含那些可以减轻许多人的压力。然而，这个系统也是有缺点的：有时候某些诊断需要排队等候很长的时间 — 特别是对于那些普通的非危及生命的手术，如膝盖和髋关节置换手术。如果他们在经济上能够负担得起，一些人宁愿花钱去私人诊所，马上就能得到治疗，这样好过等上几个月甚至几年。

专科转诊诊所是一项服务，它可以帮助您迅速找到世界一流的专科医生并接受最好的治疗。有两个主要地点，一个在温哥华，另一个在新西敏。他们还可以在加拿大医疗设备最好的甘比外科中心为您安排手术。

另一个私人医疗的选择是由卡普曼医疗中心提供的。科普曼团队的医师和专科医疗专业人员每年以会员身份为温哥华的个人、企业和家庭提供年度评估，持续保健计划和各种医疗服务。正如他们在其网站上介绍的那样，他们"重点提供疾病预防、早期诊断和健康监测，以确保您有可能得到最佳的健康结果。" 科普曼的收费标准是，儿童每年500加元，年龄在18至24岁之间的年轻人2500加元，成人费用在3500至4500加元之间。除了12个月的治疗护理，费用还包括年度全面的健康预防筛查体检。

November 24 Interesting Facts About Vancouver

11月24日   温哥华趣闻

No One Thinks the Vancouver Special is Very Special

If you look back at the home shown in the photograph on the November 8 entry of this book, you will see the Vancouver Special type of home. From 1965 to 1985, houses of a box-like structure with front balconies, low roofs, and a combination exterior of brick or stone on the lower level and stucco on the upper level were built. These houses were given the nickname **"Vancouver Special"** by locals because they were being built everywhere because the floor plan and identical upper and lower floors, made it easy to make two separate living quarters. The lower suite could be rented out to provide extra income to help with the high cost of living in Vancouver. Builders liked to build these structures as they were cheap and easy to build. However, everyone agreed that they were very ugly and the public reaction to these houses was very negative. So, in late 1980s, the city of Vancouver made changes to building and zoning regulations to stop this type of house from being built any more. In recent years, however, these houses have started to become popular again.

没有人会认为温哥华"特色"有什么特色

如果翻回到本书的11月8日所示的住宅照片，您会看到著名的带有温哥华特色的房屋类型。从1965年到1985年，许多房屋都设计成箱子状的外观，前面的阳台，低矮的屋顶，外墙的灰泥，和下层的砖石组合建成。 这些房子被当地人戏称为"温哥华特色"，因为它们随处可见，楼层的设计为上下相同的两层，分成两个独立的生活区。下面一层可以出租，以增加额外的收入，缓解温哥华高昂的生活费用。建筑商们喜欢建造这种结构的房子，因为它们造价低廉，易于搭建。然而，大家都认为它们很丑，公众对这些房子的反应全是负面的。 因此，在20世纪80年代末，温哥华市府改变了建筑和分区的规定，禁止这类房屋的建造。然而，近年来，这种房型又再度流行了起来。

November 25   # Finding Work in Vancouver

11月25日   在温哥华找工作

Websites for your Job Search

Nowadays, the majority of job advertisements are found online. There are many different kinds of job search sites that specialize in different areas or job types. There are general Canadian job sites that post open positions across Canada and then there are more specific job sites that post job openings for government jobs, healthcare jobs, academic jobs and so on. Two of the popular Canada-wide job sites are **Workopolis** and **Eluta**. For information about the more specific job sites, it is best to speak with the librarian at your local librarian and they will be able to show you how to find these sites.

您的求职网站

如今，大多数招聘广告都是在网上找到的。 有许多不同种类的工作搜索网站，专注于不同的领域或工作类型。加拿大求职网站列出了全国各地的职位空缺，然后还有更具体的工作地点，为政府职位、医疗保健工作、学术工作等提供职位空缺。加拿大两个很受欢迎的工作网址：Workopolis和Eluta。 有关更具体的工作网站的信息，最好和当地图书馆员的图书馆管理员谈谈，他们会告诉你如何找到这些网站。

November 26   Vancouver Sightseeing

11月26日   观光

Granville Island

The Granville Island Public Market, located under the Granville Street Bridge, is a centre of activity that is popular with both locals and tourists. It is one of the city's most important cultural districts with theatres, artisan workshops and craft studios. The biggest attraction on Granville Island is the Public Market that has several rows of stalls that feature fresh produce, gourmet foods, baked goods, and seafood. Outside of the market, catch a show at one of the many theatres on the island, browse an art gallery show, or appeal to your outdoorsy side with a kayaking or paddleboarding tour. The market features a very popular food court at the end of the market building that has many delicious and affordable choices. If you prefer a more formal restaurant, there are several that offer fine seafood and steaks and views of the harbour.

格兰威尔岛   http://granvilleisland.com/

格兰维尔岛公共市场位于格兰维尔街大桥下，是一个受到当地人和游客们欢迎的活动中心。它是城市的最重要的文化区。有剧院，工匠作坊和工艺品工作室。格兰维尔岛最吸引人的地方是一个大型的公共市场，有许多摊位，包括新鲜的农产品、美食、烘焙食品和海鲜。在市场之外，岛上有许多画廊、雕塑展览、陶器展览和手工艺品展览。在附近可以租个皮划艇或用桨划船旅游。走到市场的尽头那里有一个非常受欢迎的美食广场，有许多美味可供选择。如果你喜欢在正规的餐厅里用餐，有几家提供美味的海鲜和牛排，同时还可以边吃边欣赏窗外海港的美景。格兰维尔岛是一个很好的购物场所，因为它有独特的工艺品、熟练的工匠、户外服装装备商店和豪华美食店相结合。阁楼建筑式的商店陈列着第一民族艺术品、B.C省葡萄酒和其他独特的礼物。沿岛漫步，可以看到各种工匠工作室，玻璃工在那里吹各种造型的瓶子，陶工，珠宝商甚至扫帚制造商现场编织各种奇特的扫把。

November 27 Vancouver Transportation

11月27日 温哥华交通运输

Getting Out of Vancouver by Bus, Train and Ferry

Sightseeing by bus, ferry and train is such a relaxing way to see the sights compared to flying. There are many daily express bus services set up between the popular destinations of Victoria, Seattle, and Whistler. For any other location in Canada and the USA, there are national train and bus companies that can transport you anywhere in North America – if you have the time!

乘坐公共汽车，火车和渡轮去温哥华以外的地方

与坐飞机相比，乘公共汽车，渡轮和火车观光更为放松。在维多利亚，西雅图和惠斯勒等热门目的地之间每天都有许多对开的特快巴士服务。至于加拿大和美国的其他任何地方，如果您有时间的话，也都有相应的火车和巴士公司，把您运送到北美的任何地方！

开往惠斯勒和斯阔米什的巴士：
惠斯勒滑雪巴士 https://snowbus.com/
开往惠斯勒太平洋高速公路巴士 http://www.pacificcoach.com

开往美国贝灵汉和西雅图的巴士：
开往美国贝灵汉和西雅图的特快巴士 http://www.quickcoach.com/

温哥华市中心和维多利亚市中心之间的公共汽车和轮渡：
维多利亚/温哥华市中心的特快巴士 – http://bcfconnector.com/
BC 轮渡 http://www.bcferries.com/

探索北美洲的公共汽车和火车：
加拿大各地的巴士 https://www.greyhound.ca/
加拿大火车Via Rail http://www.viarail.ca/en
从加拿大到美国的火车 https://www.amtrak.com/home

November 28   Sports Teams and Special Events

11月28日   专业体育赛事和活动

World Ski and Snowboard Festival, Whistler/Blackcomb

Once per year, the World Ski & Snowboard Festival (WSSF) takes over Whistler, BC. Thousands of fans come to the charming mountain town each year to witness North America's largest annual ski and snowboard competitions, music, and mountain culture celebration. For 10 days and 10 nights, the World Ski & Snowboard Festival hosts a high-energy combination of world class ski and snowboard competitions, the largest annual free outdoor concert series in Canada, visual arts productions, film premieres, community events and an endless lineup of parties. It is a sporting event that also takes the fun and entertainment side just as seriously as the competition.

世界滑雪和单板滑雪节，惠斯勒/黑梳山 http://wssf.com/

　　每年的四月，卑诗省惠斯勒举办世界滑雪节（WSSF）。每年都有数千人来到这迷人的山区小镇，见证北美洲最大的年度滑雪比赛，同时欣赏音乐，并共同庆祝山区文化。整个比赛和活动将持续10天10夜，届时有加拿大最大的免费的户外音乐会，巨型制作的视觉艺术，电影首映式，社区活动和无尽的欢聚。世界滑雪节不仅仅是一项体育赛事，也同样是人们尽享欢乐的地方。

November 29   Vancouver Parks

11月29日   温哥华公园

Whytecliffe Park

This waterfront park located in West Vancouver near Horseshoe Bay offers an amazing view of the oceanfront with its rocky cliffs and beaches and crashing waves. In the summer, you might be able to see Sea Lions sunbathing on the beach and eagles soaring overhead. Also, you will see scuba divers visiting to see the more than 200 marine animal species that are protected in this official Marine Protected Area waters off the beach (one of the first in Canada to get this designation). In addition to walking and hiking trails, beaches and lawns for picnics, there is also a playground for the kids and picnic tables for relaxing.

怀特公园 http://whytecliffpark.com/

这个位于西温哥华马蹄湾附近的海滨公园提供了一个惊人的海滨景色，其岩石峭壁，海滩和拍击海岸的浪花。在夏天，你可以看到海狮在海滩上晒日光浴，鹰在高空翱翔。此外，你可以潜水前往受到官方海洋保护水域观看到超过 200多种海洋生物物种（加拿大第一个获得此称号）。除了在海滨小径上散步，海滩上沐浴阳光和草坪上野餐，还有一个供孩子们娱乐的操场的和野餐桌。

November 30   Stories and Advice for Newcomers

11月30日   移民的故事

Wassem

良好的人际关系会带来良好的生活质量

　　我想大多数新移民都会同意，当他们在新的城市交到了一个好朋友的那一刻，他们会觉得自己像在家一样。他乡遇故知，任何年龄和背景的人都可以成为新的朋友。最重要的是，朋友可以回答问题，与您分享故事。良好的人际关系会带来良好的生活质量，这对您的幸福和健康至关重要。当我初到温哥华的时候，我试着去参加一些活动和志愿服务，这样我就可以认识其他和我有着共同兴趣的人，或者其他移民朋友，和我分享经验。当您遇到不同年龄和不同文化背景的人时，生活会变得更加有趣，您仿佛置身于一个更大的家族，您会对温哥华的新生活感到快乐，而乐不思蜀。

December

Weather:	Average temperature: 1°C to 7°C
	Average rainfall days: 22, Average rainfall: 220 mm
Statutory holiday:	Christmas Day (December 25),
	Boxing Day (December 26)
Other special days:	Christmas Eve (December 24),
	New Year's Eve (December 31)

December is just as cold and rainy as the other winter months, but somehow Vancouverites don't notice because the whole city goes into "Christmas Craziness" mode! Whether you celebrate Christmas or not, there is a general feeling of celebration, fun and excitement in the air. We say that people get full of the "Christmas spirit"*.

People decorate the outside of their house or apartment with colourful Christmas lights and the inside of their home with a beautiful Christmas tree decorated with their collection of Christmas ornaments. Children have Advent Calendars* counting the days until Christmas, and they write a letter to Santa Claus* with their Christmas wish list of toys. Everywhere you look is Christmas. Even the stores and office towers are decorated with lights, the televisions play special Christmas cartoons, Christmas music specials and Christmas movies that they play every year. Colleagues at work go out for Christmas lunch or dinner together, schools hold Christmas concerts and parties and everyone gets together for celebrating and singing Christmas carols* during the month.

Locals also spend a lot of time doing Christmas baking and making the traditional treats of Christmas. On December 24, the children leave cookies and milk for Santa Claus plus a carrot for the reindeer as they believe that Santa Claus delivers presents to all the children of the world after they go to sleep on Christmas Eve. The whole family then wakes up on Christmas Day to open presents and have breakfast together. And later the whole family gets together for a Christmas Day dinner*. Many restaurants offer traditional Christmas Day meals for families that want to take a break from cooking, and major grocery stores also offer Christmas Dinner meals to go.

Boxing Day, December 26, is the day that everyone goes shopping for all the big sales after Christmas! Then the rest of December is spent resting and relaxing until the big year-end parties of New Year's Eve where the end of the year is celebrated with a glass of champagne and a kiss with your loved one.

Vancouver hosts a big outdoor New Year's Eve party and fireworks at Canada Place, and many hotels and restaurants offer formal New Year's Eve dinner and dancing packages where guests dress up in their finest clothes and eat, drink and dance until the midnight countdown.

12月

> 气候： 平均温度： 1°C 到 7°C
> 　　　平均降雨天数： 22，平均降雨量： 220 毫米
> 公众节假日： 圣诞节（12月25日）；节礼日（12月26日）
> 其他特殊日： 圣诞平安夜（12月24日）；除夕（12月31日）

十二月和冬季的其他月份一样的寒冷和多雨，但不知何故，温哥华当地民众在不知不觉中已经发生了很大的变化，因为整个城市已经进入了"圣诞狂热"！在空气中散发着一种普天同庆、欢乐和兴奋的气氛。这就是人们常说的，充满了"圣诞精神"。

人们在他们的房子或公寓外装饰着五彩缤纷的圣诞灯，在屋里摆放一棵美丽的圣诞树，树上装饰他们收集的圣诞装饰品。孩子们看着圣诞日历，计算着到圣诞节的天数，他们给圣诞老人写一封信，上面写着他们的圣诞愿望 – 玩具清单。圣诞的影子随处可见，商店和办公楼的装饰灯、电视台专门播放的圣诞卡通节目、圣诞音乐专辑和每年都会放映相同的圣诞电影。单位的同事们一起出去吃圣诞午餐或晚餐，学校举办圣诞音乐会和派对。这个月，大家都聚在一起，搞庆祝活动，唱圣诞颂歌。人们天天忙着购物和娱乐，整个城市充满了活力，我们将精选一些主要的活动和特殊事件附在下面。去参加这些活动，您会发现不管走到哪里，大家谈论的话题都是圣诞。

当地人也会花大量时间烘焙圣诞美食，制作传统款待客人用的圣诞礼物。12月24日，孩子们留下饼干和牛奶给圣诞老人，外加胡萝卜给驯鹿，因为他们相信，圣诞老人会给世界上所有的孩子们送去礼物，然后他们在圣诞前夜回去睡觉。全家人在圣诞节早上醒来，打开礼物，坐一起吃早餐。晚上，全家人又聚在一起吃圣诞晚餐。对于那些不想在家做晚餐的人来说，许多餐馆还专门为他们提供了传统的圣诞家庭套餐，一些大的食品店也提供圣诞晚餐外卖服务。

12月26日是节礼日，这一天几乎每个人都会去商场购物，零售店在圣诞节后会通过清仓大甩卖各种商品。然后，彻底放松和休息直到年终大聚会，新年除夕喝一杯香槟，给您深爱的人一个吻。

温哥华将在加拿大广场上燃放烟花，同时举办一个大型的户外除夕跨年度晚会，许多酒店和餐馆也提供正式的年夜饭和舞会，宾客们穿着他们最漂亮的衣服，尽情地吃喝，跳舞，一直玩到午夜的倒计时。

词汇和短语：

*Christmas Spirit圣诞精神：在十二月份（除了在拥挤的购物中心），人们会感觉到无比的温暖和喜悦，体会到彼此的慷慨和善意！

*Advent calendar圣诞日历：这是一个特殊的日历专门用来计算或庆祝圣诞节的预期（现代版本每天都有一个小糖果）。

*Winter Solstice冬至：是一种天文现象，它标志着一年中最短的白天和最长的夜晚。在北半球，冬至日在十二月份。

*Christmas foods 圣诞食品：传统的圣诞节晚餐食品非常类似于感恩节吃烤火鸡，填料有肉汤和土豆泥。最大的不同是增加了很多甜品：圣诞布丁、水果馅饼、奶油饼干、姜饼曲奇和圣诞树根蛋糕。烘焙食品和拐杖糖果等圣诞节期间也很受欢迎。

*Write a letter to Santa给圣诞老人写一封信：写一封信给他，他会给你回信的！

*Christmas carols圣诞颂歌：每年圣诞节期间唱的传统歌曲。有的是专门为孩子们编写的，而成年人唱的颂歌宗教色彩较浓。

Local Customs

当地的习俗

Good Neighbour Customs

It is customary to have a polite but formal relationship with neighbours if you live in a house. When a new neighbour moves in, it is polite to say hello, introduce yourself and welcome them to the neighbourhood. However, if you live in an apartment building, people usually don't say anything except hello to their neighbours.

The purpose of knowing your neighbours is important for safety and convenience. A neighbour can "keep an eye on your house" while you are out of town and you can do the same for them. It is customary to thank the neighbour for watching your house while you are gone with a small present from your travels. Also, neighbours can sometimes help each other out with small physical tasks such as clearing the front sidewalk of leaves and snow if the other neighbour is not feeling well. When they are feeling better, they can give the neighbour a bottle of wine or some baked goods to thank them for their help. Most importantly, when you know your neighbours then it is easier to see if there is a stranger in the area who might cause trouble.

The Vancouver City Police assist neighbours who want to increase the safety of their area with a program called **Block Watch**. Block Watch is all about neighbours helping neighbours. Households, apartments or condominiums on a block form a communication group with a map of names, telephone numbers and addresses. Participants watch out for each others' homes and report suspicious activities to the police and each other. This communication is important in reducing the likelihood of residential crime.

The City of Vancouver encourages residents to have **Block Parties** which are large outdoor celebrations with all your neighbours where there is food and drinks and a chance to get to know the people who live on the same block as you. The City of Vancouver is very supportive of these Block Parties and will even provide a one-day permit to close the street to traffic so the party can happen right on the road. They realize that Block parties are a great way to build social connections and improve your community.

Also, it is important to be a good neighbour when doing household renovations or construction to your house and property. These are the standard customs that locals do when they are having work done on their house to be considerate to their neighbours. This **Good Neighbour Policy** makes sure that there are no disputes or problems between neighbours. This policy is especially important for **Infill Building** – when an old house is torn down and a new house is built in the neighbourhood.

街坊邻里

在您家附近的街区聚会 http://vancouver.ca/doing-business/block-parties.aspx
温哥华警察局守望计划http://vancouver.ca/police/community-policing/block-watch/

如果您住的是普通的房型，通常会很容易与街坊邻居建立起友好的关系。当有新的邻居搬到您隔壁时，您可以有礼貌地说hello，然后介绍自己，并表示欢迎他们成为您的邻里。但是，如果您住在公寓楼里，除了打一声招呼以外，人们通常不会说什么。

English for Everyday Life
日常生活英语

这里是日常生活用语，您可以用来向邻居介绍自己:

"Hello, my name is Yi and me and wife Qi just moved into the house next door. We wanted to come here and say hello."

"您好，我叫义，我和妻子琪刚刚搬到您的隔壁。我们想来这里和您打个招呼"。

如果您只是想给他们留一张便条和一份小小的欢迎礼物，您可以按照下面的范文书写，并放在他们的前门廊上:

Hello, my name is Yi and me and my wife Qi want to welcome you to the neighbourhood. Here is our phone number in case you need to contact us. Also, we made these cookies for you. We hope you will be very happy here.

"您好，我的名字是义，我和妻子琪欢迎您成为我们的邻居。这是我们的电话号码，以备您需要时联系我们。另外，我们专门为您制作这些小点心。我们希望您在这里生活的愉快"。

为了安全和方便起见，搞好邻里关系很重要。远亲不如近邻。当您离开温哥华的时候，邻居可以"帮您照看房子"，您也可以为他们做同样的事情。为了感谢邻居帮您照看房子，习惯上您在旅途中买一件小礼物回来答谢。此外，平日里邻里之间也可以相互帮助，比方说，如果邻居感觉不舒服，您可以帮他们清除门前过道上的落叶和积雪等。当他们恢复健康以后，他们会回赠一瓶葡萄酒或一些烘焙的食物，以表感激之情。最重要的是，当了解您周围的邻居以后，就会更容易分辨出是否有陌生人给您那儿带来麻烦。

温哥华市的警察协助小区，希望通过一个名为街道守望计划来提高他们所在区域的安全。Block Watch是指社区里面邻居之间互相帮助。欢迎所有住宅，公寓或公寓之间的家庭成员志愿加入守望计划，提供姓名，电话号码和住址，形成一个完整的通讯链。参与者留意彼此的房屋，并向警察和邻里举报可疑的活动。这种沟通是非常重要的，它大大减少了住宅区犯罪的可能性。

温哥华市府鼓励市民举办街区聚会，这是一种大型的户外庆贺活动。与您所有的邻居分享食物和饮料，这样您就有机会认识并了解住在同一个街区所有的人。市府是非常支持这种街区聚会的，甚至可以为此提供一整天关闭该街道交通的特许证，以方便所有活动都可以在马路上进行。因为市政府意识到街区聚会是一种建立良好的社交联系和改善社区关系的最好方式。熟悉您的邻居真的很重要，因为：

- 当我们患有疾病或其他紧急情况需要帮助的时候，住在远方的朋友和亲人就不如您的邻居；
- 研究表明，当邻里之间相互了解、彼此信任的时候，街道更加安全，人们更加健康和快乐。

最后，作为一个好邻居，当您在做家庭装修或建造新房子的时候，一定要考虑到周围邻居的感受。体贴他人是成为一个好邻居重要的习俗。做到了这一点就能避免邻里之间发生不必要的纠纷。尤其是当拆除一所旧房子，盖新的时候，更要注意。

睦邻友好政策 － 建筑商的六项基本规则：

1. Get all required permits and approvals;
2. Tell all neighbours what you are doing;
3. Protect the neighbourhood, including private property, fences and shrubs;
4. Clean up;
5. Keep noisy work to allowable times; (during daytime hours, and not on weekends if possible)
6. Do not block driveways (public or private).

1. 获得所有必需的许可证和批准；
2. 告诉所有的邻居您在做什么；
3. 保护邻里周围的环境，包括私人财产，围栏和灌木；
4. 清理垃圾；
5. 注意噪声，在允许的时间内操作；（如果可能的话，在白天的时间干活，而不是在周末）
6. 不要挡阻车道（公共的或私人的）。

English for Everyday Life

日常生活英语

如果您正在装修房屋，将会产生噪音影响到邻居。为了避免邻里之间的不快，这里有一个好主意，您花一点儿时间给您的邻居写一张便条。下面是一个例子：

Hello John and Mary,

I just want to let you know that we are having our house repaired and some more room to the back of the house. The construction work will be a little noisy but the workers will try to get it done as soon as possible and won't do any work in the evenings and the weekends. They will also keep the area clean. Thank you for your patience and understanding.

Sincerely,
Lisa
PS here is my cell phone number if you ever need to reach me 555-296-7548

约翰和玛丽，二位好，

我只想让您知道，我们正在装修房子和后院。装修工程会有一点儿吵，但工人们会设法尽快完成，不会在晚上和周末做任何施工。他们将保持场内的清洁。感谢您的耐心和理解。

此致，
丽莎
附带说明：这是我的手机号码，如果您有需要请打555-296-7548

Parenting in Vancouver

12月2日   在温哥华养育子女

Special Events at School

Every school year has a regular cycle of special events during the school year. To celebrate special days like Thanksgiving, Halloween, Easter and Valentine's Day etc., elementary school children will have a small **classroom party**. The teacher usually asks the parents to bring in small cakes or cookies to these parties. In the spring, elementary schools host one day of fun sports competitions outdoors called **Sports Day**. There are no classes on this day, just fun and games with all the students in school. Parents come to watch their children participate in these games. A highlight of the school year for both elementary and high schools are the **seasonal concerts**. These concerts usually happen at Christmas time and towards the end of the school year. The children in the school participate in the shows and play music, sing, dance and do plays. Parents and members of the family can come and watch these charming performances.

学校特别活动

　　每个学年都有一些固定的特别活动。每逢庆祝感恩节、万圣节、复活节和情人节等特殊日子，小学生将举办一个小型的课堂派对。通常老师会要求父母给这些派对准备小蛋糕或饼干。春天，各小学将主办一天有趣的户外体育比赛称为运动会。这一天没有课，所有在校的学生只是参与娱乐和游戏。父母来观看自己孩子参加这些比赛和游戏。小学和中学学年的一大亮点是季节性音乐会。这些音乐会通常在圣诞节和学年结束时举行。学校的孩子们参加表演节目，演奏乐器、唱歌、跳舞和表演戏剧。父母和家庭成员可以来观看这些迷人的表演。

Stories and Advice for Newcomers

12月3日   **新移民的故事**

Cathy

我有几点想法分享给大家

大家好！我是Cathy. 来自北京。我是去年一月底登陆温哥华。现在边学习边打工。在温哥华生活的一年多，我有几点想法分享给大家，相互学习。

第一，调整好心态。无论你在国内工作文化背景是什么样，到这里或许不能很快适应。但是始终要相信自己可以通过努力获得自己想要的生活。比如，刚开始找工作，可能不会是理想的工作，但是积极学习，积累加拿大的工作经验，为以后更好的职业铺路。

第二，制定职业规划。新移民最好结合自身情况制定一个短期和长远的目标。比如，我想利用第一个三年学英语，考一个当地认可的证书。也有人选择从头开始工作，然后边打工赚钱边完成学业。

第三，学英语。在温哥华生活，英语不好的人也可以很好的生活。可是对于新移民，我建议在学英语这方面不要惯着自己。狠下心来好好踏踏实实地学。因为刚开始生活在这里学习的动力最足。例外与政府部门打交道，有时候没有英语翻译的。

第四，抓紧时间。新移民要把学英语拿文凭的时间计划的紧凑而合理。能两年学好的不要拖到好几年。

第五，关于打工。我对于新移民朋友的建议是根据自己的情况，决定是否要在最初登陆温哥华的几年里打工。如果条件允许，先专心学习，把想要学习的课程一气呵成是最好的。如果一边打工一边学习，就要把学习最为优先考虑，打工不是耽误或懈怠学习的借口，而是支持和促进你进步的工具。

第六，善于利用政府提供帮助新移民的机构。比如，中桥可以提供新移民在温哥华生活帮助。WorkBC可以为新移民提供修改简历，面试技巧等。例外在VCC，既温哥华社区学院学习，低收入家庭可以申请政府资助而免费学习英语。

最后建议新移民尽快在温哥华拿下驾照。这样出行就方便很多。以上是我这个新移民的一些小想法。希望能够给大家带来一些帮助。我们一起努力，在温哥华生活快乐而充实。

December 4   Vancouver Entertainment

12月4日   温哥华娱乐

Ballroom and Salsa Dancing

Going dancing is a wonderful way to stay healthy, have fun and meet new people. There are a few dance studios in Vancouver that teach the very popular ballroom and salsa styles of dancing and also organize social dance events. Spending the evening dancing is a wonderful form of entertainment. Here are some places where you can practice your dance skills and have some fun in the city:

The Crystal Ballroom

Richmond's newest, largest and most elegant dance studio offers a wide range of ballroom and salsa dance classes for all levels. They also host tea dances four times a week in the afternoon and Evening Dances every night so there are many chances to get out and have a great time.

Broadway Ballroom

Broadway Ballroom specializes in Ballroom dancing, including the 10 International-style dances and West Coast Swing. They host regular dance parties in their large and gorgeous ballroom with a musical format designed to keep you dancing as much as possible.

舞厅和萨尔萨舞蹈

跳舞是保持健康、快乐和结交新朋友的最好方式。温哥华有几个舞蹈工作室，教授非常流行的芭蕾和不同风格的萨尔萨舞蹈，并组织社交舞蹈活动。傍晚跳舞是一种美妙的娱乐形式。这里有一些地方可以练习和体验舞蹈技巧：

水晶宴会厅 http://crystalballroom.ca/
水晶宴会厅是温哥华最新，最大和最优雅的舞蹈工作室，有不同级别的舞蹈班和萨尔萨舞蹈课程。他们每天晚上都有舞蹈活动，值得一提的是，每周开办四次茶舞会，在那里您有很多机会跳舞，您会过得很愉快。

百老汇舞厅 https://broadwayballroom.ca/
百老汇舞厅专门从事交谊舞，包括10个国际风格的舞蹈和西海岸摇摆舞。他们在其大型华丽的舞厅定期举办舞会，设计了尽可能多的舞蹈曲目：先放两种国际风格的标准舞曲，紧接着为每种舞蹈类型再提供两首拉丁舞曲。这样可以最大限度地减少舞伴们尴尬地坐等他们熟悉的舞蹈类型的音乐。门票也包括小吃和饮料。

Best Elementary Schools

12月5日　温哥华著名的小学

Corpus Christi Elementary school (private)

Here is the description of the school from their website: "Corpus Christi School is a Catholic community called by God to share in the mission of the Church. With Christ as our center, the parish, teachers and parents work closely together in love and prayer to create a joyous and challenging place of learning. Each child will be encouraged to grow intellectually, physically, socially, aesthetically and above all, spiritually. By preparing our students to be responsible and active members of the Church, we are building God's kingdom."

科珀斯克里斯蒂小学（私立）http://www.corpuschristi-school.ca/

下面是学校网站的描述：

"科珀斯克里斯蒂小学是一所天主教社区分享教会使命的学校。它以耶稣基督为中心，与教区、教师和家长在爱和祈祷中携手合作，共同创造一个充满欢乐和挑战的学习场所。鼓励每个孩子在智力上、身体上、社交上、审美上，尤其是精神上的成长。我们正在建立神的国度，所有的学生都将负起教会的责任并成为积极的成员。"

December 6   A Different Way of Thinking
12月6日   不同的思维方式

Good Manners Highly Valued

Although Canada and the USA seem very similar to each other, there is one very big difference in everyday language and culture that is related to history. The USA is a country born from revolution while Canada was a colony of the United Kingdom and, therefore, many of its institutions and traditions are based on this British connection. One of the fundamental features of British society that you will find in Canada is the importance placed on good manners and etiquette. Canadians highly value good manners and consider it a sign of a good education and high status. Also, they believe that good manners ensure daily life proceeds in a calm and kind way. In fact, the three most important words and phrases to know and use frequently in Vancouver are "please", "thank you" and "excuse me".

Vancouver parents know that making sure their children have good manners is a very important part of their future success. Fortunately, there are companies in Vancouver that can help parents teach their children the important manners and etiquette they will need for their future professional life. One such company is called **Tablesmarts**. This company offers manners and etiquette courses that help students (for children and adults) with the confidence and skill set to integrate in a variety of social settings.

良好的行为举止

English for Everyday Life
日常生活英语

名词解释:

- *Manners (definition): polite or well-bred social behavior.*
  礼貌（定义）：有礼貌或有教养的社会行为。
- *Etiquette (definition): Etiquette is a code of polite conduct. If you practice proper etiquette, you are less likely to offend or annoy people — and you may even charm them.*
  礼仪（定义）：礼仪是礼貌的行为准则。 如果您养成适当的礼仪，您就不太可能冒犯或惹恼别人，您甚至可以吸引他们。

　　虽然加拿大和美国似乎很相近，但与日常生活有关的日常语言和文化历史背景却有着很大的差异。美国是一个从革命中诞生的国家，而加拿大是英国的殖民地，几乎所有的机构和传统都是按照英国的体制建立起来的。在加拿大您会发现英国社会的基本特征之一是高度重视礼貌和礼仪。加拿大人之所以非常重视礼仪，是因为他们认为这是一个人受过良好教育和身份地位的象征。此外，他们确信良好的举止会确保日常生活以平静和友好的方式进行。事实上，在温哥华经常听到和经常使用的三个最重要的单词和短语是"please""请"，"thank you""谢谢"和"excuse me""对不起"。

　　温哥华的父母知道，确保他们的孩子有良好的行为举止是他们未来成功的一个非常重要的保障。幸运的是，温哥华有些公司可以帮助父母教会孩子们为未来职业生涯所需要的所有重要的礼貌和礼仪。有一家这样的公司被称为Tablesmarts。该公司专门提供举止和礼仪的课程，帮助学生（适于儿童和成人）掌握各种技能，充满信心地融入各种社会环境。

Tablesmarts礼仪培训 https://www.tablesmarts.ca/

Best High Schools

12月7日   温哥华著名的中学

Mulgrave Senior School (private)

Here is the description of the school from their website: "As students move into the Senior School, we strive to grow creative, critical and independent thinkers with the flexibility of thought best suited to the changing world into which they will emerge as young adults. Subsequently, in addition to our energetic focus on academic attainment and successful university placement, our education is equally attentive to the development of the whole person beyond the institutional worlds of school, college and work. Active engagement in local service, global outreach, outdoor education, sport and artistic performance is vital in this endeavor, so the Senior School focuses on giving students the life skills necessary to manage these competing commitments on their time. Our integration of the International Baccalaureate (IB) Approaches to Learning and 21st century skills ensure our students grow as people within an educational context that is highly relevant, flexible and enjoyable."

马尔格雷夫中学（私立）　https://www.mulgrave.com/

以下是学校网站上的描述：

"当学生进入高中即将步入年轻人的时候，我们努力培养他们具有创造性、批判性和独立性的思考者，思维灵活最适合不断变化的世界。随后，除了我们对学业成就和大学成功安置的积极关注之外，我们的教育同样还关注个人的发展，这超越了学校和学院的工作范围。积极参与当地服务、全球推广、户外教育、体育和艺术表演至关重要，所以，高中重点是为学生提供必要的生活技能来管理这些竞争的承诺。我们融入了国际文凭（IB）的学习方法和21世纪的技能，确保我们的学生是在一个高度灵活和愉快的教育背景下成长起来的人。

December 8   The Homes of Vancouver

12月8日   温哥华住宅

A Welcoming Home
欢迎来家里做客

白天打开百叶窗向邻里发出友好的欢迎信息。

December 9   Best Extracurricular
                      Activities for Kids

12月9日   最佳儿童课外活动

Learning Centres and Private Tutoring

When children and teens need extra help to complete their courses, parents can get assistance from learning centres and private tutors. Except for the Vancouver School Board's summer school program, all the learning centres in the city are private businesses that specialize in different types of help – from math, science and writing help to SAT test preparation. There are too many of them to mention in this book. The best way to find one that is suitable for your child is to ask the teachers at your student's school.

Private tutoring is also widely available throughout the city for all subject areas. The price per hour ranges depending on the tutor's experience, reputation, and subject area. Science and math tutors are generally double the rate of writing tutors as there are not as many as them. The rates range from $25 to $150 per hour. The best way to find a good private tutor is through word of mouth. The parents in your child's school's Parent Advisory Committee (PAC) are also an excellent source of information about the best tutors in your area. Private tutoring can happen in a public area like a café or library or in your home.

学习中心和私人辅导

当儿童和青少年需要额外的帮助来完成他们的课程时，父母可以从学习中心和私人教师那里得到帮助。除了温哥华学校教育局的暑期计划外，市所有的学习中心都是专门从事不同类型帮助的私营企业，从数学、科学和写作辅导，到SAT考试准备。本书介绍了很多。找一个适合您孩子的最好方法是问问学生所在学校的老师。

私人辅导在全市范围内也广泛适用于所有学科领域。每小时的价格取决于导师的经验、声誉和学科领域。科学和数学辅导教师一般是写作老师的两倍，因为这方面的师资比较短缺。价格从每小时25加元到150加元不等。找到一个好的私人家教的最好办法是通过口碑。孩子学校的家长咨询委员会（PAC）中的父母也是您所在地区最好私教信息的来源。私人辅导可以安排在公共场所，如咖啡厅，图书馆或在您的家中。

December 10   Meeting Locals in Vancouver

12月10日   与当地人接触

Meet locals Everywhere you Go – from Stores to Bus Stops

We have given you lots of different ideas for where you can meet local people. But, really, the truth is that you don't need to go to a special location or do anything special because locals are all around you and everywhere you go. Standing in line, waiting for a bus, sitting on a park bench are all great opportunities to have a small conversation with a local person. It is a natural way of daily life here to have small chats with strangers. We call this "small talk" which is short conversations about simple topics. All it takes to get started is a simple "hello" and a smile.

当地人随处可见——从商店到公交车站

我们已经给您很多不同的思路，告诉您在哪里可以接触到当地人。但是，事实上您不需要去一个特别的地方或者做任何特别的事情，因为当地人就在您身边，他们无处不在。不管您走到哪儿。站着排队等候公交车，或坐在公园的长椅上，都是和当地人聊天的好时机。与陌生人闲聊是一种很自然的日常生活方式。我们称之为"闲聊"，是关于简单话题的简短对话。第一步要做的只是一个简单的说一声"您好"和一个微笑。

English for Everyday Life
日常生活英语

Small Talk寒暄

寒暄是加拿大人日常生活的重要组成部分。它被定义为非正式
的，友好的谈论无关紧要的话题。开始闲聊最常见的就是谈论天气。
关于温哥华的天气总是会有很多话要说的，因为天气的冷暖总是在变
化的！每个人都可以聊上几句。如果您想要换一个话题继续聊下去，
聊天气是一个很好的开头。下面是一个有关天气的对话：

A. Isn't this a beautiful day?
B. Yes, the temperature is perfect.
A. I love this time of year.
B. I do too. The fall colors are great.
A. They sure are.
B. I hope the weather stays nice
*A. Me too because my family is planning on going for a
hike this weekend.*
B. That sounds good, where are you going?

A. 今天天气不好吗？
B. 是的，温度适宜，不冷不热。
A. 我喜欢每年的这个时候。
B. 我也喜欢，秋色很美。
A. 可不是吗。
B. 我希望天气一直好下去。
A. 我也是，因为我的家人打算这个周末去徒步旅行。
B. 听起来不错，您要去哪儿？

关于天气的谈话引出了周末远足的话题。现在我们可以通过谈论
在温哥华徒步旅行等话题来继续谈话。谈论天气只是其他话题的一个
"过门"。

December 11   Restaurant Customs and Etiquette

12月11日   餐厅的习俗与礼仪

Paying the Bill and Tipping

The server will bring the bill to the table some time after the third course is finished, or you can ask the server for the bill sooner. Usually the bill is paid at the table. When you pay the bill, it is also common practice to leave a tip for your server. While tipping used to be considered optional and only as a reward for superior service, nowadays they are always given. In fact, the restaurant owner pays their staff very low wages per hour because they expect that the extra money will come from customers' tips.

Tips can vary from 15% to 25% of the bill. Here are examples of tips given to restaurant staff:

- Server: 15% to 20% of the bill; 25% for extraordinary service
- Valet parking attendant: $5.00 to $20.00
- Coat check: $2.00 per coat

Remember that the amount you tip reflects the total price before any coupons, gift certificates, etc. Just because you get a discount, does not mean that your server did not serve up the full order.

结账和给小费

在第三个道菜结束之后，服务员有时会把账单带过来放到桌面上，您也可以主动告诉服务员您打算结账。通常结账付款是在桌面上进行。当支付账单时，通常您是要额外付给服务员小费的。在过去，是根据服务员的工作态度、服务质量好坏给小费的，小费是自愿给予服务人员的额外花销以奖励其优质服务。现在的情况就不同了，收小费已成为一种规定。事实上，餐馆老板付给员工的工资非常低，因为他们期望额外的钱会来自顾客的小费。

　　小费大概付账单总支出的15%至25%。以下是付给餐厅工作人员小费的示例：

- 服务员：账单的15％至20％；25％为非凡的服务
- 代客停车服务员：$5.00至$20.00
- 衣帽员：每件外套2.00加元

　　请记住，您给小费的数额是按消费的总价格计算的，任何优惠券、礼品券等等仅仅是您从餐馆那里得到的折扣，它并不意味着您的服务员没有提供完整的服务。

English for Everyday Life
日常生活英语

有几种不同的英文表达方式可以用来告诉客人，由您来结账：

"*I am treating you to lunch.*"
"*我请您吃午饭。*"
"*lunch is on me today.*"
"*午餐今天我请客。*"
"*I would like to pick up the bill for this.*"
"*我想为这个买单。*"

另外，还可以用较短的表达方式，如果您在同一时间拿起账单并使用肢体语言。您可以说：

"*My treat.*"
"*我请客。*"
"*Let me.*"
"*让我来。*"

如果您的客人继续反对您付账，您可以这样说

"*You can get it next time.*"

"*下次您结账好了。*"

这意味着下次我们在一起时可以由对方支付账单。

December 12 Top English Programs for Adults

12月12日   成人高级英语课程

Private Schools and Private Tutors

Private Language Schools: Vancouver has many private language schools that offer a wide variety of English courses and test preparation courses for a fee. They are usually targeted to younger students in their twenties who visit Vancouver for short periods on temporary visas. These courses often include activities and sightseeing as well. The private schools also offer test preparation classes for all the major English language proficiency tests like IELTS and TOEFL. **Private English tutors** can also be hired to help you learn and practice your English skills. The hourly rate for private tutors ranges from $25 to $50 per hour depending on the level of experience and training. Tutors advertise their services on posters in community centres, in newspapers and also in online directories. There are also companies that provide tutors on all subjects. The **Teachers' Tutoring Service** is an example of one of the many companies that provide tutors to learners. All the tutors are BC certified teachers with many years of experience.

私立学校和私人家教

　　私立语言学校：www.languagecourse.net
　　教师辅导服务 https://tutor.bc.ca/

- **私立语言学校**：温哥华有许多私立语言学校，提供各种收费的英语课程和复习考试的课程。他们通常以二十几岁的年轻学生为对象，他们持临时签证短期访问温哥华。这些课程通常包括日常活动和观光。私立学校还提供所有的英语水平考试（如雅思和托福）的复习准备工作。以上的网站有温哥华主要的私立英语学校的目录。

- **私人英语家教**也可以雇来帮助您学习和练习英语技能。私人家教，根据经验和培训的水平，时薪从25加元到50加元不等，家教在社区中心、报纸和在线目录海报上刊登广告宣传他们的服务。还有专门提供所有各类学科私教的公司。**教师辅导服务**是一家为学习者提供辅导教师的公司。所有私教都是经过BC省认证的，且有多年的教学经验。正如其网站上说的，他们"自1983年以来一直以合理的价格向学生提供一对一高素质的专业辅导。"

December 13   Vancouver Backyard Wildlife

12月13日   温哥华后院的小鸟和动物

Moles

This Vancouver backyard animal is very secret and shy and doesn't like to come above-ground. You will know that you have moles when you start seeing piles of soil on your lawn. The moles remove the piles of dirt as they dig long tunnels and burrows under the grass. They are very active during the wet winter months and they give birth to their young, deep underground in their small burrows. Then in the summer the young moles will come above ground and move to a new territory. When they are above-ground they are at risk of being eaten by owls, cats and coyotes. The moles have soft black fur, long pointed snouts, and strong, paddle-shaped front paws with long strong nails that are used for digging. They eat many earthworms, slugs and other invertebrates. Moles can cause a lot damage to lawns, golf courses and playing fields as they can dig up to 4 meters/hour.

鼹鼠

　　温哥华居民住宅的后院还有一种动物非常隐蔽和害羞叫做鼹鼠，它不喜欢跑到地面上来。这种动物适于在地下掘土生活。当您在院子草坪上看到成堆的泥土时，您家的地下就藏有鼹鼠了。当它们在草地下挖出长长的隧道和洞穴时，鼹鼠会清除，搬移成堆的泥土到地面上。它们在地下洞穴生活，主要以地下的蚯蚓、昆虫及其幼虫为食。它们在湿冷的冬季非常活跃，它们会在小洞穴中产下幼崽，到了来年的夏天，年轻的鼹鼠会蹦到地面上，寻找一个新的属于自己的领地。可是当它们在地面上露头时，它们就有被猫头鹰、猫和郊狼吃掉的危险。鼹鼠身上生有柔软的黑色毛皮，长而尖的鼻子，和适于掘土强壮的桨状形前爪，每小时可以挖掘4米。由于它们喜好挖洞，经常对草坪，运动场和高尔夫球场造成很大的破坏。

December 14   Support for Newcomers

12月14日   支持新移民

YMCA of Vancouver Immigrant Services

The YMCA provides many opportunities for newcomers to make new friends, improve their language and improve their physical fitness. They encourage newcomers to come join their programs and meet new people and try something different. In addition to courses and workshops, they also hold regular English conversation clubs.

温哥华基督教青年会移民服务部
https://gv.ymca.ca/Programs/Categories/Immigrant-Services

基督教青年会为新移民提供了许多结识新朋友的机会，提高他们的语言和改善他们的身体素质。 他们鼓励新来的人加入他们的计划，结交新朋友，尝试不同的东西。 除了课程和研讨会之外，他们还会定期举办英语会话活动。

   # Vancouver Neighbourhoods

12月15日   温哥华社区

South Granville

South Granville is the sophisticated home to some of the greatest variety of shopping, dining, lifestyle and fine art venues in the city. Some of the finest art galleries and designer décor stores in the city are there for exploring and then enjoy stopping somewhere for lunch or dinner afterwards. South Granville is located just a few minutes away from downtown. For gourmet lovers, South Granville has a variety of fascinating stores and award-winning restaurants, while fashionistas can shop the latest trends in the many designer boutiques. To view the most beautiful mansions and parks in Vancouver, explore the nearby neighbourhood of Shaughnessy and feel like you have entered a special world of beauty, gardens and elegant residences.

南格兰维尔 http://www.southgranville.org/

南格兰维尔是城市中最有品位，最丰富多彩的集购物、餐饮、生活和美术的场所。城市中最优秀的艺术画廊和设计师装潢店都集中在这里，对于美食爱好者来说，南格兰维尔街上的餐厅屡获殊荣，建议参观访问后，选一家餐馆享用一下午餐或者晚餐。游客们喜欢住在南格兰维尔酒店，因为交通十分便利，四通八达，距离温哥华市中心仅有几分钟的车程。这里许多时装精品店引领着城市最新的潮流，时尚达人在这里可以购买到心仪的服装。南格兰维尔拥有温哥华最美丽的豪宅和公园，步入肖内西小区，看到那一座座高雅的住宅和花园仿佛进入另一个美丽的童话世界。南格兰维尔让你感受到不一样的温哥华。

December 16 Basic Everyday English

12月16日　　基本日常生活用语

On the Telephone

Understanding and using English on the phone is not easy, especially for newcomers. When you first arrive in Vancouver, try to do all your important communication in person, if possible, especially if it must be in English. This way, you can use all your tools – body language, Google images, translation dictionary and so on. However, if you must speak English on the phone, below are some phrases that will help you. Also, remember that "practice makes perfect" and every day that you are living in Vancouver, it will get easier and easier to understand and use English in every circumstance – including on the telephone.

打电话

在电话上理解和使用英语是不容易的，尤其对新移民来说。当您初到温哥华时，所有重要的沟通都要亲历亲为，特别是有些必须使用英语交流的场合。这样，您熟知的所有交流工具 – 肢体语言、谷歌图像、翻译字典等等都能派上用场。可是，有时您不得不在电话上说英语，怎么办？别着急，下面是一些对您有帮助的短语。请记住 "熟能生巧"，您现在每天都生活在温哥华，耳闻目染，慢慢您就会越来越容易在各种场合理解和使用英语，包括打电话。

English for Everyday Life
日常生活英语

下面是一些基本英语短语，您也许听到过，您可以在打电话时使用。请访问我们的网站www.mynewlifeinvancouver.com，听一听这些短语的发音，并练习会话。

Hello?
He is not home, can I take a message?
Can you please spell your name?
Speak slower please
Please call back later
I would like to speak to _____

您好！
他不在家，我能给他捎个口信吗？
您能拼一下您的名字吗？
请说慢一点
请稍后再打来
*我想和_____说话_*

December 17   Education

12月17日   教育

District Parent Advisory Council (DPAC)

Every school has a **Parent Advisory Committee (PAC)** that helps support their school with guidance, volunteer assistance and fund-raising. PACs are made up of parents who have volunteered to be a member for a period of one school year. All of the PACs are then supported by the large Vancouver District Parent Advisory Council (DPAC) which is a collection of volunteer parents working with the common goal of supporting education for all the children of Vancouver. The DPAC supports the PACs and advocates for parent concerns at the provincial government level. They also organize educational events and workshops for the PAC members.

区家长咨询委员会（DPAC）

DPAC网站：http://www.vancouverdpac.org

每所学校都有家长咨询委员会（PAC）帮助支持他们的学校，提供指导、志愿服务和筹款。 家长咨询委员会由学生父母组成，他们自愿成为一个学年的成员。所有PAC都受到大温哥华地区家长咨询委员会（DPAC）的支持，这是一个父母志愿服务的集合，其工作目标是支持温哥华所有儿童的教育，和解决在省政府一级倡导家长关注的问题。他们还为PAC成员组织教育活动和研讨会。

December 18 Scenes from Daily Life

12月18日　　日常生活中的一些镜头

At the English Class for Adults
在成人英语课上

December 19 Outdoor Life in Vancouver

12月19日 温哥华户外生活

Saltwater Fishing (Angling)

Fishing from a dock on the harbour or from a boat are two popular outdoor activities in Vancouver. Whether you fish from a dock or from a boat, you are required to purchase a fishing license called a *B.C. Tidal Waters Sport Fishing license*. In addition, if you plan on catching salmon, you must also add a *Salmon fishing stamp* to your license. The stamp is valid from April 1- March 31st of each fishing season.

Pacific Angler is the largest fishing supplies shop in Vancouver that provides fishing gear, expert advice, and courses and instruction for students who want to learn about fishing in Vancouver. Their staff are experts and can help answer all your questions about fishing around Vancouver. They also provide guided fishing trips in local waters and courses and workshops for beginners who want to learn more about saltwater fishing.

If you would prefer to fish from your own motorized boat, then you must obtain a Canadian boat license. To get this **Pleasure Craft Operator Card**, you need to take a very short online test. You can also take basic boating courses with the **Canadian Power and Sail Squadron** which is a nationwide association of boating enthusiasts who are committed to improving boating safety through training.

咸水捕鱼（钓鱼）

> 太平洋垂钓者　http://www.pacificangler.ca/
> 加拿大船只许可证　https://www.boaterexam.com/canada/
> 温哥华动力和风帆中队　http://vpsboat.org

在海港码头或船上钓鱼是温哥华两种最受欢迎的户外活动。无论您是在码头，还是从船上钓鱼，您都必须购买一张被称为*卑诗省潮汐水域运动钓鱼许可证*。此外，如果您计划捕捞三文鱼，还必须在您的许可证上添加*三文鱼捕鱼标记*。许可证的有效期为每年4月1日至次年的3月31日。

太平洋垂钓者是温哥华最大的渔业用品店，为那些想要在温哥华钓鱼的人提供渔具、专家建议、课程和教学。店内的工作人员全都是专家级的，可以回答您在温哥华附近海域垂钓的所有问题。他们还在当地水域提供指导性的钓鱼之旅，并为想要了解更多关于盐水捕鱼的初学者们开设的课程和讲习班。

如果您想驾驶自己的机动船出海捕鱼，那么您必须事先获得加拿大船只许可证。若要获取此**游艇操作员卡**，您需要在上面的网站上进行简短的在线考试。您也可以参加加拿大动力和风帆中队举办的基础划船课程，

加拿大动力和风帆中队是全国性的划船爱好者协会，其宗旨是通过培训提高划船者的安全意识。

CPS是根据（加拿大）《公司法》成立的非营利组织，其行政和教学工作由其成员们完成——不计报酬。

December 20 Tips to Learning English

12月20日   资深英语老师提供学习英语的小贴士

Be Kind to Yourself

Getting used to a new city and a new language is very exciting, but also very difficult too. Please be kind to yourself as you begin to settle down and work on improving your English. As an instructor, it makes me so sad when I hear students put themselves down and say they are too stupid to learn or they are too old or too lazy or so many other negative comments. I think that learning new things has a better chance of success when it is built on a foundation of positivity. Just start where you are and build from there. Every day your English is getting better- even the tiniest improvement is still an improvement! It takes energy to learn and practice English and negativity drains us of energy. So, please be kind to yourself and keep the faith that you will improve your English and, one day at a time, you will be able to speak and understand everyday English without any problems.

要善待自己

熟悉一个新的城市和一种新的语言是非常令人兴奋的，但也非常困难。当你开始安顿下来，努力提高英语水平，请善待自己。作为老师，当我听到学生们说他们太笨而学不好，或者他们太老、太懒或是许多其他负面的言辞时，这让我感到很伤心。我认为积极地、主动地去学习新的事物，将会有更大成功的机会。正所谓事半功倍。就从你现在的英语水平开始吧，这就是你的起点。日复一日，你的英语会越来越好 – 哪怕是最微小的改进，它依然是一个不小的进步！学习和练习英语需要能量，消极的情绪对会消耗我们的精力。所以，请善待自己，保持信心，哪怕一天就学一次日常英语，你的英语水平将会很快提高的，听说和理解都不会有任何问题。

December 21   A Little Canadian Inspiration

12月21日   一点点启示

Our hopes are high. Our faith in the people is great. Our courage is strong. And our dreams for this beautiful country will never die.

-former Prime Minister of Canada Pierre Trudeau

"I have been incredibly lucky all my life. I've had a family that has loved me and given me incredible opportunities. I've gone to great schools. I've travelled across the country. When my father died, I had millions of people supporting me in a very, very difficult time. I have received so much from this country. I realize that we're defined in life not by what we get from this world but by what we have to offer it and I know that I have a lot to offer this country, and I'm serious about devoting my life to it."

-current Prime Minister of Canada Justin Trudeau
(eldest son of former PM Pierre Trudeau)

我们的期望值很高。我们对人民的信仰是巨大的。我们敢于面对一切。我们对这个美丽国家的梦想永远不会消失。

——加拿大总理皮埃尔·特鲁多总理

"我一直都非常幸运。我有一个爱我的家庭，给了我难以置信的机会。我受过良好的教育。我周游过整个国家。当我父亲去世时，在我非常困难的时候，有数以百万计的人们在支持我。我已经从这个国家得到了很多。我意识到，我们生活的定义不是我们从这个世界得到什么，而是我们必须奉献什么，我知道我有很多东西可以奉献给这个国家，我要以毕生的精力去做这件事。

——现任——加拿大总理贾斯汀·特鲁多
（前总理皮埃尔·特鲁多的长子）

December 22   Volunteer in Vancouver

12月22日   在温哥华做义工

Volunteer with a Major Festival

Throughout the year, there are many three or four-day festivals to celebrate different special events and activities. These festivals mainly rely on volunteers for their operation. They are a great place to volunteer because you get to enjoy all the entertainment of the event for free and meet new people without a long-time commitment. Some festivals are so popular, there is a waiting list for the volunteer positions. Every major festival has a website with information about how to volunteer. The Concord Pacific Dragon Boat Festival and the Vancouver TD International Jazz Festival are two fun and interesting festivals to do volunteer work.

志愿者参加重要的节日

在一年中，有许多为期三天或四天来庆祝各种特别事件和活动的节日。这些节日主要依靠志愿者协助运作。他们是志愿者提供服务的好地方，因为您可以免费享受的所有娱乐活动，并且在很短的时间内就会交上新的朋友。有一些节日的志愿服务很热门，需要列入等候名单。每个重大节日，都有一个如何填报志愿者信息的网站。以下是为您提供可以志愿参与的两个重大节日的信息：

温哥华康科德太平洋龙舟节

志愿者是为整个网站提供优质的客户服务。节日志愿者的职责包括接待顾客，检查通行证，销售商品，并帮助建立和组织各种活动，如儿童手工艺品或划船游戏。活动结束时，主办单位还会为所有志愿者举办一个免费的烧烤聚会。

温哥华 TD 国际爵士音乐节

参加爵士音乐节的志愿者可以听到现场震撼的音乐，结交新朋友，并获得新的体验。在节日期间，您可以参加一些节目，或观看一些节目，并获得梦幻般的回报。在节日结束时，主办单位为所有志愿者举办了一个大型的节日聚会。

December 23   Healthcare in Vancouver

12月23日   温哥华的医疗保健

Vancouver Laser and Skin Care Centre

While not life threatening, nowadays many people seek medical treatment for aged or damaged skin to boost their confidence and satisfaction. For more than twenty years, Vancouverites have trusted the doctors at Vancouver Laser and Skin Care Centre with treatments to help reverse the effects of stress, genetics and lifestyle choices on their skin and appearance. The centre uses the latest products and treatments to help you improve your appearance. They have complete information in Chinese on their website, as well as a Chinese receptionist available to answer your questions and book an appointment.

温哥华激光和皮肤护理中心 https://www.vancouverlaser.com/

中文直拨电话：(604) 879-9896

虽然没有生命危险，作为一种美容方式，现如今有许多人在寻求治疗皮肤老化或受损的方法，以此提高他们的自信心和满足感，使自己变得更加美丽。二十多年来，温哥华激光和护肤中心致力于客户临床测试，突破治疗方法来帮助反向应力、遗传学和生活方式的选择对您的皮肤和外貌的影响。该中心使用最新的产品，提供最有效的审美治疗选择方案来帮助改善您的外貌。在他们的网站上有完整的中文介绍，还有一位讲中文的接待员可以回答您的问题并帮您进行预约服务。

温哥华激光和皮肤护理中心简介

布劳恩医生于1996年创立了温哥华激光皮肤护理中心，引进了加拿大第一台激光脱毛设备，在此后的20年里，温哥华激光中心成为了加拿大最大的医学美容诊所之一。布劳恩医生是阿勒根公司的三钻石级别注射医师；我们诊所的医美治疗项目从美容注射到皮肤管理，纤体瘦身可以满足不同年龄段，有任何需求的客人。温哥华激光中心接待过很多城里的名人名媛，还有明星们的光临。相信我们诊所三位拥有最高医学美容认证的医生布劳恩、布洛克和洛桑一定会让您满意而归的。

Interesting Facts About Vancouver

12月24日   温哥华趣闻

A Windmill on a Mountaintop

"The Eye of The Wind" on top of Grouse Mountain is the only working wind turbine in the world that has an actual enclosed glass viewing platform that will give you the best 360 degree views of the city. The wind turbine is an actual working turbine that provides power to Grouse Mountain.

山顶上的风车

松鸡山上的"风之眼"是世界上唯一一个封闭式的风车玻璃观景台，它可以让您360度的欣赏城市景观。风力发电机为松鸡山提供电源动力。如果您敢于站在松鸡山风力发电机的顶端，那么您将拥有这个城市最好的景观之一。

December 25 Finding Work in Vancouver

12月25日　　在温哥华找工作

Starting Your Own Small Business

If you would prefer to start a small business instead of finding employment, then the Small Business BC Centre at Waterfront Station is the first place to visit. Small Business BC's excellent approach and programs have been recognized by several national and international awards, and they have a solid reputation as an exceptional business resource. Their goal is to provide entrepreneurs with products and services that will assist them with starting their own small business and to help with every stage of business development. It is also possible for small business owners to have one on one appointments with business specialists in the areas of law, taxation, import/export rules, business management, marketing, and social media for business.

开创您自己的小企业

BC省小企业：http://smallbusinessbc.ca/

如果您想开办一家小企业，而不是找工作，那么海滨站BC省小型企业商务中心是您首先需要访问的地方。他们策划优秀的BC小企业的方案和计划，多次获得了国内外的奖项，作为卓越的商业资源他们具有良好的声誉。他们的目标是为企业家提供产品和服务，帮助他们开办小型企业，帮助企业主掌握产品，服务并支持各个阶段的业务发展。小企业主还可以在法律、税务、进出口规则、商业管理、营销和社会媒体等领域与业务专家进行一对一的咨询。

December 26　Vancouver Sightseeing

12月26日　　观光

Unusual Tours

Sometimes it is difficult to get a true sense of a city from behind the tinted windows of a large tour bus. There are some tour companies in Vancouver that try to give visitors a more close-up view of the sights, sounds and tastes of Vancouver. There are food tours where a guide takes you on a tasting tour of several restaurants and markets in Vancouver. There are walking and biking tours of the city and even hiking tours to explore the trails of the famous mountains of Vancouver. For a more relaxed pace tour, the horse-drawn carriage tours of Stanley Park let you enjoy the park at a leisurely pace.

不寻常之旅

美食之旅：	http://foodietours.ca/
步行旅游：	http://www.tourguys.ca/vancouver
马车旅行：	http://www.stanleypark.com/
骑自行车游览：	http://cyclevancouver.com/
徒步旅行：	http://www.freshadventures.ca

　　有时，很难透过大型旅游巴士的有色窗户体味到城市真实感。许多旅游公司正在努力尝试着使游客近距离感受温哥华，希望能够从视觉、听觉和味觉上让游客们体验到什么才是真正的温哥华。他们当中有的推出了食品旅游，导游带着您参加温哥华几家餐馆和市场的品尝之旅。 有的组织城市的徒步和骑自行车之旅，甚至是远足旅行，探索著名的温哥华山区的步道。为了更轻松的代步游览，斯坦利公园的马车能让您充分享受公园里悠闲的节奏。

December 27   Vancouver Transportation

12月27日   温哥华交通运输

Bike Lanes and Bike Share Program

Vancouver is a very safe and convenient city to get around by bicycle. There is a very large network of designated bike routes that are protected from traffic, but you are also allowed to ride your bike on almost all Vancouver streets. The City of Vancouver creates maps and details all the bikeways and greenways in the city. Greenways are bike paths that are in a more natural setting.

Last year, Vancouver started a public bike share program – Mobi by Shaw Go. These are bikes to loan for short rides in the city by using a Mobi pass. The passes are available for the day, month or year. Each bike comes with a bike helmet for the user to wear which is a legal requirement in Vancouver. The MOBI website has a map of all the Mobi stations and information about membership. There is also a Mobi app that you can download for your phone to use for reservations and finding the closest available Mobi bike to borrow.

Bike Hub provides biking education and training courses at community centres across Vancouver. The purpose of the courses is to improve your skills and confidence to ride your bike safely and enjoyably. Their on-bike practical courses come in 3 levels depending on skills and confidence:

Learn to Ride is two custom 90-min intro classes for those who haven't cycled in years, or ever.

Ride the Road is our most popular class for intermediate riders that combines classroom & on-road instruction for anyone who can ride, and would like to get comfortable riding on city streets

Advance Your Ride is cycling skills & safety training for all road situations.

自行车车道和自行车共享计划

自行车资讯 http://vancouver.ca/streets-transportation/cycling-routes-maps-and-trip-planner.aspx
公共自行车共享计划 https://www.mobibikes.ca/
骑自行车的教育和培训 https://bikehub.ca/bike-education

温哥华对于骑自行车的人来讲是一个非常安全和便利的城市。城市里面有一个非常大的自行车专用路线，受到交通保护，您也可以在几乎所有的温哥华街道上骑自行车。上面的链接详细介绍了城市中的所有自行车道和绿道。绿道是指在自然环境中的自行车道。

去年，温哥华启动了一个由 Shaw Go 名为 Mobi 的公共自行车共享计划。 这些是通过使用Mobi在城市短期租借自行车的方式。通票的有效期可用于当日，当月或一整年。每辆自行车都配有自行车头盔供用户穿戴，温哥华的法律要求骑自行车者必须戴头盔。上面的链接显示了所有 Mobi 站的地图，并有注册会员所需的信息。还有一个Mobi应用程序，您可以把它下载到您的手机用于预订和找到离您最近的 Mobi 自行车租赁站。

在温哥华的各大社区中心都提供有关骑自行车的安全教育和培训课程。课程的目的是提高您的技能和信心，安全，愉快地骑车。他们的自行车实践课程分为3个级别，取决于您的技能和信心：

1. 学会骑车是两个90分钟入门课程，为那些从来没有骑过自行车的人设置的。
2. 骑车上路是最受欢迎的中级车手课程，结合课堂教学和道路上的指示牌，任何希望在城市街道上愉快地骑行的人都可以参加。
3. 提升您的骑行能力是在所有的路面情况下骑自行车的技能和安全培训。

December 28   Sports Teams and Special Events

12月28日   专业体育赛事和活动

Concord Pacific Vancouver Dragon Boat Festival

Every June, the waters of downtown Vancouver's False Creek become alive with the sights and sound of 200 dragon boat teams from around the world competing in this annual competition. This festival is one of the oldest and largest dragon boat festivals held outside Asia. The festival begins with the colourful Eye-dotting Ceremony and evening opening concert, and then continues with two days of non-stop entertainment, food, and world-class competition. The festival and races over the past 25 years have developed into one of Vancouver's most anticipated annual family summer events, attracting teams of 25 people ranging in age from high school students to "grand dragons" in their 60s, 70s and even 80s.

太平洋温哥华端午龙舟节 http://vancouverdragonboatfestival.ca/

　　每年六月，温哥华市中心的福溪水域异常的活跃，歌声笑声交织在一起，200支来自世界各地的龙舟队聚集到这里展开角逐争夺年度冠军。这个节日是在亚洲以外举行的最古老、规模最大的端午节之一。由五彩缤纷的龙头点睛仪式和晚会开幕音乐会拉开了节日的序幕，接下去的两天不间断的娱乐，有世界级的舞台表演、美味的食物、装饰艺术和互动马戏表演，当然，最引人瞩目的还是最高水平的龙舟比赛。参加比赛的选手从高中生到60后，70后甚至80后的"大龙"组成的25人的船队。在过去的25年里，端午节和龙舟比赛已经成为温哥华最受期待的年度家庭夏日活动之一。

Vancouver Parks

12月29日   温哥华公园

Garry Point Park, Steveston

Garry Point Park is a large 75 acre waterfront park, located close to historic Steveston Village in the southwest part of Richmond. The park is mixture of lawns and sandy waterfront with many beached logs, signs that explain the long history of the area and a large piece of public art called the Fisherman's Memorial Needle. Kuno Garden- a Japanese style memorial garden- is also located in the park. Finally, it is one of the best places to watch the sunset in all of Richmond. Many families come to walk on the beach, have picnics and fly kites in the fresh clean sea air of the park.

史蒂夫斯顿，加里点公园

加里点公园是一个 75 英亩的大型海滨公园，靠近历史悠久的史蒂夫斯顿村，位于里士满的西南部第7大道的西南 12011 号。公园上的草坪和沙滩的混杂物与许多搁浅日志，诠释了该地区的悠久历史。公园里有一个大的公共艺术品称为渔人纪念针。还有一个日式纪念花园 – 久野花园也坐落在公园里。最后，值得一提的，它是里士满观看日落最好的地方。园内飘散着清新的海洋空气，许多家庭在公园的海滩上散步，野餐和放风筝。

December 30   # Stories and Advice for Newcomers

12月30日   **移民的故事和建议**

Jan

　　作为国际夫妇，我们来自不同的国家，从中我学到了很多东西：对待许多日常小事的处理方法在不同的国家都是不同的。起初，您会认为当地人"做错了"。也许他们太忙了，您认为他们很粗鲁，因为他们不耐烦或咄咄逼人；或者他们太慢了，您觉得他们很不礼貌，因为他们在浪费您的时间。我的建议是，您先试着调整一下自己的行为，以更好地适应当地人做事的方式！每天或每周调整一点点，用不同的方式做事，您会给当地人一个惊喜，您慢慢地也会感到在新的国度里生活得很自在。

　　期望往往会带有点挑战性。成功融入到一个新的城市和国家，在很大程度上取决于您的期望 – 如果您期望它是具有挑战性的，您就不太可能会感到困难。如果在新的地方安家需要比预期的时间更长，也请不要感到惊讶 – 通常需要两到三年的时间才能感觉自己像是一个"本地人"。

Diverse Vancouver

12月31日　　**多元文化的温哥华**

Experience First Nations Culture in Vancouver and BC

There are 198 distinct First Nations in B.C., each with their own unique traditions and history and more than 30 different First Nations languages. Therefore, it is impossible to experience all First Nations culture just in Vancouver, but the **Aboriginal Tourism BC** website is a complete guide to all Aboriginal activities, sightseeing and tour information in the whole province. You can also find information about the many art galleries, museums, and cultural centres that you can visit to experience First Nations history and culture. For something closer to home, there is a small but lovely and award-winning restaurant in Vancouver called the **Salmon n' Bannock Bistro** where you can experience First Nations culture and try authentic and delicious Aboriginal flavours. Their famous dish is a burger made with a 6-ounce wild sockeye filet, lemon-garlic mayonnaise, pickles, and kale served between two pieces of bannock (traditional Aboriginal fried bread).

在温哥华和BC省体验第一民族文化

BC省原住民旅游局 https://www.aboriginalbc.com/
班诺克鲑鱼小酒馆 http://www.salmonandbannock.net/

在不列颠哥伦比亚省有198个不同的第一民族和超过30种不同的原住民语言，每个部落都有自己独特的传统和历史。因此，想要在温哥华和BC省体验所有的原住民文化几乎是不可能的，不过，在BC省原住民旅游局网站上可以看到所有的原住民的活动信息，和省内原住民完整的观光旅游指南。你甚至还可以查找到许多艺术画廊、博物馆和文化中心的信息，你可以参观体验其中部分的第一民族的历史和文化。

然而，在温哥华有一个非常温馨可爱，并屡获殊荣的班诺克鲑鱼小酒馆，在那里你可以体验原住民饮食文化，品尝正宗的原汁原味的原住民美食。最有名的是6盎司的野生鲑菲力、柠檬大蒜蛋黄酱、腌菜和羽衣甘蓝汉堡（传统土著油炸面包）。

Index to Entries by Category

类别条目索引

Local Customs
当地的习俗

Parenting in Vancouver
在温哥华养育子女

Newcomer Stories & Advice
移民的故事

Vancouver Entertainment
温哥华娱乐

Best Elementary Schools in Vancouver
温哥华重点小学

Fun and Interesting Facts about Vancouver
温哥华的趣闻

Best High Schools in Vancouver
温哥华重点中学

The Homes of Vancouver
温哥华住宅

Extracurricular Activities for Children
最佳儿童课外活动

Meeting Locals in Vancouver
与当地温哥华人接触

Vancouver Restaurant Customs and Etiquette
温哥华餐厅的习俗与礼仪

Top English Language Programs for Adults
成人高级英语课程

Vancouver Backyard Birds and Animals
温哥华后院的小鸟和动物

Support for Newcomers
支持新移民

Vancouver Neighbourhoods
温哥华社区

Basic Everyday English
基本日常英语

Vancouver Education
温哥华教育

Scenes From Everyday life in Vancouver
温哥华日常生活中的一些镜头

Outdoor Life in Vancouver
温哥华户外生活

English Teacher's Tips to Learn English
英语老师给出学习英语的小贴士

A Little Inspiration: Quotes About Canada
一点启示：加拿大的名言

Volunteer in Vancouver
在温哥华做义工

Health in Vancouver
温哥华的医疗

Fun and Interesting Facts about Vancouver
温哥华的趣闻

Finding Work in Vancouver
在温哥华找工作

Sightseeing
观光

Vancouver Transportation
温哥华交通运输

Vancouver Professional Sports and Events
温哥华职业体育赛事

Vancouver Parks
温哥华公园

Newcomer Stories & Advice
移民的故事

Diverse Vancouver
多元文化的温哥华

Kari Karlsbjerg Bio

Kari Karlsbjerg is an experienced English as a Second Language Instructor and Tutor with a demonstrated history of working in the higher education industry in Canada and abroad. She is skilled in English as a Second Language (ESL), Academic English, Public Speaking, Curriculum Development, and International Education. She has taught English to business-people in Hong Kong, Denmark and Indonesia. Living abroad gave her a deep appreciation of the rich diversity of cultures around the world. She is married to an immigrant from Denmark and her own firsthand experience of learning Danish as an adult has helped her be even more compassionate and understanding of the unique challenges of her adult ESL students. Kari is passionate about helping newcomers strengthen their English language skills and discover the many joys and unique opportunities of living in her hometown of Vancouver. In particular, she hopes this book will help to demystify local cultural traditions, remove barriers to communication and foster genuine understanding, connection and relationships across the community. She is grateful for her friendship and wonderful partnership with Yi Zheng and his family throughout this project.

个人简历

    Kari Karlsbjerg是一位经验丰富的英语教师和导师，长期在加拿大和海外从事高等教育工作。她精通英语、擅长教移民英语作为第二语言的ESL、学术英语、公共演讲、课程开发和国际教育。她曾在香港、丹麦和印度尼西亚给当地的商人普及过英语。旅居海外使她深切体会到世界各地文化的丰富多样性。她嫁给了一个来自丹麦的移民后，开始学习成人丹麦语，亲身的经历使她更加同情和理解那些成年ESL学生所面临的挑战。Kari非常热衷于帮助新移民，加强他们的英语语言技能，发现生活在异国他乡温哥华的许多乐趣和独特的机会。特别是，她希望这本书有助于帮助读者揭开当地传统文化的神秘面纱，消除沟通的障碍，促进人与人之间真正的理解、这关系到社区乃至整个社会的和谐。在本书写作的过程中，非常感谢她的搭档郑义及其家属之间的友谊和友好合作伙伴关系。

Yi Zheng Bio

I came to Vancouver in 2010. After immigration, I enrolled in Language Instruction for Newcomers to Canada (LINC) courses which offered by Vancouver Community College (VCC). I met a great mentor Kari there, who was highly respected by Chinese newcomers. With the help of her gently guiding me day after day, I progressed quickly. Kari and I often discuss Canadian and Chinese cultures. But more than that, we talk about the problems encountered by immigrants.

Kari regards immigration as a matter of her own, and she often uses her weekend rest to solve problems for many newcomers. In 2015, under the proposal of Kari, we formed an English Study Team to organize activities regularly. To be able to help more newcomers overcome the language barriers, meet and make good friends with locals, and truly integrate into Canadian society, she wrote this book. Those who have been in contact with Kari know that she is always considerate of others and has great enthusiasm for Chinese newcomers. I would like to take this opportunity to say that Kari is the best friend of Chinese newcomers.

个人简历

　　我是于2010年来到温哥华的，移民后，我报读了温哥华社区学院(VCC)的成人英语课程LINC 。我在这里遇到了一位备受移民们尊敬的导师Kari。在她耐心的日复一日的帮助下，我进步得很快。Kari和我在一起经常讨论加拿大和中国的文化，当然更多的还是探讨移民们遇到的各种问题。

　　Kari把移民的事情当作自己的事情，她经常利用自己周末休息时间，为广大的移民朋友排忧解难。2015年，在Kari的倡导下我们组建了一个英语学习团队，定期组织活动。为了能够帮助更多的移民克服语言障碍，与当地人成为好朋友，真正融入加拿大社会，她特别写出此书。凡是接触过Kari的移民朋友，都有这样的一种感觉，那就是，她处处为他人着想。对移民极端的热忱。借此机会我想说出大家的心声 —— Kari就是中国移民最好的朋友，她不愧是当代的白求恩。